PRAISE FOR *CROSSING THE LINE*

"With a propulsive narrative and an engaging style, *Crossing the Line* is an important contribution to our understanding of the borderlands, and by extension, America itself."
—**REECE JONES**, author of *White Borders*

"In *Crossing the Line*, Towle achieves something few writers can: she catalogs years of the US government's nightmarish cruelty towards migrants without tipping into despair. It's an inspiring account of many tireless, and seemingly fearless, immigration advocates standing up for justice and humanity. Towle's personal tale, too, is a smart and moving grappling with the moral calamity that is the US immigration enforcement regime. I challenge any reader to pick up this book and not be shaken, disturbed, and ultimately committed to a better and more just world. Towle beautifully renders moments of humanity in a fundamentally inhumane system."
—**JOHN WASHINGTON**, author of *A Case for Open Borders*

"*Crossing the Line* is a well-researched yet accessible exposé of border policies that harm migrants and undermine the promise of America. From the 'family separation' policies of the Trump administration to the massive growth of immigrant detention, Towle's ability to weave together first-hand stories of accidental activists—including priests, attorneys, and concerned locals—with the broader policy context is on display in an ambitious book infused with a profound commitment to humanity and justice. Every concerned citizen should read this book."
—**AUSTIN KOCHER**, Research Assistant Professor, Syracuse University

"Thanks for lifting up these voices and not relenting. Congratulations on a compelling read."
—**LUZ VIRGINIA LOPEZ**, Senior Supervising Attorney, Southern Poverty Law Center, Immigrant Justice Project

"What grace filled and beautiful writing. Thank you for capturing our community's story!"
—**DYLAN CORBETT**, Executive Director, Hope Border Institute Regional Assistant Coordinator, Vatican Migrants & Refugees Section

"Inspiring and transporting from the opening passage . . . a journey of historical context expertly weaved into the human experience, allows the reader to relate to the current border climate on so many levels. I did not want to stop reading. Abrazos."
—**ELIZABETH "LIZEE" CAVAZOS**,
Angry Tías & Abuelas of the Rio Grande Valley

"Absolutely BRILLIANT, a masterpiece! It feels so lonely at times, like no one understands. But Sarah sees us here in the borderlands, flying the tattered flag of this country's ideals. It touched me deeply."
—**MADELEINE SANDEFUR**,
Angry Tías & Abuelas of the Rio Grande Valley

"Powerful and true. An important historical account."
—**JUAN DAVID LIENDO-LUCIO**, Team Brownsville

"Sometimes you ache for the unvarnished truth. Sarah Towle tells it in this book—the whole truth, good, bad, and ugly. She speaks for the silent hordes seeking "the lamp beside the golden door" to be opened for them, giving access to the wonder that is America."
—**MERRY HANCOCK**, Cameroon Advocacy Network

"The personal stories bring the historical narrative to life."
—**ANNE MARIE MURPHY**, author of *A Perfect Fit* (coming 2025)

CROSSING THE LINE

CROSSING
THE LINE

FINDING AMERICA
IN THE
BORDERLANDS

SARAH TOWLE

SHE WRITES PRESS

Published 2024
Printed in the United States of America
Print ISBN: 978-1-64742-579-1
E-ISBN: 978-1-64742-580-7
Library of Congress Control Number: 2024905770

For information, address:
She Writes Press
1569 Solano Ave #546
Berkeley, CA 94707

Interior Design by Tabitha Lahr

She Writes Press is a division of SparkPoint Studio, LLC.

"Let us be reminded that before there is a final solution, there must be a first solution, a second one, even a third. The move toward a final solution is not a jump. It takes one step, then another, then another."
—Toni Morrison, 1995

*To all the brave hearts and heroic souls
impacted by border violence.*

*To those who should be in this book but
whose paths I've yet to cross, may the
stories herein lift yours up as well.*

Contents

INTRODUCTION

The Subversive Act of Seeing

The mercury soared to 104 degrees Fahrenheit (40 degrees Celsius) in London in July 2022—a temperature not projected to hit the UK until 2050 under current climate-change models. Air conditioning really isn't a thing here. So I spent a sweaty month in Zoom hearings with civil rights investigators representing the US Department of Homeland Security. From my desk, overlooking a patchwork of gardens enclosed by a city block of crooked, late-1800s Victorian homes, I had become the unlikely intermediary between African nationals who had sought asylum in the US and this team of lawyers operating deep inside the monumental post-9/11 creation of the "War on Terror."

Until being given a rare glimpse inside, I was not aware that the national security behemoth included an accountability office charged with keeping a combined force of 80,000 law-enforcement agents mindful of individual liberty, fairness, and equality under the law. Then a chance discovery of a conscience-shocking wrong led to my becoming party to a legal action against the most infamous of the twenty-two Homeland Security tentacles: Immigration and Customs Enforcement, or ICE.

A former head of the Homeland Security civil rights office advised me that its attorneys would be grateful for access to those with lived experience under the agency funded by Congress to incarcerate tens of thousands of immigrants annually—a number that jumped beyond 52,000 in the Trump years—in over 200 US prisons, 70 percent of which are operated by for-profit companies. Complaints of human rights infractions against ICE and its contractors are so routine, my contact informed me, investigators struggle to keep up. What's more, evidence is often whisked away via its sub-agency: ICE Enforcement and Removals Operations, aka ICE Air, "the deportation machine."

With the support of my collaborators at the Texas A&M University School of Law Immigrant Rights Clinic and Cameroon Advocacy Network, I facilitated a series of hearings in the summer of 2022 that would have brought blood to boil even without the record heatwave. Through anger and incredulity, as well as tears shed on all sides, roughly two dozen teachers, lawyers, medical and hospitality professionals, students, technicians, and entrepreneurs from the West African nation of Cameroon recounted the details of their journeys from harm to harm.

They were among the several dozen individuals I tracked down and interviewed who had sought safety in the US at great personal risk and expense, after having been the targets of persecution at home. Rather than finding succor on arrival at the US-Mexico border, however, their human rights were systematically violated by the US Homeland Security apparatus. They were jailed by ICE for an average of seventeen months—and in odious conditions—though they had committed no crime.

Indeed, seeking asylum and a life free from cruel, inhumane, or degrading treatment is a fundamental human right, codified under US and international law. Yet, these folks had been denied their freedom and subjected to routine physical, emotional, and psychological abuse. They were kept locked up even when the coronavirus pandemic turned prisons into death traps. Then, in defiance of international treaty commitments and legal due process, ICE delivered these mothers, fathers, sisters, brothers, sons, and daughters back into the hands of their persecutors in the midst of a brutal civil war. The circumstances of their deportations were violent and egregious.

In meetings that spanned the hot summer and lasted two to three hours each, these courageous men and women gave voice to the myriad human-rights violations they suffered while captives of the US immigration detention-to-deportation pipeline. Their testimonies chronicled injustices unforetold. They represented only the tip of an iceberg—the only iceberg impervious to melting in the era of climate breakdown.

I came face-to-face with the atrocities forced upon these people while researching this book. It was not a tale I intended to tell when I landed in the Rio Grande Valley of Texas in January 2020 to see for myself what politicians and the media refer to *ad nauseam* as "the crisis at the border." At that point, my intention was to bear witness to the inhumanity Trump had wrought.

When his Homeland Security chain of command ordered Customs and Border Protection agents to tear children from the arms of their traumatized parents—and they did—the sound of grief reverberated around the globe. My shock joined that of millions. It didn't end, however, with the June 20, 2018, executive order that supposedly ended Trump & Co's policy of "family separation."

As they continued to manufacture fear about "surges" and "tsunamis" of "illegal aliens" and "invading hordes of criminals and perverts," I saw a different crisis: the hardening of the human heart; a world in which empathy had seemingly expired.

Since the Cold War ended and the Berlin Wall came down in 1989, another eighty or more walls have gone up behind it, including along the invisible line separating the US from Mexico. After then-German Chancellor Angela Merkel offered welcome to more than one million Syrian civilians displaced by war and thirty-nine thousand Eritreans escaped impunity across the Mediterranean into Italy, the European Union rolled out the razor wire and paid Libya to keep other would-be newcomers away. When, also at that time, children and families began to arrive in unprecedented numbers at the US southern border, fleeing unrelenting and escalating hemispheric violence and crippling poverty, leaders might have asked: *Why are so many people on the run?*

Instead, first the Bush-Cheney administration, then that of Obama-Biden, raised more walls, creating prisons to detain these safety seekers, before expelling them. Australia led the charge in "offshoring" asylum: sending folks in need of protection to island prisons, where they were left out of sight and out of mind. And the European Border and Coast Guard Agency, Frontex, became evermore emboldened to simply push people in need away, even if to their mortal peril.

The wealthiest and most privileged nations have been turning their backs on post-WWII human rights commitments in favor of a security-first paradigm. This betrayal of the refugee protection regime has been in motion for decades—well before the shattering events of September 11, 2001. Another forty-five countries are planning or building walls as I write. Some are terrorizing whole peoples in the name of fighting terrorism. Others have weaponized geography to do the work of walls for them—using the Sonoran and Sahara Deserts, for example, the Mediterranean and Caribbean Seas, or the English Channel to thwart human migration.

|||||||||||||||||||||||||||||||||||||||||||||||||||||||||||||||||

I arrived at the easternmost port of the US-Mexico border on January 3, 2020, with the intention of crossing the line from Brownsville, Texas, to Tijuana, Mexico, and points in between. I had only a car reservation, three nights booked at a hotel, and a single contact: Susan Law, an ally to all whose work in social justice advocacy spanned decades. She had become one of the Angry Tías & Abuelas of the Rio Grande Valley when Trump & Co began their takedown of asylum in the US. Directing me to the humanitarian crisis that awaited just a twenty-minute drive away, Tía Susan was the first of myriad mentors and guides I would encounter in what was to become a journey of awakening.

She passed me into the hands of Angry Tía Cindy Candia, who accompanied me over Brownsville's Gateway International Bridge into Matamoros, Mexico. There, living in tents, were roughly three thousand people in search of a safe and dignified life. They had been pushed back into a US State Department Level-4 "no go" zone by the leader of the free world. A good third of them were children.

Tía Cindy introduced me to five Texas school teachers who coalesced in 2018 as Team Brownsville, collectively called to see to the common good. There was much to do. And so few US citizens beyond the border knew, because in stopping safety seekers from crossing the line, Trump & Co had stopped their stories from traveling, too.

"Please, capture their tales and take them north with you," Angry Tía Elizabeth "Lizee" Cavazos implored me upon learning I was a teacher, researcher, and writer. But it was her next comment that sent me from the on-ramp of my actual road trip to the superhighway of a metaphorical one.

"We can't get our voices heard beyond the 100-mile checkpoint," Lizee stated.

That's when I first learned that the whole of my birth nation is encircled in a 100-mile law enforcement zone—not just a border, symbolized by a wall, demarcating a line. And that within the zone, the rights supposedly guaranteed to all of us by the US Constitution do not universally apply. That's when I understood that we are all negatively impacted by the "broken" US immigration system, which is failing everyone, save the profiteers and demagogues who benefit from it. That's when I committed to lifting up not just the voices of those identified by misleading labels and dangerous tropes, but also those of the ordinary people offering welcome: the folks who never stopped flying the tattered flag of US-American values in what history will remember as one of the country's darkest times.

In their accounts can be found a handbook for a more humane world.

||||||||||||||||||||||||||||||||||||||||||||||||||||||||||||||||

Expanding my witness, Angry Tía Madeleine Sandefur ushered me inside the dark, dehumanizing underbelly of the immigration detention system. There, I met people from the other side of the globe seeking asylum in the United States: Pastor Steven from Uganda; Manny and Keith from Guinea; Valery and Carl, Godswill and Benedict, Confident, Faith, and so many others from Cameroon returned from harm to harm on ICE Air. Determined that everyone should know what goes on under ICE, they became my next mentors, guides, teachers, and collaborators.

As I struggled to comprehend how the US came to incarcerate people seeking safety, Angry Tía Jennifer Harbury sent me traveling back through time to the Banana and Dirty Wars eras, when the big-stick bludgeoning of Central America and the Caribbean established the same destabilizing forces that drive people northward today.

Guides Jenn Budd and Robert Vivar in Tijuana and San Diego, as well as mentors John Fife, Dora Rodriquez, and Alvaro Enciso in southern Arizona, opened my eyes to the human toll of the forty-year-old border management strategy called "prevention through deterrence." Though it has never accomplished its creators' stated purpose—to stop people from coming—it continues to be the bedrock of Washington policymaking.

Built on cruel and racialized foundations, "prevention through deterrence" birthed the detention-to-deportation pipeline that began, mentor Guerline Jozef schooled me, with the refusal of the Reagan-Bush administration to welcome Haitians seeking asylum in the early 1980s.

〰〰〰〰〰〰〰〰〰〰〰〰〰〰〰〰〰〰

Today, the Cold War-era Military Industrial Complex has sown the seeds of a Border Industrial Complex that encircles the globe like a second equator. Cleaving north and south asunder, its walls and surveillance systems, its visa requirements and passport controls, its dictates about who is welcomed and who isn't, now separate rich from poor, white from Black and Brown, and relative safety from danger and violence in a global apartheid.

I have observed its encroachment with my own eyes for I, too, am a migrant, though by choice and privilege. To date, I have lived more years outside the land of my birth than in, having plied my trade as an educator—in classrooms; on campuses; even under the trees—on four continents, from Central America to China and Hong Kong to New York, Paris, and now London. I remember well the days before biometric passports, endless security lines, and dystopian face- and iris-scanning technology. When I first set out to work my way around the world, I had no trouble obtaining employment. But when France denied me a work visa in 2004, I abandoned my academic career—and a steady paycheck—for life as a freelance writer and sometime entrepreneur.

Still, I continue to cross borders with relative ease by virtue of my blue and gold embossed passport, professional qualifications, and skin tone. I am a white woman. Born and raised under the influence of the Civil Rights, Women's Rights, Labor Rights, and Anti-War movements, my personal identity and values were formed and forged within the promise of these cries for social justice. I reside, and thrive, in an ephemeral borderlands—one that cannot be mapped—buffeted and buoyed by a diversity of languages, cultures, colors, landscapes, and creeds.

"Your global and historical perspectives add a unique dimension, placing this border insanity into a context weary wanderers and helpers often lose sight of," Angry Tía Joyce Hamilton told me, urging me on when the thought of wading into the political minefield of today's divisive immigration debate threw my confidence into crisis. When the coronavirus pandemic forced me back home in March 2020, Tia Joyce kept my exploration on track. The ensuing three years of research, reading, and discursive learning began with her, the Angry Tías' archivist and documentarian.

She and Susan became my earliest editors, helping me to craft a narrative dedicated to the dreamers and strivers directly impacted by the many-headed Hydra that is the worldwide Border Industrial Complex: from those caught under its knee to the welcoming first responders who show us, every day, that there is a better way. I have done so with their permission and their collaboration, to the extent possible, engaging all featured storytellers in fact-, quote-, and chronology-checking; or by verifying the accounts they shared with me through resources and statements already in the public record. But any remaining errors are mine alone.

Their tales of humanity became the warp supporting the weft of my growing understanding as to how we reached this wretched place.

Rainier Rodriguez, Helen Perry, Abraham Barberi, and so many others, became lifelines and translators as I endeavored to stay connected with asylum-seeking families and individuals trapped, indefinitely, in Mexico during the pandemic. My growing contacts in El Paso—from Border Network for Human Rights to Hope Border Institute to the University of Texas and Holocaust Museum to individuals too numerous to name here—stepped me through the over-one-hundred-year history of El Paso as border-control laboratory. But my voyage into the heart of darkness took flight when I joined the team called Witness at the Border.

Thanks to the methods they developed to enable the subversive act of seeing, even from afar, I participated in tracking in real time the expulsion of 80-90 Cameroonians with credible fears of persecution, even death, if returned to their native land. That is when I unexpectedly uncovered the routine misuse of a so-called "humane" human restraint device, called The WRAP, by agents of the US federal government to force the compliance of many through the torture of the few. And how I came to collaborate with Texas A&M University Law School Professor Fatma E. Marouf to expose this heinous practice.

llllllllllllllllllllllllllllllllllllllllllllllllllllllllllll

With *Crossing the Line: Finding America in the Borderlands*, I aim to humanize today's immigration debate through the transformative power of storytelling. The work is a tapestry of original reporting, oral history-telling, historical discovery, and memoir of my own awakening to the impunity of the US Department of Homeland Security. It documents lived experiences of global migration in the 21st century as it connects historic dots that shed light on the rise of the extreme Right. It serves to show that the 21st-century shift to a security-first paradigm has obliterated the 20th-century promise of civil liberties as a human birthright.

In asking, *How did we get here?* I flesh out the root causes of forced displacement through stories I believe will resonate with readers in these deeply troubled times. The tales of humanity included in the book illustrate how the so-called land of immigrants, democracy, opportunity, and equality under the law has flouted its own commitments to protecting refugees and human rights, giving permission to other world powers to do the same. They reveal that US border cruelty is not a mere by-product of Trumpism but that it grew up all around us, hiding in plain sight, enabling him and his anti-immigrant acolytes to crank the cruelty to 11—a volume Biden-Harris never turned down.

It is the story of an "America" represented today by whip-snapping Border Patrol cowboys and elected officials so cynical they booby-trap river buoys with razor wire and circular saw blades; erect made-for-TV "walls" of shipping containers; traffic human beings with public funds; and orchestrate military maneuvers against unarmed "foes." It is the story of an "America" that existed before the US border crossed it, pushed into it, claimed it, and subsumed it. It is also the story of an

"America" many of us dream about and still aspire to, where everyone's humanity is recognized and valued: the "Beacon of Hope for those striving to live free." It is a call to action to safeguard that promise.

‖‖‖‖‖‖‖‖‖‖‖‖‖‖‖‖‖‖‖‖‖‖‖‖‖‖‖‖‖‖‖‖‖‖‖‖‖‖‖

I embarked on this odyssey with a single contact, Angry Tía Susan Law. Thanks to her invitation, when the snowbirds with whom I arrived in Texas on January 3, 2020, turned right out of the Brownsville-South Padre International Airport, toward the golf courses and beaches beyond, I turned left. Destination: the Tex-Mex border.

IN MEMORY OF

My father and first champion, Bill Towle,
Thank you for the inspiration. I will miss you forever.

My mother, Stephanie Towle,
Thank you for passing your passion for
history and love of words to me.

And Susan Law, who the world lost too soon.
May your commitment to social justice
be our collective flashlight.

PART I:
DEPARTURE

CHAPTER ONE

Confronting Cruelty

One day deep into June 2018, Rio Grande Valley lawyer Jodi Goodwin received a curious phone call. It was from a deportation officer employed by the US agency of Immigration and Customs Enforcement, better known by its acronym: ICE. He was stationed at the Port Isabel Detention Center in Los Fresnos, Texas, where Jodi's most recent clients had been imprisoned, though they were not outlaws.

Her clients were parents. They had pulled up stakes and fled brutal violence and food insecurity in their home countries in order to bring their children to safety in the United States.

They had survived the perilous journey northward along the migratory trail through Central America and Mexico only to land at the US southern border just as Trump & Co threw down the gauntlet called "zero tolerance." Anyone crossing the US-Mexico line between international ports of entry, announced Trump's first attorney general, Jefferson Beauregard Sessions III, that April, would henceforth be considered a criminal, even people seeking asylum though pursuing safe haven in the US is legal under both US and international law, no matter their means of arrival.

Agents of US Customs and Border Protection, which includes the Border Patrol, had been ordered to shackle and imprison all border crossers, even those who turned themselves in and requested asylum. Agents also had been ordered to take their kids away. Such harsh treatment was necessary, the administration maintained, to signal to other would-be border crossers: *Do Not Come. Do Not Come.*

Family separation would deter further northward migration, Trump & Co maintained. They also believed in the rightness of their actions: parents making the dangerous journey with children were no better than traffickers, they argued, so criminalization was justified, they said, leaning on the harshest interpretation of laws dating back 100 years.

US Federal Judge Dana Sabraw did not agree. Ruling in favor of the American Civil Liberties Union in the matter of *Ms. L v. ICE*, he ordered immigration authorities to stop separating families, to halt the deportations of parents without their children, and to reunify all separated families within thirty days, by the end of July 2018. This proved problematic, however, for neither Customs and Border Protection nor ICE had kept track of who was taken from whom and where separated family members were sent.

Without these data, the US Department of Homeland Security had no clue how to comply with Judge Sabraw's order.

"So irresponsible," sighed Jodi. "They had absolutely no plan."

Family members had been flung to the winds, in many cases incarcerated miles apart. Hundreds of mothers and fathers had been deported already, turning babies and toddlers too young to provide a parent's name or country of origin into orphans and wards of the US government. They risked being lost to loved ones forever, trapped inside a mysterious bureaucratic black box until they turned eighteen, when they would likely be turned over to ICE to be incarcerated as adults, and eventually sent back themselves to places they now never knew. In some cases, families following legal procedure, applying for asylum at official border crossings, were also separated.

<hr>

Standing 5'2" in boots and known to wear a white cowboy hat over her long blonde ponytail to protect her blue eyes and fair skin—when not dressed for court, that is—Jodi had been an integral part of the border-lands humanitarian network, fighting from the trenches on behalf of immigrants in the US and their families, for nearly twenty-five years. She landed in the Rio Grande Valley (RGV) in 1995, fresh out of law school and having just passed the Texas Bar. She had committed to a one-year clerkship with the US Department of Justice Executive Office for Immigration Review, though her goal was to practice public interest law on behalf of those unable to afford private attorneys.

"I thought I'd be in the borderlands for a year, then move back to San Antonio," Jodi told me. But that's when then-Speaker of the US House of Representatives Newt Gingrich pushed through Congress his infamous "Contract with America." Representing the ultra-conservative agenda still alive in US politics today, it pushed taxes on the rich to a minimum, while gutting services for the elderly, very young, disabled, and poor.

Jodi didn't need a weathervane to see which way the wind was blowing: the Gingrich "Contract"—what President Bill Clinton would liken to a hit job, calling it the "contract *on* America"—didn't just harm disadvantaged communities; it placed undue burdens on new arrivals to the US, too. So she pivoted. Deciding to stay in the RGV, she hung up her own shingle.

Jodi has since represented thousands of people seeking asylum, immigrant workers, and permanent residents pursuing citizenship. She has also held a front-row seat to the ever-increasing militarization of the US border, which triggered a boom in the country's for-profit immigration-enforcement complex.

"There was one detention center in the Valley at the start of the Obama era," Jodi states. "By spring 2018, there were at least six." And that number, she noted, didn't include the government-funded kids "shelters"—aka, detention centers for migrant youth and children—sprouting up in strip mall office suites and abandoned big-box stores all over the country, though most of us never knew.

Jodi knew. She also knew that the only way to reunite separated families was to spring the parents from ICE prison first, while simultaneously tracking down their kids, so reunifications could happen as quickly as possible.

Though Jodi acknowledges that her caseload might have been more constant—and more lucrative—had she joined a firm or legal aid practice, she appreciated the freedom and nimbleness of being a solo practitioner. Never was this flexibility more important than in the spring of 2018. She was among the first to act—a good three months ahead of colleagues who needed the go-ahead of senior partners and/

or funders before joining the effort to reunify families separated by Uncle Sam.

She also had a jump on ICE. And after Judge Sabraw's ruling in June 2018, the agency was in desperate need for her help. "The officer asked if I'd be willing to share my list."

By that, Jodi meant *not the names* of the imprisoned parents, but their "Alien" Registration Numbers (A#s). For under ICE the dehumanization of people seeking safety includes stripping them of their identity: replacing their names with a nine-digit number and a label that conjures another life-form and one to be feared.

⸻

Jodi was in a rare position to see the writing on the wall before most others. Because she provided pro bono representation at the Brownsville public defender's office, she was acquainted with most legal professionals in the Valley, and they her. When, toward the end of May 2018, a strange case shift arrived at the courthouse, she began to receive calls from colleagues, all asking the same question: *Are we prosecuting asylum seekers now?*

She went to court to see for herself. There, she discovered adults in need of protection shackled, though requesting asylum is not a crime. What's more, they were desperately seeking information as to the whereabouts and welfare of their children. This led her and her colleagues also to ask: *Are we taking their kids now, too?*

On Friday of that week, while attending a colleague's retirement party, she presciently suggested he wait a little longer to step down. "You gotta stay," she told him. "We're going to need you. Something bad has rolled into town."

He said he knew. It had rolled into McAllen, Texas, too. Their friends at the Texas Civil Rights Project had sounded the alarm that week as well.

At the Brownsville Courthouse the following Monday, Jodi saw it with her own eyes: "Moms, dads, they were distraught, beside themselves. They couldn't attend to the proceedings or respond effectively to the judges' questions. They just wanted to know what happened to their kids."

According to a second federal class-action lawsuit, *Dora v. Sessions*,

"Every single parent described the moment that their children were taken from them as the single most vividly horrifying experience of their lives: 'shattering,' 'unbearable,' 'a nightmare.'" Having fled their home countries, in large part to protect their children, they were emotionally and psychologically traumatized at losing them, most cruelly, to men in uniform.

The lead plaintiff, Dora, took off running with her seven-year-old son after years of extraordinary abuse at the hands of her husband. She arrived at the border and turned herself in to immigration agents, requesting asylum. When a Customs and Border Protection official took her boy, she begged and pleaded, explaining that after all he'd been through, he needed her. The officer told her "she deserved to lose her child and would not see him again until he was eighteen years old."

"Alma" was taken to court the day after requesting asylum for her and her two children, aged seven and nine. When she returned to the Border Protection processing center, her kids were gone. She, too, was told she would never see them again, "that they would remain in the US and she would be deported."

Likewise, "Esperanza," whose husband "gifted" her to a Mara Salvatrucha, aka MS-13, gang leader as a sex slave—she ran to save her son, who witnessed her being raped too many times to count. A Border Protection officer told her, "He belongs to the US government now."

A fluent Spanish speaker and mother of three, Jodi understood not only the tragic import of their stories but the forces they were up against. She obtained the A#s of seven women in court that first day. She followed them to Port Isabel Detention Center, thirty miles away from the Brownsville Courthouse. She told them, "I'm going to get your children back."

She hoped she could.

|||||||||||||||||||||||||||||||||||||||||||||||||||||||||

The right of asylum is an ancient juridical concept, under which any person facing persecution, or the threat thereof, may seek the protection of another sovereign authority. Before arbitrary lines were drawn on maps to create nations and states, that meant places of sanctuary, such as houses of worship and religious institutions, as well as "governable territories." In modern times, the right to safety and protection is also the domain of the United Nations Refugee Agency (UNHCR), which was born of the 1951 Refugee Convention after the shame of nation-states turning Jewish refugees back to their deaths during the Nazi era.

The Refugee Convention codified today's right of asylum, determined as having a credible fear of harm due to one's race, religion, nationality, social group, or political opinion, a definition that has deep historical roots in pre-Christian Egyptian, Greek, and Hebrew traditions. The practice has survived the ages, changing little. It was folded into Islam, which teaches that a host society is duty-bound to provide protection to those fleeing persecution. The principle of asylum was adopted by the established Christian Church in medieval times and evolved into an accepted, unquestioned aspect of Western culture. It has been recognized under international law since the ratification of the Universal Declaration of Human Rights in 1948 and was written into US law with the 1980 Refugee Act.

Grounded in the belief that all members of the human family have a right to dignity, Article 14 of the Universal Declaration of Human Rights states, "Everyone has the right to seek and to enjoy in other countries asylum from persecution." In addition, the right to dignity and freedom from torture, as enshrined in the Declaration, have become foundational to fair treatment under the law in societies around the globe. Yet, even before the 2016 election, Trump & Co were determined to strip those rights away.

In 2015, then-candidate Trump claimed, without evidence or following questionable evidence from unreliable sources, that the US asylum system allowed "alien criminals and rapists" to "disappear" into the country and run roughshod over the nation's laws, elections, and values. Intent on ending the right of asylum altogether in the US, he and his administration declared "zero tolerance" for anyone crossing the line between ports of entry. They criminalized everyone, including safety seekers, even as they cut off access to legal pathways, creating a Catch-22 for the world's most vulnerable people. Then, as if denying them their right to dignity weren't enough, Trump & Co tortured them by taking their kids.

Such cruelty for cruelty's sake is part of the historic playbook of dehumanization, stretching as far back as time. Not simply a violation of the Declaration, it is a crime against humanity.

Regarding the US immigration system, Jodi states, "It has never been fair or humane, not under Clinton, either Bush, or Obama. But zero tolerance brought a new level of cruelty to US immigration that I had never witnessed before." She continues, "A body politic that will separate families will stop at nothing."

Especially when that body politic gives total power over the lives of others to bureaucratic agencies that know no accountability and fail to keep records.

‖‖‖

On arrival at the US southern border, adults and youths—including those rendered "unaccompanied" when taken from their loved ones—are funneled into two different government-run pipelines, each including its own alphabet soup of departments, offices, and agencies. Everyone's first contact, whether presenting at a port of entry or between ports, is with Customs and Border Protection. Port officers wear blue, while agents operating between ports, the US Border Patrol, wear green.

Once in Border Protection custody—what the agency refers to as an "apprehension," whether a person is caught crossing the border, has turned themselves in to Border Patrol, or has lawfully requested asylum at a port of entry—everyone is detained in a processing facility. These are secured prisons. They are kept so cold, ostensibly to kill bacteria, they are known as *las hieleras*, aka "iceboxes," or "cold houses." There, everyone is sorted by age and gender, and caged in *las perreras*, "dog pens," where by US law they may remain for no longer than seventy-two hours. That's when safety seekers should be released and allowed to pursue their asylum claims while living with family, friends, sponsors, or even on their own in the US. But most adults are transferred to a "detention center," while children under eighteen and labeled unaccompanied are sent to a "shelter." Both terms are euphemisms for jail, however, for in neither type of facility is one allowed to come and go.

Adults are shackled in five-point restraints—wrists and ankles bound in metal cuffs and tied into a heavy waist chain—as one would treat someone considered a danger to society. They are then handed off to ICE.

Children, however, are passed to the Department of Health and Human Services, which sends them, in turn, to the Office of Refugee Resettlement, if there is bed space available in its network of one-hundred-plus facilities licensed by state-based departments of child and welfare services. If the Resettlement Office is out of beds, Health and Human Services will place children in what are variously called Emergency or Temporary Influx Shelters. These are notoriously militaristic congregant settings run by contractors that typically have no background, qualifications, or training in the care of kids.

Whether in emergency congregant or licensed settings, freedom is denied these children; their fate is little discussed. These factors, compounded with the traumas that caused their flight, the horrors experienced while in flight, and the shock of being lost to parents and other loved ones, whether pulled apart or not, can intensify in the young brain to the point of toxic stress. In this state, a child's mental and emotional, even physical, development simply shuts down.

To minimize the too-often irreversible ill effects of this phenomenon, guidelines laid out in a 1997 legal landmark, the Flores Settlement Agreement, demand that children be removed from custody, whether under Health and Human Services or the Resettlement Office, within twenty days of arrival and placed, ideally, with a parent; with another relative if a parent cannot be found; or in a home-like setting, if there is no parent or relative available to receive them—in that order.

With their parents locked up somewhere in the clandestine network of two-hundred-plus ICE prisons that make up the US immigrant-detention complex, many of the children taken from parents in the spring of 2018 had no one to go to and nowhere to go.

That's why Jodi's priority was to get the parents out of jail first, and as quickly as possible, too. Because once the Resettlement Office's "system of care" kicks into gear, children have a tendency to disappear inside the "next best thing" to being with a parent or other relative: the US foster care system. There, they can get swallowed up and lost track of altogether, often for years. There, like their adult counterparts, they—even toddlers—are put into "removal proceedings" and expected to represent themselves to immigration judges, without lawyers.

And although the Departments of Homeland Security and Health and Human Services are both cabinet-level US agencies, they are not historically in the habit of talking with each other or sharing information. That might not matter in the case of individuals arriving alone. But when it comes to parents and children deliberately separated, it matters a great deal. As Jodi states, "Reunification is next to impossible if information is not routinely captured and shared."

Trump & Co did not track who was taken from whom, whether and where they were jailed, or if they were summarily deported without due process, because reunifying the families they tore asunder was never a part of their master plan.

<hr />

At the Port Isabel Detention Center, following her May 2018 Brownsville courtroom epiphany, Jodi emptied her pockets and purse of car keys and cell phone, passed through the metal detectors, then spread-eagled her arms and legs for a wanded pat-down. She approached the clerk's security window and pushed seven forms through the gap between glass and narrow laminate counter, each one filled out with the A#s of the seven mothers she'd come to see. Then she settled into a hard-backed, scoop-seated immovable metal chair in the cheerless, institutional, high-ceilinged waiting room where there was nothing to do but watch someone else's choice of movie from a soundless TV screen.

Jodi met with all seven mothers that day. Each recounted her story—slowly, haltingly, wiping away tears that would not stop flowing—of her last moments with her child or children. Jodi carefully recorded what details they could remember, taking down their names as well as the names of their missing kids; their country and town of origin; the identities or characteristics of their Border Protection handlers, if remembered, if they even knew.

By the end of the day, Jodi held not just these seven horror stories. She also learned that inside the Port Isabel Detention Center there were at least four dorms of seventy women each, all of them robbed of at least one child.

That meant 280 women and many more children needed representation. And this was just one detention center!

She asked herself, "How am I going to be able to find all these kids?" Leaning always on the "child's' right to protection" argument, both Health and Human Services and its Resettlement Office shield their youthful "inmates" from view—and themselves from scrutiny. These are impenetrable bureaucracies, even denying attorneys the names and locations of their under-age and tender-age (younger than twelve) clients.

"I wanted to cry," remembered Jodi. "But there was no time. There was too much work to do." She knew she couldn't manage that many cases. "Most lawyers handle only about twenty-five cases in a single year."

<hr />

After that first day at Port Isabel Detention Center, Jodi gathered her networks. She called Kimi Jackson, then-director of the South Texas Pro Bono Asylum Representation Project (ProBAR), and asked for help with locating kids. She joined her list of names with those being collected by the Texas Civil Rights Project and the San Antonio–based Refugee and Immigration Center for Education and Legal Services (RAICES). In all, she organized 250 attorneys and legal advocates from all over the nation to provide pro bono support for the families broken apart by Trump & Co.

She took statements, wrote briefs, and completed asylum applications—called I-589s. She advocated on behalf of her clients with ICE, argued their cases, and mentored others to argue cases, too. Her mission was to make certain all parents separated from their children had a fighting chance at getting their kids back. She did all this while single-mothering two teenaged daughters and a young son, and without taking on a single paying client for nearly four months. Jodi grew so broke that when a water pipe burst in her house one long weekend when she and her kids were away, leaving it damaged down to the subflooring and in need of a total renovation, she had to move them into a rented two-bedroom in downtown Harlingen, Texas, a thirty-minute drive from home. Putting family reunifications before all else, it would be another two years before she could afford to restore her beloved *ranchita* to livable condition once more.

By the end of the summer of 2018, Jodi had single-handedly reunited thirty-four families—the number would eventually rise to thirty-seven—and played a significant role in bringing 450 families back together again. Even during her own family's summer trip to France that August, planned and paid for before the house flood, she was working on reunifications.

Sadly, not everyone found each other again. Coerced into signing papers they did not understand, some parents were subjected to a tried-and-true US practice called "voluntary departure" and deported before their kids could be found. Emergency Influx Shelters erected in Tornillo, Texas, and on the Homestead Air Reserve Base in Florida, stood on federal lands where Trump & Co claimed exemption from Flores regulations. Kids were incarcerated there for months, many used as bait by ICE to hunt down relatives living undocumented in the US. When these people, too, got deported, many youth were left cut off and alone, without loved ones or advocates.

Some were sent to foster care; others languished in the custody of the Resettlement Office until their eighteenth birthdays. There were still an estimated one thousand children not yet reunited with their families five years later when, on October 16, 2023, the American Civil Liberties Union announced a settlement in *Ms. L v. ICE*. Those who might have gotten into scraps during their prolonged imprisonment accumulated criminal records while on the inside and were transferred to ICE custody upon "aging out" to remain incarcerated as adults. They may still be locked up today.

But the forced separation of families wasn't the only dark tide to flow through South Texas that spring.

CHAPTER TWO

Aunties and Grannies Get Angry

Jennifer Harbury had been keeping her eye on the Rio Grande Valley bridges. A longtime civil rights attorney and dedicated refugee advocate, she had lived in the Valley for four decades. She knew that any shift in border activity at California ports of entry meant something was on its way east. And by all accounts—increasing intimidation and abusive behavior by ICE and Border Protection agents; Trump & Co's suspension of the Legal Orientation Program for new arrivals seeking asylum; and near-blanket denial of humanitarian release into the US of pregnant women—whatever was coming wasn't good.

Sure enough, evil reached the Hidalgo International Bridge port of entry, just south of McAllen and the last stop before Brownsville, in the final days of May 2018. Jennifer messaged her colleague Kimi Jackson at ProBAR right away: *Urgent help needed!*

Forty people were stranded on the bridge. They had been there for five days. They had no food, no water; they were completely exposed to the elements. Some were barefoot, their shoes having fallen apart on their trek across Mexico. All were desperate.

Kimi lost no time. She contacted her trusted comrade in LGBTQIA+-rights activism, Cindy Candia, as well as her friend, a retired adult literacy educator and Presbyterian Elder, Joyce Hamilton. The three sprang into action, calling on others to help them form a caravan to deliver to the bridge as many sandwiches as they could make, as well as snacks, diapers, Pedialyte, whatever they could pull together in a heartbeat.

Cindy, an ex–correctional officer and the daughter of migrant farmworkers, emptied her cupboards into a large picnic cooler, "because my husband and I were between paychecks at the time." On the hour-long drive from Harlingen, she and the others couldn't stop asking: *Why isn't Customs and Border Protection letting them in?*

What the three women found at the bridge that day, June 3, 2018, defied explanation and challenged the imagination: a scrum of men, women, babies, and children pressed up outside the commodious and air-conditioned Border Protection office at the bridge's north end. Under the eyes of US federal agents, they'd been sleeping on bits of found cardboard, washing in a nearby water fountain, and taking turns using the bathroom at the duty-free shop in Mexico, known only by the acronym UETA.

"They were literally stuck there," Joyce recounts.

The triple-digit Texas sun scorched the asphalt, burning their feet. There was nowhere to sit. Babies needed new diapers, women needed clean underwear. Everyone needed a change of clothes and a bath. Some needed medical attention. Then-McAllen resident and freelance writer Daniel Blue Tyx called it "a refugee camp on the bridge."

Back at home that night, Kimi tapped out a call to action on her Facebook page, describing what she'd seen and asking for volunteers and money to help support the needs of those trapped at the Hidalgo-Reynosa port of entry. She included a shopping list.

Nayelly Barrios was among the first Valley residents to receive Kimi's message. A poet and immigrant from Mexico, the then-University of Texas-RGV professor lived close to the bridge, in Edinburg, Texas, and was on summer break. She dashed right over with supplies from Kimi's list, but not without first sharing the call for help with her Facebook friends. She received $200 in donations overnight.

When Joyce and Cindy met Nayelly face-to-face for the first time four days later, the refugee camp on the bridge had grown in size from forty to seventy. Border Protection agents were still processing asylum claims then, but slowly—around ten per day—meaning more people were joining the bottleneck than leaving it. By day, they were forced up against the outer metal barrier of the walkway to allow the thousands of quotidian pedestrian border-crossers to pass on the left. Their long, single-file line extended from the empty customs office, which could have accommodated a hundred people, to the bronze plaque, marking the official US-Mexico boundary.

On June 11, Nayelly sent a frantic group message to Kimi, Cindy, Jennifer, and Joyce: she'd arrived at the bridge to see US officials pushing the entire line of asylum-seeking families and individuals back—all the way to the international midpoint, or "limit line." There, no longer in US territory, they would not be able to exercise their legal right to request asylum in the land believed, by people and cultures the world over, to be the "Beacon of Hope."

That day, Attorney General Sessions, the son of an avowed Alabama segregationist, announced that the Trump administration had rolled back asylum protections for victims of domestic and gang violence. The rule change would affect nearly every individual and family running from the Northern Triangle countries of Honduras, El Salvador, and Guatemala, where decades-long corruption and US-backed military training, along with a surfeit of weapons, had bred cultures of impunity.

Meanwhile, the hemispheric "fruit basket" suffers longer periods of drought or more frequent drenching rains every year, either burning up or carrying away crop yields that once sustained subsistence farming. Whole communities throughout Latin America are facing starvation even as they do the backbreaking work of harvesting the sugar, coffee, avocados, blueberries, bananas, and other produce that grace our tables.

Following Sessions's announcement of zero tolerance for anyone crossing the line between ports of entry, the people on the bridge were determined to seek safe haven in the US the so-called "right way": by presenting themselves and requesting asylum at a recognized port of entry. It was the only legal pathway left to them. Yet, they were made to add their names to a list, then wait in Mexico for their turn to request protection.

This practice, called "metering," created a bureaucratic wall more impenetrable than the physical one. Only an audience with Customs and Border Protection officials would kick-start the asylum process— and you never knew when your name would come up. So there you had to remain, in danger and squalor, in towns the US State Department decreed were as dangerous as any war zone. Because just as Prohibition one hundred years earlier gave rise to a shadowy, criminal market for gangs (aka the mafia) to traffic in liquor and other then-illicit substances, the late-20th century phenomenon of hardening borders has opened up lucrative human trafficking rings the world over.

Trump & Co's twin policies—of zero tolerance for those who crossed between ports; and metering for those who presented at the bridge-based Customs and Border Protection offices—proved a boon for organized crime. Stuck between the "rock" of persecution back home and the "hard place" of a hostile and unwelcoming nation, the waiting asylum seekers were rendered sitting ducks for drug cartels and transnational criminal organizations. They represented easy money—a means through which to extort family members in El Norte, anxiously awaiting the arrival of a loved one.

The most desperate chose the river, risking death or "apprehension" and arrest, which meant prolonged detention and the removal of their children. But for those wishing to cross "legally" and too afraid of losing their kids, staying put on the heavily patrolled international bridge, even without food and water or a change of clothes, was the safest place to be.

McAllen was not just a borderlands flashpoint for Trump & Co's family separation debacle in the spring of 2018. It was a place where the right to asylum was eroding as well. Waiting your turn on the bridge in the Rio Grande Valley heat could take days, or weeks—no one knew.

Cindy, Nayelly, and Joyce were angry. What they encountered on the Hidalgo International Bridge was injustice, plain and simple. Jennifer, an expert on torture, saw crimes against humanity. She was angry, too.

She asked Kimi to invite everyone to her house to brainstorm a coordinated response to the humanitarian crisis unfolding not only at the bridges, but at courthouses, ICE detention centers, Resettlement Office shelters, bus stations, and hicleras all across the Rio Grande Valley. But Kimi's hands were full. She was already working around the clock, alongside Jodi Goodwin, to provide pro bono counsel to the women at Port Isabel Detention Center who'd been robbed of their kids. And more were being taken away every day.

Kimi passed the task of coordinating everyone's schedules to Joyce, who set the date—June 13. Folks were invited from as far as San Antonio. Cindy thought it wise to have members of the press involved. She brought along a couple of activists from NETA-RGV, an independent bilingual media platform founded upon Trump's election to support and amplify the voices of Rio Grande Valley residents. Their presence was critical: when Jennifer suggested they mount a fundraiser, the NETA crew agreed to take that on. They brought in $72,000 the first month. Donations only went up from there.

NETA-RGV had the organizational infrastructure. The angry women who'd gathered that evening had neither formal organization nor name. But that wouldn't last long. At one point during the meeting, Jennifer remarked, "You all sound like a bunch of angry tías." In fact, they *were* all aunties. The comment lightened the mood a bit. It made them all laugh. But it got them thinking, too.

||||||||||||||||||||||||||||||||||||||||||||||||||||||||||||

The next day, June 14, Joyce was at the Brownsville Courthouse with her birder friend, Swiss-born, US-naturalized Madeleine Sandefur, the wife of a US airman from Kentucky she'd met in Paris in the 1970s. In addition to both being Texas Master Naturalists, and on the front lines of a public protest to save South Padre Island habitats from the development of SpaceX and liquefied natural gas export terminals, the two had helped to organize the local gathering of the Women's March, which brought an estimated seven million people into streets worldwide on Inauguration Day, 2017. Eighteen months later, the women brandished placards with a different message: they decried the separation of families at the US-Mexico border.

Madeleine was instrumental in getting the protest off the ground. And Joyce, alongside Cindy, had not stopped her continued round trips from Harlingen to the Hidalgo International Bridge, with massive shopping sprees in between. They had been so busy that when a reporter asked them, on mic, what they thought of Sessions using the Bible to defend family separations, they responded with mouths agape and blank stares.

"We were like deer in headlights," Joyce said.

Pointing the mic back to himself, the reporter paraphrased what Sessions had said: "I would cite you to the Apostle Paul and his clear and wise command in Romans 13, to obey the laws of the government because God has ordained them for the purpose of order."

A woman of faith, Joyce had a few choice spontaneous words to say about that! Though typically reserved, when the mic was thrust back in front of her, she railed at the travesty of invoking the same biblical passage that had been used to justify slavery to defend tearing children out of the arms of loving parents. How dare he! It was not Christian!

Jennifer, who stood next to Joyce on the courthouse steps, commented that she sounded more like a rampaging *abuela* (grandmother) than an angry tía. And the name of the group was born: the Angry Tías & Abuelas of the Rio Grande Valley.

Before the march was over that day, Madeleine, also an aunt and grandmother, had joined their ranks as well, "Because this was not what I signed on to when I became a US citizen." A former executive assistant and office manager, Madeleine took on the responsibilities of financial liaison and administrative coordinator.

Another incensed auntie at the demonstration, Elisa Filliponc, jumped into the fray, too, becoming the sixth Angry Tía. Elisa lived just a block from the Brownsville bus station and within walking distance of the city's bridges. She volunteered to keep an eye out there.

||||||||||||||||||||||||||||||||||||||||||||||||||||||||||||||||||

Days later, Lizee Cavazos, a mental health professional, waded into the effort. A naturalist, bird enthusiast, and friend of Tías Madeleine and Joyce, Lizee agreed, at first, to help orient refugees coming through the McAllen bus station one day each week. But on hearing the agonizing cries of children separated from their parents at McAllen's hielera, the Ursula Processing Center, she was moved to full-time activism.

That famous recording now heard 'round the world had been leaked to a trusted member of the press, Ginger Thompson at ProPublica, by Tía Jennifer. She had obtained it from an unnamed whistleblower inside Ursula. It would sweep across a shocked nation, and globe, inspiring a popular movement under the banner *Families Belong Together*, which resulted in spontaneous protests in 750 cities worldwide—600 in the US alone—and, alongside Judge Sabraw's ruling in *Ms. L v. ICE*, brought Trump & Co's family separation policy to its knees.

"When I heard the cries of children in Border Patrol cages," states Lizee, "I realized then, if I don't act to stop Trump's crimes against humanity, then I'm complicit in committing them."

By July, families in search of safety were being released into the US once again. With the cork on the border backup popped like that of a champagne bottle, the lines of people blocked at the bridges began to advance northward once more, now in greater numbers. From Ursula, ICE agents bused safety seekers in five-point restraints to the McAllen bus station and dumped them there. They had no money, little, if any, English, and no idea how to get where they were going.

Anywhere from two hundred to one thousand seekers of asylum landed there every day between July 2018 and July 2019. Before she knew it, Lizee was working full-time at the station alongside Jennifer's longtime friend and colleague Susan Law.

Retired human resources director of Texas RioGrande Legal Aid for 42 years, Susan was a beloved ally to all: wise, passionate, and supremely dedicated to social justice. "Her compassion for humanity and for alleviating human suffering was at the core of her character," Tía Joyce recalls. She put in a lifetime, whether in the company of rebels, sinners, fools, or saints, trying to right the bent arc of justice, and she was always willing to push boundaries in that pursuit.

It was fitting, then, that on behalf of the Tías, Susan and Lizee joined forces with Sister Norma Pimentel, executive director of Catholic Charities of the Rio Grande Valley. Sister Norma's McAllen-based Humanitarian Respite Center was already set up to assist refugees who were being left, stunned and resourceless, and expected to get out of Texas, stat.

Tías Susan and Lizee became an inseparable pair. They organized and trained a small army of volunteers, who met them at the McAllen bus station every day, seven days a week, *for a year*, helping folks prepare for bus trips that might go on for two or three days. With the funds raised by the Tías, Susan and Lizee provided the safety seekers with food; travel money; maps of the US marked with their individual itineraries; a list of key English phrases and practice in how to pronounce them; and—until bus station authorities stopped them—backpacks that had been stuffed with essentials, including diapers and small toys for children, by a fast-growing team, mostly from Harlingen, working out of the fellowship hall at Tía Joyce's church, when it was available, or her house, when it was not.

"It was a HUGE operation," she remembers. "We needed a lot of space."

CHAPTER THREE

Like Stones in David's Sling

On another hot Texas evening in late June 2018, shortly before 11:00 p.m., Tía Elisa's phone rang, waking her up. She had been monitoring the Brownsville bus station, stopping by several times a day. But so far things were business as usual. At one point, she'd scratched out her phone number on a Post-it, leaving it at the Greyhound ticket counter.

Elisa roused and reached through the dark for her phone. Though the call was from an "Unknown Number," something told her to pick it up. On the other end of the line was a Greyhound ticketing agent named Mario. He said a woman, newly released from ICE detention, had been dropped off at the bus station. It would be closing in ten minutes.

Could Elisa help her out, so she wouldn't have to sleep on the street?

Elisa pulled on the same jeans and T-shirt she'd taken off just hours before. She holstered her gun, "this being Texas," and hurried to the station just a block from her house. With Tía Madeleine's blessing, she checked thirty-year-old "Jessica," a mother from Honduras, into a hotel. Elisa was back first thing the next morning to help set Jessica on her way to South Carolina where she was hoping to be reunited with her young daughter.

Mother and child had crossed the Rio Grande with a trafficker and turned themselves in to Border Patrol when zero tolerance was roiling. Like Jodi's clients, they were taken to the Ursula hielera, wet and cold, with nothing but a shiny silver mylar blanket and each other for warmth. Jessica had to sleep sitting up, her back against the bars of the crowded "dog cage" into which the two were thrust. Her daughter slept in her arms as she shifted, cold and uncomfortable, throughout the long night. The next morning, a Border Protection agent "kindly" offered to take the little girl to "get cleaned up" so Jessica could "get some rest." He assured the exhausted mother that they'd be back in thirty minutes.

Jessica had not seen or heard from her daughter since.

Many more distraught mothers and fathers as well as aunts, uncles, older siblings, and cousins would follow in Jessica's footsteps—from the Ursula hielera to ICE detention centers to street corners and bus stations, where they were left resourceless, if they weren't deported without their kids first. After Jessica, Elisa found a group of four or five women at risk of being forced to sleep on the Brownsville streets. Then it was eight or nine; then a dozen. So, Elisa brought to Brownsville the strategy of welcome piloted in McAllen by the Angry Tías & Abuelas.

Michael Seifert, a former Roman Catholic priest turned border advocacy strategist for the American Civil Liberties Union of Texas, described to me how Elisa would introduce herself to the individuals stranded by ICE: "She'd earn their trust, then tell them, 'I can sit with you here all night or we can find a place for you to sleep safely.'" Their confidence won, she'd send them to homes of welcome with trustworthy local families, where they could rest and take a warm shower, before resuming their epic journeys.

Mornings, Elisa was back at the station, handing out pre-stuffed backpacks delivered to her house by Joyce as well as gift cards so folks had a bit of emergency cash. She helped them purchase tickets and she got them on their way. And because she lived so close to the bridges, her house became a way station for donations of clothing, hygiene supplies, and water, which she carted over to those stuck on the other side.

For three weeks, Tía Elisa worked around the clock and largely alone, eventually recruiting a group of neighborhood youth, who dubbed themselves *Los Primos* (the cousins). Then, just when the numbers were becoming too much for her and Los Primos to handle, five Texas teachers stepped into the effort, too.

They would become like the five stones in David's sling when the crises spawned by zero tolerance stomped like a clumsy Goliath into their Tex-Mex backyard.

|||||||||||||||||||||||||||||||||||||||||||||||||||||||||||||||

That summer, Juan-David Liendo-Lucio, his wife, Dr. Melba Salazar-Lucio, and their friends and colleagues from the Brownsville Independent School District, Sergio Cordova, Mike Benavides, and Andrea Rudnik, went from merely protesting family separations to supporting the needs of individuals and families forced to endure unspeakable conditions both north and south of the line.

Why did they do it?

"Because we are blessed when we help others," states Juan David.

"It started like a call from God," he continues. There *was* a "call." But it came from Michael Seifert.

"The multiple crises rolled into the valley like a glacier, imperceptibly at first, then suddenly taking over," states Michael, adding that no one was prepared. "A lot happened in a hurry. We had no idea how bad it would get, or how long it would last. And the needs were so great."

Not everyone was willing to help, however. *They aren't really our people*, was a common refrain, even within communities of Mexican origin. "But Melba and David are different," says Michael. "It's never about them. No matter how busy they are, they always show up and with smiles on their faces. They make the hard work fun."

He emailed David and Melba, requesting urgent help at the McAllen bus station. This is how they recall the origin story of what would become Team Brownsville:

DAVID: *Michael Seifert said ICE was just dumping asylum seekers in McAllen, right out of detention, dazed and confused, and without resources. I told Melba. Then I called Sergio. He and Mike Benavides drove.*

SERGIO: *We walked into chaos. There were hundreds of people. They had nothing but what they'd been wearing when they crossed. Many were victims of family separation and had no idea what had happened to their children. They were terrified.*

MELBA: *Another volunteer, Cindy Candia, of the then-forming Angry Tías & Abuelas of the RGV—although we didn't know that at the time— ran over to us. "Thank God you're here!" she said.*

DAVID: *As soon as we saw what was happening, we asked, "What do you need?" Cindy told us, "Get backpacks, toilet paper, water, snacks, diapers, whatever!" Mike and I left Melba and Sergio at the station. We went to the Dollar Store and emptied the shelves. Everything we bought was gone by the end of the day.*

MIKE: *We stayed there all night. The second time we went to McAllen to help, Cindy suggested we check the bridges and bus station in Brownsville. Sure enough, the same issues had come to us. We resolved to stay and help right there at home.*

Whether they knew it or not, Mike, Sergio, Melba, and David were following in the footsteps of decades of Rio Grande Valley humanitarians before them.

⸻

The US southern borderlands has always been a place of interchange, where languages and cultures met, mingled, and created something dynamic and unique. Not too long ago, families crossed the international bridges regularly, and easily, living binational, bicultural lives. It was the era of "natural migration," with people coming and going between work and home, crossing from one country to the other to go to school, attend a wedding, or receive specialized medical care. Border officials, many from the borderlands themselves, ushered familiar folks through the international boundary without checking passports. They opened ports of entry when US farms needed laborers. They waved the workers southward again, laden with goods purchased in US stores, when the seasonal harvest was over. Having grown up there, Mike, Sergio, Melba, and David remember those days well.

In the late 1970s and '80s, however, a new population began to arrive at the US frontier, not as part of their daily lives, but to start new ones. This was the era of the Dirty Wars, when civilians throughout Central America were too often caught in the crosshairs of the violence sweeping their native lands. Nearly one million Central Americans arrived at the US border between 1981 and 1990, but the same president who exalted the US as "the exemplar of freedom and a beacon of hope"—Ronald Reagan—slammed US doors shut on them. Most were "apprehended," detained, and deported right back to where they came from, without access to due process under international asylum treaties and US laws.

The religious faithful of the US borderlands found it impossible to reconcile the actions of their government, which refused protection to the very victims it created. Springing out of the Arizona desert and quickly spreading east and west along the nearly two-thousand-mile US-Mexico frontier, and many points north, a 20th-century underground railroad was born. Based on the perennial principles of welcoming the stranger, healing the sick, and giving water and nourishment to the thirsty and hungry, participating congregations offered food and shelter to the traumatized and destitute refugees pouring into their backyards. They shielded folks in search of safety in open defiance of an immigration "system" they felt betrayed both religious beliefs and national values.

At the movement's height, 580 houses of worship of all religious denominations provided sanctuary to refugees. One such refuge was the Casa Romero, established in 1982 in San Benito, Texas, just west of Brownsville, in honor of the Salvadoran Catholic Archbishop Oscar Romero who was felled by an assassin's bullet in 1980, while saying Mass. The modest shelter initially cared for about 150 souls each month. But Sister Norma Pimentel, who worked at Casa Romero as a young novitiate of the Missionaries of Jesus, remembers that within two years a similar number sought shelter there each day.

||||||||||||||||||||||||||||||||||||||||||||||||||||||||||

While the reasons for their displacement have changed over the years, Central Americans have never stopped traveling north in search of safety. In 2004, tending to the needs of two hundred refugees would have been considered a busy day for Rio Grande Valley humanitarians, like Sister Norma. Fast-forward ten years to 2014, and the borderlands saw those numbers double when roughly seventy thousand families and an equal number of children traveling alone arrived at the border in a single year.

In 2018, the numbers of southern border crossers surpassed anything witnessed before, even during the Dirty Wars era, for it wasn't just Central Americans asking for protection in the US anymore. These

21st-century refugees included cultures, colors, and creeds from across the globe, according to Brownsville native son James Pace, author of *Mother of Exiles: Interviews of Asylum Seekers at the Good Neighbor Settlement House, Brownsville, Texas*.

"But one thing remained constant," James told me before his death in 2022: *they were all running for their lives.*

As in the Reagan '80s, however, instead of asking, *Why are they coming?* and addressing the root causes of forced displacement and migration, US federal and state governments continued to cling to a singular border management strategy: "prevention through deterrence"— known officially in the US legal code as a "consequence delivery system." The theory behind it goes like this: if we make accessing the US as difficult and painful as possible, safety seekers will be scared off from coming.

The manifestation of that theory is that instead of providing financial support to borderlands humanitarians already doing the work of welcome, which politicians maintain will "pull" people to the border, more and more money is earmarked year-upon-year for building walls, hiring more law enforcement agents, constructing more prisons, and extending the border into Mexico, and beyond, with training and weapons for other national and sometimes local police forces. It's also made manifest in how US Border Protection and ICE agents and officials are indoctrinated to treat their fellow humankind, even children. Cruelty for cruelty's sake, so the theory goes, will repel people; it will keep them away.

But it hasn't.

Sister Norma was one of very few people outside the US Department of Homeland Security ever to be allowed a peek inside the now-infamous Ursula hielera in McAllen. "That experience has marked me forever," she told the *National Catholic Reporter*.

She describes seeing close to one hundred children packed into cage-like cells, with no showers, few mats to sleep on, and no room to sit or lie down, in frigid temperatures, all crying and pulling on her dress, saying, *Please get me out of here.* The memory remains for her "like a dagger in my heart."

As in the '80s, scores of people seeking asylum forcibly returned to their respective countries by the US, particularly to El Salvador, faced death or serious abuse, according to a February 2020 Human Rights Watch report. And deliberately rubbing coarse salt into the psychological wounds of those who did earn release, ICE stopped delivering them directly to area shelters and respite centers per agency practice to that point. From 2018, agents simply loaded them into unmarked white buses with blackened windows and dropped them off, penniless, hungry, filthy, and confused, sometimes in the middle of nowhere, often in the middle of the night.

It was humanitarian crisis upon humanitarian crisis.

After responding to the chaos in McAllen, David, Melba, Sergio, and Mike began working with Tía Elisa to replicate in Brownsville what the Angry Tías were doing at the bus station. They handed out backpacks stuffed with clean socks, travel snacks, bottled water, soap, a toothbrush, and toothpaste. They sent folks in need of asylum to their final destinations with food and maps marked up to explain their itineraries, noting where they would need to change buses. They coached the non-English-speaking travelers in handy phrases and taught many how to use ATMs and vending machines.

Simultaneously, the nationwide movement united around the cries of "kids in cages" demanded that Trump & Co stop separating families just as Judge Sabraw ordered. Stating, "Lots of people are going to be happy about this," Trump rolled his eyes, pulled out a black Sharpie, and grudgingly signed an executive order ending the practice on June 20, 2018. But as his government had made no provision for reuniting stolen children with their aggrieved parents (as Jodi Goodwin was now learning), no one knew how many families had been torn apart, nor how they would be put back together again. The administration's only real response was to pivot toward jailing whole families together, indefinitely, or slow their ability to cross the line through metering.

The call for a whole-scale mobilization attracted the support of over 250 national and local organizations, celebrities, politicians, and other public figures, coalescing as *Families Belong Together*. Capping off months of building global outrage, more than one thousand people gathered in Brownsville on Thursday, June 28, 2018. They met in Linear Park, across from the federal courthouse where parents who'd fallen victim to zero tolerance had been prosecuted while terror stricken and shackled in five-point restraints.

For Andrea Rudnik, the national mobilization was the catalyst that moved her from outrage to action:

ANDREA: *We all marched together under this banner that Mike made of baby onesies strung on a clothesline. It read: R-E-U-N-I-T-E. People came from all over the state. Speakers from Rio Grande Equal Voice Network and Los Union del Entero, even child speakers of undocumented parents, really opened my mind to the plight of immigrants in our own community. Even after living in the Valley for over three decades, I had no idea.*

But while family separation brought Trump's immigration agenda to their eyes, the horrors of metering brought it to their doorstep.

Driven to ports of entry by the threat of criminalization under zero tolerance, determined to enter the US through the only legal pathway available to them, people were suddenly being told: *There's no more room. The president says the US is full.*

Border Protection agents added safety seekers' names to a handwritten list and told them, simply, *You'll have to wait.* They were not told for how long. They were afraid to remain in Mexico. As in McAllen, the Brownsville bridges became "refugee camps," too.

Andrea, an Episcopal Seminarian, could no longer look away.

ANDREA: *If the Church has any message at all, it is to take care of our neighbors. I wanted to do something but I didn't know what. Sergio suggested we gather water and snacks and go together to meet the people stuck on the bridge.*

SERGIO: *She said, "Yes, I can do that." Then she couldn't stop. None of us could.*

MELBA: *So, in addition to helping orient people at the bus station, we started trudging across the bridges, carrying water to the asylum seekers, bags of clothes, shoes . . .*

MIKE: *We rigged tarps over the walkways of the bridges to shield the asylum seekers stranded there from the sun. We brought mats for them to sit and stand on to keep their feet from burning on the scorching hot asphalt.*

SERGIO: *I remember a colleague donating all these trial-sized toiletries. I posted a picture on Facebook. I wrote, "Look what my friend gave me!" After that, people kept showing up with supplies for me to take over.*

MIKE: *Then we got the idea to bring dinner. It was just boxes of pizzas at first, when it was just twenty to thirty people.*

DAVID: *Yes, crossing over to feed people was Team Brownsville's idea.*

MIKE: *People like to say that we were the love child of the Angry Tías, and it's true—our action was born out of theirs. We might even have become part of their group: The Angry Tías y Tíos.*

ANDREA: *But the Tías are spread across the Valley, as is their work. We're here, focused on our community. Our identity has always been tied to Brownsville.*

SERGIO: *And we were already a team. We've been colleagues and friends forever.*

These five Texas teachers worked together all that summer, uniting as Team Brownsville. A nationwide force for welcome formed around them.

SERGIO: *I started making these little videos, which I posted to Facebook. They got shared and shared.*

MIKE: *People sent money along with donations.*

SERGIO: *They really wanted to help. There was one day—I posted that I would be at Sam's Club all day, accepting donations. I parked my seven-passenger Honda Pilot in a visible place and opened up the hatch. People showed up with stuff from their houses or stuff they'd just bought at Sam's. By the end of the day, I couldn't fit another thing in the car.*

MELBA: *I remember this woman—her name was Susan. She was from Austin, and she came up to me at the bus station. She was wearing a hot pink embroidered Mexican dress. And she just handed me $1,000 in $10 bills to give to the folks seeking asylum so they'd have money for their bus journey. It was like that.*

ANDREA: *We wanted the asylum seekers to know: We see you. We hear you. We recognize your pain, and we will do for you what we would do for a neighbor.*

SERGIO: *Because they are our neighbors! My mother immigrated from Mexico. She met and married my father here, so I was born here—a first-generation US citizen. I kept thinking: if my mom had stayed in Mexico, that could be me there on the bridge with my kids. Just because she crossed when she did, I have what I have.*

Being born in the US makes you lucky, but it doesn't make you better. Humans are humans. Our hearts all beat the same blood. We all suffer the same pain.

CHAPTER FOUR

Welcoming with Dignity

Throughout the summer of 2018, refugees kept traveling north. The rules were unwritten, and unspoken, but they were heard loud and clear: there would be no governmental support for these newcomers. It was up to local shelters, respite centers, and volunteers to help safety seekers with a meal and a bath; to offer them some pocket money, and onward passage to their next destination from McAllen, Brownsville, and eventually Harlingen. ICE brought them in busloads, unshackled them, and left them, fifty at a time, hundreds a day, until as late as 9:00 p.m.

Fortunately, folks compelled to show welcome kept coming south, too, like Woodson Martin, a San Francisco Bay Area executive at the cloud computing company Salesforce.com, whose border work began in Calais, France. While volunteering in a refugee camp there with his wife, Kelly, and two sons, the Europeans chided him: "Don't you all have your own refugee crisis?" they asked. So immediately upon returning to the US, he flew to Texas and went straight to the bus stations. Tía Susan and Sergio put him right to work.

"I planned to go for a week, maybe two," Woodson told me. But he stayed for the bulk of his corporate sabbatical, from June 2018 to March 2019.

Then there's the story of Brendon Tucker. Though his path to the borderlands was circuitous, he seemed destined to become the Tías' favorite nephew and Team Brownsville's prodigal son.

Tucker, as he is affectionately called, hails from Texas Hill Country, located along the axis marking the geographical midpoint of the continental US. Known for its tall rugged limestone and granite hills, beautiful lush valleys, mystical underground caverns, and Canyon Lake—where Tucker grew up—Hill Country is one of the reddest regions in one of the reddest states, where Hillary Clinton claimed only 27 out of 254 counties in the 2016 presidential election.

Tucker grew up politically conservative, he says, "because that's what I was taught." His high school history class watched *The O'Reilly Factor* on Fox News every day. On the sites of his father's home construction business, the radio was tuned, almost invariably, to Rush Limbaugh. But a series of unexpected life events changed Tucker's point of view, forever.

First came the low-level charge for marijuana possession when he was still a teen. That landed him a sentence of ninety days in jail or a stiff bail. No one posted bail, so Tucker did the time. One of few white men on the inside, he learned firsthand about the racial injustices baked into the US prison system.

Then, with a Class-A misdemeanor on his record, Tucker discovered how too many are forced to live in the so-called Land of the Free: juggling several minimum-wage jobs—none with health care—and still barely making ends meet. He worked in sales for popular retail chains and, for a time, he rented out short-term furnished apartments to families of cancer patients receiving treatment at the Houston Medical Center. One day, he found some of his previous tenants living in the hospital parking lot in their van. They were paying for their loved one's cancer treatment out of pocket and had run out of rent money. Meanwhile, it was not unheard of for Tucker to sell five pairs of the same designer sunglasses to a single client—one pair for each boat and car.

"That's when I discovered income inequality and the broken state of health care in the US." This was particularly true in Texas, which boasts the nation's highest rate of medically uninsured.

In early 2018, he was back in Hill Country, managing the family Sno Cone business and working with his dad to fix up houses. Now, however, he had his radio tuned to Amy Goodman and *Democracy Now!*. "When I heard Reverend William Barber II speak about his revival of Dr. King's 1960s Poor People's Campaign," Tucker says, "I knew I wanted to be part of it."

He jumped into his old jalopy of a car and drove straight to Washington, arriving for the May launch of Barber's National Call for Moral Revival, a forty-day coordinated act of civil disobedience intended to focus popular attention on the "triple evils" of racism, poverty, and militarism. There, Tucker learned that Brownsville would be hosting a *Families Belong Together* rally on June 28. He reversed course, returning to Texas to attend the same event that drew Jodi Goodwin, as well as the newly formed Angry Tías and soon-to-be Team Brownsville.

‖‖‖

The march attracted people from all over Texas and beyond, including a young mother named Ashley Casale and her then-seven-year-old son, Gabe. They had driven 2,054 miles from upstate New York as soon as school let out that summer to agitate for the reunification of separated families. Denied access to every Resettlement Office shelter they tried to tour and every interview they tried to conduct, from Raymondville to Harlingen to Brownsville, mother and son pitched a tent in front of Casa El Presidente, a "tender age shelter" managed by Austin-based government contractor Southwest Key. When Tucker steered his old car into the Casa El Presidente parking lot to join their vigil it sputtered and gave up the ghost—his fate in Brownsville sealed.

The redneck-turned-revolutionary remained encamped in front of Casa El Presidente for about two months, even after his companions left to get home before the start of a new school year. Brownsville residents grew curious as they passed by the tents and signs stating SILENCE IS BETRAYAL and WHAT IF IT WERE YOUR CHILD?

Some folks stopped, like Methodist Deaconess Cindy Andrade Johnson and her husband, Mike. They brought Tucker home from time to time for a meal and a shower, when they weren't hosting asylum seekers brought to them by Tía Elisa. Team Brownsville urged their growing local following to bring Tucker water and sandwiches.

Just about then, ICE had another unwelcome surprise for municipal leadership and humanitarians throughout the RGV, informing them to expect a further increase in asylum-seeking families coming through their towns. Valley providers had to dial up a system of welcome quickly. Sister Norma took the lead.

〰〰〰〰〰〰〰〰〰〰〰〰〰〰〰〰〰〰〰〰〰

"When Sister asks you to do something," says retired social worker and then-volunteer director of Brownsville's Good Neighbor Settlement House, Jack White, "you jump, and ask how high later."

Jack recalls Sister Norma inviting him to McAllen when the number of refugees passing through the Catholic Charities Humanitarian Respite Center was reaching record highs of eight hundred to one thousand a day. They came in for a meal, a rest, a shower, some toothpaste or deodorant, maybe some aspirin and a change of clothes—all provided to the Respite Center through charitable donations. They left as soon as they could get a bus out of the station down the block. Those whose buses did not leave the same day were invited to grab a blue, plastic-covered, five-inch-thick single mattress from the stack that climbed to the center's ceiling. There was often no floor space left at lights out. Volunteers marked pathways on the floor with blue electrical tape to keep pallets from creating an obstacle course for people needing the bathroom and shower facilities in the night.

"People were traumatized," states Jack. "They didn't know where they were going or how to get there. They had no money, no English, no direction. When the bus station closed, they were pushed outdoors. If not for the Respite Center, they'd be forced to sleep on the surrounding streets."

Sister Norma requested that Good Neighbor Settlement House fold emergency relief for refugees into its mission as a homeless shelter. Fortunately, Jack's particular genius is in raising armies of volunteers, according to James Pace, whose mother, Zenobia, was one of five Methodist women to found the Good Neighbor Settlement House in 1952. Sixty years later, in 2012, Jack prevented the downtown community center from having to shutter its doors by increasing its volunteer workforce. In 2018, Good Neighbor's wheels were turning smoothly thanks to three full-time paid staff members and a cadre of unpaid helpers who, together, clocked in hundreds of thousands of hours annually.

Jack and volunteers, with the blessing of Good Neighbor's board, became immediately enmeshed with Team Brownsville. In addition to buying meals and bus tickets, handing out pre-stuffed travel packs and individualized itineraries, they ran a round-the-clock escort service to the Settlement House, located just a few blocks away, for those unable to leave for hours, or even days. There, staff and volunteers were moving nonstop, feeding people, outfitting them with new clothes, and bedding them down for the night after a warm shower.

Tía Elisa no longer had to hunt up local hosts. But on the bridges, the work continued as the numbers of asylum-seeking families and individuals continued to back up.

MIKE: *We calculated that the population grew each week by ten. On average, for every ten that crossed, twenty more took their place.*

MELBA: *We realized pretty quickly that buying food was too expensive.*

SERGIO: *So we started cooking food and taking it over.*

Tucker joined them to deliver meals and water, tarps and diapers, flip-flops and clean underwear—whatever was needed—to the refugee camps on the Brownsville-Matamoros bridges. But just as Ashley and Gabe had to prepare for Back-to-School, so did the five Texas teachers.

SERGIO: *We asked Tucker if he'd like to join us as Team Brownsville's chef.*

He signed right on.

DAVID: *Team Brownsville never missed a dinner from that moment forward.*

||||||||||||||||||||||||||||||||||||||||||||||||||||||||

Tucker cooked all that fall from a small efficiency apartment the team rented for him near the Gateway International Bridge. Decorated with Poor Peoples' Campaign posters, they dubbed the apartment "Tucker's Place." Some dubbed him "Super Tucker," as he made the trip into

Matamoros nearly every day, sometimes more than once. Others called him *"Güero Loco,"* the crazy gringo!

ANDREA: *We created a GoFundMe to raise money for the rent and Tucker took over. He was really enthusiastic and full of energy. He cooked. We cooked. Volunteers came to cook. The apartment was always crowded with people. When school started up again, and we could cross less often, we took turns helping "Super Tucker" take dinners over and man the bus station.*

SERGIO: *I kept making videos and they kept getting shared until one day I got a call from a* New York Times *reporter. "We would love to do a story on you," he said. It ended out on the front page!*

The donations really started to flow just as Tucker was lured away by a group of young activists who wanted to start a similar kitchen in Tijuana. He left Brownsville right after Thanksgiving to cook for the latest arrivals of a migrant caravan the United Nations estimated to total 7,322 individuals at its peak. A smaller group had set off from San Pedro Sula, Honduras, on October 13, adding Guatemalans, then Mexicans, all along the 2,500-mile trek to the US. But they were blocked from advancing northward by an unwelcoming president just in time for the 2018 midterm elections. Trump ordered an equal number of National Guard reservists to meet the caravan of people who carried children in their arms and all that they owned on their backs. He weaponized the footsore crowd fleeing harm to whip up a panic about barbarians storming the nation's gates in order to get his base to the polls that fall.

It was the second time he manufactured a crisis for the cameras that year—the second time he played politics with human lives, putting thousands at grave risk.

Shelter populations exploded, causing encampments to pop up all across the southern side of the line. In Tijuana, a population of mostly women and children moved into a tent city that formed the previous May when about 150 people traveled as a group from Central America's homicide capitals to the steps of the El Chaparral-San Ysidro port of entry. The El Chaparral tent city had grown steadily since then, with the second group, or caravan, adding thousands more.

Throughout the winter of 2018–2019, however, the San Ysidro port was effectively closed. Wait times for an audience with Customs and Border Protection officials stretched out for months, sending those coming behind them on a course for the Rio Grande Valley, where folks were still getting across the line, if slowly. Fortunately, another Team Brownsville volunteer was able to step in when Tucker left. Already a familiar face at "Tucker's Place," Rio Grande Valley lifer Gaby Zavala knew all too well what it meant to be a family separated. Hers had been ripped apart when she was in elementary school. When family separation became government policy, she was alarmed.

Gaby was then working as a liaison for global media outlets, connecting reporters with local figures. "That's how I met the members of Team Brownsville," Gaby recalls. Charged with scouting up a story for Hilary Andersson of the BBC, she set up an interview with Sergio and Andrea in the fall of 2018.

"Afterward, they took me to Tucker's Place. I cooked with him, I crossed with him. When he left to set up a kitchen in Tijuana, I became him."

When across the border in Matamoros, Gaby began to hear the stories: families and individuals were being extorted by Mexican border agents to keep their place in line; Cubans were forced to pay more than Central Americans; those unable to pay were disappearing from the line altogether. "They were sitting ducks," says Gaby.

The practice of metering asylum provided the cartels with a market opportunity they were happy to exploit to their fullest advantage. False promises of getting folks past US Border Patrol and on their way to loved ones in El Norte pushed many to try their luck with the river and organized crime, for whom trafficking people provided a safer payday than moving drugs. The cost to sneak a human into the US doubled to $5,000, then climbed to $6,000, the fee rising alongside safety seekers' increasing desperation. The local gangs made it increasingly clear: *Under pain of torture or even execution, the only route available to the US is with us.*

"I was learning firsthand how our immigration policies were affecting—and destroying—real lives."

As the calendar turned from 2018 to 2019, Gaby founded the Asylum Seeker Network and was off to Austin, to advocate for immigrants' rights among Texas state legislators and policymakers.

ANDREA: *Things got very hectic with first Tucker leaving, then Gaby. We scrambled to make sure there was always someone to cook and serve.*

They let go of "Tucker's Place" and moved into the Good Neighbor Settlement House, with Jack White's blessing.

MIKE: *Good Neighbor had much more room to cook and pack and store food supplies. And it was already supporting refugees released at the bus station whose buses did not leave right away.*

But the numbers of asylum-seeking families and individuals continued to back up.

MIKE: *By example, in December—we'd been taking dinner to the asylum seekers for about six months at that point—I overheard someone say that, for many, it was the only meal they got all day.*

So, Mike started a breakfast club.

MIKE: *I woke up at 6:00 a.m. and bought breakfast tacos in Brownsville. I'd pull the tacos and a couple of coffee carafes over in a canvas wagon, then cross back in time to get to work by 8:00 a.m.*

But it was becoming clear to everyone that metering was not going away. And the Team Brownsville co-founders were running out of money.

SERGIO: *In January, we relaunched the GoFundMe campaign. That brought in money, but it also brought us volunteers from all over the country—Houston, Dallas, Austin, the Bay Area, greater New York—and from all religious denominations.*

ANDREA: *I came up with the idea of organizing a rota. I'd assign a day to each group of local and out-of-town volunteers, and make a weekly announcement about who was doing what and when on a new Facebook page: Team Brownsville Volunteers.*

The first time Kathy Harrington cooked was Christmas Eve, 2018.

KATHY: *That dinner was for forty-seven people. I'll never forget it. I had no idea what was coming. They ate like they were starving. I was shocked. Once you see something like that, you just can't look away.*

Borderlands Pastor Abraham Barberi and his congregation at One Mission Ministries took Wednesday nights. Jodi Goodwin came with her kids on Sundays, dragging over home-cooked meals from Harlingen. In cowboy boots and hat, her blue jeans secured by a wide leather belt fastened with an oval silver buckle, Jodi provided Know-Your-Rights workshops to the crowd. She'd been counseling individuals and families by WhatsApp. But as the numbers grew, she realized it would be more efficient to educate everyone stuck in the Matamoros bottleneck as a group.

At least one member of each asylum-seeking family gathered around her as they ate—leaning against a traffic barrier, floppy paper plate in hand or propped on their knees if they were able to secure a spot to sit on the roadside curb. She taught them how to advocate for themselves upon being called by border officials for review, for metering also thwarted safety seekers' access to legal representation.

"My mission was to counteract the harms our government was inflicting on these people by setting them up for success," states Jodi.

‖‖

The collective effort that sprang to life in Brownsville the previous summer seemed, finally, to have found its flow with the new year. Then, one January evening at 5:00 p.m., Jack White received his first-ever phone call from ICE.

"They don't usually direct communications to people like me," Jack recalls. But they wanted him to know, "as a courtesy," that instead of dropping off individuals newly released from ICE prisons at the bus station throughout the day, as they had been, they would henceforth be delivering them directly to Good Neighbor Settlement House. He could expect two hundred to three hundred people the very next day…starting at 7:00 a.m.!

This gave Jack less than twelve hours to turn an operation staffed by three into a round-the-clock system. "It was then we went into madness. What followed was expansion to a twenty-four-hour, seven-day-a-week service. We put Band-Aids over Band-Aids; our medical clinic was overwhelmed; showers broke down. We had to reconfigure food preparation to provide for both refugees as well as our homeless. We had to set up sleep spaces in spare rooms over the food bank and in the community room, where we packed in up to three hundred a night."

The local police chief called ICE to castigate the agency for causing an untenable public safety crisis. But somehow the RGV humanitarian community managed. When Good Neighbor hit capacity, Victor Maldonado, director of the former Casa Romero— now called the Ozanam Center—offered overflow shelter for refugees coming through Brownsville. Farther-flung shelters, such as La Posada Providencia in San Benito and Loaves & Fishes in Harlingen, became additional ICE drop-off points for families when the increasing numbers became too much for Sister Norma's respite center in McAllen and the Brownsville shelters that spring. Tía Joyce organized a team of Harlingen and San Benito volunteers to help transport folks in motion from the bus station to area shelters, as well as the airport. And as the winter of 2019 rolled into spring, Gaby Zavala switched her focus back to direct-aid grassroots advocacy to run a daytime respite center at the church of Pastor Carlos Navarro, the Iglesia Bautista West Brownsville.

Gaby crossed paths frequently with Pastor Carlos in Matamoros when his Golán Mission brought goods and food to those encamped on the bridges. One day, after witnessing the crush of humanity overwhelm Good Neighbor's infrastructure, Gaby presented him with a plan.

"She told me, 'I have a dream; I just need a place,'" Pastor Carlos states.

The two phoned Brownsville's emergency management team, convincing them to let Iglesia Bautista open a day shelter for women and children. The facility had a large nursery full of toys, they argued, where volunteers could tend to the kids while their mothers—many of whom hadn't slept in weeks—could rest on Red Cross–donated cots scattered through class and worship rooms.

"Oh, and don't worry about the lack of showers," Pastor Carlos remembers Gaby telling them. "We'll set up temporary privacy showers in the church parking lot."

When the municipal authorities responded favorably to the pastor's offer to help, he left the decision to his congregation. "We began receiving people the very next day," he recalls. "I took care of their food and spiritual sustenance. Gaby took care of the social side of things: filling out forms, getting them to planes and buses on time, finding them legal representation."

"We even set up clothing and vanity stations. About twenty-five volunteers a day from Pastor Navarro's mission helped the women and children to create outfits from the donations and fix up their hair," says Gaby.

IIIIIIIIIIIIIIIIIIIIIIIIIIIIIIIIIIIIIIIIIIIIIIIIIIIIIIII

The "holy chaos," as Sister Norma dubbed it, ticked along until July.

SERGIO: *Mike and I were chosen GoFundMe Heroes of the Year, which brought a lot of awareness and helped us to raise a lot of money. It also attracted more volunteers from all over the country.*

That's when Austin-based Ann Finch suggested the team incorporate as a nonprofit organization, recalls Woodson, who went from lending a hand at the bus stations to helping expand Team Brownsville's humanitarian assistance program. He did this, in part, by leading large groups of Bay Area volunteers to the Brownsville/ Matamoros border with Kelly and the boys. The team's incorporation became effective on May 10, 2019, with Andrea, Woodson, and Ann serving as officers alongside Sergio and Mike as elected members. Kathy was eventually brought onto the board as well, taking over for Ann. They established leadership committees to help scale the effort; set up more economical arrangements with local vendors; sourced bulk purchasing options in Mexico; and raised funds by tapping the generosity of family foundations and individual donors, as well as running frequent Facebook campaigns.

SERGIO: *Things became less grassroots, then. But we had access to a lot more money.*

It was a welcomed trade-off, according to Mike.

MIKE: *In December, I was buying breakfast for forty people. By May, I was feeding one hundred and had exhausted my savings.*

One year after the launch of zero tolerance, the team was humming like a finely tuned engine. Andrea oversaw the rotation of an ever-growing community of local, state, and national volunteers; Sergio kept his eye on the bus station; Mike continued to run the breakfast club; and they all took turns escorting local and out-of-town helpers to bring dinner. As demand grew and grew, Woodson quietly modernized a Matamoros restaurant, Gorditas Tía Raquel, "one pot and pan at a time," to avoid cartel extortion. "We furnished the kitchen so they could produce hundreds of meals a day for over a year. It was a big deal. They were so committed."

||||||||||||||||||||||||||||||||||||||||||||||||||||||

By mid-summer, Team Brownsville and its extended ecosystem of volunteers were serving about two hundred people a day. Though metering had slowed Customs and Border Protection processing to a trickle, people in search of protection were still eventually getting through.

MIKE: *They were stopped here long enough that most of them became like family. We heard their stories. We knew why they left home. We knew what they aspired to be. We knew when they crossed. We knew when they'd been released from detention and were on their way to their loved ones.*

Then, without warning, the bottleneck at the Gateway International Bridge began to grow again: On July 19, 2019, Goliath stomped back into town, bigger and angrier than ever. That's when the Trump administration erected the most impenetrable wall of all thus far: the Migrant Protection Protocols (MPP), which didn't protect anyone at all.

Rolled out in San Diego on January 24, 2019, and otherwise known as the "Remain in Mexico" program, MPP didn't just slow the processing and eventual release into the US of those seeking safety. It barred folks in need of protection from entering the US until their asylum claims were resolved.

Translation: you'd be living in a tent for at least ten months if you were one of the lucky one percent whose asylum review was successful.

MIKE: *I remember our first victims of MPP. A Cuban couple—Dairon Elizondo Royas and his wife, Elizabeth. On the day of their metered hearing with [Border Protection], I said goodbye and wished them well. But they were back in Matamoros the next day. They'd been told they had to "Remain in Mexico" for the duration of their asylum trial, rather than in the US with their family, which was common practice before Trump.*

The shelter and tent city populations exploded again. Customs and Border Protection closed the Hidalgo port of entry in McAllen, pushing those fleeing harm to Matamoros. Instead of adding twenty and losing ten a day, the community began to grow at a rate of over one hundred each week. No one was getting into the US, and few were leaving Matamoros. They were literally stuck.

And that was just one tent city along the two-thousand-mile border. The policy would eventually stop more or less seventy thousand individuals in their tracks.

In Matamoros, tents crawled from the foot of the Gateway International Bridge, across the Civic Plaza, and right up to the doorsteps of local businesses as well governmental offices, including the headquarters of the Mexican agency tasked with immigration control: the National Migration Institute. When the plaza became full to bursting, tents worked their way up the embankment—or berm—of the levee park before they spilled onto the floodplain overlooking Matamoros all along the Rio Bravo, as the Rio Grande is called in Mexico.

Suddenly, bus stations, respite centers, and shelters all over the Valley went shockingly, eerily quiet. The thrum of controlled chaos at the McAllen bus station dimmed to whispered echoes. Brownsville's cathedral-like bus depot fell hauntingly silent, too. And Good Neighbor staff and volunteers stacked up and cleared away their surfeit of donated sleeping mats.

In the words of Tía Joyce: "When MPP came to the bridges south of the Valley, the bus stations in McAllen, Harlingen, and Brownsville went empty overnight."

PART II:
INITIATION

CHAPTER FIVE

Flying the Tattered Flag

The Rio Grande Valley has been inhabited for as long as history remembers. Home to at least eight nations, including those of the Americas' first peoples, it has flown seven flags—one its own, as an independent country that lasted less than a year, in 1840. The hunter-gatherers of the Coahuiltecan roamed the area before the Spanish, then French, then Spanish—again—laid claim. And it was part of the vast northern territory of Mexico when the doctrine of Manifest Destiny augured the 19th century westward expansion of the United States by Anglo colonial settlers.

As the new nation exercised what its leadership believed was their "God-given right" to push their ways into the old, hostilities grew.

First came the Texas Revolution (1835–1836), when Anglos new to the region, many of them enslavers, rebelled against Mexican President Antonio López de Santa Anna's attempts to outlaw the practice of humans owning other humans. The settlers won, giving birth to the Republic of Texas, a newly declared nation-state bordered by the Gulf of Mexico to the east, the Louisiana territories to the north, and Mexico to the west and southwest. Inevitably, the US annexed the Republic of Texas—in part to strengthen the political power of the Confederate South—to create the twenty-eighth US State.

The pretext for annexation was a ten-year border dispute. Mexico drew its northeasternmost border at the 315-mile-long Nueces River, which flows into the Gulf at Corpus Christi. Texans claimed the border was farther south, along the Rio Grande. Between the two rivers of contested territory lay a vast patch of desert filled with wild ponies and pecan trees. Though perfect for cattle grazing, what Washington powerbrokers and industrialists really wanted were Mexico's territorial holdings to the West, particularly California.

When a US Army brigade advanced south across the Nueces, their Mexican counterparts moved north, crossing the Rio Grande at Matamoros. This gave President James K. Polk, an ardent expansionist, just what he wanted. Calling it "an invasion," he weaponized the tit-for-tat to spark the Mexican-American War.

The bloody two-year contest ended in 1848 with the Treaty of Guadalupe Hidalgo. Mexico paid dearly. It agreed to the Rio Grande as the Texas boundary; and it ceded to the US ownership of California, as well as everything in between—today's New Mexico, Arizona, Nevada, Utah, and Colorado—a bit more than half of what was then Mexico.

Anglo settlers surged into the region then—the second mass migration of Europeans since the Spanish incursion 350 years before. They flooded to the safest places: military forts, like the one built by Major Jacob Brown where the Rio Grande empties into the gulf.

Charles Stillman, a Matamoros businessman, saw nothing but opportunity when the spoils of war brought Texas right to his doorstep. One of about three hundred non-Mexicans living in the region at the time, Stillman took advantage of an imposed Anglo legal code, one that most Mexicans did not understand, to gobble up thousands of acres just north of the Rio Grande in the area of Fort Brown. He transformed the former military outpost into a vibrant and strategically important international trading port, complete with saloon, brothels, and casino.

He founded the settlement in 1848. He named it Brownsville. He would amass from it a vast fortune. His son, James, would become a titan of the US financial industry as president of National Bank (now Citibank), and an ally to history's most recognizable robber barons: 19th-century businessmen intent on pushing the US colonial project even farther south, who became rich through ruthless and unscrupulous practices. Only now it was the Monroe Doctrine, not Manifest Destiny, that justified continued US expansion, but of a different kind. First articulated by the fifth US president, James Monroe, it asserted that the New World and the Old World were to remain distinctly separate spheres of influence. Thus, any future actions by European powers to stake a claim to any part of the Western Hemisphere would be viewed as a threat and potential cause for war.

This was not put forth in the spirit of altruism. Rather, it gave the US carte blanche to do as it pleased in Latin America and the Caribbean. Which it did, leading to the endemic hemispheric issues that have resulted in forced displacement and propelled increasing numbers of people northward to the US southern border year upon year and decade upon decade.

I learned all this Texas history on my first full day in the Valley, January 4, 2020, while waiting to hear from Angry Tía Cindy. Tía Susan had arranged for Cindy to take me over the border to the encampment, with the caveat that the Tías didn't really organize volunteers. But after being oriented by Tía Cindy, she expressed, "I feel certain you will find much to do."

Cindy had told me only to meet her "at the bridge" and to "bring $1 in quarters." She hadn't said which bridge—there are two in Brownsville—or what time. So I went downtown early to grab a breakfast of fresh-picked fruit and homemade kefir at the Saturday farmer's market in Linear Park. Then I schooled myself up on the history and culture of the RGV, passing several hours at the Historic Brownsville and Stillman House Museums.

I wandered Brownsville's historic streets, mostly empty on this holiday Saturday, peering beyond boarded-up windows and peeling paint to find architectural souvenirs of the town's more prosperous past. I found respite at the post-Gothic Immaculate Conception Cathedral built by French missionary Father Pierre Yves Kéralum. Bathed inside and out in South Texas light, it welcomed and calmed me with its quiet beauty. And when I got hungry, I Googled "best Mexican food near me," which led me to Las Cazuelitas, a nondescript canteen on E. Adams Street.

I arrived just shy of closing time, a little before 2:00 p.m. As I tucked into a meal of tacos wrapped in homemade corn tortillas, my phone pinged. It was Tía Cindy.

"Change of plans," she texted. "Meet me at the bus station instead."

She'd forgotten to mention the time again. But before I could wipe my fingers clean of taco drippings to text her back, my phone pinged once more:

"4:00."

⁣⁣⁣⁣⁣⁣⁣⁣⁣⁣⁣⁣⁣⁣⁣⁣

The bus station took me aback: More modern than the Brownsville airport circa January 2020, and cleaner than any US bus station I'd ever been in—and I've frequented a fair few—its ceilings soar overhead, supported by brick columns that reach for the sky. Light and airy, painted a cheery yellow, it's bigger and taller than the cathedral I'd just found solace in two blocks away.

I looked around, not completely certain which of the women pictured on the Angry Tías' website was Cindy. I spotted a gringa with dirty-blonde hair pulled back in a messy ponytail sitting on the far side of a tired folding table. She looked official and friendly, just waiting to offer help. As I approached, the lettering on a small, handwritten sign taped to the left-front corner of the table came into view. TEAM BROWNSVILLE, it said.

"Are you Tía Cindy?" I asked.

"No, but she's here. I saw her taking care of a Mexican family that was just released on bond. She'll be back."

As we waited, we chatted. Also a volunteer, Lindsay hailed from one of the reddest areas of North Carolina. A practicing Quaker and wife of a dairy farmer, she worked as a school librarian to help make ends meet, "money always being tight on a farm," especially, she conceded, with the uncertainty then being kicked up by Trump's US–China trade dispute.

Lindsay had taken a few days away from the kids and cows to do the same as me: bear witness to the two-thousand-mile humanitarian crisis that started a few hundred yards away, across the Gateway International Bridge in Matamoros.

"My mission is to carry back to my friends and neighbors the reality of how the actions of our government—and this president—impact the lives of immigrants." In other words, that the people they'd voted for were not welcoming the stranger, feeding the hungry, clothing the naked, or giving the thirsty to drink, in keeping with their faith and values.

"They're not bad people," Lindsay stated, referring to the folks back home. "They're just maybe in denial that you can't 'make America great again' while condoning treating others in a way that's in opposition to biblical principles."

Her mission—which I learned as Lindsay sat cutting paper cows and goats and sheep out of white cardboard—resonated. Suddenly, she looked up. And pointing her scissors toward a brunette carrying an overstuffed bag from Subway, she said, "That's Cindy."

On introducing myself, Tía Cindy pulled me into a warm, welcoming hug. "Thank you so much for coming to Brownsville," she said. "I've just bought this family dinner." She was flanked by a man, woman, and four children, ranging in age from maybe one to thirteen. They looked exhausted, but relieved. All smiles, they embraced me as well.

"Give me a few minutes to get them bus tickets. Then I'll take you across."

Just then, a clean-shaven man with closely cropped hair, wearing khaki shorts and an untucked button-down blue-and-white gingham shirt, came bursting through the automatic double doors at the back of the station.

"I need hands!" he shouted to no one in particular, then spun around on his heels and disappeared back through the double doors again.

"Go help Sergio," Tía Cindy said. "I'll catch up to you at the bridge." She was off.

Abandoning the info-table and her craft project, Lindsay leaped up, explaining that Sergio was one of the Team Brownsville leaders. I followed her following him out into the bus station parking lot, trotting to keep up. Sergio led us wordlessly across E. Jefferson Street to a storage shed behind a former taxi dispatch storefront.

He keyed open the padlock that secured the metal grill over a wooden door, then started hoisting out a caravan of folded-up canvas handcarts. No sooner had we dragged the first round of the empty carts back to the bus station parking lot, when several SUVs pulled up, disgorging a dozen or so people. They looked oddly familiar. Introductions were made all around as back hatches were flung open to reveal hundreds of juice boxes and stacks of aluminum trays, containing freshly quartered oranges, along with still-packaged ground cloths, sleeping bags and pads, fleeces, boxed lanterns, T-shirts and socks, winter jackets with tags still on, and various other items, including a large black garbage bag filled with used clothes. All these items were loaded into the now unfolded canvas wagons. I took charge of the Hefty bag of donations.

Just when we were about to go, Tía Cindy appeared, carrying a machete still in its packaging. She hid it in my wagon under the bag of clothes. "They'll want us to pay duties on these used things, which should distract them from the contraband beneath." She winked.

"What's it for?"

"Firewood," she said, matter-of-factly. I didn't understand, but she hurried off before I could ask.

||||||||||||||||||||||||||||||||||||||||||||||||||||||||||||

As we walked, each of us pulling a now heavily burdened wagon, I learned that Team Brownsville had out-of-town groups lined up for the next two months. The volunteer battalion helping Sergio that night was from Brooklyn, New York, the place I called home when I met and fell in love with my husband before moving to China in 1994. Unlike Lindsay, who came to the border seeking language and methods to reach across the ever-widening political divide cleaving her North Carolina community, this single-minded crowd representing the Brooklyn Heights Synagogue had come to serve. Among them were a lawyer, several teachers, a pregnant rabbi, a nurse, an IT guy, and two teenagers skipping school for a few days of "real-world education." They swept Lindsay and me into their mission.

Our wagon train passed through the bus station, out the front door and to the right; it continued down E. Adams to the municipal car park, hooking left onto E. 14th Street; then headed straight and across the main drag of E. Elizabeth Street to the foot of the Gateway International Bridge. I scrambled to find the quarters Cindy had instructed me to bring. I now understood why: to feed the turnstiles that mark the pedestrian entry to the in-between—the place that demarcates *la línea*, the line, separating not just nations but Global North from

Global South; the wealthy world from the poor one; and relative safety from the reality of daily violence. A toll of $1 per person, in quarters only, dropped one at a time into a coin slot, unlocked the three-armed, hip-high barrier giving way to those with the privilege to cross.

On this evening, a blue-uniformed agent of US Customs and Border Protection welcomed us by holding open the solid metal security gate to the left of the turnstiles. This made it easier to enter the border boundary pulling wagons full of food and drink and goods. We handed over to him our quarters with a dozen or so "buenas noches!" answered with as many "gracias!" accompanied by the musical clinking of coins as they fell into his pocket.

I wondered out loud if that was kosher; Tía Cindy leaned in and whispered, "Don't ask."

Once through, the sound and scenery shifted suddenly, as if we'd been sucked through a portal. The swoosh of a car en route to Mexico, accelerating on its ascent up the bridge, contrasted with the hum of standing engines on the side destined for the US. Drug-sniffing dogs handled by high visibility-vest-wearing Border Protection officers weaved in and out of the barely moving vehicles. They waved this or that one over to be searched. The shouts of Border Protection agents mingled with the perfume of petroleum exhaust.

Beyond the cars, on the opposite side of the bridge, a long line of people bound for the US stretched up to the apex at the middle of the bridge, perhaps farther. They appeared patient, though the line did not move. I reckoned that would be us before the night was over.

As they and the northbound vehicular traffic stood, unmoving, we rolled south, up and over the Rio Grande, single file so as not to block the faster moving foot traffic that passed us on our left. Sometimes we pulled up, waiting for we-knew-not-what obstacle in front of us to clear.

Halted at the midway point of the in-between, I caught my breath while peering through the chain-link fencing that stretched the bridge from end to end. There flowed the infamous river, slow and sickly brown. It resembled more a wide, still creek than the grand waterway of my imagination.

To my right, on the US side, standing tall and rigid and rusted, was a wall demarcating a line drawn on a map after a bloody war of aggression. It wasn't the wall that Trump promised Mexico would pay him to build. This one predated that pipe dream by a decade. Dating to 2008, it provides a cautionary tale: when erected, it cut off the then-popular golf course in the area of the old Fort Brown, creating a dead zone between border fortifications and the north bank of the Rio Grande. The golfers stopped coming. The once-manicured greens turned to fields of weeds and brush that eventually took over. The course went bankrupt depriving its operator, the University of Texas at Brownsville, of both community and income. It is now the playground of venomous river snakes and rats and other critters brought up with the waters en route to the Gulf of Mexico.

Looking toward the Mexican side, I spied several people carefully descending the river's precariously steep bank. Others were already bathing and doing laundry in water known to be contaminated by human sewage as well as pesticide and factory runoff.

When our caravan continued, rolling downhill into Mexico, I nearly lost control of my laden wagon. It nipped at my ankles, prompting the man behind me, one of the Brooklynites, to reach down to slow it. I thanked him and, turning to face him, I asked, "What's your name?"

Before he could answer, I knew. There was a flash of mutual recognition. Roy and I had played in a rock band together in our early twenties. We dated for a little while, too, probably breaking up the band. I was embarrassed, remembering the shitty way in which I'd broken things off. I wanted to apologize. But the years between us and the improbable circumstance of our reunion robbed me of words. What were the chances of meeting a long-lost friend while lugging handcarts full of food and camping supplies to refugees trapped on the Mexican side of the Tex-Mex border?

〰〰〰〰〰〰〰〰〰〰〰〰〰〰〰〰

We made it through the border patrol checkpoint, machete and all, passed over the empty southbound traffic lanes to Mexico's interior, wove our wagons through the standstill traffic heading into the US, then confronted the sight for which we were unprepared: the tent city that hugged the dual-nation border complex fanned out in all directions, spreading across the town's Civic Plaza to the steps of its commercial and governmental enterprises as well as through a chain-link and barbed-wire barrier and up the levee embankment to the tree-lined river park and floodplain above.

Also right there, standing in a peaceful scrum that ran at a diagonal to the hundreds of humming cars, were the first of thousands of people waiting for dinner that night.

Several jumped into action, setting up tables and delivering the clothes and camping gear to a canvas tent tall enough for an adult to stand in. It popped out from the others like a sore thumb. From it hung a handwritten sign: LA TIENDA #1. We emptied the carts of that night's dinner onto the tables and prepared to help serve, cafeteria style.

"¡Hola! ¿Que tal?" we chorused as we spooned rice and beans and meat stew cooked by the Matamoros canteen onto wobbly paper plates. Someone handed out tortillas, another topped off each plate with the oranges we'd schlepped over, others offered up juice boxes of grape, apple, or punch. For two hours, folks kept coming. As the sun dropped behind the archway of the Gateway International Bridge, I fished out the last spoonful of beans from the second industrial-sized cooking pot I'd handled that night.

"Sergio, no hay más frijoles," I announced. *There are no more beans.*

"Not surprised. We served probably two thousand tonight," he said.

But people were still coming, so he instructed me to drizzle bean juice over the rice, "to give it flavor."

It was dark by the time we finished. We'd had no time to get a good look at the encampment. That would have to come. It was against Team Brownsville's rules for volunteers to wander around Matamoros at night. A State Department Level-4 "no travel" zone, it was considered too dangerous for US citizens, though that hadn't stopped Trump's Homeland Security apparatus from pushing roughly seventy thousand men, women, and children into homelessness and potential harm in northern Mexican border towns.

We cleaned and packed up with the light from the head beams of cars still lined up to drive into the US. Then we followed Sergio back over the bridge. It cost $0.30 to cross north, coins I did not have. Roy lent me the change.

We climbed the bridge from Mexico, exhausted and cheerless, knowing we were leaving refugees trapped in tents in Matamoros to go back to beds. When we hit the still-long line of human traffic backed up on the right, everyone waiting their turn to go through US Customs and Border Protection, Sergio stopped to usher us bearers of dark-blue-and-gold-embossed passports to their left. Our entitlement as US citizens extended to skipping directly to the front of the line, which we did.

As we passed the stalled queue, Sergio called out, "Who's up for breakfast?"

He did not mean who would join *him* for breakfast. He was asking who would be back at the bus station first thing the next morning to repeat the same routine.

"We meet at eight."

CHAPTER SIX

An Epiphany of Epiphanies

In the calendar of saints, January 6 marks the Epiphany, when the three Magi, or Wise Men, rocked up into Bethlehem, guided by a star. They traveled to meet the baby Jesus. They brought gold, frankincense, and myrrh: gifts fit for a king.

On the Sunday before Epiphany in homes all over the Latin Americas, families gather to exchange gifts and share a feast topped off with King's Cake, Roscón de Reyes. Shaped like a crown, the round, center-less pastry is encrusted with dried fruit, representing the Wise Men's jewels. Hiding inside is a small figurine symbolizing the Christ Child. The person who bites into it is anointed king or queen for the day, adorned with a gold crown, and given chocolate coins wrapped in gold foil to pass around.

On this Epiphany Sunday in Brownsville, Texas, in the year 2020, Dr. Melba Salazar-Lucio pulled into the bus station parking lot with enough Roscónes de Reyes to feed a small town—for that is exactly what she intended to do. One of the five founding members of Team Brownsville, she was heading across the border with a large company of volunteers to bring to fruition a project that had been in motion for weeks.

It began as a literacy lesson. Melba, who led Team Brownsville's *Escuelita de la Banqueta*, had instructed her teacher-volunteers back in November 2019 to coach the children of the Matamoros tent city in writing letters to Santo Clós or Los Reyes Magos, following their own family traditions. They asked the kids to express their thanks and dreams, inviting them to state what gifts they might like to receive in celebration of the holiday season.

Despite all that these children had been through—from forced displacement to dangerous flight to homelessness at the foot of the world's richest nation—they gave thanks in their letters, particularly to God and the camp volunteers. Their requests were not for toys or technology, but for basics: warm socks and something soft to cuddle at night.

Melba collected all those lovely little handwritten notes of thanks and dreams and dispersed them to teachers all over the United States. They, in turn, put together drives to fulfill the wishes of each child, throwing in additional goodies besides.

Gifts flooded in, from New Jersey to Oregon and everywhere in between. Melba placed them, along with a note from each giver, into hundreds of brand-new, child-sized backpacks, and tagged each one with the name of its recipient. She stuffed a few extras as well, for more recent arrivals.

||||||||||||||||||||||||||||||||||||||||||||||||||||||||||

Joining that day was a group from Austin that had been coming to Matamoros one Sunday every month to help out with Melba's open-air school since it began in fall 2019. Lindsay, the Brooklynites, and I helped them to stack jumbo boxes of King's Cakes into twice as many wagons as held the previous night's dinner. In and among the roscónes, we arranged the tiny backpacks into orderly squads of pink and blue, plaid and tie-dye. The energy was chatty and cheerful as we made our way on this crisp, bright, clear day over the bridge. The name tags fluttered, tossed by a gentle breeze brushing the Río Grande.

"School before cake!" Melba instructed through a small, blue megaphone once we'd reached the encampment. In a bright yellow high-visibility vest, she was easily spotted in the crowd.

Out of la tienda #1 came a pile of folded square plastic tarps. These were unfurled and laid on the asphalt where we'd set up dinner the night before. Where one tarp ended, another began, covering the plaza from la tienda #1 to within a few feet of the bumper-to-bumper US-bound traffic.

Each ground covering constituted a "classroom" big enough for a teacher, or two, and six to eight kids. The teachers all claimed one and pulled out their lesson materials. In the "class" closest to la tienda #1, two Latinx thirty-something men tag-teamed reading *The Cat in the Hat,* first in Spanish, then in English. One held the book high in his left hand so the children, sitting in a semicircle around him, could see the pictures. The other sat adjacent, his eyes trained on the book as he read. Parents wishing to enjoy the read-aloud stood at the tarp's edges, for footwear was not allowed in "class." The children's kicked-off flip-flops and sneakers scattered the sidewalk school's "hallways."

In other classrooms, a volunteer from Austin practiced basic math skills, using dice and some printed worksheets. A teacher from Brooklyn led an English lesson through song. And all the way at the end, closest to the traffic, Lindsay introduced her students to the names and sounds and habits of farm animals, using the cardboard cutouts she'd been preparing at the bus station the day before.

〰〰〰〰〰〰〰〰〰〰〰〰〰〰〰〰〰〰〰〰

I took a seat on the last available tarp, prepared to read aloud a beautiful bilingual picture book, *Bolay,* by Mexican author Irma Uribe Santibáñez. She had written it after visiting the stadium-turned-shelter for the seven-thousand-plus-strong caravan that passed through Mexico City in late 2018—the same caravan that Tucker left Brownsville to go cook for; the same caravan that Trump tried to weaponize to get his base to the polls that November.

While Trump alleged that "many gang members and some very bad people" were mixed into the caravan, Irma found folks who were bruised and battered, uprooted by the region's endemic problems: gang violence, police corruption, crop failure, and virtually nonexistent economic opportunity. As US federal agents laced more concertina wire into the already angry border fortification from Tijuana to Mexicali, sympathetic Mexican citizens, like Irma, lugged blankets, food, and water to the shelter-stadium. They offered the exhausted parade of men, women, and children a respite midway through their journey.

Irma talked with the migrants. She listened to their stories. She asked them, *Why?* Knowing all that might befall them on the migratory trail, why had they given up everything to reach the USA. The answer was simple and always the same: *We are running for our lives.*

Bolay resulted from Irma's experience with these travelers. Named for a mythical jaguar who aids those seeking a better future by leaving paw prints that mark the way to safety, it's a freedom-trail story for today's global migration crisis.

The world is currently experiencing the largest movement of people since World War II. As of spring 2020, according to the UN Department of Economic and Social Affairs, an estimated 281 million people were living outside their country of origin, including corporate migrants and international educators, like me, who enjoy freedom of movement by virtue of our citizenship. But an unprecedented 114 million, as of this writing—folks from Honduras to Haiti to Cameroon, Syria, Sudan, Afghanistan, and Ukraine—are now forcibly displaced and stateless because of theirs.

That's more than one in every one hundred people on the planet today uprooted and driven from their birthplace by violence, persecution, climate-related disasters, and crushing poverty—80 percent from the Global South. One-third are estimated to be children.

|||||||||||||||||||||||||||||||||||||||||||||||||||||||||||||

The kids huddled on my sidewalk classroom that day ranged in age from about three to twelve. One little boy shivered with fever. I gave him the sweatshirt I'd removed with the heat that accompanied the rising sun. Joyful, curly-haired, five-year-old Sarita jumped up and wrapped her arms around my neck on learning that we shared the same name. My oldest pupil, a Guatemalan girl in traditional dress, appeared to understand neither Spanish nor English. She stared not at the pictures but at my mouth as I read aloud in alternating languages. Her long, dark, unbrushed locks surrounded delicate features. But it was her peculiar gaze that pierced my heart. In her light-brown eyes was unfathomable sadness.

"It's the look of the traumatized," Team Brownsville's Mike Benavides schooled me. Mike knows. A veteran of Desert Storm and part of a bomb squad, he returned home from the Gulf War with greatly reduced hearing and post-traumatic stress disorder. It took a long time, but thanks to a loving extended family as well as a medical and psychosocial safety net provided by the US Department of Veterans Affairs, Mike overcame the worst of his anxieties and was able to rejoin society.

"I was one of the lucky ones," he admits.

He became a special ed teacher in the Brownsville Independent School District, a job he loves. He told me that whenever he gazed on the faces of adults and children stranded in Matamoros, he saw deep trauma caused by the wounds of dark experiences, like his own.

"It's a blank and fearful expression—the same thing I used to see when I looked in the mirror." It's a wound that is further opened and infected, Mike says, by such policies as Remain in Mexico and Family Separation, which leave safety seekers torn from loved ones, heartbroken and alone, rejected and in limbo.

When our hour of lessons and read-alouds came to a close, the Roscón de Reyes were finally passed around. My quiet little friend from Guatemala gripped her cake with both hands. She savored it, eating slowly, without a word, staring into the middle distance.

Except for the chatter of volunteers and the rumble of idling vehicles, the entire camp of 2,500-3,000 people fell silent.

I got up from my classroom. After an hour sitting on the hard pavement, my hips and back were screaming at me. *Imagine having to live like that*, I thought to myself.

Through her blue megaphone, Melba led the children away from the plaza so we teachers could tidy up our tarps. We picked them up, shook off the crumbs, folded them, and returned them to la tienda #1.

I noticed the other teachers returning their books to a mobile book cart: "Melba's Library," they told me. She kept stacks of donated children's books available at all times for the refugees to borrow. They were always returned. I added my copies of *Bolay* to the unruly rows, and neatened them. (That night, when we crossed back over with dinner, I would see that someone had taken care to cover the library with a tarp to shield the books from the elements.)

Melba began reading out names and handing out backpacks, one by one. The children, so patient, seemed to settle in, seeing exactly what I saw: With seven hundred or so kids—roughly one-third of the total camp population—this was going to take a while!

I picked my way around the expanse of bodies hemmed in by traffic and the city of domed camping tents that from July 2019, crawled across parking spaces, delivery lanes, and pedestrian passageways of the Matamoros Civic Plaza. They created an obstacle course for townspeople as well as day-trippers from Brownsville drawn to Matamoros's famous Garcia's Restaurant. By January 5, 2020, they climbed from the plaza up the artificial river levee, a joint project of Mexico and the US dating to 2009 and dedicated to protecting the city's more than half-million inhabitants from flooding during the summer hurricane season.

I found the best route up and over the top of the levee at the northernmost end of the plaza, just to the right of two battered dumpsters overflowing with garbage that, even in January, were swarmed with flies. At the sign denoting Mexico's 0-km mark, a flight of crumbling stairs built into the levee slope provided passage from the hot plaza asphalt to the cool, tree-lined park that paralleled the Río Bravo.

Mounting the staircase, I passed through an opening in the chain-link and barbed-wire barrier that, before Trump, kept Matamoros-based visitors to the park safely away from the snarl of border traffic. Now it was festooned with freshly laundered clothing. Men's ripped jeans, women's floral print blouses, and children's brightly colored sweaters, T-shirts, and leggings hung from the inhospitable metal like holiday decorations.

Above that, single-use plastic shopping bags, snagged by barbs, struggled in the wind to be free.

With the children hovering around Melba, and the adults hovering around them, the camp that stretched between river and levee seemed nearly empty. It was quiet, peaceful even, the hum of engines replaced by the seven songs of the great-tailed grackle and the rhythmic sound of someone chopping wood.

I remember thinking how much more comfortable it must be to live up here under the trees, surrounded by birdsong and away from the hard pavement and stench of car exhaust. But this city of tents was perched precariously on a floodplain.

Dropping from the levee, the land leveled off before beginning to slope gently and relentlessly downward until, suddenly, it plunged over the side of an eroded cliff to the water below. Parallel to the berm wall ran a dirt road newly forged as vehicles bringing in water, firewood, and other materials trampled the grass. Though in pre-MPP times, the park would have been frequented in the dry season by joggers and picnickers and young people at play, it was designed to be submerged when the rains came or the floodgates upriver were opened, at which point it became the playground of river snakes and rats and other critters brought up with the rushing waters en route to the Gulf of Mexico.

In contrast to the mosaic of tents pitched on the plaza, here under trees denuded of their lowest branches were clutches of shelters. Covered by tarps sewn together and strung up with ropes, they formed multi-family compounds. Central to each tent and tarp setup was an outdoor kitchen, a *cocina*, that served many. Makeshift stoves had been constructed out of dried mud, adobe-style, or from old propane tanks cut through to make space for kindling and wood. A rigged grill perched on the top.

As there were no barriers, I waltzed right into a compound where a woman stirred rice in a deep metal pot stained black with soot. The smoke from the fire caught in the corners of her eyes, causing her to squint and grimace. She wiped away tears with the back of her free hand.

I apologized for the intrusion, in Spanish that had lain dormant since my five years living between New York and Central America in the '80s and '90s. I introduced myself. She stopped stirring, put down her too-short spoon, wiped her sooty hands on her skirt apron, and gave me her right to shake as well as her name: "Esther." We began to chat.

I asked where she got water to cook with, hopeful she wasn't tapping the contaminated Río Bravo. She pointed to water tanks that dotted the floodplain, all branded with the name ROTOPLAS. There were eight of them, I would later find out, each capable of holding 2,500 liters. They had been brought in and were maintained by borderlands' pastor Abraham Barberi and his flock at One Mission Ministries. They predated the arrival of a tall, thermos-like structure that sat at the edge of the eroded cliff bank. Called an AquaBlock, it pumped river water with the help of a generator, then pushed it through a filtration system.

"They say it's clean enough to drink," Esther said, sounding skeptical.

"Who are *they*?" I asked.

"Tucker and G-R-M," pronounced *Hey-Erey-Emey*. She lifted her eyes to the heavens and made a swift sign of the cross. Then, bowing her head, Esther held her clasped fingers to her lips, kissed them, and throwing her hand open, she tossed both kiss and prayer to the wind.

Sunlight glinted off the polished chrome siding of the potable water station as an industrial-sized construction bucket sat under an open faucet, catching the water that fell out in an anemic trickle. It was, indeed, as clear as anything you'd see running from a kitchen tap in El Norte. Faucets extruded from each of its four sides. More empty buckets—some stacked, some strewn—stood in the dirt beside it, available for community use.

Before its installation, Esther said, there had been no potable water in the camp. At first, the refugees had to wait for Pastor Abraham to bring bottled water each day. In addition to producing a lot of waste, it meant that she could not cook: "Bottled water was only for drinking and cleaning teeth." But in addition to the 16,000 liters of water Pastor Abraham trucked in daily to fill the Rotoplas tanks, he also delivered five-gallon jugs to each family twice a week. Those enhancements to camp life, plus the filtration station installed by GRM, all made it possible to feed her family again.

||||||||||||||||||||||||||||||||||||||||||||||||||||||||

"Where do you get your cooking oil?" I asked, looking at the raw ingredients of her family's coming lunch. "Your rice and corn meal? Your beans?"

Esther described the camp's "free store" system to me. It was run by residents, referred to as "store managers." Cooking utensils and foodstuffs; tents, sleeping bags, jackets, and mats; diapers, feminine hygiene products, toilet paper—they could all be obtained at these *tiendas*, like la tienda #1, where the Escuelita classroom tarps were housed and where I'd helped to deliver a machete and other supplies the night before.

The tiendas were stocked by Team Brownsville and the Angry Tías. Before this system had been established, Esther recalled, necessities were distributed from the canvas wagons pulled over the bridge from Brownsville. But when the camp population exploded with the onset of MPP, lines became too long, it was impossible to know who got what, and frustration mounted. It was not uncommon for fights to break out.

Someone hatched the idea of buying a large, multi-person tent and some storage containers and identifying a resident couple to keep track of what came and went. Yami, Josué, and their two daughters, who were among the first asylum-seeking families to be trapped in Matamoros by MPP, had established their temporary home right at the base of the bridge. They became the first store managers. Theirs was la tienda #1. The system worked so well, three more tiendas were added as the camp grew. The managers worked so hard, Team Brownsville and the Tías raised money to pay them, kicking off a culture of building occupational capacity within the camp.

Donations and purchased items were stored in the tiendas, which store managers distributed to the residents of their catchment area on demand. When an item was given out, it was then added to a list to be replenished. That way, when a new family showed up, which they often did at night after the volunteers had crossed back into the US, the store managers were ready and equipped to support them.

<hr/>

Esther and her family fled home, she told me, when gang pressure to "rent" their fifteen-year-old daughter had become too much. The entire family was threatened. They were already being extorted for "protection" money on their *pupuseria*, identifying her instantly as hailing from El Salvador, where the pupusa is the national dish. But that insurance, it turned out, didn't extend to the safety of them or their kids. If Esther and her husband didn't agree to turn their eldest over as a sex slave, the gang would murder them instead.

"It would kill us if they touched her," she said.

"Do you feel the children are safer here?"

"We never let the children out of our sight."

It was not unusual for the cartel to disappear the children, she said. They'd been known to snatch a sleeping child from a darkened tent in the dead of night. They would hold kids for ransom. Rape was an additional and constant threat—no matter one's age or gender.

A common cartel tactic is to rape and torture their captives as their loved ones listen over the victim's own phone. Only receipt of monies demanded—typically in the thousands of dollars—will secure the release of one's daughter, son, mother, wife, husband, brother, sister, etc. So, in addition to the "free store" system, the tent city camp residents elected nation-group leaders, who organized nighttime patrols to mitigate the cartel's penchant for kidnapping.

The encampment was therefore active around the clock. The men seen sleeping in hammocks under the trees during the day had likely been on duty the night before. But no one ever slept through the night, Esther professed. It was impossible to sleep deeply, or for very long. Every noise produced fear of an imminent threat. To be sick while living in a tent under menacing elements, both natural and human-made, was an experience she wished on no one.

I asked Esther about the clusters of trees curiously wrapped in tarps that I'd noticed dotted here and there throughout the encampment. These were outdoor bucket shower stalls, she said. And then I saw it: Tarps served as privacy walls; one untied corner created a movable door; carefully laid stones or boards were floors that lifted feet out of the mud. In one, a bucket rigged in the trees and cleverly tied suggested a pulley system that, with a tug, would bring water down over the bather's head.

"Were these the work of the nation-group leaders, too?"

"No. The first of these came in September 2019, thanks to Gaby and Tucker of the R-C-M," pronounced *Erey-Sey-Emey*.

Gaby later confirmed, when I met her, that a fifteen-year-old girl from the encampment got sucked into the undertow that month, while bathing in the Río Bravo—just months after Salvadoran father, Óscar Alberto Martínez Ramírez, and his 23-month-old daughter Valeria died in roughly that same spot. Gaby watched it unfold in almost real time while waiting for a prenatal checkup at her Brownsville obstetrician's office. Another resident of the camp filmed the incident, sending it to Gaby with an urgent request for help. Through competing reactions of fury, shock, and horror, Gaby watched as two other teens pulled the girl, unconscious, from the murky water. Gaby held her breath as they tried—and failed—to resuscitate the young woman.

"If paramedics hadn't arrived when they did—or at all—she would have drowned," Gaby relayed. "And she would not have been the first."

Having faced the same issue when she and Pastor Carlos Navarro opened the Iglesia Bautista Respite Center in Brownsville that spring, Gaby knew just what to do. "They needed wash water," she said. "They needed to get out of the river."

She set up a GoFundMe campaign, raising enough money to buy two 275-gallon water tanks. She sourced the tanks in Brownsville, then she sourced some friends and a truck to help her transport them over the border. One of those friends was Tucker. He had just returned to Brownsville from Tijuana and points in between. He was hesitant to help her at first as she was then nine months pregnant and her doctor had ordered her to stay in bed.

"When she refused to stay put," Tucker also later told me, "I realized, you do not say 'No' to a pregnant woman about to pop!"

He helped Gaby sweet-talk both US and Mexican border officials into letting her drive the tanks into the encampment and up onto the levee park. Gaby insisted that they set up a few temporary privacy showers right away. "And a good thing, too," Esther concluded, bursting into laughter, "because Gaby gave birth to baby Scarlet the very next day!"

<hr />

As Esther brought that camp legend to a close, a dangerously frail older man passed through her compound. He wore baggy blue jeans held up with bailing twine and no shirt. He carried a load of split branches slung under one arm. When he heard me ask Esther—remembering the machete I'd hauled over the night before—if he'd cut that wood himself, he let his load drop and answered: "Pastor Abraham brings the wood in."

Pastor Abraham came every day, I was informed, en route from his home in Brownsville to his church in Matamoros. He often stayed the night in the encampment to pray with the refugees. He brought in the earliest portable potties, too, which could still be found at the northernmost end, near the bridge. He helped to form the night patrols. He was a great friend and comfort to the camp residents.

"Where can I find him?" I asked. He'd just left, the old man told me, but I would meet the good pastor the next day, rolling into the camp with wood and other donations he distributed from the back of his pickup.

As for Gaby, the two pointed south. I could find her at the Resource Center Matamoros," they said—now I knew what Erey-Sey-Emey, RCM, meant. "Located across the street from the encampment, you can't miss it," they assured me. "There's always a crowd of asylum seekers waiting right out front."

The old man gathered up his firewood, gave us a wave, and carried on. Esther and I posed for a selfie, then I left her to finish preparing her family's lunch of rice and beans. The sound of children at play was beginning to compete with the great-tailed grackles' many-throated calls, suggesting that Melba's Epiphany party had turned a corner, closer to completion.

||||||||||||||||||||||||||||||||||||||||||||||||||

A rope line strung between trees and covered end-to-end with freshly laundered clothing drying in the sun blocked my path. I pushed aside an upside-down SpongeBob SquarePants appliqué and stumbled into another multi-tented family compound, turning my ankle in a narrow ditch.

"What are these for?" I asked a woman as I limped toward her. She was sweeping the dirt "floor" of her compound with the leaves of several tree branches she gripped in both hands. In that instant, I noticed that many of the living areas were surrounded by trenches lined with pebbles. Each somewhat-circular canal met a straight one at the lowest point in the sloping landscape, then ran downhill in the direction of the river cliff, petering out along the way.

"They help to move rainwater away from the tents," answered "Miriam."

She invited me to rest on an overturned construction bucket placed beside a table made of found scrap lumber that rested on legs resembling gnarly, twisting tree branches felled by a machete then whittled to a sort of smoothness. Laughing, she told me of Dr. Jill Biden's visit just a month before. The then-presidential candidate's wife tromped around the camp much as I was, though wearing calf-high rubber boots, followed by a Secret Service detail, a cadre of reporters, and accompanied by Sister Norma.

"You're lucky to be here in the dry season. Most of the time, it's either too hot or too wet here on the banks of the Rio Bravo. When the rains come, it becomes too slippery to walk."

She pointed out how her two-person tent had been raised up on forklift palettes. Others sat upon mounds of built-up earth.

"Who digs the canals and builds the mounds?"

"Tucker and the men from R-C-M."

Miriam, the wife of a Guatemalan border cop, had been forced to flee when her husband was murdered by the gang he'd been investigating. She took off with three small children and all the evidence he'd collected. She faced similar risk because she knew too much.

She had presented the evidence to US Customs and Border Protection authorities not once, not twice, but three times, at three different ports of entry, she said. In each location, she had requested asylum for her and her kids. In each location, she had been kicked back to Mexico. Matamoros was her last stop. There was nowhere else to go.

"At least this camp isn't in chaos. Matamoros isn't safe. But as long as we stay up here on the hill, it's better than some of the other places we've been."

There was truth to what she said. The encampment was clean. Floors were swept, even if they were dirt. Children and adults were washed, their clothes laundered, their hair combed and plaited. And residents were free to come and go. Though both US and Mexican governmental oversight were absent, and the usual international players—the UN, the International Red Cross, and Doctors Without Borders—were nowhere to be seen, a community sprouted from sheer necessity. There was a beating heart within the patchwork of tents and tarps, sown from shared experience and common understanding. It had a lifeblood and culture all its own, sustained by a network of grassroots humanitarians—the Tías and Team Brownsville, Gaby's RCM, and GRM—which I had yet to identify, as well as Pastor Abraham and Sister Norma, whom I had yet to meet.

Placing a premium on the fundamental human right to dignity, these borderlanders and visiting volunteers were doing all they could to make squalid conditions as livable as possible for the victims of MPP. They kept them from dipping into squalor, while also fighting for the inhumane program to be overturned so that these people, who were simply searching for safety and a better life for their kids, could continue northward.

"It's not who we are," stated Jill Biden, while at the camp. Joe had condemned Trump & Co's Remain in Mexico program as "an abomination." He promised to end it, if elected, giving camp residents and humanitarian volunteers alike hope that this purgatory would end with the return of a Democratic US administration.

This is where I found them in January 2020, one month after the Biden-campaign visit: harmed but hopeful.

<hr>

I interrupted my self-guided tour with a pit stop. Lined up in parallel to the levee and dirt delivery road, and stretching southward in the direction of two white canvas domes, was a row of thirty Port-a-Potties. Remarkably, they did not smell. A man stood by, handing out toilet paper and disinfecting each stall after each use.

"When did these arrive?" I asked.

"Last month," he said. They had been delivered just in time for the future First Lady's flyby visit. Paid for not by Mexico or the US, but by Team Brownsville.

Nearby, the twin domes that stretched over a metal skeleton had been erected then as well. Under the canopy, lined up in tidy rows like city blocks and separated by straight passageways, were the same synthetic camping tents that covered the plaza below like wild dandelions. They contrasted comically with the hodgepodge of tent and tarp compounds to their north. The wall-less covering promised little shelter from wind or cold or slanting rain, and no shelter at all from the caprices of the cartel. Only white plastic ground cloths separated tent floors from the mud to come.

"Who keeps the toilets so clean?" I asked, pulling out of my reflections to attend to real needs.

"We do," the steward stated, puffing up his chest and pointing to his blue T-shirt emblazoned with the RCM logo and large block letters that spelled STAFF. He handed me a wad of TP and, with a flourish, held open a potty door for me as I stepped inside.

<hr />

I continued my wanderings, following the thrum of a generator. It drew me into a comparatively posh U-shaped compound of four canvas-colored Better Shelters. Built by the IKEA Foundation, they are common in refugee encampments worldwide. These were not lived in, however. They were linked to something resembling a holiday camper van. A carpet, rolled out on the dirt under a canopy of trees standing between the camper van and Better Shelters, suggested this was a meeting place for the community—a place to find respite and someone who cared. So, physically tired from my early morning teaching and mentally tired from dusting off my once-fluent Spanish, I pulled up an empty camp chair, and took a seat.

Just then, stethoscope draped from his red T-shirt-clad shoulders, a man came to the open door of the camper van. He was dashing, with almond-colored eyes, olive skin, and a neat, closely groomed beard. Glancing at the clipboard in his hand, he called a name—his next patient. A deep, pleasant laugh caught my attention, and I turned to see another man dressed in a similar red T-shirt tussle the hair of a little boy before giving him a gentle push toward the doctor, who beamed at the child as well as the young mother holding his hand.

My eyes fell on the red logo painted on a side window of the camper: GRM. The acronym then stood for Global Response Management— it is now called Global Response Medicine—and it was the camp's medical provider. The camper van—I would later learn—was the team's Mobile Medical Unit, or MMU; the Better Shelters were their patient examination rooms. I had never heard of GRM before. It was not then a known player in the world of international medical organizations, but Matamoros would soon put it on the map.

A woman about my height, also in a red GRM staff T-shirt, joined me under the trees. With wavy blonde hair, she could have been my sister. She was from Temple University in Philadelphia, she told me. This was her third two-week tour of duty with GRM since then-director Helen Perry had arrived in Matamoros the previous October.

"That's how GRM staffs up," she said, with volunteer medical professionals from US universities. They rotated in and out to support a skeleton crew of veteran military medics as well as camp residents with medical credentials—like the handsome doctor, Dairon, and the affable man I'd seen comforting the little boy moments before, Ray. He was Dairon's translator. Both men were asylum seekers trapped in Mexico by MPP. They worked full-time with GRM, my doppelgänger informed me, providing a permanent presence for the far-flung veterans that ran the global operation.

"Ask Helen about how she got the MMU up here," the woman teased as she was called away to dress a nasty skin wound—"a little problem that can become a big threat living in these conditions." Unfortunately, Helen was not on-site at the time of my visit and Ray and Dairon were busy with patients. So my questions would have to wait.

||||||||||||||||||||||||||||||||||||||||||||||||||||||||||

I returned to the plaza from the south end of the camp. Another staircase built into the levee embankment, this one decorated with bright-colored graffiti and tiled mosaics, led me straight to the Resource Center Matamoros across a little-used side street that dead-ended just there. On the camp-side sidewalk, a cell phone charging station sprouted a tangle of cords attached to devices of all makes and sizes. This being Sunday, the two-story RCM office suite was locked up tight.

I arrived back at la tienda #1 just in time to help the other Escuelita de la Banqueta volunteers pull the now empty handcarts back over the bridge and through the bus station. We wiped them clean, refolded them, and returned them to the Team Brownsville storage shed. Then I followed Roy and the group from Brooklyn to the Good Neighbor Settlement House to begin preparing the evening meal.

This had been the life of Team Brownsville and its cadre of rotating volunteers since the summer of 2018: Prepare, pack, pull over breakfast; prepare, pack, pull over dinner; then wake up the next day to do it again.

Back at the bus station that evening, on our way to transport dinner to the encampment, I spied Sergio, who'd led the Team Brownsville dinner crew the night before. He was sitting with a teenage boy wearing a stiff orange baseball cap. An orange mesh string-bag slumped on the floor at his feet—the mark, I would learn, of one just released from US immigrant detention. Headphones passed over the crown of the cap to cover his ears. Music blared from them so loudly, I could hear it from where I stood several feet away. I tried to catch the young man's attention, but he avoided my gaze. His eyes remained fixed on the floor; his expression flat.

He'd just been sprung from Casa Padre, Sergio informed me, a youth "shelter" housed in a defunct Walmart run by Southwest Key. It was his eighteenth birthday that day. Southwest Key could detain him no longer. Sergio was helping to get him on his way.

"Where will he go?" I asked.

"Where he should have gone all along: to the loved ones who've been waiting for him since his arrival in the US over two years before."

"But wait," I said, doing a quick mental calculation. "Family separation started in April 2018. It was over by June. That's less than two years ago."

"Oh, the government was taking children long before then. It still is," said Sergio, just as the boy's bus departure was announced.

That's when I understood that what Ronald Reagan professed to be a "Beacon of Hope" for folks in need of safety worldwide is neither a North Star nor a mythical jaguar's paw prints leading to a promised land. It is, for many, an abrupt dead end, where they are not welcomed but shackled, disappeared into a shadowy prison system, and deported; or pushed back onto the mean streets of Mexico. It began long before Trump. He just exposed it.

It was for me an Epiphany of epiphanies. And it was only the beginning.

CHAPTER SEVEN

From Mosul to Matamoros

Helen Perry's road to Matamoros began in the Iraqi city of Mosul—a proving ground of killing that became a laboratory for life-saving in 2017. That's when Iraqi Special Operations Forces, backed by US airpower, moved to recapture territory lost to the Islamic State of Iraq and the Levant in 2014. In direct violation of international rules of combat, ISIL, aka ISIS, folded Mosul's 1.5 million residents into the bloodiest urban battle since World War II.

They detonated grenades on families who dared to hide rebel soldiers. They took hostages, turning men, women, children, and the elderly into human shields as they dotted them atop the roofs of buildings to protect their snipers and to keep US bombs from falling.

The world's usual medical responders, like Doctors Without Borders, the International Red Cross, and those associated with the UN World Health Organization, couldn't get close enough fast enough to save the lives of innocents hit by weaponry so fierce they would bleed out within minutes. With the most accessible facility twenty miles from the front lines, a modern response was needed in this swiftly shifting theater of war.

A group of US veterans and medics, who had voluntarily jumped into the fight against ISIS to care for civilians caught in the crossfire, conceived of an emergency medical model focused completely on trauma care: stop the bleeding, start the breathing, and treat for shock; then transfer to the nearest available field hospital or state medical center.

To receive UN funding, its founders created a non-governmental organization (NGO). They called it Global Response Management (GRM).

Alongside Iraqi medical teams, they drove pickup trucks stocked with basic medical supplies to within a mile of the urban battlefield. They trailed Iraqi forces with medical necessities strapped on their backs. As mortar rained from the skies just ahead of them, they felt the earth shudder underfoot. They went "farthest forward" in a wartime experiment that would be life-changing not only for those they saved, but for themselves.

They treated the injured in bombed-out schools, empty butcher shops, by the sides of roads—applying chest seals over gunshot wounds; wrapping tourniquets to lost or mangled limbs; and administering antibiotics to stave off infection. In nine months, this nimble battlefield-based emergency medical team served ten thousand patients and worked with other entities to establish a trauma referral network that covered almost 100 square miles and expanded to multiple cities. Born out of the ashes of a 21st-century guerrilla war, GRM cheated death with a 94 percent survival rate for those they were able to stabilize and transfer to intensive care.

When Helen, a former early childhood educator turned US Army nurse then on reserve status, found out about the group's methods and successes, she felt drawn to help. "I loved the model," says Helen. "It was so grassroots. The idea was simple: let's just help people."

She arrived about six months into the experiment, in September 2017, and stayed for three weeks. "It was eye-opening how much was being done with so few resources." The following year, Helen joined the GRM board. "I truly believed in the work."

When the hell on earth that was that battle of Mosul finally drew to a close, the GRM team resolved to bring their model of "high-risk, low-resource medicine" to the world's most dangerous conflict zones. They cast their gaze across the globe for other under-resourced flash-points: Yemen torn apart by civil war; Bangladesh overwhelmed by nine hundred thousand Rohingya chased out of Myanmar; the Mexican side of the US border.

||||||||||||||||||||||||||||||||||||||||||||||||||||||||

On seeing a video of the Matamoros refugee camp, Helen says, "I just had to go witness it to believe it for myself." After a solo reconnaissance mission in early September 2019, she put out a call for help, returning in October with six other volunteers. These included Blake Davis, a firefighter and paramedic from South Portland, Maine, and Sam Bishop, a special operations combat medic in the US Army's 3rd Ranger Battalion.

Sam, who was finishing his fifth year on active duty after tours in both Afghanistan and Iraq, had been contemplating medical school. In July, while still in the Middle East, he heard Helen speak on *EMCrit*, a podcast about emergency intensive care, trauma, and resuscitation. He reached out and agreed to help draft GRM's trauma manuals as a way to start racking up volunteer hours for future med-school requirements.

Then came Helen's late September call for veteran military medics to join her on the Tex-Mex border over the long October holiday weekend. In what would turn out to be a happy accident, the trip happened to fall as Sam's military service was concluding. So he went.

"I didn't get involved initially out of a passion for border issues," states Sam. "I backed into that. Matamoros wasn't even on my radar."

Armed only with backpacks filled with basic medications and blood pressure cuffs, Helen, Blake, Sam, and the others stepped off the Gateway International Bridge and into an ad hoc settlement of then roughly 750 tents. With an estimated three to four people living in each tent, they calculated a population of 2,500–3,000 people hoping to gain asylum in the US—up from about 200 just two months before, when MPP began in Brownsville.

"The place was mobbed," states Blake. "But the numbers were still too low to warrant intervention by the UN or Doctors Without Borders."

⸻

The UN must be invited by the country in which a refugee camp is located. But calling the UN institutions to the US-Mexico borderlands would be both a politically dangerous acknowledgment, by Mexico, that its northern neighbor had violated international law, and an admission that it was not up to the task of handling the fallout. As both the US and Mexican governments looked away from the mounting human crisis on their shared doorstep, the GRM advance team saw a gap they knew they could fill. The board was initially split. Some members felt their work belonged squarely in conflict zones where no other organization dared to go. But there, on the ground, Helen, Blake, and Sam were keenly aware that, while not a battlefield, Matamoros was no less perilous. Here, innocent people were caught in the crosshairs of a different kind of war—undeclared but no less political.

They ducked into Garcia's Restaurant, a local draw for residents on both sides of the border, to talk through whether the GRM model of care was justified. While there, the skies opened up, dropping two inches of rain in an hour.

"When we came out," recalls Blake, "the plaza was flooded. Everyone was soaked. There was this young mother with her newborn baby, two to three days old. They had neither tent nor sleeping bag. Another mother, holding her one-year-old close to keep her warm, was shaking and in tears. She looked absolutely traumatized, not knowing what to do."

That night, the temperature plunged to a near-freezing 33°F (0°C).

"Back in our comfortable hotel," continues Blake, "we couldn't sleep, thinking about all the kids that might die of hypothermia overnight."

They concluded that the model developed in Iraq—to respond to immediate needs and refer bigger issues to local partners—was applicable where hostile powers gave up sobbing mothers and their infant children as fodder for the ravenous appetites of organized crime syndicates.

<hr />

"The next day we stopped at Walmart on our way to the bridge and spent $40 on a blue pop-up tent—the kind you pitch in your yard in the summertime—and a plastic set of mobile drawers," says Helen. From the tent, they hung a sign: MEDICO. People immediately began queueing up. Sam and Blake ran triage, while Helen and an ER doc from the University of Pennsylvania handled patients.

"We saw ninety-seven people that first day. It was like an assembly line of care," recalls Sam.

Everyone was sick, but with mostly preventable issues: diarrhea, urinary tract infections, sore throats, and coughs; asthma, infections, allergies, and pink eye—in some cases so far progressed, kids were going blind; skin rashes from bathing in the fetid river. They saw side effects kicked up from people running out of meds for chronic illnesses like high blood pressure and diabetes. They witnessed evidence of a brutal journey rife with sexual assault, "lots of bruised genitals and STDs." They took blood pressure readings and measured the middle-upper arm circumference of children for signs of malnourishment.

They existed outside any formal health system. Yet no international NGOs had been asked to serve their population; no infrastructure had been established to meet their myriad needs. Deaconess Cindy had been coming across the border every Tuesday and Thursday, since the start of metering, bearing over-the-counter pharmaceuticals and requested medicines. Gaby tried negotiating low fees for sick-care with Matamoros doctors and pharmacists. But many Mexican doctors flat out refused to treat Haitians and Africans, as well as members of the LGBTQIA+ community.

"Migrants are at the bottom of the food chain in Mexico," says Sam. He, Helen, and Blake saw the same yawning gap the GRM founders witnessed in war-torn Iraq, though this time on the edge of the world's richest nation. They took a meeting with local officials of Mexico's National Migration Institute to pitch their no-cost solution to a problem neither country could just will away. The officers did not officially say "Yes." They did not wish to give anyone a reason to stay put. They did not wish to attract others from coming.

But neither did anyone say "No," for no one relished the idea— the potential political fallout—of people dying in their own front yard. So the GRM leadership set about re-creating the dual-mission model established from their improbable start in Iraq: to bring life-saving, low-resourced health care to conflict areas, while enhancing the capacity of local experts. They found their Matamoros partners, however, in unexpected places.

"Deaconess Cindy funded the majority of medications we needed through her ministry," states Sam. She carried on marching needed medicines and supplies over the border twice weekly, just as before, becoming crucial to maintaining asylum seekers' basic health as well as GRM's bottom line. And when she and her GRM collaborators shifted to buying what they could at the nearby Garcia's pharmacy, the local economy benefited as well.

The team gained a firm toehold in Matamoros thanks to the rare diplomatic talents, street savvy, and local knowledge of bilingual, bicultural, binational Pastor Abraham. As we've seen, he, like Deaconess Cindy, had been supporting the safety seekers since the earliest days of the encampment. Critically, he quietly aided the medical team in gaining access, affordably, to resources in cartel-controlled Matamoros.

They found two doctors, including Dairon; two translators, one being Ray; and a pharmacist from the refugee community itself. And Gaby got the crack medical team off the street.

She had spent the whole of that long, hot summer baking on the tarmac of the treeless Matamoros town plaza, feeling the crushing weight of humanitarian needs grow with the weight of her coming child. Between helping applicants fill out asylum forms, replace missing documents, gather evidence to support their claims, and obtain access to health care, she scoured the available area real estate for a cool, comfortable space where she could consult with the refugees out from under the punishing Rio Grande Valley sun. When she first toured the vacant dentist office just across the street from the growing encampment, she saw endless possibilities. The idea began to take shape in her mind of creating a resource center, where folks might review their asylum claims with pro bono attorneys; make photocopies and phone calls; attend workshops to help them build strong asylum cases; see a doctor, a pastor, a priest.

"The landlord said it was mine as long as no migrants lived there."

All Gaby needed was the deposit and first month's rent, as well as occupants, for this was not the single-desk storefront she originally envisioned, and could afford.

Fast-forward to October 2019 and GRM was now in Matamoros and needing shelter from the elements, too. But it was the arrival of Charlene D'Cruz, also that month, that enabled Gaby to seal the deal.

An immigration attorney with borderlands experience dating back to the Dirty Wars era, Charlene knew that once placed into MPP and kicked back into Mexico, refugees would have little to no success winning their asylum claims, for they would have little to no access to legal representation. That was the point of the program: to end asylum in the US as we know it by denying due process under both US and international law.

With the backing of a consortium of over forty US law firms, Charlene relocated from snowy Wisconsin. The financing made it possible for Gaby to secure the lease on the office suite.

⸻

"The mission was growing into something we never thought it would be," says Melba, reflecting on the mood change that occurred with the arrival of MPP. "Before that, migrants still had hope of getting across the border, getting to their families, and eventually winning asylum. But MPP offered only 'false hope.'"

By then, many of the local volunteers thrust into humanitarian action with family separation more than a year before were reaching a breaking point. Some had already stepped back, suffering burnout and sympathetic trauma. Others forged on, exhausted and losing hope. But the newcomers and one particular returnee brought renewed energy, recounts Andrea.

"Tucker came back to Brownsville in summer 2019, and just in time,'cause we at Team Brownsville were heading back to school. Other groups, like GRM, started to show up, too. There was a bit of jockeying as we tried to figure out how to share our minimal resources, and not duplicate efforts. But there was so much need, we learned how to function collaboratively pretty quickly."

In late October, the Resource Center Matamoros opened its doors, with Gaby and Tucker at the helm of camp management, working out of the apartment. GRM moved its clinic out from under the blue tent and into the garage, where there was sufficient space to store medications and supplies. Charlene took over the top-floor suite, creating a legal aid office.

In addition to Pastor Abraham and Deaconess Cindy, they joined forces with Team Brownsville and the Angry Tías, longtime Matamoros shelter provider Larry Cox of Casa Bugambilia, and local community organizer Gladys Cañas Aguilar of Ayudándoles a Triunfar, as well as countless others from both sides of the line too numerous to name. Working in collaboration was essential, Helen informed me, "because maintaining a healthy community extends in all directions, from check-ups and medicines to food and exercise, sleep and education, water, and, of course, hygiene.

When Blake first arrived, for example, there were only six Port-a-Potties to support the needs of 2,500–3,000 people. "The smell was horrid," he recalls. "The refugees were forced to climb the levee and defecate on the riverbank."

It was unhealthy and unseemly. Their presence angered Matamoros residents, who wanted their town back. An immediate priority for the burgeoning collective, therefore, was to expand the number of potties and move them off the Civic Plaza. And while the Rotoplas tanks brought wash water into the encampment, bottled drinking water resulted in a lot of plastic trash that needed to be burned—producing toxic fumes—or hauled away.

"My first mission," says Blake, "became getting more potable water into the camp."

With Team Brownsville's funding, GRM negotiated the eventual installation of two AquaBlock portable filtering systems, like the one I'd seen on my Epiphany tour through the camp.

⸻

Until February 2020, when they finally established a full-time presence in Matamoros, Helen, Blake, and Sam staggered their time in the tent city on a volunteer basis, adding nurse practitioner Andrea Leiner to their ranks in December. As the days grew shorter, auguring the start of a new year, they sought funds to sustain the growing operation, while building a cadre of rotating medical professionals, who committed to tours of duty of at least one week.

Between nursing duties at the Florida hospital where she then worked, Helen cold-called every migrants' rights and refugee advocacy group she could find on Google. A chat with Yael Schacher of Refugees

International led to connections with foundations focused on border issues, resulting in a $50,000 donation. Helen used some of the funds to buy a secondhand camping trailer, turning it into a doctor's office on wheels. She stripped it out, converted the living area into a rolling examination room, and retrofitted the kitchen with additional refrigeration to keep medicines cool. Then she hauled this Mobile Medical Unit to Texas. She drove it over the Gateway International Bridge and pulled it right up onto the Rio Bravo levee park as 2019 was coming to a close. It would remain parked there until March 2021.

But what really captured the imagination of all involved, compelling everyone to coalesce under a single banner, was the possibility of replacing the flimsy camping tents with Better Shelters. Deployed in refugee situations worldwide, these affordable temporary shelters are big enough for a family of five and tall enough for a grown man to stand up in. They offer forcibly displaced persons a safer, more secure, and more dignified home away from home.

Team Brownsville agreed to bankroll the project, with the help of Catholic Charities, whose executive director, Sister Norma, was invited to join the coalition. With her lifetime of ties to religious and border control communities on both sides of the line, the groups felt that she would be the perfect liaison between them and Mexico's National Migration Institute.

Thus was born the Dignity Village Collaborative. Meetings among GRM, RCM, Team Brownsville, Pastor Abraham, and the Angry Tías took place every Sunday. These were followed by sitdowns each Monday at the Migration Institute's office with Sister Norma and at least one representative from each group present.

GRM brought in engineers from Villanova University to develop a plan for laying out a refugee community on the levee park. An architect from the Better Shelter Foundation reviewed the Villanova blueprint to make certain the proposed village complied with the UN Refugee Agency's "standards of dignity." Once approved, the Dignity Village Collaborative bought the first four of a projected 150–200 Better Shelters. In late November 2019, they pitched their rollout plans to Mexico.

"You can't have dignity living in a tent meant for weekend camping," they began. And Migration Institute personnel strung the Dignity Village Collaborative along with smiles and nods. But their "No" rang out loud and clear when the refugee camp awoke, on December 5, to the sound of contractors building a tent to cover tents: the two dome-shaped structures I'd seen on Epiphany Sunday, 2020.

What local officials and residents wanted, it turns out, was for the refugees to get off their plaza—not a reason to stay. GRM could keep the four Better Shelters they already had, to use as patient examination rooms only—not living quarters. They could erect no more.

By the time Sam Bishop planted stakes in the RGV in February 2020, becoming GRM's full-time project manager for Matamoros, the team on the ground had grown significantly. Professional medical providers had been brought on, as planned. But not from the local healthcare establishment, as anticipated. Rather, the professional skills and expertise they required emerged from within the refugee community itself.

The two trained doctors, two Spanish–English translators, and pharmacist who became part of GRM's full-time staff gave living proof to Trump's first Big Lie, declared in June 2015, that *other countries are not sending their best*. Indeed, Doctor Dairon, Professor Ray, and Perla Vargas were just three of the many individuals trapped in camping tents on a floodplain who would be an asset to any nation. Their stories offer a glimpse into the vast human potential that refugees offer—potential that should be honored and warmly embraced.

Their stories force us to ask the question: *Who are the real barbarians at the gate?*

CHAPTER EIGHT

The First Big Lie

Dairon Elizondo Rojas was one of Cuba's best.

When he finished his medical training as an intensive care physician, he was chosen to represent the Cuban government in Venezuela. Part of a long-standing agreement between the two countries, Cuba plucked the most promising of its fresh graduates to help bolster the Venezuelan health-care system. Although Dairon had no say in the matter, he welcomed the opportunity. It was a contract of only two to three years. While away, his housing, food, and travel expenses would all be covered. He would be paid well, in Cuban terms, directly into his national account. So, when he returned home, he'd have several years' salary entirely banked. The South American sojourn would also provide him with valuable international experience before settling down back home.

"But it was all a fiction," says Dairon.

Not only was he sent to a country then caught in a downward economic spiral, where hospitals didn't even have lights, much less supplies, he and his wife, Elizabeth, were housed in terrible conditions in the most crime-ridden "red zones" of Caracas. There, they were robbed often at gunpoint. The food they were promised was nonexistent and Dairon and the other young Cuban recruits were made to work long days for weeks on end without breaks—even when patients stopped coming.

As hospital supplies dwindled, so did people in need of care.

The Venezuelan government had to justify the continued funding from Cuba, however. So, Dairon was badgered to invent patients and illnesses the Venezuelan leadership could turn into cash. The few sick he and his colleagues did see were forced into the intensive care unit, even if unwarranted, because of the higher price tag for that level of supervision.

Dairon never expected the job would entail shaking down his own government. He found it intolerable to make up patients to raise funds that were not being used to support hospitals. He grew hungry and fearful. He couldn't sleep. But he couldn't go back to Cuba because he'd be penalized for not finishing his contract.

Being made to march in a pro-Maduro government rally was the final straw. That's when he and Elizabeth decided to join the parade of Venezuelans then fleeing their homeland for the US. They were caught at the border with Colombia, however, and deported.

Back in Cuba, things went from bad to worse. He was returned without his things. He was not allowed access to the $7,000–8,000 he'd earned while working in Venezuela, a great sum in Cuban currency. He was persecuted, called a traitor, a worm, a deserter. He was constantly surveilled, repeatedly arrested, and always beaten; cited again and again for speaking out against the government—a crime in Cuba. One beating left him with broken ribs and blackened eyes. But the worst blow of all was being fired from the hospital where he held the position of intensive care chief and stripped of his diploma.

It all added up to one thing: he was destined for a life behind bars if he didn't get out of Cuba. No longer a doctor, he was en route to becoming a political prisoner.

On June 15, 2019, Dairon flew to Panama, where Cubans may fly round-trip without a visa to shop. He posed as a watchmaker on a supply run. Elizabeth pretended to be his assistant. There, they changed their last names and dyed their hair and set out for the US border to join Dairon's father in Louisiana.

They crossed through Central America, on foot, by bus, and in taxis. In Chiapas, Mexico, they obtained transit documents and took the first transport they could catch to the US border. They landed first in Reynosa. But the metering list there was already endless and there was no room at any of the local shelters. So they continued to Matamoros, arriving exhausted.

"I hardly slept the entire trip—too worried about being killed or abused or robbed to let sleep come," recalls Dairon.

They asked for asylum at the Customs and Border Protection office on the Gateway International Bridge. Officers took their names and photocopied their passports and sent them back to Mexico.

"I didn't know about metering or about Mexico being declared a 'Safe Third Country'": another new rule, implemented by Trump & Co in July 2019, that required safety seekers to request and be denied asylum in a pass-through country in order to be eligible to apply for asylum in the US. Running for his life, Dairon did not have time to study what critics were reasonably calling an "asylum ban." It went into effect while he was in motion.

"I was focused only on getting to the US and to my dad. We expected to be allowed to enter on arrival, but we were stopped by the Trump administration. I thought it was the end of me. I doubted everything."

Dairon and Elizabeth found sanctuary in a church. But they had no food, no privacy, no bathroom. He took a job in a *maquiladora*, one of thousands of borderlands sweatshops whose parent companies are headquartered in the US: a qualified ICU doctor now working a mechanical job, twelve hours a day, four days a week—for pennies—in a stationery factory. On the other three days, he worked odd jobs where he could find them, leaving the church each morning at 4:00 a.m., exposed, frightened, seeing danger around every corner; returning each day at nightfall. "Luckily, nothing bad happened."

Between jobs, Dairon would go to the bridge to see where his and Elizabeth's names were on the list. One day, about two months after taking the factory job, he saw a blue tent on the Civic Plaza. Curious, he picked his way around the tents to take a look. As he approached, a small hand-lettered sign came into view. MEDICO, it read.

He approached a woman sitting there. It was GRM's Helen Perry. He told her he was a Cuban medical doctor, a trained generalist. She interviewed him right there. She checked out his credentials. She offered him a job on the spot.

The change was immediate and profound. Dairon found hope again. He was practicing medicine and discovered a new sense of pride in taking care of people trapped in his same situation. "It was extremely rewarding to care for people's health for no other reason than they needed me and I could."

When it was his and Elizabeth's turn to request asylum, they learned they'd been shifted into MPP. Now stuck in Matamoros, he worked every day. "What else was I going to do?"

Because ICU training is rigorous and general, he could see all ages of patients and treat most issues. He became an invaluable member of the GRM team. Not only was he a permanent fixture as others, both staff and volunteers, rotated in and out, but he was also a consultant and trainer for new volunteers.

Perhaps most importantly, he became an empathetic confidant to the tent city refugees. He was always there, always looped into decision-making, standing in for Helen or Sam or Blake when they were not on-site.

There was only one issue: Dairon did not speak English. He could not speak directly with his Anglophone colleagues. He needed an interpreter.

||||||||||||||||||||||||||||||||||||||||||||||||||||

He found that person in Professor Rainer Rodríguez. A fellow Cuban refugee, Professor Ray fled a different threat: homophobia.

Ray knew he was different from a very young age. He tried to hide it, understanding even as a small child that his kind were hated. He didn't want the violence and brutality that shadowed members of the LGBTQIA+ community to affect his mother, so he hid his identity.

Succumbing to an internalized homophobia, Ray learned to hate himself. He tried to be what society wanted him to be. But it was unsustainable. Eventually, he began to hate the system that hated him.

Professionally, Ray wanted to be a university educator and translator of English. He worked hard, pouring himself into his studies, which he finished in 2009 with top marks. He was then obliged, as Dairon had been, to fulfill two years of government-mandated community service. He joined the faculty of the Technical University of Havana. But with Cuba's historic revulsion of gays, he was forced to continue to hide his true self or risk being kicked out of the academy.

As part of his English-teaching duties, Ray was obligated to impart Cuba's revolutionary ideology to his students, values he was coming to question as no longer aligned with Cuba's reality. Eventually, he just refused to do it.

First came the "meetings," where colleagues asked him to change. Then came their demands to correct his political views. Then came the homophobic comments; the admonishments to not be "so gay." Finally, he was let go.

After that, Ray couldn't find a steady job. Every background check resulted in the same dead end, with his one and only previous employer: the university leadership that had kicked him out of his profession.

He tried working as an independent tutor and a tour guide but he couldn't get a license. He did it anyway, as a matter of survival, suffering several run-ins with the Cuban police.

What are you telling these people? they would ask, suspicious that Ray held ulterior motives as a self-employed contractor. "Once you are on the police radar in Cuba, you cannot be free," Ray tells me.

He took a job in Fiji, where he earned $150 every fifteen days. "It was basically slavery," says Ray. "But it was out of Cuba."

He returned home just as the Cuban government was clamping further down on basic freedoms. This enraged people, leading to the brazen scapegoating of identifiable minority groups. "Hostility toward gays grew higher than ever."

Now Ray faced unemployment as well as hate crimes for which there was no hope of holding anyone accountable, especially the police. In early 2019, he was robbed. When he went to the police, they blamed him and detained him in handcuffs for forty-eight hours. They pushed him around, deprived him of food and water, and abused him verbally with homophobic slurs. He realized then that if he didn't get out of Cuba, he would be killed or imprisoned for good.

On April 9, 2019, he flew to Panama with a childhood friend, Tito. "I didn't want to leave home. I was driven away," he states.

The trip to the US southern border was brutal. Ray and Tito were shaken down at every step. A $1,000 fine in Panama; $750 to get across Nicaragua; $100 a night for a patch of floor in a flop house shared with two hundred others. Someone agreed to drive them to Mexico. But elevated the price ten times before they set out. They rode buses that were full to bursting, for which they paid steep fares; they walked the soles of their shoes bare, then the soles of their feet. They had to pay $1 to be told which van to get on; $5 to be directed to the best route across a river. "It seemed like every one hundred meters or so we were milked for more money."

At each new border crossing he joined a queue of three to four hundred, or more, folks on the move, with locals and law enforcement officers alike preying upon them in a vast, unregulated extortion scheme. From country to country, their biometric data were taken, meaning governments *could have* tracked and traced and defended their human rights—if they wanted to. They just didn't want to.

When Ray twisted an ankle running down a hill while crossing the border between Costa Rica and Nicaragua, he was forced to stay put until it healed. "I saw two hundred people come through where I was staying every day. Groups of ten and twenty at a time. The place went from empty to full every day for ten days while I was there."

In Choluteca, Honduras, crowds of people fought to get a $35 place on the next bus to the Guatemalan frontier. When it stopped just south of the border and ordered all the passengers off, a boy led them through a wooded pathway to a creek, then held out his hand—another $5.

When Ray and Tito ran out of money, Tito handed over his gold engagement ring to a trafficker who promised to get them to Guatemala City. "That was a new low point," said Ray. "I sat down and cried and cried."

But the worst had yet to come.

By the time they reached Tapachula at Mexico's southern border, Trump & Co were mounting a full-throttled pressure campaign to make Mexican President Andres Manuel Lopez Obrador, AMLO, stop everyone from transiting through his country, effectively extending the US southern border as far as the Mexico-Guatemala frontier. That's when journalists started to send word that US Customs and Border Protection agents could be seen in southern Mexico training up a new law enforcement corps, la Guardia Nacional, courtesy of US taxpayers.

Ray and Tito steered clear of the authorities for seven days as they waited to see if their transit documents would be approved. Once in hand, they made a beeline for Matamoros, arriving on May 12, 2019, a little more than one month after leaving Havana.

"We went straight to the border and asked for asylum. But Border Protection sent us back to the Mexican side and told us to ask the authorities there to put us on 'the list.'" Pushed back into Mexico by agents of the US government, Ray became metered asylum seeker #1545.

He and Tito joined the line of humanity that had all but ceased to move. With only ten or so people getting into the US each day, it could be months before their numbers came up. They noted the tents pitched at the bridge-based border complex and despaired at having to live in one. They ate only when Sergio or Mike or Andrea of Team Brownsville showed up with pizza or sandwiches or tacos. But they were on the list, so hope prevailed, however slim. And they stayed, waiting for their turn to request asylum, per their right under both US and international law.

As they did, more people seeking safe haven came behind them. When the MPP curtain officially fell in the RGV on July 19, 2019, the line stopped moving altogether and the tent city exploded.

Ray and Tito were shifted into the MPP program by the US government. But they wouldn't know this until July 31, the day their numbers were finally called. They went to the bridge, filled with relief. But rather than being allowed to enter the US to pursue their asylum claims, they were pushed back into Mexico again. This time with a court date—three months into the future.

Throughout the interminable wait, Ray had seen the same woman coming every day to the bridge to hand out shoes and water and other things. Her name was Felicia Sampanora-Rangel and she traveled with a translator, a woman from Honduras. On the day MPP began in the RGV, Felicia arrived alone.

Ray approached her. He offered her his services. She was a teacher; so was he. When she started a weekday school on the sidewalk of the Civic Plaza that fall for the children trapped in Matamoros, Ray was one of her first teachers. That brought him to the attention of the GRM team, for whom his English skills were in high demand.

On October 20, Ray started translating for them as well. He could be found at the GRM clinic from ten to four every day, even on Sundays; then at Felicia's Sidewalk School from five to six Monday through Friday afternoons.

Like Dairon, Ray pokes holes in the age-old nativist trope that immigrants are a strain on a host county's economy. Quite the opposite.

Both men found pride in their work and would become integral to the running of the burgeoning Matamoros refugee camp.

The same could be said for Perla Vargas.

<hr />

Perla had been a certified pharmacist for twenty-two years when she arrived in Matamoros with her daughter and two granddaughters. Back home in Matagalpa, Nicaragua, she made no secret of her allegiance to the Partido Liberal Constitucionalista (PLC). The political successor of the country's original Democratic Party, the PLC has traded the country's top jobs with the Sandinista Party since the overthrow of the US-sponsored Somoza family dictatorship in 1979.

The mother of three was also a volunteer counselor at her local PLC office for youth and women. In 2011, however, the PLC began to lose its grip on power, first failing to hold onto its majority in Congress, then losing the presidency. Being part of the political opposition grew increasingly dangerous.

It started with Perla getting vocal pushback for her liberal viewpoint. Then, it became more difficult to get—or keep—a job if you didn't show your support for the Sandinista government. When the Sandinistas tried to raise the official retirement age, popular protests were met with violence, says Perla. Any critique or disagreement with the party could result in persecution, including sexual assault by the authorities, which the government did little to stop.

By 2018, Nicaragua was embroiled in civil unrest reminiscent of the US-backed Contra-war era. Government-sanctioned brutality led to an increasing civilian death toll, as well as documented instances of torture, the ransacking and burning of buildings, and death threats against journalists. Opposition figures argued that the government was responsible, a view supported by some international press outlets and human rights watchdogs such as Amnesty International.

On September 29 of that year, President Daniel Ortega declared political protests "illegal," compelling the United Nations to condemn the action as a violation of the human right to freedom of assembly. Then a youth group leader with whom Perla worked was assassinated.

Death threats posted to Perla's Facebook page followed. Her cousin, also active with the PLC, was found dead.

Petrified that she would be next, Perla fled south to Panama in April 2019. Her intention was to relocate there, where she could be close to family in Nicaragua, but far enough away to feel safe. Her son joined her, also afraid for his life, followed by one of her two daughters as well as her two grandchildren. When a paramilitary force believed to be in league with the Sandinista government began to hassle them, the family was forced to flee again. This time they went northward.

They had to pass through Nicaragua under cover of night, avoiding urban areas. Though she longed to, Perla didn't dare check on her home in Matagalpa. From Nicaragua, they traveled by sea to El Salvador, then by bus through Guatemala to Mexico, where the trek continued, sometimes by transport, other times on foot. They found safety in numbers, joining groups of other safety seekers they met along the way. They walked mostly at night from dusk to dawn; they rested during the heat of the day.

Perla, her daughter, and two granddaughters arrived in Reynosa in August 2019. They knocked on the door of US Customs and Border Protection and requested asylum from political persecution. Though hunted, Perla was bused to Matamoros by officials of the US federal government and left her there to fend for herself with two small children in tow.

Just one of now thousands of refugees, Perla moved as if by instinct. She found la tienda #1, securing for her family a tent, sleeping mats and bags, and fresh clothing. In November, she needed a doctor. One of her granddaughters had fallen. She suspected a broken wrist.

She located the nascent clinic, recently set up in the garage space at the newly opened Resource Center Matamoros. There, Perla noticed a messy pile of donated medications. She wondered if there might be a role for her here. She offered her services as a pharmacist, handing her relevant papers over to Blake. Her job was to control and stock medications, keep track of expiration dates, fill prescription requests, and liaise with Gladys Aguilar, now working with the Angry Tías, and Deaconess Cindy when supplies were running low. She even trained assistants from among the encampment residents whose numbers swelled the Matamoros tent city to three thousand.

Perla fled political persecution only to be persecuted by politics. She, Ray, and Dairon all brought north with them important skills and expertise beneficial to any society and nation, home or host. But that wasn't the only thing the three had in common.

Fleeing Cuba, Nicaragua, and Venezuela, they ran from three of the roughly twenty-three nations subjected to what writer, researcher, and *Democracy Now!* co-host Juan González refers to as "economic warfare." Warfare that economist Agathe Demarais, moreover, contends has backfired again and again and again. Whether leveled as trade, banking, or financial embargoes, such sanctions have almost never worked to achieve their purported foreign policy goal: to force regime change from the grassroots. Rather, in crippling whole economics, sanctions disrupt the lives of innocent people, forcing displacement and exacerbating northward human migration.

Now, a doctor, linguist, and pharmacist had been trapped on a floodplain by Trump, a man with authoritarian tendencies and access to the largest, most troubled, and least transparent law enforcement agency in the land: the same force that when ordered to kidnap children, did.

CHAPTER NINE

Sounding the Alarm

In April 1989, as I was preparing for the first of what would become five long-term witness trips to Central America, unarmed pro-democracy protesters gathered at Beijing's Tiananmen Square. They were there to mourn the death of Communist Party leader Hu Yaobang. He'd been a vocal advocate for Chinese liberal reform. The mourners' grief turned to grievance, leading to a demonstration of over a million people in Beijing that spread to more than four hundred cities across China. Their demands included the rights to political participation, due process under the law, free speech, and freedom of the press—hard-won ideals now taken for granted in the democratic West.

The world watched, riveted, hopeful that the Chinese leadership might finally throw off the yoke of its authoritarian past. But by the end of May, then-Paramount Leader of the People's Republic Deng Xiaoping had had enough. He declared martial law, mobilized three hundred thousand troops, and ordered them to clear Tiananmen Square.

In the wee hours of June 4, troops armed for battle marched behind tanks that rolled through Beijing, killing an estimated ten thousand Chinese citizens. Equal numbers were thought to be wounded, but no one knows for sure, because tyrants invent their own reality and share their own numbers.

The near-revolution was televised—but only to a point. When the tanks started firing, Deng Xiaoping shut down all international news outlets, because tyrants prefer to control the narrative by inventing their own news.

Decent people around the world recoiled. And then there was Donald Trump.

The Atlantic City hotel and casino mogul was impressed with the "law and order" tactics of China's leadership: "They were vicious, they were horrible, but they put [the protests] down with strength. That shows you the power of strength," he told *Playboy* in 1990.

Fast-forward thirty years to the summer of 2020: the same man ordered the same agency responsible for tearing families asunder at the US southern border to clear peaceful protesters from Lafayette Square, just across the street from the White House. Using tear gas and flash bangs, men in uniform marched on the park so the president could have his picture taken in front of the St. John's Episcopal Church, which neither invited nor welcomed him. The violent escort services were provided, in part, by agents of US Customs and Border Protection. The largest federal law enforcement agency in the land, it had been conscripted—alongside National Guard reservists, Park Police, and specially trained prison guards—to act as a US president's personal security detail.

The peaceful protest was part of the Black Lives Matter movement against police brutality and systemic racism that erupted nationwide after George Floyd lost his life under the knee of a Minnesota cop. All that summer, Customs and Border Protection Predator drones, unmanned aircraft intended for spying on suspected enemies, could be seen circling high over US cities where Black Lives Matter demonstrations were ongoing. Customs and Border Protection drones were even spotted flying over the skies of Minneapolis, which may not seem troubling until you learn that Minneapolis lies outside the agency's jurisdiction.

It is little known, but the whole of the US is encircled in a one-hundred-mile policing zone that emanates inward from east–west sea coasts as well as north–south land borders. More shocking still is that this zone, which is patrolled by Customs and Border Protection, con-tains nine of the US's ten largest cities and two-thirds of the country's population. But even more disquieting is that, owing to a series of dubious Supreme Court decisions beginning in the 1970s, everyone's Fourth Amendment rights to protection from unreasonable searches and seizures by Customs and Border Protection, the Border Patrol, and

ICE have long ceased to exist in this vast borderlands region, especially if you are a person of color.

In the summer of 2020, it appeared that Supreme Court Justice Thurgood Marshall's 1973 prediction, that nobody was protected from law enforcement overreach, had come true. The Border Patrol Tactical Unit, BORTAC, wielded stun grenades, projectiles, and chemical irritants against Black Lives Matter demonstrators in Portland, Oregon. It was suspected of being the mysterious, plain-clothed police apparatus that disappeared Portland protesters into unmarked vehicles.

For context, considered the Marine Corps of the US federal law enforcement community, BORTAC was deployed in Iraq and Afghanistan. It is allowed to function without oversight or accountability. It was now being deployed, as Paramount Leader Deng Xiaoping's military had been, against its own people.

"Trying to solve the issue of police brutality with the use of the most brutal arm of law enforcement puts at risk the rights of all US citizens," says immigration attorney Charlene D'Cruz. "The history of ruthlessness by federal agents on the US-Mexico border was already well documented. But their impunity was ratcheted up many times since Trump's inauguration."

And that is a genie not easily stuffed back into its bottle.

||||||||||||||||||||||||||||||||||||||||||||||||||

Charlene lived and worked for twenty-three years in the town where George Floyd begged for, and was denied, his life's breath. A teacher and legal-aid attorney, she defended vulnerable people whose rights were routinely violated by landowners, schools, and the government. Growing up surrounded by the stories of her own family's struggle to get out from under the knee of British imperialism, Charlene is no stranger to the savage inequalities that Black and Brown people face daily, in the US and elsewhere. She is well versed, personally and professionally, in the reality of injustice on the part of US law enforcement. But Customs and Border Protection, she says, is in a class all its own.

"They have eviscerated due process and the rule of law at the border."

Charlene's immigrant advocacy dates back to the 1980s when Central Americans were running from the violence caused by the US-supported Dirty Wars. Right out of college, she worked, unpaid, for as many as eighty hours a week to help refugees detained in the middle of the Arizona desert at the site of a former Japanese internment camp. Charlene first put her stamp on the world of migrant advocacy then, essentially running both legal and non-legal systems for what would become the Florence Immigrant & Refugee Rights Project.

At the height of the 2018 family separation crisis, she was back at the border, this time in Tijuana, helping to reunite parents and children separated by zero tolerance. Then, as metering evolved into MPP in 2019, Charlene pivoted again. She coordinated a nationwide legal defense system, with the goal of pairing every person and family forced back to danger in Mexico with a pro bono lawyer, preferably bilingual, to provide remote advocacy; help fill out the notoriously confounding I-589 immigration forms; build case files; and prepare clients via WhatsApp and videoconferencing for court hearings.

She tapped local attorneys to facilitate "know your rights" workshops in northern Mexico shelters and tent encampments. Then she relocated to the Rio Grande Valley in October 2019, setting up a legal clinic in the former dental suite turned Resource Center Matamoros.

||||||||||||||||||||||||||||||||||||||||||||||||||||||||||||||||||||||

I first learned about Charlene from a lawyer traveling with the Brooklyn delegation. "This woman will restore your faith in humanity," she told me. "Tireless in her efforts to defend asylum seekers' rights, Charlene is perennially overworked and understaffed."

I decided to go introduce myself and see if I could help her out.

At 9:00 a.m. on Epiphany Monday, a line of fifty people—at least— snaked from the reception area of Charlene's upper-floor office suite, down and around the landing of two half-flights of stairs, then spilled out the door and onto the street between building and encampment. They did not appear to be moving.

I climbed the stairs, gingerly dodging the knees of people seated on the steps. I jumped to the front of folks awaiting an audience with

Charlene just as I'd been allowed to jump the Customs and Border Protection queue the night before.

"Lo siento," I was told. "I'm sorry. But Charlene's gone to the bridge." For, as early as November 2019, Charlene's responsibilities had expanded to include arguing for the rights of the critically ill and infirm who, by Customs and Border Protection's own field guidance, should have been exempted from the Remain in Mexico program.

Though MPP rendered all safety seekers vulnerable—to homelessness and hunger as well as cartel kidnapping and other violence—Border Protection officials were expected to grant those with urgent or documented health issues and mental or physical disabilities a "vulnerability exemption." It should have worked like oil to lubricate the rusted doors of welcome, permitting vulnerable individuals and their caregivers to enter the US under humanitarian parole and continue onward, where treatment could be pursued while their asylum cases were adjudicated.

But Border Protection officials refused to play by their own rules.

So, in addition to preparing asylum seekers for their day in court, Charlene was also expending precious hours walking the sick, pregnant, injured, and chronically impaired to the Border Protection office on the Gateway International Bridge to argue for their exemption rights. To bolster her points, she took to bringing along a consultant from the GRM team. Always made to wait, sometimes for hours, they seldom achieved first-time success.

"I would present the paperwork. I would make the legal arguments. And we'd get pushback. Every. Single. Time."

<hr />

The legal-medical partnership began when a refugee family presented at GRM with a two-year-old so sick she looked more like a child of eight months. GRM doctors diagnosed acute and chronic malnutrition, and worse: A recent illness had led to septic shock, a life-threatening emergency caused when the body's immune system goes into overdrive in response to an infection, shutting down organ function and potentially leading to death. The child needed medical attention stat, and appropriate care could not be found in Matamoros. A GRM doctor alerted Charlene, who pulled together the paperwork. The two crossed the child together to argue for an emergency "vulnerability exemption" to get her into a Brownsville hospital right away.

It was a cold day for Texas, 44°F (7°C) and raining. The Border Protection supervisor took a look at the child dying in her mother's arms and said, *We're not taking them.*

But Charlene persisted. She insisted. She refused to leave. Finally the supervisor called for a government-affiliated medic to come to the bridge.

"Why waste more time?" Charlene pleaded. "It's cold and raining and this child is dying! Why won't you let us just get her to the hospital?"

Finally, a nurse practitioner showed up at the bridge. Within forty seconds, she confirmed a major sepsis manifestation. "This kid has to get in," she agreed. But as soon as her back was turned, the supervisor denied the child entry again.

It was now two hours and ten minutes since they'd first made their appeal and the child was crashing. Panicked, Charlene picked up her phone and called everyone she knew. She begged them to call Brownsville Port Director Tater Ortiz to demand that this child and her family be let through. She implored them to spread the word, by word of mouth and on social media.

"In maybe ten to fifteen minutes, a thousand people had called the port director. They let us in," Charlene recounted.

The entire process took three hours and thirty-seven minutes, "and a year off my life," says Charlene. It was neither legal, moral, necessary, nor fair. It was a US federal agency playing politics—or God—with a child's life.

"They are indifferent to human life," states Charlene. Fortunately, this life was saved.

Then came the near-death experience of seven-year-old "Amy."

||||||||||||||||||||||||||||||||||||||||||||||||||||

In early December, when Amy's mom was in Charlene's office for her initial legal intake, Charlene learned that her little girl had been born premature and with significant health complications. Amy had required multiple surgeries, which had not been performed well. They left her with an unintentional connection between her colon and her skin, through which stool would freely pass. The condition, called a "colocutaneous fistula," is rare and incredibly complex.

Amy needed to be housed in a clean and sanitary environment—not in a tent under the elements. She needed specialized care. Fistulas invite infections that can threaten other organs. Most dangerously, says Helen, "if stool drained into her abdomen, Amy would die."

GRM doctors wasted no time: They located a pediatric surgeon in Louisiana, with a program in place to support such patients and their families. With a letter in hand signed by Gregory F. Shay, M.D., they took the little girl and her mother to the bridge.

By the time the supervisor deigned to give them an audience, Amy was covered in fecal matter. Border officials took mother and daughter into custody, and Helen and Charlene went back to work. But that's when the good news ends, for the family was then separated.

They shackled Amy's mom and sent her to ICE detention. They took Amy to the Valley Baptist Hospital emergency room. There, doctors agreed she needed surgery. But because it couldn't be performed in Brownsville, attendants cleaned Amy up, put her in a diaper, and discharged her back to her Border Protection custodian, who sent the seven-year-old child back to the encampment, unaccompanied, at approximately midnight.

"Border officials either didn't understand or didn't care to understand," recalls Charlene. It was another 24 hours, at least, according to Helen, before Amy's mother made it back to the camp. So, Charlene crossed them over again. And again. And again.

It took a week, ten hours on the bridge, a court hearing, and the help of multiple doctors, but border officials finally relented. Amy made it to Doctor Shay in Louisiana.

ıı

Charlene and the GRM team eventually found a way to beat Customs and Border Protection agents at their own game: they tracked serious cases on a three-tier basis, according to the level of health severity. A level-3 case indicated that professional attention was needed, but the condition had not yet progressed to urgent or chronic. These cases they put on round-the-clock watch. Level 2 was a case in the balance—it could resolve back to a 3 or tip toward 1. At level 1, the case had evolved into an emergency. It was time to go to the bridge.

Initially, even Tater Ortiz and his crew found it hard to turn the level 1 cases away, though they tried. For example, the eight-year-old boy that presented at GRM with a stomach ache. His mom had done all the normal things moms do, including take him to the hospital in Matamoros. They said it was nothing he couldn't ride out and sent them back to the tent encampment. But the boy didn't get better.

As it happened, a team of volunteer doctors and medical students from Temple University was with GRM at that time. They had with them a portable ultrasound machine that connected to a smartphone app. Imaging revealed that the boy's appendix was on the verge of rupture. They laid him in one of Team Brownsville's canvas wagons and ran him across the bridge as quickly, and as gently, as they could. The bridge supervisor made them wait an hour.

"Don't do this," the doctor implored. "We know it's going to burst. Get your physician's assistant; get somebody up here." But the official would not be moved.

An hour later, the kid was finally in an ambulance. On arrival at the Brownsville ER, his appendix exploded. Another life saved. But only in the nick of time.

⁂

Customs and Border Protection, which includes the Border Patrol, is not only the largest law enforcement agency in the US; it is also the most dangerous. It suffers neither oversight nor accountability. It has grown from an "underfunded frontier agency," writes Reece Jones in his page-turning 2022 publication, *Nobody Is Protected*, "into a modern, sophisticated paramilitary force" that operates outside the reach of the US Constitution.

From Brownsville to San Diego and one hundred miles north, the terror the Homeland Security Border Protection regime incites in the US borderlands has only increased with the decades. Tucson-based writer Todd Miller, describes the evolution of Border Protection check-points taking over the borderlands in his 2017 book, *Storming the Wall: Climate Change, Migration and Homeland Security*, as, "like a heat wave. It happens gradually, then overtakes you."

Its agents assert the power to board public transportation and to stop and interrogate people without warrants or reasonable suspicion. They search children on their way to school; parents on their way to work; families en route to doctor's appointments. When the Obama administration tried to curtail racial profiling by law enforcement officers, the Department of Homeland Security agencies pushed back, hard. "We can't do our job without taking ethnicity into account," one official told the *New York Times*. "We are very dependent on that."

The agency entrusted with keeping the homeland secure has spawned a culture known to rip children from the arms of parents and other loved ones and to allow kids in custody to die from such easily treatable conditions as septic shock, dehydration, and the flu.[1] It hunts people with tactics, like high-speed chases, that the Southern Border Communities Coalition calculates have led to death or serious injury of about three hundred people from the time they began tracking in 2010 to the close of 2023. The Border Patrol shoots to kill—even unarmed youth.

Yet the agency remained essentially invisible to folks living beyond the one-hundred-mile border perimeter until the Trump-era crises of family separation and "kids in cages." It was further unmasked when it used tear gas on peaceful protesters in the US capital, disappeared Portland demonstrators into unmarked cars, and surveilled the skies over US cities outside its jurisdiction. As with Deng Xiaoping turning tanks on his own people in 1989, Trump's deployment of Customs and Border Protection as a national police force is nothing short of chilling.

In this context, as Justice Thurgood Marshall warned, "Nobody *is* protected." For wherever armed officers are given free rein to act with impunity, the results are never good for democracy and the rule of law. All our rights are put at risk.

---

1. Seven children died within a 10-month period in 2019, during or after incarceration in filthy, crowded, medically negligent conditions by Border Patrol and Customs and Border Protection. Say their names: Mariee Juárez, 20 months; Wilmer Josué Ramírez Vásquez, 2 years; Jakelin Caal Maquin, age 7; Felipe Gómez Alonzo, 8; Darlyn Cristabel Cordova-Valle, 10; Juan de León Gutiérrez, 16; and Carlos Hernandez Vasquez, 16.

Even today, most Chinese people will call the Tiananmen Square Massacre *jia xinwen*—"fake news"—as penalties are steep for those who dare to speak of it. When I lived and worked at China's Nanjing University in the mid-1990s, I was cautioned by my government handler—all of us "foreign experts" had them—that I would face immediate deportation if ever caught discussing any of the three Ts: Tiananmen, Taiwan, and Tibet.

Zero tolerance woke me up to the inhumanity of US immigration policies. MPP drove me to the border to bear witness to the humanitarian crisis it caused. Witnessing opened my eyes to the systemic cruelty of the prevailing border management strategy: "prevention through deterrence." And watching how Charlene's advocacy on behalf of innocent children was met with agency intransigence again and again and again made me realize that in a world where security is prioritized above all other things, there can be no expectation that human rights values will prevail.

Deterrence has failed us all. It regularly flouts human rights and due process under the law, destroying more and more families and lives each year. It gave rise to worldwide markets in human trafficking, which in turn emboldens organized crime, fueling the relentless militarization of the US-Mexico borderlands.

For four decades, at least, the US has been sending conflicting signals: We are the Beacon of Hope; but, *Do Not Come. Do Not Come.* When all we ever needed to ask is, *Why?*

Why are so many people running for their lives?

|||||||||||||||||||||||||||||||||||||||||||||||||||||||||||||||||

As I flew home in late January 2020, my road trip cut short by the specter of pandemic, a question became lodged in my heart and would not let go: *How did the so-called leader of the free world get here?*

By the time I landed in London, Milan had followed Wuhan into COVID lockdown. And I would have the next two years of near-full-time isolation to wrestle with that conundrum before resuming my project to cross the two-thousand-mile US-Mexico line.

PART III:
ENCOUNTER

CHAPTER TEN

Déjà Vu at the Border

The gang came for "Sam" on his fifteenth birthday. He'd said "No" to them before. This time, they gave him an ultimatum: Join us or die. Poor though his family was, however, Sam did not want to enter a world of crime and brutality from which death was the only escape. But the gang, born in Los Angeles in the '80s, deported back to Central America in the '90s, and known as Mara Salvatrucha or MS-13, doesn't give third chances. The final time they came for Sam, it was to run him over with a car.

They left Sam for dead. Remarkably, he pulled through. When he awoke three days later, with a head injury and badly bruised body, his mother pressed a wad of cash into his hands—about $30, maybe a little more. It was all her savings, plus what she'd been able to beg off friends. Like so many other Northern Triangle mothers, she faced a Sophie's choice: aware that she couldn't protect her boy from the gangs, and that the police wouldn't, she determined that the only way to save his life—maybe—was to kick him out of the nest.

Along with the money, she gave Sam one simple word of parental advice: "Run!"

Sam traveled on foot and by bus from Honduras, his country of birth, through Guatemala. In Mexico, he rode the back of La Bestia, The Beast, the perilous freight train that has taken the lives of so many. En route to El Norte, Sam witnessed fellow safety seekers miss their step and get sucked between train and rails. He suffered their screams as their bodies were shredded. He learned quickly how to identify and to steer clear of the gangs that knew no borders and preyed upon people on the move.

He met other boys whose loved ones had been exterminated when they, like him, turned down MS-13 or Barrio 18 or one of several organized crime syndicates that had popped up in Mexico since the Dirty Wars transformed into the Drug Wars. He met families who, robbed of every penny they'd painstakingly saved to pay a coyote to get them to safety in "the Beacon of Hope," were reduced to riding the dangerous rails with him. Like them, young Sam ran toward the promise of a better life.

He made it to the Mexican state of Tamaulipas, across the US border from Texas, where he tried first to swim across the Rio Grande but nearly drowned. He was plucked from the swirling waters by members of one gang or another—Los Zetas, the Gulf Cartel—who detained him and tried to turn him into a drug mule when they found he had no one in El Norte to extort.

Fortunately, Sam got away. At the Mexican border town of Reynosa, a recognized US port of entry, Sam approached the Customs and Border Protection officers and requested asylum. They labeled him a "UAC"—then-government-speak for an "unaccompanied alien child" (the acronym has since been changed to UC in recognition that no human is an alien)—and passed him into the bureaucratic tangle that is the Office of Refugee Resettlement. The Resettlement Office locked him up in a series of detention shelters for kids until his eighteenth birthday, when the agency could not legally hold him any longer. At that point, he was turned over to ICE and imprisoned with adults until someone agreed to be his sponsor and got him out.

Able to walk free after more than three years of incarceration, Sam had no resources and few skills, for while in US custody, he received little education. He was also weighed down by trauma, not just related to the horrors he fled. But from September 2006 to March 2007, while a captive of the Nixon Center, in rural Texas, operated by then-federal contractor Away From Home Inc., Sam experienced "grave and repeated sexual, physical and emotional abuse."

Sam made the first attempt on his life while at Nixon. This was after he tried to escape. But in 2004, Nixon had modified both facility windows as well as the compound's exterior privacy fence, adding nine feet of metal to make it more "secure," which is to say, more difficult to leave. His bid for freedom denied, Sam resorted to more drastic measures. He wasn't the only one. Yet, instead of investigating why kids, like Sam, kept trying to run away from Nixon, the Resettlement Office continued to fund and populate the facility.

This led, finally, to legal action that Sam joined with ten other young men. All alleged experiencing beatings and molestations by Nixon staff; that the abuse was "widespread, rampant, open, and notorious"; and that they had no meaningful method of reporting their abusers. Memos and other correspondence from visiting child-welfare experts to federal employees of the Resettlement Office's Division of Unaccompanied Children's Services suggest that the basic protocols were not in place at Nixon, leaving "inmates" at serious risk of abuse. The warnings dated as far back as 2005. The legal action was therefore brought against the Resettlement Office representatives James De La Cruz and Maureen Dunn, among others, for failing to ensure the safety of unaccompanied youth in their care.

||||||||||||||||||||||||||||||||||||||||||||||||||||||||||||||||||

I learned of Sam's journey and plight from Tía Jennifer Harbury, the lead attorney in the case brought on behalf of the children by Texas Rio Grande Legal Aid of Weslaco, Texas. His isn't the only horror story Jennifer's had to negotiate. A lifelong human rights activist and civil rights attorney, Jennifer has spent more than forty years standing up to the USA's habit of bullying its southern neighbors. From her home in the RGV, Jennifer has been a longtime champion of the humanitarian front against the US government's unnecessary border cruelty.

It was Jennifer who passed, from whistleblower to press, the secretly recorded audio of despondent children inside Ursula, crying for their missing parents, that woke the world up to Trump & Co's family separation policy. And as one of the first borderlands to discover people being metered and succumbing to dehydration in triple-digit heat on Tex-Mex bridges, Jennifer was instrumental in sparking the birth of the Angry Tías and Abuelas of the RGV.

"It was the most brutal thing I've ever seen," Jennifer recounts. Which is saying a lot, for in the 1990s, Jennifer exposed the complicity of the US government and Central Intelligence Agency (CIA) in the commission of war crimes, including unlawful confinement, torture, and genocide.

||||||||||||||||||||||||||||||||||||||||||||||||||||||||||

Hailing from Connecticut, a graduate of Cornell University and Harvard Law School, Jennifer grew up with a fierce commitment to justice as well as a deep-seated belief in the democratic ideals of her birth nation—values instilled in her by her immigrant father. A Dutch Jew, he fled WWII Europe with his parents and siblings when he was just eleven—not much younger than Sam when he fled MS-13. Much of Jennifer's extended family perished at the hands of the Nazis.

The earliest years of her career found her working with small legal aid organizations in Texas and Florida, representing farmworkers in employment and civil rights disputes. It was the early '80s, and from her unique vantage point, Jennifer saw indigenous Guatemalans streaming into the US; and, just as Charlene D'Cruz had observed from her post in the Arizona desert, that US immigration officials were detaining them, then sending the terrified and traumatized right back to the scepter they fled, without legal due process.

They were not even given the support of translators of indigenous languages still spoken by half a million Guatemalans today, to whom they might have explained the reign of terror that had forced them to flee. So Jennifer went south to find out for herself.

She traveled first to Mexico to gather information and testimonies from the refugees that populated the camps sprouting up just north of the Guatemalan border in Chiapas. She interviewed sympathetic members of the religious community, who gave her ample evidence to support refugees' persecution claims. Wanting to know why, in particular, indigenous Guatemalans were running, and what happened to them when they were returned, she relocated to Guatemala City in the mid-1980s. But she didn't stop there.

In 1990, she was cleared to venture into the jungle to meet with members of the Revolutionary Organization of the People in Arms, one of the guerilla groups of the Guatemalan National Revolutionary Unity, a popular movement and political party that formed to resist the brutal repression of the Guatemalan military and oligarchy against its own people, especially the indigenous and poor. There, she met Comandante Everardo.

||||||||||||||||||||||||||||||||||||||||||||||||||

Born Efraín Bámaca Velásquez, Comandante Everardo was a Mayan who, like many of his compañeros and compañeras, had been forced from childhood to work for poverty wages on corporate plantations that had appropriated ancestral Mayan lands, then cultivated their yields for export to the US and Europe off the backs of the territories' traditional stewards. Growing up toiling others' fields, Bámaca was gripped by an unquenchable desire to go to school: "I wanted badly to learn things, to know things . . . to read and write." But persistent, nagging, insatiable hunger drove him to help his father at an age still younger than Jennifer's dad when he set sail across the Atlantic.

Unable to shake his longing for literacy and learning, Bámaca ran away from the plantation on his eighteenth birthday. In the mountains, with the Guatemalan National Revolutionary Unity, he found a university under the trees.

"These were the people who taught me to read and write, who taught me history, who gave me books," he told Jennifer.

He was a voracious student and learned quickly, rising within the ranks to become a comandante, known by his *nom de guerre*, Everardo. He was fair, dedicated to the Mayan people and their cries for justice, and beloved by his troops.

||||||||||||||||||||||||||||||||||||||||||||||||||

To understand the forces that drove Everardo to take up arms, we must do some time-traveling. Our first stop: The period of Guatemalan history known as the Ten Years of Spring, which came to an abrupt and violent end in 1954. That's when the CIA orchestrated a covert military coup d'état to depose the democratically elected Guatemalan president,

Jacobo Árbenz, on the grounds of stopping communist infiltration of the Americas.

Ten years earlier, in 1944, a popular uprising toppled the military dictatorship of Jorge Ubico. Guatemala's first-ever democratic election followed. Juan José Arévalo became the country's first president. Making good on his campaign promise to bring democratic reforms to Guatemala, Arévalo set up a social security system, instituted a minimum wage, and redistributed fallow land to landless peasants. Allowing for near-universal suffrage, he turned Guatemala into a democracy for the first time since its independence in 1839.

When Jacobo Árbenz succeeded Arévalo in 1951, he built on his predecessor's agenda. He nationalized and redistributed to the country's poorest people unused lands claimed by the United Fruit Company (today's Chiquita). These were part of the company's "stock of territory kept in reserve," for which Árbenz paid the price of the company's own valuation. Even with money in the bank, however, the US-based entity, notorious for its exploitative labor practices and accustomed to earning huge profits off the sweat of cheap labor, played the Cold War card. Unleashing an influential lobbying campaign, filled with much unverifiable fake news, it persuaded a McCarthy-era US government, then in the grips of a global contest against the Soviet Union, to overthrow the nascent Guatemalan democracy.

Secretary of State John Foster Dulles and his brother, Director of the CIA Allen Welsh Dulles, harnessed the era's politically distorted "moral panic"[2] over the "threat of communism" to convince Congress to surge funds to prop up US corporate interests in the country. Under that misdirection, the US military intervened on behalf of United Fruit rather than allow a sovereign nation to bring economic security to its most vulnerable citizens. Upon toppling Árbenz in 1954, the CIA brought back to heel a nation previously tamed in the name of US capitalism. That takes us back to the turn of the 20th century and the era of the "Banana Wars."

---

2. Moral panics are the phenomena of mass hysteria, based on irrational fear, that a person, group, ideology, or thing threatens the values, interests, or well-being of an entire community or society. Moral panics are often whipped up through demagoguery—appealing to prejudices that prevent rational thought—with the aid of the media, particularly disinformation machines like Fox News, Breitbart, and Newsmax, exaggerating perceptions of danger through propaganda, political sloganeering, and stereotyping.

II

Starting with the 1898 Spanish–American War and continuing into the 1930s, US military forces launched a series of occupations, police actions, and interventions in Central America, the Caribbean, and the Philippines. Each event was branded and sold to US citizens as an act of aggression necessitating a call to arms, much as their forbears claimed the Mexican-American War (1846–1848) had been provoked. In reality, these contests were carried out against a largely unarmed "foe" at the behest of US banks and big business, like United Fruit, which had significant financial stakes in the production of bananas, tobacco, sugarcane, and other products throughout the region. United Fruit had come to control vast territories and transportation networks all along the Central American Caribbean coasts of Honduras and Colombia, as well as in the West Indies, maintaining a virtual fruit monopoly in Costa Rica, Honduras, and Guatemala on lands held for centuries by native peoples. Indeed, the company treated these land holdings, and the people that lived on them, as their own personal plantations and expendable labor forces, earning the countries to which they belonged the moniker "Banana Republics."

In addition, the US government had its eye on both Nicaragua and Panama at that time. If it could obtain control of the Central American isthmus, into which it might carve a deep canal, linking the Atlantic and Pacific Oceans, it could dominate the Americas and broaden US economic and geopolitical influence worldwide. The most familiar names of the Robber Baron era, the Vanderbilts, Rockefellers, Carnegies, Morgans, Fricks, and Fords of shipping, steel, railway, and banking fame, were ready and willing to support whatever project prevailed. Frank Stillman, son of Brownsville's Charles Stillman, head of National City Bank (today's Citibank), was ready to provide the financial backing. They all looked forward to making big bucks at the intersection of government policy, corporate self-interest, and military might. And they did.

Eventually, one of the top enforcers of this "Banana War" strategy saw through it, blowing the whistle on the bloody wars they created. In 1935, the exquisitely named Major General Smedley Darlington

Butler, a senior US Marine Corps officer, penned a book called *War Is a Racket* in which he outed the US as an imperialist aggressor that had misappropriated its own armed forces to operate as "gangsters for capitalism."

For the thirty-three years and four months that "Old Gimlet Eye," as he was known to "the Boys," was on active military duty on three continents, he was, in his words, "a high class muscle man for Big Business, for Wall Street and the bankers." He made Mexico "safe for American oil"; Haiti and Cuba "a decent place for the National City Bank boys." He helped "rape half a dozen Central American republics," including Nicaragua, which he "purified" for Wall Street. He "brought light to the Dominican Republic for the American sugar;" and he "helped make Honduras right for the American fruit."

In other words, US industrialists and agriculture concerns snatched up lands they wanted and brought out the big guns if the people who lived there, like Comandante Everardo's indigenous ancestors, resisted. Indeed, a lot of blood has been shed historically for literal and figurative "bananas." Today, it's being shed for mining, fossil fuels, timber, petrochemicals, and other extractive industries, monoculture crops and hydroelectric power, though under the misdirection of the Drug War, Cartel War, and the War on Terror.

|||||||||||||||||||||||||||||||||||||||||||||||||||||

The Banana Wars came to a brief end with President Franklin D. Roosevelt's 1934 Good Neighbor Policy. He repudiated US interference in the domestic affairs of its southern neighbors, advocating instead that they be left alone to develop their own economies and governments. Reciprocal trade with the US would follow—a win for all.

That paradigm fell in line with Latin America's emerging post-colonial movement to exert their rights as sovereign nations. Aiming to get out from under the knee of US corporate capitalism, they signaled that the first beneficiaries of the development of their resources would henceforth be their own people. This is indeed what happened in Guatemala, for a decade, giving rise to the democratic elections of Arévalo and Árbenz.

But Roosevelt's Cold War–era successors, Harry S. Truman and Dwight D. Eisenhower, ascribed to a different foreign policy mandate. They believed that the first beneficiaries of Latin American resource development should be its investors—mainly US corporations and US banks. They worried that Guatemala's "experiment with democracy" posed a destabilizing threat to the capitalist order, potentially inspiring other nations in the region to agitate for land reform, labor unions, and voting rights as well. They hid their pro-corporate priorities behind the threat of a "communist takeover on our doorstep" to justify the need for war.

||||||||||||||||||||||||||||||||||||||||||||||||||||||

Roosevelt's Good Neighbor Policy was relegated to *el dompe* of history when the CIA, under Eisenhower, overthrew the Árbenz government in 1954, kicking off the Dirty War era that Jennifer, Bámaca, and I were born into. The military dictatorship the US installed promptly took back the lands distributed to the Guatemalan poor, returning them to the United Fruit Company. Voting rights were snatched away as well. They put Guatemalan liberalism in its place in order to guarantee the continued control of US businesses over sovereign politics. Then, to further deter neighboring nations from similar social justice organizing, the military government, with active US participation, unleashed a reign of terror in the country's highlands that quickly reached epic levels of barbarism.

Having tasted the sweet fruits of social justice and political participation, Guatemalans found the renewed disenfranchisement and oppression too bitter a pill to swallow. The first wave of civilian fighters took up arms in 1960. The future Comandante Everardo would join the revolutionary forces some fifteen years later.

The civil war that ensued was marked by abductions, torture, and disappearances; the dumping of bodies scarred by violent mutilations in public places; and the strafing, bombing, and burning to the ground of hundreds of remote villages. The more brutality the military got away with, the more brutal it became, leading to a culture of impunity in Guatemala that targeted, above all, the Maya. No one was spared: not women, the disabled, nor the elderly. All indigenous peoples were considered suspect, profiled by race. Even small children were labeled "subversives," disemboweled alive, their heads smashed against rocks.

It is within this context that Jennifer Harbury stepped, in 1990, into the hidden jungle encampment of the Mayan resistance group led by Comandante Everardo. At first, Jennifer took the baby-faced soldier to be a much younger man. But when he spoke, she recognized a person wise beyond his thirty-three years. The two felt the spark of a connection they knew could not be: Everardo belonged in the mountains with his battalion; Jennifer was needed at the front lines of the civil rights battles being waged in the US. But the two corresponded. And in handwritten letters that read like poetry, Everardo confessed his love for Jennifer, which she reciprocated.

In 1991, they were wed. In 1992, Everardo was captured by the Guatemalan military. He was detained by Guatemalan officials in the employ of the CIA. They faked his death, then disappeared him so that they might torture him for information, which they did, possibly for as long as three years. Honorable to the end, he never spilled any secrets of the Guatemalan National Revolutionary Unity. He knew them all.

IIIIIIIIIIIIIIIIIIIIIIIIIIIIIIIIIIIIIIIIIIIIIIIIIIIIIIIIIIII

We might never have learned the truth of Everardo's fate if it weren't for Jennifer's love of both man and justice—as well as her profound knowledge of international law. In her search for Everardo, which included a Freedom of Information Act lawsuit against the CIA and three hunger strikes—one in front of the US White House—Jennifer exposed US complicity not just in the extended torture and death of her husband, but in the thirty-six-year Guatemalan genocide.

What's more, her quest for justice for Everardo led to a historic judgment issued by the Inter-American Court of Human Rights. The court, based in San José, Costa Rica, found Guatemala guilty for failing to undertake an effective investigation to redress the crimes committed. It determined that Guatemala violated the American Convention on Human Rights and the American Convention to Prevent and Punish Torture. The ruling set new regional standards with regard to truth, justice, and reparations in the context of the Dirty Wars that devastated

Central America throughout the 1980s and '90s, for Guatemala as we've seen was not unique: Nicaragua and El Salvador also tried to get out from under Washington's knee at that time, with tragic results. The Reagan and George H.W. Bush administrations used the Soto Cano Air Base in Palmerola, Honduras, as the staging ground for US-backed and -trained paramilitary armies ordered to keep the region safe for United Fruit and its like. Even today, impunity is alive and well in Guatemala and the region, according to the Inter-American Court of Human Rights.

I followed Jennifer's quest for truth when I lived and worked in the Northern Triangle. When our paths crossed again in the RGV in 2020, I did not at first recognize the Angry Tía as the celebrated lawyer who cracked the thin veneer of what we internacionalistas knew in the 1980s: that the US government was not protecting us from communism at all. Under that pretext, it was protecting capitalism from the barefoot mothers and illiterate fathers who longed for the dignity of being able to feed, clothe, and educate their children—the same forces that push people to the US border today.

Thanks to Jennifer, who refused to look away, we know that the men involved in torturing Bámaca to death, like Colonel Julio Roberto Alpírez, studied at the School of the Americas—a US Army training center located at the former Fort Benning (now Fort Moore) in Columbus, Georgia, notorious for institutionalizing state-sponsored torture, murder, and political repression throughout Latin America. The School of the Americas (SOA) has trained tens of thousands of soldiers and police in counterinsurgency tactics and combat-related skills since its founding in 1946, in the early days of Guatemala's Ten Years of Spring. The terror SOA graduates have rained on the region is so widely documented, the havoc they have wrought so total, that the School was forced to rebrand itself in 2001 in an attempt to whitewash its reputation. It is now called the Western Hemisphere Institute for Security Cooperation. But that does not change the fact its alumni, like Alpírez, were paid handsomely by the US CIA for information extracted through the cruelest of means.

We know that the targets of these US-trained monsters included guerrilla fighters, as well as union leaders, activists, students, teachers, and religious leaders, among them US citizens, such as Sister Dianna

Ortiz, whose abduction and torture by the Guatemalan military was discredited and denied by US federal investigators and State Department officials. We also know that the Dirty Wars were not limited to Central America. US-backed campaigns of political repression, involving CIA-backed coups d'état and intelligence operations accompanied by assassinations of opposition leaders and voices were persistent in Latin and South America from 1968 to 1989 under Operation Condor.

⁙⁙

The US-sponsored Central American Dirty Wars saw the military slaughter of an estimated 30,000 Nicaraguans; 75,000 El Salvadorans, with untold numbers more disappeared; and 200,000 Guatemalans, 83 percent of whom were Mayan. They created some of the most barbaric killers history has ever known: people transformed into monsters by their CIA and CIA-trained minders, who for decades were given free rein to torture, mutilate, rape, recruit child soldiers, and carry out village-to-village massacres with impunity. They committed some of the most egregious human rights violations under the eye—and the cover—of the US government. They are protected by the CIA still.

When the Dirty Wars ended with the demise of the Soviet Union and the fall of the Berlin Wall, and the truth of Comandante Everardo's death came to light, Bill Clinton apologized for the US's "big stick" bludgeoning of Central American nations and populations. He had the US military advisors pack up and go home. But they left behind a region awash in armaments as well as a generation of now-unemployed officers who had amassed personal fortunes as CIA informants and knew only one skill: how to bend people to their will.

Overnight, these thugs morphed from highly paid CIA assets into drug lords. They swapped their uniforms for *guayaberas*, says Jennifer, becoming the heads of drug mafias, aided and abetted, again, by US foreign policy. For in a truly twisted and myopic move, US law enforcement under Clinton rounded up, jailed, then deported the same displaced Central American youth who, in the absence of welcome, decent housing, and educational opportunities, found brotherhood within gangs, minted on the mean streets of Los Angeles, that would become MS-13 and Barrio 18.

This is how the US government came to supply today's drug lords with their own personal paramilitaries. Now, instead of righting that wrong, states Jennifer, "our immigration policies criminalize and punish their victims."

Until the US acknowledges and addresses the true cause of ongoing Central American immigration—the Frankensteins it created in order to protect US and foreign corporate assets—"people like Sam will keep roaring north," says Jennifer. These Frankensteins now rule the region with such impunity, the notion of "government" throughout Central America has grown elusive. Indeed, they even own the police, as Sam's mother well knew back in 2006—the year *before* Congress authorized $1.3 billion be sent to the region under the Mérida Initiative, aka Plan Mexico, to "secure" it for transnational corporate investment—funding which eventually totaled $3 billion.

From Banana Wars to Dirty Wars to the moral panics kicked up by the so-called Drug and Cartel Wars and the War on Terror, we're all trapped in a vicious situation 100 Percent Made in the USA. It's a modern problem requiring creative thinking, but which, in the words of Reverend John Fife, co-padre of the 1980s Sanctuary Movement, "we keep addressing with Medieval solutions."

CHAPTER ELEVEN

Modern Problems, Medieval Solutions

The night of Dora Rodriguez's high school graduation started much as you'd expect: music and dancing, girls in dresses, boys in starched shirts, punch and presents. Suddenly, in the midst of the joy and celebration, everyone hit the floor. "There was bombing everywhere. Gunshots. The music stopped. The lights went off. We raced to shelter under the tables."

That was the night, Dora recalls, that the US Dirty War in El Salvador crossed her threshold. It was 1979. Following the Sandinista Party victory in neighboring Nicaragua, El Salvador became ground zero for the US strategy of containing the so-called communist threat in the Western Hemisphere.

Dora was just a teen. Her family was poor. She grew up in a Christian base community,[3] built with the financial and spiritual support of the Maryknoll Sisters, a group of Roman Catholic religious women who've devoted their lives to the needs of the poor, the ailing, and the marginalized throughout the world since their founding in 1912.

"They were our angels," recalls Dora, "especially Madre Magdalena. She made a big impact in our lives. We were so in love with her and her good heart."

---

3. Part of the liberal renewal of the Catholic Church kicked off by the Second Vatican Council (1962–1965), *Comunidades Eclesiales de Base* were established to spread Christian principles more broadly throughout poor, rural regions of Latin America then served only intermittently by itinerant priests. Nuns and lay figures, called Delegates of the Word, harnessed biblical teachings to encourage popular participation in self-governance and communal betterment. Such grassroots activism, though positive and uplifting for many, threatened traditional structures of elite power.

In addition to helping the families obtain resources to build sturdy homes, Magdalena organized youth groups to study the Bible and engage in community service projects. Following an evening meeting with Madre Magdalena some months after the truncated graduation celebration, Dora heard gunshots, yelling, screaming. "I remember it like it was yesterday."

The whole community was paralyzed in the grip of terror. Finally, everything went quiet. Doors were cracked. Eyes peered out. Bodies slipped through.

Quietly, folks made their way through the dark in the direction of the gunshots, arriving at the home of Dora's friend and fellow youth leader, René. He lay dead in a pool of blood in his own home.

"That night we realized the military had been turned on its own people, especially if you were organized by an American nun."

As in Bámaca's Guatemala, the US-backed regime in El Salvador labeled anyone who participated in labor unions or student protests, or who took on leadership roles in Christian base communities, as "insurgents"—a threat to the status quo. Entire social groups became victims of state-sponsored violence, as did the religious leaders then decrying the poverty, injustice, and oppression of the majority at the hands of an elite minority as a social injustice and a destabilizing force. These views, birthed from the Second Vatican Conference of the Catholic Church in 1968 and known as liberation theology, became a political lightning rod for the world's most economically unequal region, where still today the richest 1 percent have accumulated more wealth than the remaining 99 percent. Anyone associated with the Liberation Church, like Dora, became a target.

"My mom, of course, got very worried for me. I was always talking about injustice and what was not right. She was really very scared."

Dora's aunt and uncle, then living in Los Angeles, offered her travel money and a place to live with them. At least until the war ended and she could safely return home.

|||||||||||||||||||||||||||||||||||||||||||||||||||||||||||||

It took Dora three tries to get into the US. Her first trip to the border, by bus, found her in Tijuana with five friends, all age-mates, all fleeing the violence that had rocked their quiet community. But as soon as they stepped foot on US soil, "the lights came on and we heard voices and it was Border Patrol."

They were arrested and sent back to El Salvador within a week, despite the cornerstone principle of the 1951 Refugee Convention to which the US is a signatory: the guarantee of *non-refoulement*. The principle states that no one shall be returned to *any* country where they face serious threats to their life or freedom, or where they fear torture, cruel, inhuman or degrading treatment or punishment and other irreparable harm. Dora and her friends fled such threats. Yet, US border officials offered them no access to lawyers and no legal due process. They were shackled and refouled—that is, returned to potential peril.

The ink had barely dried on the 1980 Refugee Act when Reagan & Co were already flouting it. Passed by Congress in the waning months of the Carter administration, the law expanded asylum eligibility in the US and created the Refugee Resettlement Program to assist newcomers and aid them in achieving economic self-sufficiency as quickly as possible.

Reagan & Co made an end run around the 1980 legislation by characterizing all Salvadoran and Guatemalan war refugees as "economic migrants," coming to the US to "steal" jobs and "drive down the wages" of US citizens. They refused to acknowledge the human rights atrocities committed by these governments, leery of exposing the role played by the US. As a result, asylum approval rates for Salvadorans and Guatemalans remained a steady 3 percent throughout the 1980s.

"I remember being forced onto a plane with a lot of other deportees and my shoes full of mud and my pants all wet. And I was terrified because I thought, now the government knows I left. What are they going to do with me?" But no one asked Dora if she feared for her life and needed protection.

Back home, Dora went into hiding. She spent her nineteenth birthday underground. Then, on March 24, 1980, Archbishop Oscar Romero was assassinated.

In a sermon broadcast the day before, the archbishop rebuked the US government for backing El Salvador's military junta. He denounced the death squads. He spoke directly to them: "I implore you, I beg you, I order you," he shouted. "Stop the repression!"

The next day, a red Volkswagen Passat pulled up in front of the Carmelite chapel of San Salvador's Hospital de la Divina Providencia, where Archbishop Romero was celebrating Mass. A bearded stranger stepped out of the vehicle gripping a rifle. He lifted it, steadied it, then sent a single .22-caliber bullet right into the archbishop's heart.

I remember the news piercing my heart. Like Dora, I grew up in a Catholic home. These things simply didn't happen to the Church leadership.

Archbishop Romero's assassination put El Salvador on the map for me. A year later, on the anniversary of the monsignor's death, I was in DC, protesting US involvement in the escalating war there. Reagan continued to maintain that his administration's proverbial hands were clean. But news, though suppressed, did leak through from intrepid journalists on the ground.[4]

The archbishop's murder "was another horrible, scary moment for us," states Dora. And things only got worse. In December of 1980, three Maryknoll Nuns and a lay missionary—all sisters of Madre Magdalena—fell victim to the escalating violence toward Church members. They were kidnapped upon leaving the airport in San Salvador, raped, and shot in the head, execution style. Their bodies, recovered two days later, had been hidden in a shallow grave.

Dora's second failed attempt to reach safety in the US preceded that incident. That time, her family in Los Angeles hired someone to traffic her for the tidy sum of $2,500—that's $9,000 today—from El Salvador to Los Angeles.

---

4. Hat tip to Raymond Bonner and Alma Guillermoprieto, correspondents for the New York Times and Washington Post, respectively. Their coverage of the US Dirty Wars included the December 1981 massacre in El Mozote, El Salvador when roughly 900 men, women, and child non-combatants were slaughtered by the US-trained Atlácatl Battalion. The story of the carnage, replete with photographic evidence and survivor testimony, ran the day before Reagan swore to Congress that the Salvadoran military had been reined in and would henceforth comply with internationally recognized human rights conventions. Reagan discredited Bonner and Guillermoprieto, calling their reportage "fake news." Military funding went through at a rate of $1 million a day throughout the 1980s, eventually totaling $6 billion, though human rights abuses never stopped.

The southern border being firmly closed to citizens of countries allied with US government and corporate interests, those in need of safe haven were forced to cross the line without the knowledge of border authorities. Official US foreign policy, in other words, had created a new market: human trafficking.

"They had announcements on television, in the newspaper, everywhere: We will take you to Los Angeles, easy trip. We will take you by airplane from the border. You don't have to ever suffer; we will take care of you."

Dora's family paid half the money up front. The other half would be paid upon successful completion of the voyage. She embarked, part of a group of forty-five, in June 1980. The trip took ten days. From El Salvador, they traversed Guatemala by bus.

"But if you don't have legal papers to enter Mexico, you have to cross the Suchiate River in large tubes. I didn't know how to swim, so they had to tie me into one. I was lucky not to drown!"

They spent a couple of nights in a "nasty, run-down hotel, with women and men all thrown in together. There was no separation of rooms because all they wanted to do was save money."

Then the forty-five were crowded into an old US Blue Bird school bus transformed into private transport emblazoned with Playboy bunny stickers and shout-outs to Dios. At times they rode all sitting on top of one another, trying to catch a breeze through half-opened windows. At other times, the traffickers ordered everyone off the bus. "They did that a couple times, whenever they thought it was a checkpoint in Mexico."

The forty-five, including many teenagers, several small children, and one young woman then seven months pregnant, were made to walk through fields of cotton and other crops to avoid the Mexican Federal Police—*los Federales*. "They told us to keep walking, that the bus will meet us just up ahead. We walked sometimes for six hours. It was horribly hot. And also very dangerous because there were pesticides in there. The guide kept giving the little ones medicine to go to sleep so they wouldn't cry."

Finally, they arrived at the border with Yuma, Arizona. But no sooner had the forty-five jumped an irrigation canal when floodlights flashed on again. Helicopters appeared out of nowhere, descending from the sky. The group, instantly triggered by traumatic memories of being under bombardment back home, ran helter-skelter in all directions.

The Border Patrol calls this "dusting." It's a common tactic to create deliberate terror and scatter would-be border crossers. It worked, of course. The chopping of helicopter propellers was quickly followed by the sirens of a squadron of Border Patrol vehicles.

Dora's second attempt to get to safety met with the same end as the first: they were refouled right away. But the traffickers' deal was payment in full on arrival to the *interior* of the US—not the border—and they wanted their money. They had also agreed to bring Dora and the others back to the US a second time, at no extra cost, if they were caught and deported on the first try.

They reassembled the forty-five without delay. It was the height of summer.

||||||||||||||||||||||||||||||||||||||||||||||||||||||

Same routine, almost—the Suchiate River; the same nasty hotel; the sleepless, bumpy bus ride; the acres of DDT-laced cotton. But this time the journey through Mexico took them farther east to the lonely border outpost of Sonoyta. Just north lay the sleepy town of Lukeville and Arizona's otherworldly Organ Pipe Cactus National Monument.

"The story told to us was that we were going to jump the barrier into the US—it was just barbed wire, not a wall at that time—and walk in the direction of a helicopter that was waiting to take us to California."

Walking straight into the area immortalized twenty years later by Luis Alberto Urrea's Pulitzer Prize–nominated and bestselling exposé, *Devil's Highway*, they were doomed before they even began.

In the pale light of dawn on June 28, 1980, the Salvadoran traffickers separated the forty-five, sending the families, mainly women and children, off with a Mexican counterpart in the direction of Yuma to the west. The remaining twenty-six, "Young people like me in their teens," says Dora, "nineteen, seventeen, a woman seven-months pregnant, couples," were to cross the Sonoran Desert with the two Salvadorans guided by a local man and his twenty-something son.

"It was very hot and unbearable. They never told us that we needed a lot of water to cross the desert. We didn't have enough food. We didn't have appropriate shoes or clothing. They told us, *Within half an hour after you cross, there's going to be the road and somebody is going to be waiting for you guys.* So a lot of women had high heels on when we started crossing. We all had our luggage of clothing, carrying them with us. One woman, she had rollers in her hair because she thought as soon as she crossed, she was going to meet her husband. But it was an evil, evil lie. She never met him. She died in the desert."

|||||||||||||||||||||||||||||||||||||||||||||||||||||||||||

The four traffickers set off in the predawn dark followed by the twenty-six as the temperature began to climb. The air would reach as high as 117°F (47°C). Right away, the kid and his father got lost.

"They didn't know where they were walking. And the breeze was just like a fire in your face. And right away you start hearing everybody screaming because the cactus were getting into our feet and our shoes."

There is one type of cactus in the Sonoran, la cholla, that is particularly mean. It jumps on you, literally. It hooks into your skin with a barb. When you pull it off, it takes your skin with it, creating an open sore that gets instantly infected in the sweaty, sandy desert conditions.

The first death came within an hour. Her name was Berta. "She was young but she was very heavy and she had a heart attack because of the heat."

Panic set in. "All of us under a tree with all the luggage, crying. And when the young guy saw that, he got very scared and he left. He abandoned us."

The father stayed, however. He helped to bury Berta and remained with the group until the end. He witnessed twelve more agonizing deaths from exposure to the elements, leading to hypothermia. He was begging for death himself shortly before the thirteen who survived, including Dora, were finally discovered, melting into the desert floor, on day five.

He was arrested and sentenced to fifteen years in prison for human trafficking and murder. But was it right to lay the blame solely at his feet?

Reverend John Fife of Tucson's Southside Presbyterian Church, and his friend Jim Corbett, a Quaker philosopher, human rights activist, and son of a transplanted Wyoming rancher, didn't think so.

Jim, John, and many others reasoned that if the US government had welcomed Salvadorans fleeing a war it created, as well as a genocide of Guatemalan indigenous people it fueled and funded, then Dora would not have been pushed to hire a trafficker. Indeed, if the US had not fomented these Dirty Wars, there would have been no reason for Dora to flee her home and country. A market niche would not have been opened to create an industry dedicated to human trafficking. Dora would not have had to walk through the Sonoran Desert—one of the hottest places on Earth—in the middle of the summer, in the middle of a heat wave.

The man took the fall for what a growing number of borderlanders believed was a crime against humanity caused by the US government.

My first glimpse of the irreverent reverend was of the heels of his cowboy boots and the calves of his blue jeans as he stepped out of his truck. I had beaten him to our meeting place at the Southside Presbyterian Church, where he was still fighting the good fight decades later. It was midday in September and the sun bore down from a cloudless, multi-blue sky that seemed to have no end. I waited from the air-conditioned comfort of my economy-class Budget rent-a-car, taking in Southside's unique construction. Far from its European-origin denomination, this house of worship was modeled after the Great Kiva of the Anasazi Pueblo Culture of the US Southwest.

When I reached out my hand to shake his, Reverend Fife waved off my use of honorifics, telling me to call him John, instead. From cowboy boots to silver tooled belt buckle to the swear words that colored his speech, John was like no other "man of the cloth" I'd ever met. I liked him instantly, and feeling a little starstruck, paid a nervous compliment to his church, which he proudly explained was built from local materials—pine logs, saguaro cactus ribs, adobe, and flagstones—"in honor of the elders who were struggling for justice and the embrace of diversity long before us."

As we walked into the building together, I remarked on the lizard and snake door handles and other nature iconography woven into the structure throughout. "They represent the beings that move between the creation and us," John told me in his characteristic drawl.

Like every Kiva, this one is built partly underground. A hole, called a sipapu, drilled into the lowest point creates a passageway to an underworld that is cherished, not feared. "The Christian traditions have their angels in an imagined, unperceived heaven," states John, "while the deities of the American First Peoples are drawn from Earth, from our natural surroundings, from creation."

"They are a lot smarter than we ever were," he concluded, after a pensive pause.

On the far side of the Kiva sits a bronze sculpture by a Guatemalan woman who once took refuge at Southside. Her husband, like Dora, also sought safety in the US by way of the vast Sonoran. He died in the desert. A machete and laborer's hat, memorializing his loss, sit beside the eye-level figure of a peasant girl. Her hands, face, and tattered clothing mark her as one who knows hard work. She sits under a portal, which represents the sanctuary she found at the church. On its frame scurries a creature meant to evoke the over ten-year infiltration of the Southside Presbyterian community by the FBI and Immigration and Naturalization Service—the precursor to ICE. Beginning in December 1983, it was intended to bring down the Sanctuary Movement, and John Fife with it.

Fortunately, it did not succeed.

John and I settled around a wood table in the Kiva office and I asked him how he came to be the Father of the Sanctuary Movement, another honor he shrugged off.

"It wasn't just me," he said.

|||||||||||||||||||||||||||||||||||||||||||||||||||||||||||

John did not foresee, as a young man from Pittsburgh, Pennsylvania, with Scotch-Irish roots, that migration would become his issue. "I mean, I grew up in the Appalachian Mountains, listening to Bluegrass music on WWVA out of Wheeling, West Virginia."

By chance, he was offered a summer internship on the Tohono O'odham Reservation while still a seminarian. He remembers asking, when the interviewer wondered if he was interested, "What's a reservation?"

The admission that he knew nothing about Native American history or culture was followed by silence; then the sound of a deep inhale. Finally, his interlocutor said, "Well, the Church has done a lot of damage to Native Americans over the years. You probably can't do too much more in three months. Why don't you come out?"

So John found himself in southern Arizona in 1963.

"I fell in love with the people, the desert, the border culture, the mountains, the cheap tequila. Everything."

He and his wife Marianne decided to return and settle in the Southwest as soon as they could. But first he had some "fetching up" to do as part of the Civil Rights Movement.

"I took a job in Canton, Ohio, doing community organizing. I was working with street gangs in '67, '68, '69, when the cities were on fire after decades of Jim Crow and segregation and lynching and all that shit that went down just to maintain an unjust, racist system. And it was a good education—an education on the streets. I found my hope within the Civil Rights Movement. And we got traction. Then I heard that this church in the oldest, poorest barrio of Tuscon was looking for a pastor. I beat the drum and got the job and I stayed for more than thirty-five years."

John and Marianne planted stakes in Tucson in the last two decades of the Cold War when the long arc of justice seemed to be bending in favor of equality under the law for all US citizens. Voting rights had been won; public schools had been ordered to desegregate; and the heinous assimilationist practices of separating Native American families and whitewashing the kids in abusive, faraway boarding schools were finally coming to an end. The Anti-War Movement would soon bring the troops home from the nightmare of Vietnam, and bring into the White House a president dedicated to returning human rights to US foreign policy. But even before the New Right under Reagan wrestled the country's top job away from President Jimmy Carter in 1980, refugees were crossing the line at the US southern border.

They landed on John's literal doorstep.

"Nicaraguans were being welcomed because they were from a country with socialist leanings. But folks who were fleeing wars that we supported and funded and created were getting deported back to their deaths. So we started a legal aid project."

Dora's group provided the spark.

|||||||||||||||||||||||||||||||||||||||||||||||||||||||||||||||

"After we bury Berta with her stuff, and say a prayer around her," continues Dora, "we keep on walking. Because we don't want to be close to a dead body. We keep walking until the sun comes up. By early morning we cannot walk anymore because of the heat."

Records show that the summer of 1980 was one of the hottest ever in the Sonoran Desert. Experts say the ground had likely heated up to a blistering 120°F (49°C) when the now twenty-five laid down to rest. They tried to seek relief, in vain, under the beautiful, but shadeless, palo verde trees.

On the second day, they lost more people.

On the third day, their prospects were grim.

"We start drinking our own urine, shaving lotions, anything we can get hold of that is liquid. Some people started having delusions, thinking they were surrounded by water and pouring sand into their mouths."

Eventually, the men in the group left with one of the Salvadoran traffickers, Elias, to try to find help. The other, Carlos, stayed behind. "He said, 'I want to be here for the women,'" Dora recounts. "He said, 'I want to take care of them.'"

But he took advantage of them, she believes. With Dora were three sisters, aged twelve, fourteen, and sixteen. "And you know, every time I tell my story, this is the part that I still struggle to say, because they were so young. And their mother had worked so hard in Los Angeles for five years to save so much money to bring her three daughters to her. But Carlos, I truly believe, he raped the sisters and he killed them."

Dora was dying, drifting in and out of consciousness. She had rolled herself into a ball in the shade of two palo verde trees growing side by side. "I remember hearing screaming and me not able to get up, not able to open my eyes. Just listening . . .listening. Carlos was totally crazy, saying that he will kill us all. And I could hear him saying, 'Oh, I'm not going to touch Dora; she's dead anyway.' That's what I think saved me."

||||||||||||||||||||||||||||||||||||||||||||||||||||||||

On the fifth day, Dora was overcome with an awareness that she was passing. "I remember repeating over and over one Bible verse that my mom taught me. She said it would protect me throughout the journey: Nothing will strike you, on your left or your right."

With no strength remaining, she just lay on the desert floor, staring into the sky. "It was so blue, blue, blue, blue. I had never, ever seen the sky so beautiful blue, dark blue like the ocean. And stars, so many stars."

But that must have been a delusion, or a dream, because it was high noon when she was shouted awake by a man dressed in green: "Wake up, wake up, don't go, don't go," he said.

She begged him for water: "'No water,' he told me. 'Just a little bit in your lips.'"

Dora's face, mouth, and throat were covered with angry, oozing sores. She smelled of burning flesh. She was spiked, like a porcupine, head to toe, with cactus thorns and barbs. Her hair was so burned from the sun, it was frizzled all the way up to her scalp.

"I had to cut my hair very, very short after that. There was nothing left."

||||||||||||||||||||||||||||||||||||||||||||||||||||||||

Thirteen of the twenty-six sent into Organ Pipe Cactus National Monument that June 1980 survived. The other thirteen died an agonizing death; fourteen if you count the unborn child. "It was a pretty odd number," says Dora. "Thirteen lived and thirteen died."

They were discovered stripped down to their underwear, unable to take the heat anymore. Their clothing was scattered everywhere.

"We finally took a helicopter," Dora states, rolling her eyes to emphasize the irony. "But it belonged to the Border Patrol and it took us not to California but to the town of Ajo, Arizona."

The thirteen spent seven days under Border Patrol observation, getting rehydrated and regaining their strength. And as soon as they could walk, Border Patrol threw the book at them. They were transferred to prison. The government required a bond of $2,500 to secure their release—money the refugees did not have.

A Presbyterian pastor by the name of David Sholin and a Catholic priest named Gary MacEoin stepped in to stop the deportations of the thirteen survivors. They pulled in Margo Cowan, attorney for Manzo Area Council, to do the legal work. A scrappy four-women social-justice operation born from President Lyndon Johnson's War on Poverty, *Las Mujeres de Manzo* added immigration defense to their portfolio when the infamous 1970s Supreme Court decisions, allowing for racial profiling in Border Patrol policing, resulted in their neighbors being arrested after church or during weekend soccer games.[5] The initial strategy was to keep the thirteen safe from deportation until they had a chance to request asylum, at which point, under the 1980 Refugee Act, they'd be protected while their claims were adjudicated.

John jumped into the effort when Pastor Sholin and Father MacEoin convinced the whole of Tucson's Ecumenical Council to get involved. He brought along his good friend and partner in social justice activism, Father Ricardo Elford, with whom he organized a series of prayer vigils, following Archbishop Romero's assassination. That is where John first met Quaker rancher, Jim Corbett.

"A more brilliant man you will never meet," John remarked of Jim.

This grassroots alliance of faith-based leadership, pro bono lawyers, and community advocates saw themselves as a social justice bulwark for Central Americans picked up by Border Patrol, incarcerated by the Immigration and Naturalization Service, and deported as soon as the government could organize a plane.

"That's all we thought we were doing, at first," says John. "Then we realized that nobody was getting political asylum if they were from Guatemala or El Salvador." And news was trickling back that deportations were, indeed, leading to refoulement: returned refugees were being killed on arrival.

---

5. The four celebrated Mujeres de Manzo, lifelong activists at the forefront of human rights organizing in Southern Arizona, include public defense attorneys Margo Cowan and Isabel Garcia, as well as historians and professors Guadalupe Castillo and Raquel Rubio-Goldsmith.

So efforts escalated. In early 1981, Margo led them in educating the six hundred Salvadoran refugees then locked up in El Centro Detention Facility in California.

"We rented buses for the weekend," John recalls. "We rented a hotel to house people. And volunteers would go into the facility and teach folks how to fill out political asylum applications."

"We got the whole detention center organized," adds Margo. "The refugees began filling out applications themselves. They passed on their knowledge of the asylum process to those coming in behind them," she describes. "They kept a list for us of people most at risk."

"Then we had to raise funds to bond people out," states John. Once the federal government became hip to the team's strategy, it hiked the bail required to $3,000–4,000 per person, "astronomical sums in those days." So the organizers created a bail fund. Tucson residents rose to the occasion, putting up their houses as collateral. One priest put up his inherited South Dakota family farm.

"We raised a little more than $2 million," says Margo. Then, once they got refugees sprung from jail, "we had to find allies for them to go to."

"We were resettling people all over the country," recalls John.

‖‖‖

News of the Arizona-based action began to spread among faith-based and legal aid organizations from Texas to California. One day, John received a curious letter. It was from a Lutheran pastor in East LA.

The letter described how a fourteen-year-old Salvadoran kid had been chased down the street by a federal age. The boy had run into his church, blasted down the center aisle, made a turn at the altar, and dashed into the rectory. There, he threw open a closet and, diving in, hid behind the robes and vestments.

Seconds later, continued the pastor's story, the officer also burst into the church. He called for backup as he searched the edifice, eventually finding the boy. And right before the pastor's eyes, the immigration cop cuffed the kid, and dragged him out into the street, kicking and screaming.

The letter concluded with the pastor asking, *Why can't the church be a sanctuary from such intrusions, even by civil authorities, as it was in Europe in the Middle Ages?*

"Quite frankly," states John, "I threw the damn letter in the wastebasket. But it soon started to make sense to adopt a medieval solution to the equally medieval practice of raising walls against people in need."

"Of course, Corbett was way ahead of me," remembers John. Jim had already decided it was a moral imperative to bring safety seekers, like Dora, out of the desert before they succumbed to hyper- or hypothermia or were apprehended by Border Patrol.

"We know what they're getting deported to," he told John. "Death."

<hr />

Jim drew strength from the abolition movement of the 19th century, when people of faith formed an Underground Railroad to move runaway slaves to safety in places as far away as Canada. "And he said to me, John, those were the truly faithful. They were the ones who got the faith right."

Jim recalled the unwillingness of the Church in Europe to protect Jews fleeing Hitler, calling it "the darkest chapter in Church history."

He told John, "I don't think we can allow that to happen in our lifetime."

He and a Mexican priest in Nogales, Padre Ramón Dagoberto Quiñones, formed a bridge. Quiñones sheltered refugees at his church, Our Lady of Guadalupe, south of the line. "He had a parishioner who lived on a hill right above the border. It was nothing more than a cyclone fence then, which she could see from her window. Quiñones would send refugees to her. She would tell them where the smugglers (whose intent to save lives I differentiate from traffickers, who move people for money) had cut holes into the fence. She would then instruct the folks seeking safety to follow the silhouette of a bell tower of a Catholic Church on the other side in Arizona. When they showed up there, the priest," a former boxer from New York, Father Tony Clark, "called Corbett or me. And we'd send someone to pick them up."

They brought the refugees into their homes, at first. But it didn't take long before the numbers soared. "That's when Jim said to me, 'Well, can we bring him to your church?'"

And that's when John remembered the letter from the pastor in East LA. It was March 1982, a year and a half after the tragedy that almost took Dora's life triggered the Tucson samaritans into action.

The Sanctuary Movement was born. "Because word got out that you could get food and protection at Southside Presbyterian Church in Tucson. We housed the refugees we'd smuggled as well as those who made it to us on their own."

When Southside ran out of room, John, Jim, Margo, and the others located havens for refugees at another church or synagogue or Quaker meeting house until 580 houses of worship of all denominations in more than thirty states were sheltering people in need of refuge from detention and deportation by the federal government and law enforcement. This represented close to seventy thousand people in a nationwide act of mass civil disobedience.

"We reached back to an ancient Church tradition and called our sacred places Sanctuaries for Central American Refugees."

CHAPTER TWELVE

The Long View

Five years after Dora cheated death, another Salvadoran teenager fled to El Norte. Her name was Jenny Lisette Flores. She was then fifteen. She did not know it, but she was about to make history.

Jenny was on her way to reunite with her mother, one of 334,000 Salvadorans—roughly 25 percent of the population—to be displaced by the strife then rocking their country. But Jenny did not make it across the border undetected. She was apprehended by US Border Patrol near San Ysidro, California, on or about May 16, 1985, and passed into the custody of Commissioner of the Western Region of the Immigration and Naturalization Service Harold Ezell.

Ezell's INS detained Jenny, curiously, in a defunct and dilapidated 1950s-era Pasadena motel called the Mardi Gras. Few area residents knew that the old roadside eyesore was still in use; they certainly did not suspect it was being used to warehouse refugees fleeing war.

The Mardi Gras was surrounded by a razor-wire-topped chain-link fence and an improvised entry/exit enclosure called a sally port. Grasses shot through the cracked and unkempt concrete parking lot like fountains. There, Jenny's welfare was wholly neglected.

Conditions at the makeshift prison, run by the private, for-profit government contractor Behavioral Systems Southwest, Inc., were deplorable and unsanitary. Men, women, and youth of all ages and genders, and with no relation to one another, were forced to share crowded sleeping quarters. Basic necessities, like soap and toothpaste, were few. No recreation was allowed; neither were visitors. There was little food, no supervision, zero education, no books, no toys, nothing to do to pass the time except to play beside a drained pool. In the event of an accidental fall, no medical care would be provided.

Ezell famously said, referring to refugees crossing the border without authorization, "If you catch 'em, you ought to clean 'em and fry 'em yourself." His policy was to detain people fleeing north for as long as possible, as punishment, before deporting them. He felt such practice would deter others from coming to the US.

As for children and youth, like Jenny, Ezell used them as bait. Agreeing to release them only to a parent, without the force of law behind him, Ezell dangled the kids in front of their undocumented loved ones to lure them out of hiding. Then he cuffed them, too, and deported everyone right back to the dangers they'd fled.

Jenny's mother knew this, so she refused to step forward. To do so would be tantamount to suicide.

Also imprisoned with Jenny at the motel-turned-detention-center were sixteen-year-old Dominga Hernandez-Hernandez and 'tween-aged Alma Yanira Cruz. A few of the story's details have become fuzzy with the passage of time, like Alma's exact age and whether it was her mother or Jenny's that worked in the home of actor Ed Asner. What's important is that the star of the legendary *Mary Tyler Moore Show* and its spin-off, *Lou Grant,* made no bones about using his celebrity to broadcast his distaste for the US Dirty Wars. When he heard of the government-sanctioned abuse that Alma, Jenny, and other children were facing in detention, he called LA's Center for Human Rights and Constitutional Law.

‖‖

Run by attorneys Carlos Holguín and Peter Schey out of a 1920s Craftsman house with bad plumbing and a warped roof, the Center for Human Rights was then a hub for the immigrant-rights movement. From as early as September 1984, Holguín and Schey, the grandson of a Mexican immigrant and immigrant son of Holocaust survivors, respectively, knew that Ezell had gone rogue. And they were ready to sue. All they lacked was a plaintiff.

Now, thanks to activist-actor Asner, they had not one, not three, but potentially thousands, for the injustices were not limited to California:

over in Laredo, Texas, Ana Maria Martinez Portillo faced similar conditions in a prison run by Corrections Corporation of America (now
CoreCivic). In addition to suffering the daily humiliation of incarceration, she and other youth were also forced to strip naked and withstand
body-cavity searches. Ana Maria, too, was just sixteen.

"The call from Ed Asner was the trigger we needed," Carlos told me.

He and Peter agreed to represent Jenny along with all other children
being detained by the US government nationwide. In conjunction with
the National Center for Youth Law and the American Civil Liberties
Union of Southern California, they brought a federal class-action lawsuit on behalf of these young people, who were suffering irreparable
harm but had no legal recourse. Jenny Flores was the lead plaintiff.

Filed on July 11, 1985, the goal of *Flores v. Meese* was to establish policy based on commonsense ground rules regarding the care
and rapid release of unaccompanied migrant children in US custody,
while exposing the unconstitutionality and sheer immorality of Ezell's
practices. Messrs Schey and Holguín argued that children should not
be detained, but released as quickly as possible to a responsible adult.
And if detained, for example, in the event no adult relation could be
found, that their needs as children be met and their rights as humans
protected. And that they should never be subjected to invasive vaginal
and rectal searches.

The case would wind its way through the US legal system for
more than a decade. Resistance came from the government, to be sure,
but also from a little-seen yet already very potent counter-movement
sparked by a small-town Michigan ophthalmologist. Though it had
nothing to do with eyesight, it did possess long-term vision. And that
vision, in the mid-1980s, was beginning to come into focus.

‖‖‖‖‖‖‖‖‖‖‖‖‖‖‖‖‖‖‖‖‖‖‖‖‖‖‖‖‖‖‖‖‖‖‖‖‖‖‖

John Tanton was a first-generation immigrant of English and German
lineage, whose father immigrated to Detroit from Canada. The younger
Tanton eventually moved his growing family to the rural wilderness of
his wife's youth: a farm in the thumb of Michigan's mitten on the shores
of Lake Huron's Saginaw Bay.

His boyhood love for the surrounding nature turned Tanton into an early environmentalist. Fresh out of the University of Michigan in 1964, he joined the Sierra Club and the National Audubon Society, organizations established to advocate on behalf of wildlife and the land in the face of ever-encroaching industrialization and urban development. But a 1968 bestselling book caused Tanton's activism to take a radically different turn.

Called *The Population Bomb*, the book regurgitated the argument of 19th-century cleric and amateur demographer Thomas Malthus, who believed that population growth, unless controlled, would outpace agricultural growth, leading to mass starvation. "The Bomb," as the book by Paul and Anne Ehrlich was known, took that argument to a new catastrophic end, predicting that worldwide famine due to overpopulation was imminent.

Tanton bought into the Ehrlichs' hair-raising premise hook, line, and sinker, becoming an overnight evangelist for "zero population growth." To that end, he helped to open Planned Parenthood clinics all over northern Michigan. His motivation, however, was not to support the beneficent cause of family planning. He did not aspire to justice for women denied access to health care and social services. Neither did he believe, as the national organization now espouses, that reproductive choice should be the right of women, not the state.

Tanton's letters from that time reveal a greater interest in the view—straight out of the same eugenicist playbook that inspired Adolf Hitler half a century before—that a better human race could be fashioned through such practices as abortions and forced sterilizations. He worried about "less intelligent" people being allowed to have children, and he felt that "modern medicine and social programs are eroding the human gene pool" by reducing infant mortality.

Critics of "The Bomb" sounded the alarm that the book's dire projections could be harnessed to justify the oppression of minorities and the marginalized by folks, like Tanton, who held white-supremacist views. Indeed, once in Washington, DC, as a member of the national board for the nonprofit named eponymously for the movement it represented, Zero Population Growth, Tanton directed his colleagues' attention to another threat to the environment and, in his opinion, the likeliest cause of the coming population explosion: immigrants, especially those coming from Asia and Latin America.

"I've come to the point of view that for European American society and culture to persist requires a European American majority, and a clear one at that," Tanton wrote in December 1983. Tanton's followers and intellectual doppelgängers today have since repackaged this view as the Great Replacement Theory.

I was not yet old enough to go to school when the 1965 Immigration and Nationality Act, also known as the Hart–Celler Act, abolished a quota system, in place since 1921, that favored immigrants from Northern Europe. Now the height of the Civil Rights Movement, the quotas were increasingly under attack for being racially discriminatory. The 1965 law, referred to as the INA, caused John Tanton to fret that white Americans were becoming an endangered species—replaced by the "wrong sorts of people" being allowed to immigrate to the US. He tried to convince conservationists and birth-control zealots alike that limiting immigration was the only way to curtail population growth *and* save the environment.

But in this era of righting the bent arc of justice in the US, Tanton met resistance. "It was a forbidden topic," he is on record saying decades later. "I tried to get some others to think about it and write about it, but I did not succeed. I finally concluded that if anything was going to happen, I would have to do it myself."

And that is just what he did.

From the wilds of upstate Michigan, John Tanton sowed dystopian seeds of division like a racist Johnny Appleseed. He tended to the roots of hate, and grew "into tall oaks—guiding and shaping the public discourse in history-changing ways"—the xenophobic demonization of folks in search of safety that threatens to tear US democracy asunder today.

As Reece Jones documents in another must-read book, *White Borders*, Tanton spent the remainder of his days, from the mid-'60s to his death in 2019, skirmishing in service of a wider war. He founded so-called "think tanks" with money raised from a handful of wealthy donors, like the Mellon-family heiress Cordelia Scaife May. He had her Colcom Foundation funnel millions of dollars to elect politicians with known links to the KKK, like Alabama's Jeff Sessions and Kris Kobach of Kansas. He funded anti-immigration activists to release position papers at the local and national level. With arguments based on pseudoscience and questionable research, they championed the end of birthright citizenship and pushed for limits on asylum; a reduction in legal immigration through refugee caps; the building of a wall on the US-Mexico border; the criminalization of all those daring to enter the US without authorization; and punitive federal opposition to adherents of Fife's Sanctuary Movement.

Sound familiar?

By 1985, when Messrs Holguín and Schey filed *Flores v. Meese* on behalf of Jenny and other children detained by Harold Ezell, John Tanton had already founded the Federation for American Immigration Reform (1979), whose acronym, FAIR, suggests the opposite of what it really is: a hate group. He had also birthed the Center for Immigration Studies (CIS), whose animating principle has always been that immigrants are criminals and perverts and a burden on the US economy, and whose statisticians will torture any data set to make sure that belief appears true. Both CIS and FAIR have long been ground zero for stirring up moral panics through misinformation and fake news.

Next up in the Tanton network would be USEnglish. It pushed onto the 1986 California state ballot a measure called Proposition 63, which kicked off the English-Only movement just as I steered my professional aspirations toward a career in bilingual education. Proposition 63 passed in California with 73 percent of the vote, declaring English the official language of the state, and leading to similar campaigns in roughly thirty more.

Tanton also developed a publishing wing, The Social Contract Press, through which he reissued a translation of *The Camp of the Saints*, the 1973 French novel that has become the bible of white supremacists and Great Replacement conspiracy theorists worldwide. Tanton called it "the *1984* of the twenty-first century" for its Orwellian depiction of Western culture under siege by swarthy refugees.

Throughout the '70s, this small-town Michigan eye doc became the unlikely architect of the modern-day anti-immigration movement. The many-tentacled Tanton network went to bed with local and federal law enforcement agencies, as well as members of Congress, harnessing racist tropes and fearmongering tactics that would transform issues of equal justice under the law into wars about culture and identity.

In 1994, the godfather of the anti-immigration movement celebrated one of his most foundational successes of all—this time his mouthpiece was INS Commissioner Harold Ezell.

|||||||||||||||||||||||||||||||||||||||||||||||||||||||||

Squat and ruddy-faced, Ezell was not an anti-immigrant ideologue when he traded in an executive position as Hot Dog King with Wienerschnitzel International for a civil servant role in 1983 as western regional commissioner for the Immigration and Naturalization Service. He enthusiastically endorsed Ronald Reagan's 1986 amnesty program—the most recent attempt by Congress to enact immigration reform—which supported granting legal residency to the roughly three million undocumented immigrants then living in the US as it also championed increased enforcement.

By the end of the '80s, however, California was heading into the worst economic crisis since the Great Depression—ripe turf for Tanton's gospel of fear and loathing. And Ezell, whose bluster made him a media favorite, was the perfect proselytizer. He and some friends had formed a citizens' group called Americans for Border Control. Their actions included cheering on INS raids on Orange County businesses that hunted undocumented workers for him, as commissioner, to jail. When the group caught Tanton's eye, he funded them through yet another one of his organizations: US Inc. He guided and financed Ezell's foray into politics as the co-author of the 1994 state ballot initiative called Proposition 187.

Before long, Ezell was bellowing out all the old tropes: scapegoating immigrants for the state's financial woes with messages of invading criminals and rapists coming for your daughters and jobs. The intent was to drive public sentiment against immigrants, for sure. But more than wanting a clampdown on immigration or for Congress to enact just immigration reform, Tanton's goal was to stop Latinx folks from becoming a demographic—and therefore democratic—force in his version of "America." His objective was to stop allowing more non-whites in—whether through legal avenues or not.

Prop 187 sought to deny public benefits, like health care and education, to anyone living in California without legal authorization. It directed teachers and health-care professionals to tattle on their students and patients, respectively, and turn them into the INS. Tanton money flowed to white suburbanites in Orange County and the San Fernando Valley to *Get Out the Vote* for Prop 187, which proved instrumental. The measure won the day by a 59–41 percent margin, prompting then-Republican California Governor Pete Wilson to order the referendum's immediate implementation.

Fortunately, Prop 187 was immediately challenged—also argued by Holguín and Schey—and was found unlawful on the grounds that it gave ordinary citizens right-of-way to target individuals based on racial profiling—a violation of the Equal Protection Clause of the 14th Amendment, which is meant to protect every US resident regardless of citizenship status. It also violated the 1982 Supreme Court decision in *Plyler v. Doe*, another landmark case Holguín and Schey played a part in bringing to trial, which gives all children—also, regardless of citizenship—access to free public education, also under the Equal Protection Clause of the 14th Amendment. Finally, the courts reiterated that immigration is a federal issue and not the purview of state lawmakers.

So why was Tanton celebrating?

Because with Ezell's help he'd finally managed to turn a "forbidden topic" into a national bogeyman. What's more, first winning, then losing, the battle for Prop 187 taught the Tanton network of anti-immigration groups how to better fight for their cause. A blueprint emerged that the organization replicated nationwide:

- Fund citizens groups to drum up populist fear and anger against foreign nationals, especially non-whites;
- help craft legislation and laws for state and local governments;

- inspire a pipeline of true believers to enter politics, and, in the process;
- transform them into a powerful lobbying force whose influence would eventually reach the White House.

Dan Stein, FAIR's president since 1988, has publicly stated that Proposition 187 has "a direct lineage to Trump." It provoked "an escalating curve, from 1994 all the way to 2016," when it became a key policy plank for Trump & Co: a literal *Who's Who* of Tanton network insiders, including Attorneys General Jeff Sessions and Bill Barr; FAIR pollster Kellyanne Conway; Trump's ICE Senior Advisor and CIS policy analyst Jon Feere; acting US Citizenship and Immigration Services Director Ken Cuccinelli and FAIR-staffer turned USCIS ombudsman Julie Kirchner; Gene Hamilton, who held prominent positions in the Departments of Homeland Security and Justice; and immigration czar Stephen Miller, himself advised by another Tanton network hardliner, Roy Beck, who worked as a Washington editor for Tanton's Social Contract Press before founding NumbersUSA in 1997.

<hr>

Prop 187 wasn't the only thing that happened in 1994 to create a through line to Trump, while also fertilizing the root causes of forced displacement and migration to El Norte. There was also the North American Free Trade Agreement (NAFTA) and its complement, Operation Gatekeeper.

Negotiated by the elder Bush, NAFTA opened borders to the free and unfettered flow of products and profits. It encouraged transnational corporate capitalism to flock to Latin America and the Caribbean with promises of low to no taxation and environmental regulation. It forced a race to the bottom in wages, locking into poverty labor forced off the land by industrial plantations, cultivating mono-crops for export, like bananas and palm oil, and into factories, called maquiladoras. Operation Gatekeeper, enacted six months after NAFTA, closed the same borders to the flow of people NAFTA's neoliberal economic experiment would inevitably displace.

Gatekeeper's two-pronged mission was to put more "boots on the ground" by increasing the number of Border Patrol agents, while also expanding the strategy tested in El Paso the previous year. Originally called "Operation Blockade," then subsequently stripped of its military connotations as Operation Hold the Line, the strategy was the brain-child of then–Border Patrol Chief Silvestre Reyes. It represented an ideological shift in border policing from the practice of hunting down, apprehending, incarcerating, and expelling undocumented individuals once inside the US to keeping folks out of the US altogether.

Posting four hundred agents on the banks of the Rio Grande in highly visible positions, Reyes claimed to have deterred unauthorized border crossings from Ciudad Juárez. The true effectiveness of the strategy was debatable even then, documents border scholar Timothy Dunn. Pinching off the route through El Paso forced border crossers to go around in a phenomenon of nature called the "balloon effect." It gave human traffickers reason to blaze new, more expensive, trails into the US. But Clinton's Immigration and Naturalization Service was convinced. Hold the Line was sold to Congress as a way to prevent northward migration through deterrence, spawning Operation Gatekeeper, which surged to the border updated surveillance technology; erected walls and fences; added more interior checkpoints as far as one hundred miles from the line; built more detention facilities; and, of course, delivered more sophisticated weapons to Border Patrol agents.

Operation Gatekeeper kicked off the militarization of the US southern border. And sure enough, when a NAFTA-related influx of surplus US corn was dumped upon the Mexican market, prices paid to small and peasant growers plunged by 66 percent, driving the country's agricultural economy into chaos. Hundreds of thousands of farmers were forced to abandon traditional family lands to search for work elsewhere. Some went to urban areas to work for pennies in the sweat-shops-cum-toxic-waste-dumps—the maquiladoras erected in northern Mexico's Free Trade Zones, starting in 1965. Others headed for El Norte where Mexican migrant laborers have long kept the US economy churning through seasonal agricultural employment.

Suddenly, however, they found they could not cross the line. It was tightly closed to them.

The first physical US-Mexico border barriers put in place under Operation Gatekeeper went up in easy-to-cross areas. Starting at Imperial Beach, California, they moved east. They forced folks already in El Norte to stay, undocumented, whereas those trying to get in were pushed into geographically harsher, more isolated, more dangerous terrain—through deserts, over mountains, across rivers.

This was not done blindly. It was backed by the theory, outlined in a document entitled "Border Patrol Strategic Plan: 1994 and Beyond," that when faced with the threat of their own mortal peril, migrants would send word back home: *Do Not Come. Do Not Come.*

Thus was born the US policy of "prevention through deterrence," what I prefer to call "deterrence through cruelty" because its intention was to inflict deliberate harm.

In the words of then-Immigration and Naturalization Service commissioner Doris Meissner, "We did believe that geography would be an ally to us. It was our sense that the number of people crossing the border through Arizona would go down to a trickle once people realized what it's like."

So, where did all that leave Jenny Flores and the class-action lawsuit Messrs Holguín and Schey brought in her name? Well, it was still winding its way through the US justice system—bouncing from local to district appeals to the highest court in the land—when Operation Gatekeeper began. Before we circle back to find out how it settled, let's meet one Border Patrol agent who saw through the cynical cruelty and is now a fierce advocate and activist for Border Patrol accountability and immigrants' rights.

CHAPTER THIRTEEN

The Education of a US Border Patrol Agent

She had no idea what she was getting herself into. Raised in Huntsville, Alabama, Jenn Budd graduated from Auburn University in 1993 with student loans soon coming due and a burning desire to put as much distance as possible between her and an abusive childhood home. Before realizing her goal of becoming a civil rights lawyer, she decided to get some real-world experience, while paying down her debt. She answered a recruitment notice for the US Border Patrol.

"I needed to get out of Alabama," Jenn recounts. "California sounded exotic and friendlier to gays, and the Border Patrol paid well compared to other law enforcement agencies. I would be working outdoors, hiking, and riding horses."

She liked the sound of that. She signed the contract on her birthday in June 1995. She had just turned twenty-four. What Jenn didn't know was that she was about to enter the US's most troubled law enforcement agency—one whose mandate was ill-defined and shape-shifting from its earliest days.

The first agents needed only their own horse and saddle to apply. The government provided a badge, oats and hay, and a revolver. "There was no training. Many of the newly hired agents were not sure exactly what they were supposed to do," documents Reece Jones.

When Jenn joined the Border Patrol, during its Operation Gatekeeper expansion, applicants no longer needed their own horse, but they did need a high school diploma. A training academy had been established in Georgia, with a program that lasted four months, in contrast to the six months required in most places to become a cop. But it was little more than induction by propaganda, according the Jenn. The focus was on physical testing. There was limited Spanish-language instruction; no expected crash course in immigration legislation. "Constitutional law wasn't taught at all. There was nothing to help you understand the power of your role, nothing about US history or the history of the Border Patrol."

It was more like being inculcated into a cult, states Jenn: "We were told, *You're great, you're heroes, you keep America safe from criminals and drug dealers*. We were told, *No one understands the important job you do*, that kind of thing, until we believed it. And we did."

||||||||||||||||||||||||||||||||||||||||||||||||||||||||||||

At the academy, Jenn would have learned that the Border Patrol was officially founded on May 28, 1924, to police the terrain between designated international ports of entry to stop people entering the US "without inspection." She would have learned that the twin missions of the force in the early 20th century were to stop persons Congress deemed unwelcome, while also—this being the era of Prohibition—interdicting the illicit importation of alcoholic beverages. She would have been instructed, as well, to celebrate the memory of the first appointed agent, Jefferson Davis Milton, originally from Confederate Florida, who joined the Border Patrol at the ripe age of sixty-two and remained in service until 1932.

She would *not* have learned, however, that the Border Patrol's roots—and Milton's—stretched all the way back to the Slave Patrols and fugitive bounty hunters of the southern slave states. Nor that Milton, a Texas Ranger from the age of seventeen and son of an enslaver, became the living link between Slave and Border Patrols. She would not have known that Milton brought to the force a "shoot first and ask questions later" attitude steeped in Slave Patrol traditions.

From the earliest days of white European colonization of the Americas, the economy of enslavement ran not by the rule of law but under the brute dictates of plantation justice. Said "justice" was enforced by vigilantes who hunted human beings attempting to flee a lifetime of labor enforced through the cruelest of means. In times of rebellion, the plantation Slave Patrols could expect the support of their colony's militia, whose authority to crush future uprisings was written into the Constitution of the new US nation.

When the Civil War (1861–1865) finally brought that Mephistophelian bargain to an end, the Slave Patrols morphed into the Ku Klux Klan. Some went west, like Jeff Milton, to aid the project of eliminating Native Americans as well as help settle scores with Mexican Americans displaced from the lands claimed by Anglo newcomers, like Charles Stillman. The Rangers relied on the same raw, physical violence as their Slave Patrol forebears.

Washington lawmakers, meanwhile, were putting legal limits on who could be included in the democratic experiment. Following Congress's first-ever immigration legislation, the Naturalization Act of 1790, which declared white skin as the baseline qualification for becoming a US citizen, came the 1875 Page Act. It sought to check the numbers of Chinese laborers lured to the West, first by the 1848 discovery of California gold, then by the construction of the transcontinental railroad. The 1882 Chinese Exclusion Act, which didn't even *try* to couch its racism inside clever language, made it harder for Chinese laborers punted over the borders into Mexico or Canada to get back in; and impossible for new Chinese arrivals to gain entry at all.

Of course, Congress needed an armed guard to enforce this legislation as well as an office to maintain the force. So, in 1904, the first US Immigration Service was born, and under it came the Mounted Guard of Chinese Inspectors. The Mounted Guard, headquartered out of El Paso, was made up of former Slave Patrollers, Klansmen, and Texas Rangers. They roamed the borderlands, hunting down Chinese immigrants with the same dehumanizing methods used against once-enslaved Black people. One of them was Jeff Milton. In 1924, he handed off to the Border Patrol the same culture of impunity he'd been brought up with as a Texas Ranger.

||||||||||||||||||||||||||||||||||||||||||||||||||||||||||

Jenn would also not have learned at the Border Patrol Academy in 1995 that six decades earlier, El Paso Mayor Thomas Calloway Lea Jr, got so worked up about a typhus outbreak in southern Mexico that he convinced Congress to let border officials fumigate all "dirty, lousy, destitute" Mexicans crossing into his city from Ciudad Juarez. Harnessing the same belief that would later move Trump & Co to shut the border, ostensibly against the coronavirus, Lea argued that all border crossers were crawling in lice and communicable diseases.

This is precisely when Mexicans got caught up in the nationwide backlash against forty years of immigration from Southern and Eastern Europe. This is also when John Tanton's intellectual hero, US lawyer and conservationist Madison Grant, became a household name with his 1916 publication, *The Passing of the Great Race*.

In Grant's book, we hear the language echoed by Tanton network acolytes and Fox News talking heads today: that too many non-whites will augur the eventual collapse (read: replacement) of the gene pool of the "greatest, most desirable, and superior human race." Buying into Grant's quack science that there is more than one breed of human, the then-reigning eugenicists of the Church, academy, media, and political leadership painted all those not of Northern European stock as something to be feared: a "diseased, and criminally inferior" devil walking among the folk. They whipped a moral panic that non-whites posed a threat to the future greatness of the US nation.

It was perhaps the country's first Culture War, and it played an active role in Congress passing the Emergency Quota Act of 1921. Known as Title 8, § 1325, of the US legal code, this is when we first see humans referred to as "aliens" and when entry into the US without inspection by a border agent first becomes criminalized. The legislation also put the first numbers on how many new immigrants would be allowed on US soil. The follow-up Immigration Act of 1924, Title 8, § 1326, also known as the National Origins Act, further tightened the quotas, made them more durable, and stipulated penalties for what was now "unlawful" entry.

Mexicans, who had moved throughout the region without issue for centuries, were no longer allowed to cross the line unless they could pass a literacy test and purchase a visa. And from 1917 in El

Paso, Jenn's precursors separated men from women, forced them to strip naked, and sprayed them down with such toxins as kerosene, sodium cyanide, sulfuric acid, and gasoline, while their clothes were similarly "laundered."

Jenn would not have been taught that it was a seventeen-year-old girl that finally faced down the indignity and injustice. Making her way to work in the US on January 28, 1917, Carmelita Torres—aka the "Latina Rosa Parks"—refused to submit to the disinfection process. She sparked a riot among the mostly young domestic workers employed in El Paso homes. They shouted and hurled stones, first at the immigration officials, then at the gawkers who gathered to watch. The crowd grew to several thousand and the rioting continued on January 29 as men also refused to submit to the "Border Bath," joining Carmelita and the women.

The El Paso border inspectors finally agreed to accept health certificates issued by Mexican doctors for the daily crossers. But the practice of stripping naked and fumigating Brown-skinned people crossing the line in El Paso went on for the next forty years. During that time, the agency that in 1924 would become the US Border Patrol experimented with several toxic products including Zyklon B, later used to exterminate Jews in the gas chambers of Nazi concentration camps. It became the chemical of choice at the makeshift border "laundromat."

||||||||||||||||||||||||||||||||||||||||||||||||||||||||||

One thing Jenn might have learned, had history been taught at the Border Patrol Training Academy, was that the agency she joined was called upon in the 20th century to manage the importation and exportation of Mexican workers. They came as miners, machinists, ranch hands, and farmworkers. Easily exploited and more easily expelled if they dared to complain about their abysmal wages and even worse living conditions. They aided the US captains of industry in building the railroads and fueling the steel industry. They herded and slaughtered livestock. They cleaned and painted houses. They tended gardens and plumbed buildings. They cared for children and the elderly.

For decades, Mexican laborers had helped the US economy expand and grow. They crossed the line liberally, until the Title 8 border restrictions of the 1920s made such movement—and such people—"illegal." From that point, treaties had to be negotiated when labor was needed to keep crops from dying in the furrows and factory assembly lines from failing to meet their projected yields. There is no finer example of this than during World War II.

With men and boys off to war, the US population needed to be fed, no matter who picked the produce. So, a political compromise was forged: the southwestern land barons could have their cheap labor as long as it was kept temporary and marginalized, out of sight so as to remain out of mind. The resulting temporary worker treaty, signed with the Mexican government on August 4, 1942, was called the Bracero Program. It would remain quietly in place until 1963.

Braceros were seasonal migrant workers hired by US scouts onto cattle ranches in Texas and New Mexico as well as the vast fruit, vegetable, and cotton plantations of Imperial Valley, California. Throughout its twenty-one years, more than four million Mexican farm laborers turned a former desert into some of the most productive lands on the planet. The US Border Patrol was tasked with opening the valve at picking time, then chasing Mexican laborers south again when the season was over, expanding their historic role from vigilante people hunters to official people herders to "henchmen for the wealthy, too," states Kelly Lytle Hernández, author of *Migra! A History of the U.S. Border Patrol*.

Braceros suffered both extreme exploitation and extreme discrimination, auguring the program's eventual demise with the Civil Rights–era farm workers rights campaigns of Cesar Chavez and Dolores Huerta. In Spanish, *bracero* means "arm," and that's how these workers were viewed, writes historian Pauline R. Kibbe, not as a "human being at all, but a species of farm implement that comes mysteriously and spontaneously into being coincident with the maturing of the cotton . . . and when the crop has been harvested, vanishes into the limbo of forgotten things—until the next harvest season rolls around."

Given the racist and violent history of the Border Patrol, had Jenn learned it, she may not have been shocked by the derogatory language inculcated at the Border Patrol Training Academy. Her instructors, many of Mexican American heritage themselves, used terms like "wetbacks" and "toncs" to refer to border crossers. Unable to work out the difference, Jenn raised her hand to ask, causing her fellow trainees to erupt in laughter.

"There are many racist terms used for Latinx by white Americans: beaners, spics, etc. But 'wetback' and 'tonc' originated with Border Patrol. Texas agents used the term 'wetback' because those who crossed through the Rio Grande often carried dry clothes in packs they held above their heads." If they made it through the rushing water alive, they changed into dry things, placing their wet clothes in the packs, which they slung across their backs again. "This is where the term came from," says Jenn. "Agents could look around at a group of Latinx people and see the ones with wet backs to tell who was undocumented and who wasn't."

"And tonc?" I asked. Jenn hesitated, clearly not wanting to go there. She took a deep breath. "We were told to tell outsiders, press, and public that it's an acronym for 'temporarily out of native country.' But that's a fake thing. The truth is, it's the sound a flashlight makes when it's used to beat someone in the head."

Mexicans were not the only targets of derision at Border Patrol Academy. Sexist jokes abounded as did unbridled gender-based discrimination. When Jenn joined the agency, there were about five thousand agents, only five percent of whom were women. This gender imbalance exists in the force still today, though the ranks have swollen to more than twenty thousand.

In her brilliant and heartbreakingly honest memoir, *Against the Wall*, Jenn details what she calls the "rape culture" of the US Border Patrol. I urge you to read her book for that side of the Border Patrol impunity story. Suffice to say, Jenn suffered greatly as part of a federal law enforcement branch whose officers, while mandated to keep us safe from criminals and perverts, are too often the perverts and criminals themselves. Yet, they are rarely, if ever, held accountable for their actions.

After basic training, Jenn went to work in the Border Patrol's Campo Sector, located twenty-eight miles east of the San Diego Sector to the border of Arizona. She remembers her first arrest—called an "apprehension" in Border Patrol-speak. She was still a trainee, out with a superior patrolling in a van. They came upon a group and she confronted them, nervous, expecting to find criminals with loaded guns. But it was a family with a baby, Jenn remembers, and clearly in distress.

"Aren't they all drug runners?" she asked her colleague, for that's what she'd been taught to believe at the Academy.

"No, they're just migrants, crossing in search of work," he said.

Jenn remembers that as a cautionary moment. "I felt like a Nazi," she told me. The majority of border crossers she encountered throughout her time on the force, "I'd say 99 percent," were poor Mexicans looking for work or Central Americans fleeing violence. "They were just people looking for a better life," says Jenn.

One time, Jenn encountered a large group in the Tecate mountains. She was alone, with only a six-shooter revolver, a baton, and one pair of handcuffs. So, she radioed in for transport, which took hours to come. As she and the group sat waiting, perched on the surrounding boulders, they chatted.

"One of the guys spoke English. He was older, graying at temples. He was better educated than me. He had a law degree. He asked me if we treated Canadians coming across the border the way we treat Mexicans. I realized we didn't. He asked me, *Why do you think that is?* I realized it was about race, about skin color."

She learned a lot about the people she was arresting, while walking them in or waiting for transport, "about who they were and what they had run from."

There was no wall in Campo when Jenn first went on patrol in 1995. There wasn't even a fence, just some barbed wire. "It was more a community back then."

The only east–west road through town ran north of the line, making the border hard to grasp, fluid. Mexican kids crossed the line to play soccer on the flatter US land. Families of both nationalities lived on both sides and crossed daily, unthinkingly, for parties and dinners and school. So did the wildlife that understood nothing of borders and visas and passport controls. "We helped them when their cattle and pigs were lost or injured."

With money appropriated for Operation Gatekeeper, however, the border fence was under construction. It was coming in Jenn's direction from Imperial Beach, north of Las Playas, Tijuana. It hit Campo Sector sometime in 1996 and kept going.

"The fortification created an obstacle course for migrants," says Jenn, forcing them into less populated and more inhospitable territory. That, plus the increase in agents, from fewer than five thousand in 1996 to roughly nine thousand in 1998, made it harder for folks in search of life. The numbers of dead began to grow each year. Border crossers were succumbing to the weather—freezing to death in winter and expiring from dehydration, one of the most painful and protracted ways to die, in the hotter months—as agents were instructed to chase them farther and farther into the dangerous wilderness.

"We always had deaths but not at the level we had after the first wall went up," says Jenn.

The views of human rights groups began to reach her ears: "Your fence is killing people," they said.

"I started to realize that pushing people east to die was US government policy. And that the policies I was enforcing were affecting innocent people, not those with criminal records."

CHAPTER FOURTEEN

The Longest War

"Only the very poor and very desperate will cross on foot through the desert," states Jenn, who as a Border Patrol agent from 1995–2001 wasn't just hunting people. She didn't know it at first, but she was also a foot soldier on the front lines of the US's longest-standing conflict: the so-called War on Drugs.

That war was officially declared by President Richard Nixon on July 17, 1971, just weeks after the publication of the *Pentagon Papers* blew the whistle on decades of lies behind US involvement in Vietnam. Nixon was desperate for a distraction. He proclaimed illegal substances his "public enemy number one," and went after the hippies and Black Panthers that threatened his reelection by vilifying their substances of choice: marijuana and heroin.

But the US Drug War had been raging already, undeclared, for most of the century. The enemies in this war have never been clearly identified, though lots of money has been pumped into stopping them. Its victims are far more obvious: the non-white and immigrant low-level users who've always been the go-to scapegoats, the "folk devils," for all manner of US social pathologies.

Congress's first-ever federal ban on drugs, for example, was the Smoking Opium Exclusion Act. Passed in 1909, it criminalized only the drug's recreational use, targeting the Chinese. Its medical use, as morphine, continued unabated.

During 1920s Prohibition, the Mounted Guard cum Border Patrol would add hunting down Blacks and Mexicans to their mission, specifically those transporting liquor, while in the country's interior, organized crime cemented its role in US society. What's more, as Prohibition laws created new outlaws, they created the need for more police. That's when the all-but-then-defunct Ku Klux Klan sold itself as a "law-enforcement" outfit and was drafted into a new role, stopping not the organized criminal operations making bank off the forbidden liquid intoxicants, but those who partook of it: Black people, immigrants, and the poor who filled the burgeoning US carceral system.

In the 1930s, during the Great Depression, the Drug War's targets became Mexicans and marijuana. Hate toward them was stoked as a means to distract poor whites from their twin plights of joblessness and hunger. They were primed to blame "the other," whose interests and needs were much like their own.

〰〰〰〰〰〰〰〰〰〰〰〰〰〰〰〰〰〰〰〰

Thus were sown the seeds of the historic braid that weaves mind-altering substances, discrimination, and punitive law-and-order policing to create the largest for-profit prison system in the world. Like all wars of choice, however, victory has proved elusive. Marijuana, opium, heroin, and their highly addictive, low-cost derivatives continue to flow northward thanks to the simplest of capitalist principles: supply and demand.

As Benjamin Smith details in his pager-tuner, *The Dope: The Real History of the Mexican Drug Trade*, the US is flooded with narcotics and synthetic and designer drugs, like methamphetamine and fentanyl, not by chance. Organized crime is now transnational and seemingly unstoppable as a by-product of the so-called War on Drugs. Violence in civil society is off the charts on both sides of the line, where enforcement bodies are corrupted and governing bodies have been captured. And that's just one of the Drug War's many twisted legacies. Here's another: Roger Ailes, communications guru for Nixon, who honed the tactic of ginning up racial animus by tying it to drug abuse, went on to build the Fox News juggernaut that traps way too many people in the Tanton-network, fake-news alternate reality that drives us apart today. And another: Rudolph Giuliani, of Trump & Co fame, filled his pockets exporting law and order policing to Mexico *before* it became one of the homicide capitals of the world. But the destructive and costly hypocrisy of the so-called War on Drugs reached an apex in the 1980s under Ronald Reagan.

As his wife, Nancy, headlined a public relations campaign that admonished us to "Just Say No" to drugs, Reagan's National Security Council and CIA joined the drug protection and gunrunning rackets. They did so to finance the same Central America Dirty Wars that upended Dora's and Jenny's lives and would eventually force Sam to run north as well. It was a tangled, covert, almost incomprehensible morass that has come to be known as the Iran-Contra affair.

It began when Congress pulled the plug on funding the Nicaraguan counter-revolutionaries, owing to their penchant for committing outrageous human-rights abuses. The Contras were intent on rolling back the fortunes of the Sandinistas, who sent packing the notoriously brutal and corrupt US-backed Somoza family dictatorship. And Reagan, like so many of his presidential predecessors, was intent in maintaining the power of US banks and business in the region. So, he and Marine Corps Lieutenant Colonel Oliver North—the modern equivalent of Major General Smedley Darlington Butler and then part of Reagan's National Security Council—sought financial aid for the Contras elsewhere.

In a complex and highly secretive three-way deal, they sold $30 million in US military equipment to Iran—despite a US-imposed trade embargo with the country at the time—ostensibly to buy the release of seven US hostages being held in Lebanon. Three hostages were eventually freed. But once the weapons deal was uncovered, some $18 million of the proceeds had gone missing.

Where did it go? To the Contras.

|||||||||||||||||||||||||||||||||||||||||||||||||||||||||||||||

The story doesn't end there, however, for Reagan's VP, Bush 41, had his own pet project at that time. Called the Task Force on South Florida, it was mobilized to stop the flow of Colombian cocaine into Miami via the Caribbean. And it succeeded. But as the Task Force and Drug Enforcement Agency, created by Nixon in 1973, gushed about all their high-profile drug busts, the Colombian trafficking networks just blazed a new trail.

Bush's approach, known as "the kingpin strategy," produced another "balloon effect"—the unacknowledged Achilles' heel of US anti-narcotics and anti-immigration efforts from the get-go. For when you squeeze one part of a blown-up balloon, as we've seen with Operation Gatekeeper, the air doesn't just disappear. It goes elsewhere, stretching the boundaries of its container.

With their Caribbean path cut off in the mid-1980s, Colombian traffickers formed alliances with Mexican marijuana movers, who'd been in business since the early-20th-century Mexican Revolution. Up until then, the Mexican drug traders were largely homegrown, plowing proceeds back into their communities' infrastructure with the knowledge and gratitude of townspeople as well as the protection of local police. Once they became the highly paid risk-takers of Colombian narco-traffickers, the transnational organized crime syndicates of today were unleashed.

The two-thousand-mile US-Mexico border provided all-new trans-shipment routes for Colombian cocaine just as Reagan & Co turned a collective blind eye to the Nicaraguan drug traffickers—and Contra supporters—who were also ferrying massive amounts of the white powder into the US. Whether through direct funneling of funds, weapons acquisitions, or "charitable" contributions, they propped up the Contras' counterrevolutionary war in Nicaragua with cocaine profits.

Simultaneously, their product joined that coming up from Colombia to spark a drug epidemic that ravaged US inner cities nationwide. As the ubiquitous public service announcement cracked two eggs over a frying pan, telling us as they sizzled, "This is your brain on drugs," cocaine poured into the US. The market was so flooded with the expensive narcotic that prices plummeted, driving enterprising manufacturers tuned into market forces to come up with a new method for unloading what had traditionally been the plaything of wealthy white people. They were responding to simple capitalist principles once again.

The Iran-Contra affair coincided with the development of a simple to produce, highly profitable, and extremely addictive, smokable form of the drug that could be sold in smaller quantities to more people. Suddenly, neighborhood kids that I'd watched grow into teens from my Brooklyn brownstone stoop were awaiting my middle-of-the-night returns from work at New York's Village Vanguard to apologetically mug me of my tip money.

||||||||||||||||||||||||||||||||||||||||||||||||||||||||||

This is when the formally hiding-in-plain-sight Mexican drug economy organized and globalized. Now assuming much of the risk for their Colombian suppliers, Mexican traffickers, like their 1920s Prohibition forebears, commenced building their own paramilitaries. This was no small feat in Mexico, however, which possesses some of the world's most draconian gun control laws. There is only one place in the entire country where one can legally buy a gun. And only if you're a cop.

So the Mexican drug lords found a way to exploit loose US gun legislation. Since the 1970s, as illicit drugs have surged north, high-powered weapons caches purchased by third-party, or "straw," buyers north of the line, particularly at Texas gun shows, have surged south. It's all been brilliantly documented by intrepid "narco-journalists," like Anabel Hernández García, who continues to investigate the potential collusion of US and Mexican government officials and drug lords despite death threats; and Ioan Gillo, whose latest book, *Blood Gun Money: How America Arms Gangs and Cartels*, draws on his coverage of the Mexican drug trade since 2000.

The transformation in the Mexican drug trade coincided with the 1994 launch of NAFTA, which opened the US-Mexico border to the flow of goods, and Operation Gatekeeper, which closed it to the movement of people. Congress surged money to the borderlands then, to expand the human and policing resources of a law enforcement agency that, as we've seen, was built on rotten, racist foundations and already famous for its near-total absence of accountability.

The field office in remote Douglas, Arizona, in particular, boomed. Its officers became so freewheeling they were referred to internally as the Douglas Mafia. Similarly, in California's Campo Sector where Jenn Budd then worked, suspicions grew that its chief had earned his nickname: Dirty Cop. Also that the Border Patrol's internal policing unit, the Critical Incident Investigations Team, could not be trusted to police itself. It was—until disbanded at the end of 2022 thanks to Jenn's activism—more of a Critical Incident Cover-Up Team.

"I was arresting people who weren't dangerous, who weren't even criminals. But at the station, I was surrounded by men wearing the same uniform who were breaking the law and nothing was happening to them," Jenn states.

As the 20th century drew to a close, she decided to leave the "cesspool" of unethical and immoral behavior at Campo and move into San Diego Sector Headquarters Intelligence to work with a smaller group of agents more dedicated to upholding the law. There, she discovered that the extent of agency impunity was far worse than she imagined. She figured out who was actually smuggling drugs into the US. And it wasn't migrants.

<hr>

"Everything is laid at the foot of Mexico as if the corruption stops at the border," Josiah Heyman, professor of border studies at the University of Texas at El Paso, told me. What's overlooked, he says, are the many ways the movement of illegal goods coexists alongside legal trade, crossing the line in trucks and cars and factory trains, to get through checkpoints.

"Drugs don't just land in little baggies on the streets in Chicago any more than the US-manufactured guns just happen to kill people in Guerrero. There has to be a system implicated in that kind of cross-border commerce. And that logically, absolutely lies within US Customs and Border Protection."

It only takes one customs agent to wave across the line a tractor-trailer packed with heroin, or a car hiding opioids wrapped in plastic in its gas tank, to satisfy the US appetite for mind-altering substances, writes Tony Payan in *The Three US-Mexico Border Wars*. We tend to want to believe in the incorruptibility of our law enforcement institutions. But as the US southern border is the riskiest point in the journey of any drug stash, payments for those willing to participate are at a premium.

Money buys protection. Always has. Always will. Corruption knows no borders.

CHAPTER FIFTEEN

Collateral Damage

Robert Vivar was a "good immigrant" by the Tanton network definition. He came to the United States in what they would deem the "right way": his parents got in the invisible line so often invoked by Fox News talking heads and applied for a shot at the "American Dream" for themselves and their eight children before leaving the land of their birth, Mexico.

Robert and his family entered the US at the San Ysidro, California, port of entry in September 1961 with proof in hand that they'd been approved for "legal permanent residence." He was just six years old, making him a "documented childhood arrival" in the eyes of the US government.

Robert's older brother Martin enlisted in the US Army at the age of seventeen with his parents' consent, serving with the 11th Armored Cavalry "Blackhorse" Regiment in Vietnam. Young Robert helped establish a Reserve Officers Training Corps (ROTC) program, hoping to serve his adoptive country, like Martin. But the war in Vietnam ended a few months after he graduated. So Robert went to work.

He landed a job as a ticketing agent for Aeroméxico at the Los Angeles International Airport, LAX, and turned out to be a natural logistician. He climbed the ranks to become the manager of Aeroméxico's LAX operations. In 1990, Robert took on a consulting gig with a low-cost Mexico City–based airline company, TAESA (Transportes Aéreos Ejecutivos SA). His job was to help the burgeoning airline forge new routes into the US.

When he rose to the position of TAESA regional director, he moved his wife, daughter, and son to Illinois where he was responsible for setting up the company's Midwest operations. But after one cold Chicago winter, the family was longing for the warmth and blue skies of LA and their expansive network of friends and relations. Though Robert loved the atmosphere of airports and the beauty of aircraft, he decided to embark on a new career path as he neared his fortieth birthday. In 1994, he returned his family to Corona, California, where he grew up, and joined a construction company.

|||||||||||||||||||||||||||||||||||||||||||||||||||||||

Meanwhile, an hour's drive away in California's San Fernando Valley, roughly 75 gangs were at war. Among them were young refugees who had escaped Reagan's Dirty War in El Salvador: some, scruffy teenaged heavy metal fans; others, defecting conscripts of rapid response battalions trained by US advisors. All had landed in the chilly Los Angeles of Harold Ezell just as the Tanton network's anti-immigrant project was gaining ground. The newcomers found themselves unwanted and un-welcomed in Reagan's "Beacon of Hope."

Marginalized in neighborhoods where the Bloods, Crips, Asian Boyz, and Mexican Mafia governed the streets, the Dirty Wars refugees turned to each other. They found fellowship and protection, as well as identity and respect, among others just like them. "Because we all want connection," states Geraldo Lopez, a former gang member turned leader in gang prevention and violence intervention for Homies Unidos. "It's part of the human experience to be part of something, to feel valued, to feel we belong."

Out of unwelcome, a clique is born. Ranks close and the clique becomes a club, then a gang. Fists turn into machetes turn into guns. Petty crime leads to prison time, a veritable university for more serious, violent crime; and from which the formerly traumatized graduate with the name of their new family emblazoned on their bodies: the Mara Salvatrucha gang, aka MS-13, or Barrio 18. What Geraldo calls "the tragic outcome of a tragic environment."

The public panic about both crack and gangs had politicians from Reagan and Gingrich to Clinton and Senator Joseph Biden (D-DE) eagerly pressing the buttons marked "tough on crime" and "illegal aliens" through the '80s and into the '90s. The Los Angeles Police Department's Community Resources Against Street Hoodlums, or CRASH, brought a "crush it and jail it" mentality to the streets, unleashing more violence. CRASH become, according to historian Kevin Starr, "the most badass gang in the city." Broad new legislation ushered in policies aimed at curbing the growth of gang culture by justifying large-scale removals of noncitizens to their countries of origin.

For almost a decade, as Robert thought he was living the "America Dream," the earth had been moving under his feet, though he did not feel it.

IIIIIIIIIIIIIIIIIIIIIIIIIIIIIIIIIIIIIIIIIIIIIIIIIIIIIIIIIIII

It started with Reagan's 1986 Anti-Drug Abuse Act, which created huge—and clearly racialized—sentencing disparities between users of crack and those of its powdery older cousin: five grams (one teaspoon) of the cocaine derivative triggered the same five-year minimum sentence as five hundred grams (one pound) of the product consumed by the Wall Street elite.

His 1988 amendments to the Immigration and Nationality Act then invented the concept of "aggravated felony." It defined the term narrowly, limiting it to murder and trafficking in drugs or firearms. But it made immigrants deportable for such offenses and mandated indefinite detention for all noncitizen "aggfels" until their deportation could be realized.

As Robert reinvented himself as a construction engineer, Clinton's 1994 "Crime Bill" brought 100,000 new cops onto the nation's streets and built 125,000 new prison cells. It amped up federal surveillance capabilities, including wiretaps and mail searches, and backed programs that encouraged police officers to carry out more drug-related arrests, pulling the so-called Drug Wars squarely into the '90s. Finally, it further enlarged the definition of "aggravated felony."

As with the 1909 Opium Ban, both the 1986 and 1988 Acts as well as the 1994 "Crime Bill" criminalized drug use, rather than responding to it as a medical or mental health issue, or the consequence of social ills that government *could* remedy, if only there existed the political will. Instead, these measures increased the numbers and scope of law enforcement and, as with 1920s Prohibition, continued to expand the US incarceration industry.

The 1996 Antiterrorism and Effective Death Penalty Act added still more bullet points to the "aggfel" category. But the coup de grace came later that year when Clinton signed the Illegal Immigration Reform and Immigrant Responsibility Act into law.

Pronounced IRA-IRA, it expanded the list of "aggravated felonies" yet again as it simultaneously closed off pathways for relief by stripping federal courts of their ability to hear civil rights cases on behalf of immigrants. Since then, even a misdemeanor can leave an immigrant subject to criminalization as well as mandatory detention and deportation, with little hope of appeal.

There would be no more second chances for noncitizens. Even now, the category of offenses considered "aggravated felonies" apply *only* to immigrants and may not be "aggravated" at all. They include civil transgressions that might warrant a wrist-slap, monetary fine, or community service for a US citizen, like me. What's more, the application of IRA-IRA was made retroactive.

|||||||||||||||||||||||||||||||||||||||||||||||||||||||||||||

Two years after NAFTA and Operation Gatekeeper, the Clinton trifecta "Crime Bill," Antiterrorism Act, and IRA-IRA—set into cement the US immigration system's predilection for cruelty. Centering imprisonment and punishment as core components, they turned the historic braid that weaves together racialized immigration policies, hyper-punitive "law and order" policing strategies, and the so-called War on Drugs into a knot. They greased the engine of the growing detention-to-deportation pipeline and caused the already crowded US prison-industrial complex to swiftly metastasize into the largest immigration-detention system in the world.

And if that weren't already enough, the exaggerated "aggravated felon" category led to immigrants, even legal permanent residents and veterans of the US armed forces, paying their debt to society not once, but twice, for the same mistake: first under the state or federal penal systems; then under the Immigration and Naturalization Service, and now ICE.

The crime-trifecta forced a double jeopardy upon them, alone.

Robert likely paid no heed to these changes because he was not the target. The net was intended to sweep up the street gangs. Indeed, by the year 2000, US authorities had deported twenty thousand members of MS-13 and Barrio 18 back to El Salvador, offloading a shameful reality, 100 Percent Made in the USA, onto a country with fragile institutions trying to recover from a needless twelve-year war.

Stepping off chartered deportation planes, these English-speaking youth dressed like Hollywood movie stars and covered in tattoos were joined by equally disaffected youth who, as another tragic side effect of war, suffered a generational loss of education. By 2004–2005, the three Northern Triangle countries suffered some of the highest murder rates in the world.

In a war, however, there is always collateral damage, and in this war there have been too many innocent victims to count. Each new tough-on-crime law whittled away Robert's rights, as a non-citizen, a little more. With each stroke of the presidential pen, his status as a permanent legal resident was becoming more precarious. With each new tightening of the screw and each new offense added to the "aggfel" list, immigrants caught up in the US judicial system were becoming more and more deportable.

Few of us clocked any of this, including green card holders and members of military families, like Robert. Then, a once-upon-a-time misdemeanor and a cry for help found him caught in the implacable machinery.

It would propel him into exile—kicked out of the only home he'd ever known.

|||||||||||||||||||||||||||||||||||||||||||||||||||||||||

"I had developed a drug problem," Robert tells me as we sit in his crowded office, half a block from Tijuana's infamous Chaparral tent city. He was on the phone with Representative Mark Takano (D-CA) when I arrived. They were discussing the latest news in their effort to bring unjustly expelled veterans home under the Honoring the Oath Act (HR5151) and other bills. He flashed a warm, gap-toothed grin and waved me into a tattered chair that faced his wide metal desk topped with a black Dell computer. As I listened to him cite chapter and verse of the US Legal Code, sounding more like a member of the US Bar Association than co-director of the Unified Deported US Veterans Resource Center, I took in the railroad-style, one-room storefront.

On the wall behind Robert hung a banner: STOP THE DEPORTATIONS OF MILITARY VETERANS, it read. A water cooler stood next to a standing fan, which worked hard to push the sticky September air around the room. *Know Your Rights* brochures and manuals neatly littered every inch of a white, thigh-high bookshelf with an invitation, handwritten in blue and red magic marker, to FEEL FREE TO TAKE ONE. A stained Mr. Coffee machine stood in salute formation atop a four-drawer filing cabinet.

A second desk tattooed with a bumper sticker announced the group with whom Robert shared the space: VETERANS FOR PEACE. Above it hung the five medallions of the US global security regime: the Army, Navy, Coast Guard, Air Force, and Marine Corps. Everywhere, framed pictures of veterans—some marked with a somber RIP—danced on the stuccoed walls alongside stars painted red, white, and blue. None hung quite straight. All faces pictured were Latinx.

"When you consider the opioid crisis," explained Robert, "there's no such thing as recreational use." He continued, "It's a big lie. First, you're getting together with friends, experimenting with drugs, once in a blue moon, because everyone else is. Or you're using stimulants to stay awake through back-to-back job shifts. And before you know it, you're a full-blown addict."

It didn't help that Robert's experimentation with methamphetamines coincided with an epidemic pushed onto the US public by Sackler family–owned Purdue Pharma. For the longest time, he was a "functional addict," going to work as expected, showing up like a responsible husband and father for family and community events.

"But you get to a point where addiction takes over every part of your life. And you start doing things that you never thought you could be capable of, things that can lead to legal trouble."

Robert agreed to boost some boxes of Sudafed in exchange for a fix. Subsequently taken off pharmacy shelves in 2006, the active ingredient in the otherwise benign decongestant, pseudoephedrine, was then being chemically modified to produce crystal meth.

Robert got caught. He was arrested for shoplifting.

"At first, it was a relief," says Robert. He knew he had slipped into addiction and he wanted help. He pled guilty, on the advice of his public defender, believing he would do time, but in a rehabilitation facility. And that would have been true if, like me, Robert was a US citizen. But he had never naturalized. For him, being a legal permanent resident, or green card holder, had always been enough.

He had no idea that a guilty plea would compromise his residence status; nor did his court-appointed attorney. She knew nothing of how the spate of immigration laws had been stacked against Robert. She failed to clock that the plea agreement she handed him to sign translated his shoplifting charge, through the lens of IRA-IRA, into one of "theft with the intent to manufacture." This transformed him on paper from a shoplifter into a "drug trafficker," and plunged him squarely into the now greatly expanded legal category of "aggravated felon."

Robert was branded a "criminal alien" and jailed until deportation. He tried to appeal, but IRA-IRA made it impossible for even a judge to take into consideration Robert's life history, his professional achievements and what he meant to his family, or that his offense was a misdemeanor for his citizen fellows. Once upon a time, a judge could have given Robert a second chance and sent him to rehab.

Instead, he fell victim to the place where racialized laws and ineffective legal counsel meet. "I trusted the attorney. I believed that she'd worked in my best interest and that I would be sent to rehab. So I signed."

Robert could blame her, and maybe should. But he doesn't. He understands now that this is precisely what the crime-trifecta laws were written to do.

It wasn't until he was returned to the detention center, however, lashed in five-point restraints, "because that's how ICE transports everyone, even non-criminals: to court, to the doctor, to the border," that Robert discovered he would not be getting the help he desired. He had to kick his addiction and clean up on his own—in prison.

Stripped of his rights, he was also stripped of his green card, and his dignity.

"I didn't wish to give up my legal residence status just like that," states Robert. So he set about learning everything he could about the law and appealed to overturn the lower court decision, *pro se*, on his own. Imprisonment was just too much to bear, however. No good to his family locked up and unable to provide, he grew depressed, despondent, demoralized. When his case stalled out within the ever-increasing backlog of the US immigration court system, now choked by IRA-IRA cases, Robert agreed to "voluntary deportation" to the now foreign country of his birth.

"That's the point of immigration criminalization," Robert explains. "To wear you down to the point when you agree to 'self-deport.'"

Eight months after losing his case, Robert was shackled in five-point restraints again, bused to the San Ysidro port of entry, and escorted across the border into Tijuana. He was dumped there by ICE with nothing to his name but a US driver's license and a criminal record for the aggravated felony of drug trafficking: a crime he did not commit.

He spent three months pounding the pavement. "I couldn't even get a job as a parking lot attendant, let alone with an airlines or in a hotel. I had no connections. Even if I got an interview, I was found to be 'overqualified.'"

Traumatized at being separated from his loved ones and growing financially desperate, Robert risked everything: "I went back to the US undocumented."

Forced, now, to live in the shadows, Robert never touched drugs or alcohol again. "I could not afford to get caught a second time. So, I dedicated myself to a quiet life of working and taking care of my family."

He had to, for as an "aggfel," Robert could no longer seek asylum or citizenship. He suffered a twenty-year ban on ever being able to return home, and had little hope of ever recovering his previous status as a legal permanent resident.

Robert made a mistake. Lots of us do. And yet he became collateral damage in a war said to be about drugs, but which served him up as fodder to fuel the flames of a manufactured crisis stoked every day by the Tanton network propaganda machine: that the newcomer cannot be trusted and that the US border is spinning dangerously out of control.

CHAPTER SIXTEEN

The Border Hardens

It was a beautiful, fresh, blue-sky day. The fall season and the sense of new beginnings were in the air. As I walked my five-year-old to her third day of kindergarten in downtown Brooklyn, she stretched an arm upward, pointing. "Look, Mama," she said. "What's that funny cloud?"

"Oh no!" I exclaimed, on seeing the steel-gray streak cleave the firmament like the mark of a wrathful Sharpie. "There must be a terrible fire in Lower Manhattan."

I did not know that just moments before, at 8:46 a.m., terrorists linked to al-Qaeda turned American Airlines Flight 11 into a missile and drove it into the North Tower of the World Trade Center. As I exited the school building at roughly 9:03, United Airlines Flight 175 rammed the South Tower a mile away from where I stood. That's when I realized this was no tragic accident.

Within 1 hour and 42 minutes, both 110-story towers collapsed, killing nearly 3,000 people , including 343 firefighters, 72 law enforcement officers, and everyone on board both planes. Forty-four more people died when a third hijacked plane crash-landed in Pennsylvania; and 184 people lost their lives when a fourth aircraft struck the Pentagon. Another 25,000 or more were physically injured. But no one would escape the fallout of the single deadliest terrorist attack in human history.

Watching the buildings come down from the roof of the Victorian-era brick-and-brownstone where my family and I then lived, I felt the shock waves that would reverberate around the globe. One week after September 11, 2001, President George W. Bush (43) signed into law a joint resolution authorizing the use of force against those responsible for attacking the US. His War on Terror unleashed the already-extant Border Industrial Complex, reveals Todd Miller in his 2019 exposé, *Empire of Borders: The Expansion of the US Border Around the World.* What Todd dubs the War on Illegality and Israeli anthropologist Jeff Halper calls the Securocratic War spun quickly, following 9/11, into a lucrative export as physical, technological, and bureaucratic barriers went up everywhere.

Bush 43 also announced the US government's intention to create a comprehensive national bulwark: The Department of Homeland Security became operational in March 2003.

Ezell's Immigration and Naturalization Service—given the "death penalty" for having approved visas for two of the 9/11 hijackers—was replaced by three agencies: the US Citizenship and Immigration Services, ICE, and Customs and Border Protection. The latter agency brought three existing forces under one roof: The blue-uniformed police at air and land ports of entry; the brown-uniformed officers in charge of Air and Marine Operations; and the green-uniformed Border Patrol, aka the "Green Monster," whose jurisdiction included the one-hundred mile national perimeter, within which lives two-thirds of the entire US population.

The Border Patrol that Jenn Budd knew was no congressional afterthought anymore. It was now tasked with "coordinating and unifying all national security efforts involved in antiterrorism, border security, immigration and customs, cybersecurity, and disaster prevention and management."

Note: not a word about managing the unique humanitarian needs of refugees and people seeking asylum appeared—then as now—in the agency's mission description.

The post-9/11 Border Patrol suddenly saw itself as the premier US federal law-enforcement agency of the land: "the marines of CBP," conditioned, like Texas Ranger turned Mounted Inspector turned Border Patrol agent Jeff Milton, to "kick ass, and ask questions later." State-of-the-art toys were surged to the southern and northern borders, from sophisticated surveillance cameras and automatic weapons to helicopters, planes, ATVs, and predator drones. We can now add to that cache the high-altitude observation blimps and watchtowers that can "see" for miles in all directions, as well as shockingly cute robotic dogs that can be weaponized in an instant and ordered to kill.

The Green Monster's new recruits no longer needed even a high school diploma to apply. They were inducted into an agency already known for its immoral and unethical behavior; inculcated by a generation of Tanton network acolytes, who populated both Border Patrol Academy and union, to view folks running for their lives and in need of safety not simply as "dirty and diseased," but also a security risk—a potentially dangerous invading force.

It was as if no one in the Bush 43 administration recognized that the 9/11 terrorists arrived not by land or sea, but by air via international airports.

⠀⠀⠀⠀⠀⠀⠀⠀⠀⠀⠀⠀⠀⠀⠀⠀⠀⠀⠀⠀⠀⠀⠀⠀⠀⠀⠀

The first Department of Homeland Security secretary, Tom Ridge, was given a bottomless pit of cash to create this new army. Since then, the post-9/11 funding flood has never stopped, Todd shows in his 2014 book, *Border Patrol Nation: Dispatches from the Front Lines of Homeland Security*. A hiring surge ensued that shoveled new recruits through the Border Patrol Academy—further shortened from four months to fifty-two days—and into the field faster than the time it took to complete their background checks. As a result, the agency infamous for its abbreviated and questionable training tradition added 17,000 agents by the end of Bush 43's administration. Many of these were unfit to carry a badge and gun, James F. Tomsheck, an eight-year Customs and Border Protection assistant commissioner of internal affairs turned whistleblower, admitted years later.

The lax hiring practices created a "perfect storm for corruption and misconduct," Tomsheck stated in 2014, adding that 5 to 10 percent of Border Patrol agents and officers were then actively corrupt: stealing government property; leaking sensitive information; abusing detainees; and taking bribes from drug- and people-traffickers to look the other way as trucks packed with contraband crossed the line.

Other high-ranking Customs and Border Protection officials have pegged the corruption rate at closer to 20 percent.

Between 2005 and 2012, at least one officer was called out for misconduct every single day, making the corruption that Jenn encountered in her days seem almost quaint. The conservative CATO Institute found that from 2006 to 2016, Border Protection and Border Patrol disciplinary infractions outstripped all other federal law enforcement agencies. The Customs and Border Protection commissioner under Bush 43, Ralph Basham, admitted in 2014, "We found out later that we did, in fact, hire cartel members."

But cartel members weren't the half of it. Polygraph exams, implemented only after, rather than before, the hiring tsunami, discovered that drug pushers and abusers, as well as kidnappers and sexual predators, had also been added to the force. White supremacists rode into elevated leadership roles from the twenty regional "fiefdoms," like the Douglas Mafia, based in the most corrupt town on the US-Mexico border, according to a 1996 *Los Angeles Times* report. That's where Carla Provost, Trump & Co's Border Patrol chief from August 2018 through January 2020, got her start in 1995.

"After 9/11, anti-immigrant groups, seeking to reduce both illegal and legal immigration to the US, got into bed with Border Patrol through the union," Jenn Budd states. Called the National Border Patrol Council, the union endorsed Trump for president in 2016—the first time the Border Patrol agency had ever backed a presidential candidate. (ICE's union soon followed—another historic first.) Council representatives, fruit of the Tanton network loins, are regulars at agency conventions and frequent speakers on the Breitbart-sponsored podcast *The Green Line | The Truth Straight from the Border*. The members-only website is peppered with resources for agents and their families produced by the usual Tanton organizations, many now labeled as "hate groups" by the Southern Poverty Law Center for their false attacks on immigrants, as well as their "ties to white supremacist groups and eugenicists." And then there was the July 2019 scandal of the secret Facebook group "I'm 10-15"—code for "undocumented immigrants in custody"—that posted lewd and threatening images of Latinx lawmakers and which counted among its 9,500 members Border Patrol Chief Provost.

According to the Southern Border Communities Coalition, which has tracked Customs and Border Protection-related violence since January

2010, about three hundred people have died as of the end of 2023, following encounters with US border agents. Many more suffer life-altering injuries. And this is a likely undercount for the Department of Homeland Security does not keep reliable, consistent data on fatalities and other harms caused by its officers. It is not obligated to do so by Congress.

Cultures of violence and impunity reign within Homeland Security agencies, perpetuated by the ever-increasing pot of billions funneled to them year after year after year. In the weekly newsletter he co-produces with journalist Melissa del Bosque, *The Border Chronicle*, Todd writes that the US government allocated more money for Customs and Border Protection and ICE operations in the 2023 fiscal year than ever before: over $29.8 billion, topping the previous record spending year of $25.4 billion in 2020. Juan González reports in *The Current Migrant Crisis* (2023) that $333 billion have been shoveled to Homeland Security agencies tasked with immigration enforcement between 2003 and 2022.

‖‖‖

The corruption, the racism, the incompetence, the hubris, the abuse of excessive force, the normalization of cruelty—all of it came together in the horrific public torture of Anastasio Hernández Rojas by seventeen federal law enforcement agents, representing Border Patrol, Border Protection, and ICE. The man who "was beloved by all who knew him," states María de Jesús Puga Morán, Anastasio's partner of more than twenty years, was cuffed, hog-tied, beaten, and tased until brain-dead on May 28, 2010. He died three days later, on May 31.

María and I met in December 2022, just a month after she and her legal team went before the Inter-American Commission on Human Rights in Washington, DC, to demand justice, once and for all, for the unnecessary brutality Anastasio suffered. I wanted to learn more about the man who Homeland Security agents felt had to be "removed" no matter the cost.

At the time of his death, Anastasio had been living in the US for twenty-seven years, contributing to his community as both engaged neighbor and taxpayer. Yet, he had no path to US citizenship. A resident of San Diego, he worked in construction from the age of fifteen, evolving into a sought-after drywaller and plasterer. He was on the verge of launching his own business, building and maintaining swimming pools, when he was picked up by the San Diego Police, allegedly for lifting some food items from a convenience store.

Anastasio's ultimate foe, therefore, was likely the Secure Communities program, or S-Comm as it's called in the military parlance of post-9/11 Homeland Security agencies. Piloted under Bush 43 and expanded to cover 1,595 jurisdictions in 44 states and territories by the time President Barack Obama took office in 2009, S-Comm allows cops to talk instantly to ICE through the FBI via shared biometric data.

When in effect, it works like this: An individual is booked into a local jail; his or her fingerprints are taken and irises scanned and sent to the FBI to be checked against criminal databases. In S-Comm jurisdictions, these data are also sent to ICE to assist that agency's mandate of hunting down and removing people.

Suffice to say, S-Comm can be, and has been, highly abused.

During Obama's administration, S-Comm kick-started deportation proceedings against many upstanding community members just living their lives, earning him the moniker of "deporter in chief." Harsher even than IRA-IRA, 26 percent of those deported under S-Comm from 2008 to June 2010 were classified by ICE as "non-criminals." They had no police record of any kind.

Among those who were deported, 79 percent, like Anastasio, were picked up for lower-level offenses, some potentially fabricated, for which people were not charged—just expelled.

||||||||||||||||||||||||||||||||||||||||||||||||||||||||||

María and her family filed suit for Anastasio's wrongful death and civil rights violations in 2011. They received a $1 million settlement. But no one—not the seventeen named agents caught on a passerby's camera beating Anastasio to death, not their supervisors, nor the agencies that train and employ them—has ever been charged criminally.

A federal grand jury investigation followed. But the sealed ruling came more than five years later, in 2015. It cleared everyone involved, citing *a lack of demonstrable evidence that agents at the scene acted with the intent to deprive Anastasio of his rights and his life.* The shocking video evidence suggests otherwise.

Not only was no person or agency ever held accountable for the extrajudicial killing of Anastasio Hernández Rojas by US federal law enforcement agents, but no agent in the history of the US Border Patrol or its antecedents—the Mounted Inspectors, Texas Rangers, or Slave Patrols—has ever been convicted of a killing while on duty.

||||||||||||||||||||||||||||||||||||||||||||||||||||||

"What do you want people to know?" I asked María.

"I want people to understand that federal agents got away with killing my husband in public. That this happens at the border every day, and until there is justice it is going to keep happening."

She paused, then continued: "We are a family destroyed." María's eldest son remains traumatized and unable to function fully in society to this day. "He has yet to overcome what happened to his papa," she states.

"I don't want any more families destroyed like mine. We don't want to see any more killings by the Department of Homeland Security."

This is what border securitization looks like. It is wholly incompatible with human rights imperatives and justice under the law—a reality that is not limited to one side of the line.

CHAPTER SEVENTEEN

Kidnapped by Uncle Sam

L ife had all but stopped in Matamoros by the summer of 2011. A bloody turf war had broken out the year before between the Gulf Cartel and Los Zetas. With links to the Guatemalan Military Special Forces unit, *los Kaibiles*, as well as the Mexican Army's Special Forces Airmobile Group (GAFEs), Los Zetas were then the most powerful, well-armed, and technologically advanced transnational criminal organization in Mexico.

They were also the most feared.

The Inter-American Court of Human Rights and the UN-backed Truth Commission declared los Kaibiles, in 1999, guilty of the worst human rights abuses of Guatemala's thirty-six-year genocide. The GAFEs, meanwhile, were some of the most elite, expert, and notorious killers ever to grace the Mexican military, and planet. After being trained in the US between 1996 and 1998, some among them discovered there was much more money to be made as the pet paramilitary for the Gulf Cartel. A decade later, Los Zetas had not only broken away to form their own transnational criminal organization, but they had replicated and extended their reach by franchising their brand.

In 2010, Los Zetas' territory spanned the length of Mexico's Gulf Coast all the way to the Texas border. They sought control of the hydrocarbon-rich Burgos Basin beneath the Mexican state of Tamaulipas as well as the drug- and human-trafficking routes above. Their battle with the Gulf Cartel put a price on the head of anyone passing through. It also terrorized the residents of the historic and formerly laid-back border town of Matamoros

Folks still attended Mass and the occasional baby shower or *quince-añera*, but afterward they went straight back home, locking themselves behind closed doors. Everyone was at risk, even the poor of La Colonia Derechos Humanos, a shantytown built atop a city dump, where Larry and Nancy Cox created and managed a refuge on "land no one else wanted."

Until they were targeted for extortion.

First came the suspicious phone calls from strangers, who knew way too much about them. Then, one night, the steady *thwomp*, *thwomp*, *thwomp* of helicopter blades hovering over their home brought Larry outdoors at 3:00 a.m. Despite the darkness, he could see men through the open side door of the low-flying chopper. At least one wielded an assault rifle. From an upper-floor window, Nancy watched in horror as a red dot danced about Larry's head and shoulders. When it landed on his chest, he saw it, too, and beat a hasty retreat back inside.

Finally, news reached them that some toughs had been wandering La Colonia, threatening to "skin and peel" them, and asking which was their bedroom window. That's when Larry and Nancy decided it was time to go.

Nancy left with the two youngest of their three children the next day. Getting eleven-year-old Keyla across the border would be more complicated, however, as she was not officially adopted. "But we had to," Larry told me. "As long as she remained in Mexico, she'd be vulnerable to kidnapping, or worse." A means to get to him.

||||||||||||||||||||||||||||||||||||||||||||||||||||||||

The violence that menaced the Coxes, their fellow Tamaulipas residents, and all those traveling through, was far from random. It was the inevitable result of corruption aided by law and order policies and cash influxes from north of the line—just one more by-product of the so-called US Drug War.

In 2000, Mexico's dominant political party of seven decades was in decline, fracturing the political landscape. Narco-traffickers flush with cash took advantage of the power vacuum. They paid off "great swathes of the Mexican security state and its security forces," documents Benjamin Smith. The result was what political scientists call "state capture"—the phenomenon of private interests infiltrating and influencing government. Six years later, $1.3 billion from Washington under the Mérida Initiative, bought Mexico more cops and training and arms and aircraft. It was meant to make Mexico safe for global investment. But it made an already bad situation worse. The country's homicide rate spiked, increasing by 50 percent each year from 2008 to 2010. (Congressional funding for the Mérida Initiative, aka Plan Mexico, would eventually total $3 billion.)

There was money to be made by anyone wishing to participate in a vast protection scheme that benefited drug running and hydrocarbon theft at the top end to gunrunning as well as kidnapping and extorting people in motion among the heavily armed foot soldiers. Safety seekers too poor to pay ransom and unwilling to become drug mules or sex slaves—like Luis Fredy Lala Pomavilla—were turning up by the hundreds in unmarked mass graves by the time Larry, Nancy, and the kids fled Matamoros.

When Luis Fredy, en route to El Norte from Ecuador, survived a mass execution by Los Zetas in Tamaulipas in August 2010, it was already open season on all those trapped between the transnational criminal organizations—aka the cartels—street gangs, and corrupt state authorities who would do them harm upon reaching the highly militarized, bureaucratized, and securitized US border. Still is.

||||||||||||||||||||||||||||||||||||||||||||||||||||||||||

Waking at the crack of dawn on June 7, 2011, Larry sent up prayers of gratitude for Texas Representative Kay Granger (R-TX), Katherine Brown of the US Department of Homeland Security, and Jason Monks of the US State Department in Matamoros. They'd arranged everything after he had reached out for help. The plan was for Larry to walk Keyla to the Customs and Border Protection office on the Gateway International Bridge and request humanitarian parole, which would keep her safe while the Coxes sorted out her status north of the line.

In an email dated June 5, Larry had suggested informing his and Nancy's friends at Desarrollo Integral de la Familia (DIF)—Mexico's office of child-protective services—of their intentions to remove Keyla from the country. Nancy had worked with them for years, so they knew the Cox family well. And Larry, who wanted everything to be above-board, thought it a professional courtesy, at least. At most, they might also be able to help.

But his powerful advisors on the US side of the border said, *No. Not yet. Let it come from the top.* He trusted their advice. He had to. He had too much to do to pack up the family's belongings as well as organize for the continued care of the residents at their refuge: Casa Bugambilia.

A doctor, Nancy had dedicated her life and her practice to providing free care for the medically fragile and physically challenged indigent of the Mexican border town. It started in 1997 with "drive-by consultations" administered out of the back of a rattle-trap van she kept stocked with antibiotics and bandages as well as alcohol, aspirin, and syringes. She drove the streets like a peddler of Good Humor Ice Cream, but instead of sweet treats, she peddled physical and emotional healing. If she met someone in need of long-term care, she found them shelter. She took those with more critical conditions to the hospital, advocating on their behalf with her colleagues who preferred paying costumers; paying for their care if needed.

Larry made Doctora Nancy's acquaintance in the year 2000. He'd heard about this celebrated "Mexican Mother Teresa" and wanted to meet her. He was immediately caught up in her mission, joining her effort as a "full-time volunteer."

The two fell in love while driving the streets of Matamoros, administering to the city's forgotten, tossed aside. They came to realize that, in addition to medicine, these people needed nutritious food and clean water, sanitation, and a roof over their heads. Most of all, they needed welcome and a community of belonging. So Larry harnessed the good-will of the United Methodist Church, which sent scores of volunteers to help raise a refuge out of the muddy and rutted dirt streets of La Colonia Derechos Humanos.

Casa Bugambilia opened in 2003 with a clinic, communal kitchen, fellowship hall, and twenty beds for those needing long-term care. Nancy was their doctor and surrogate madre; Larry their padre and provider. Refuge residents, proprietors, and volunteers became a unique and committed blended family. And it just kept growing.

At its height, Casa Bugambilia housed ninety-three people from fourteen countries, speaking at least eight languages. It included an apartment for Larry and Nancy on the top floor extension of a small school, built by its humanitarian offshoot, Juntos Servimos (Together We Serve), which constructed sturdy, if simple, homes, and provided daycare and early childhood education for the kids of the maquiladora workers of La Colonia Derechos Humanos's shantytown.

<hr/>

At 6:16 on the morning of June 7, Larry received the go-ahead from Danielle Gonzalez, casework coordinator at Congresswoman Granger's office: "Larry, Call Mr. Monks to arrange logistics on the MX side," the email read. "Once logistics are in place, let me know an approximate time and location. We will let CBP know of the circumstance," referring to the direct threats Larry and Nancy suffered and the danger that posed to Keyla. In closing, Ms. Gonzalez reminded Larry that the decision to grant humanitarian parole was solely up to Customs and Border Protection officials, so "be sure to have all Keyla's documents with you."

This was easier said than done, given the circumstances of Keyla's birth. Her biological mother had been gang-raped by five men on her twelfth birthday. Not yet physically developed for childbirth, she struggled to push Keyla into the world. She was on the edge of death when a student doctor at the public hospital where she labored went in with forceps. He saved the mother, but crushed Keyla's skull in the process, collapsing a portion of her brain. The prognosis was not good: She would live but likely not long. She might learn to walk or talk, but she would never be self-functioning.

Soon after, the twelve-year-old mother, herself motherless, disappeared. Keyla's care fell to her great-grandmother Antoñia, who was living on the streets.

Antoñia needed help with baby Keyla, who was prone to shaking fits. She sought out Nancy and Larry, approaching them for the first time in 2001 at the intersection of two muddy streets of La Colonia.

Derechos Humanos is not a pretty place. The poverty is grinding. The stench of rotting garbage is compounded by the toxic fumes of unregulated maquiladora runoff and human waste that courses past the dump they called home en route to the Gulf of Mexico. On that wretched, inhospitable corner, Doctora Nancy diagnosed Keyla, aged three, with childhood epilepsy. She provided Antoñia with anti-seizure medication. It became Larry's job to refill the prescription every three weeks and to track Antoñia down to give it to her.

In July 2005, Nancy invited Antoñia and her developmentally disabled ward to live with them at Casa Bugambilia. The sixty-two-year-old woman was not well. She struggled to support Keyla, then almost six. Keyla still did not then talk. She walked, but with difficulty, unable to balance. At the refuge, however, she began to sing, in her way, and to dance, responding to the music that filled the dining room and kitchen at all hours.

Also about that time, Larry and Nancy took in two abandoned siblings, a boy and a girl. Though born in the US, they were left at the nearby fishing village—a place even more isolated and destitute than La Colonia Derechos Humanos. On the occasion of their baptism, Antoñia leaned toward Larry and asked if he thought Keyla could be baptized, too. Larry reassured Antoñia that "God sees each child as unique and of sacred value." He promised to have Keyla baptized, even if he had to do it himself.

That's when Antoñia pulled Larry and Nancy into an even deeper confidence: "If anything ever happens to me," she said, "I want you to care for Keyla. I want you to be her parents."

"That day, Keyla entered our family and our hearts as our daughter," says Larry.

Antoñia died less than a month later from complications due to a staph infection.

|||||||||||||||||||||||||||||||||||||||||||||||||||||||||||

Per Ms Gonzalez's instructions, Larry phoned Mr Monks in the early morning light. Monks agreed to retrieve Keyla from the safe house where Nancy had placed her the week before. Monks would deliver Keyla to Larry at the foot of the Gateway International Bridge on the Matamoros Civic Plaza. Larry wanted to get an early start, hopeful to be with the rest of the family, now the guests of a church parsonage near Los Fresnos, Texas, for dinner.

The sun hovered just above the horizon when Jason Monks pulled into the Plaza in an armored car. Behind semi-darkened window glass, Keyla appeared nervous and disoriented. Larry noted that she'd lost weight after just one week away from him, Nancy, and the little ones. But seeing her father put her world right again.

They waved *¡Adios!* to Mr Monks, and commenced their journey toward safety on the US side of the bridge. As they joined the northbound foot and vehicular traffic that Tuesday morning, father and daughter walked hand in hand. She hummed, throwing upward glances at him while smiling her wide, crooked-toothed smile. He labored, patiently, to match her halting gait. Eleven years old the previous August, Keyla was a lithe and wiry 4'10" and 75 pounds. At 6'3", Larry had to stoop to be heard by her over the din of rush-hour traffic.

He chatted about all the adventures they were going to have from their new home in the US, like visiting the San Antonio Zoo. At one point, Keyla looked up at the clouds in the sky and pointed. "Mira Papi. Hay montañas en el Cielo," she whispered.

Look, Daddy. There are mountains in the sky.

At another, Larry bent his gray head toward her shock of thick, dark hair, styled like a pageboy's. Positioning his bearded and mustachioed mouth as close to her ear as his middle-aged girth would allow, he said: "*Uno once . . .*"

". . . *Quince-cincuenta-y-tres,*" Keyla responded without missing a beat. Then she reversed the game: "1-11," shouted Keyla,.

"15-53!" concluded Larry.

It was one of several memory games he'd taught her over the years, since Antoñia's passing. At that time, Keyla was fearful and confused, easily reduced to tantrums and tears. Larry empathized deeply, having lost his mother at about the same age. He tried to reassure her: "I told her that Toñia was now living in heaven right beside my mother, Tony. I told her that Toñia and Tony were together and doing very well."

Keyla calmed, seeming to understand. She commenced asking about Toñia and Tony daily. That's when Larry recognized she was capable of learning. It would take patience and kindness and lots of repetition, as well as dedicated eye contact, for her eyes did not focus.

He would lock his gaze on hers from just inches away and teach her words in a sequence to aid her memory development. He started with *¡Excelente!* Then he added *¡Fantastico!* She would touch his face and voice box to "listen" better.

In time she could repeat *¡Excelente! ¡Fantastico! ¡Fabulosa! ¡Poderoso! ¡Tremendo! ¡Increible! ¡Estupendo!* One day she shocked him by adding her own: *¡Maravillosamente Bien!*

Another time, when Keyla was eight and they were driving in the car, she looked up at the clouds in the sky and pointed. "Mira, Papi. Hay montañas en el cielo," she whispered.

Look, Daddy. There are mountains in the sky.

"She had jumped from my ongoing explanations of the surrounding environment—narrated too many times to count—to create a metaphor."

He decided to teach her the telephone number at Casa Bugambilia so she might find them again in the event she ever got lost. Over time, as she did most things, Keyla turned the mnemonic into a game and a song:

"Uno-once," she would prompt.

"Quince-cincuenta-y-tres," Larry would respond without missing a beat. Then he'd reverse the game: "1-11," he'd offer.

"15-53!" Keyla sang out in conclusion.

||||||||||||||||||||||||||||||||||||||||||||||||||||||||

On reaching the Customs and Border Protection offices, they took their place in line and Larry dutifully turned off his smartphone, in part because that's what the agency's signage demanded; in part, out of habit. Larry had made many requests for humanitarian parole over the years, having crossed dozens of physically disabled and vulnerable children over the line to receive specialized medical care, to be fit for wheelchairs or prosthetics, or to meet with eye surgeons or occupational therapists, all willing to help him and Nancy at little, or no, cost. He knew the border drill well.

What he didn't know, and would not find out until he turned his phone back on later that evening, was that Congresswoman Granger's office had sent him a second email that morning. Time-stamped 8:57, it hit his inbox while he and Keyla were waiting to pass through US customs, after he'd shut his phone down.

The subject line read, "URGENT—You need to call DIF before you leave with Keyla." In the body of the message, Ms Gonzalez wrote, "Call me urgently, I think we have a solution."

But it was too late. Not only was Larry informed that humanitarian parole for Keyla had been denied, but a Border Protection agent appeared without warning to take her away.

"What's going on?" Larry demanded, confused.

Officer de los Santos, of the US Citizen and Immigration Services, stepped in and introduced himself just as Keyla was taken into a separate room. Larry could see her through the glass. Her body had stiffened in fear. Her smile, usually bright enough to light up any room, had disappeared into a tight, taut scowl. He kept his eyes trained on hers, trying to exude calm, trusting that it was just a glitch. After all, they had the weight of the US State Department on their side. They would be reunited in no time, he told himself, and on their way to live happily ever after in Texas with their family.

Larry waited for seven hours. No one talked to him.

Finally, Officer de los Santos returned to inform him that he would have to leave the bridge. Keyla would be spending the night in custody.

Traumatized and exhausted, Larry stammered that he'd be back first thing in the morning. Officer de los Santos said that wouldn't be necessary: Keyla was now in the custody of the US Department of Health and Human Services and would be passed to the US Office of Refugee Resettlement the next morning and flown to Chicago. Larry had never heard of this alphabet soup of US agencies. They had never come up in his communications with Congresswoman Granger, Mr Monks, or Ms Gonzalez.

"What about her medications?" Larry asked, grasping at straws.

No one else on the bridge that day but Larry knew that Keyla suffered complex and partial epilepsy, cerebral palsy, static encephalopathy, pseudobulbar palsy, and microcephaly. They did not know that his wife was a doctor and that she had worked tirelessly with a pediatric special-ist from the University of Cincinnati, Dr David Franz, to bring Keyla's seizures under control. They did not know that Larry had taught Keyla to walk and to talk, despite early medical prognoses that she would never achieve either.

They did not know these things. And they did not appear to care.

Larry insisted on being allowed to see Keyla once more, to admin-ister the second of her twice-daily doses of Epival, necessary to control her seizures. It was the only medication he had with him.

Terrified, she wrapped her arms around his waist and, clutching him, crying, she refused to let go. But the sun was setting. There was nothing more he could do until morning.

"It was the only time I ever lied to her," Larry recounted, trauma-tized again by the memory. "Perhaps it was the fatigue on my part of too many sleepless nights from the personal threats I received leading up to our leaving. I decided to do what I was told to do, sure I could fix it the next day. I told her, 'You are going on vacation; you are going to be fine.' I had to pry her body off mine. I had to push her away."

<hr/>

We'll never really know what happened that day. Some of the many people I interviewed say it was Nancy's sister's doing. She could never bear that her smarter younger sister had become a doctor and local hero, when she had barely finished school. She hated that her more beautiful younger sister married a man who adored her, when she was betrayed by the father of her only child. Now her lucky younger sister was fleeing the violence that plagued their birthplace, while she was stuck, living with their elderly parents.

It is said she beat Larry and Keyla to the Customs and Border Protection offices that day, and that she arrived angry and jealous. That, in spite, she leveled an accusation against Larry that he could never bring himself to utter.

If not for that, the border authorities would have sent Keyla back to DIF or to family that had already rejected her in Matamoros. US border policies, as we've seen, have never been sympathetic to Mexicans, including children, and especially not likely "public charges" and "wards of the state." If precedent had prevailed, the two would have been stopped and sent right back where they came from.

It is also possible that border officials were responding to the inadvertent commission of an international crime—one that Congresswoman Granger, the US State Department, and their colleagues at the Department of Homeland Security should all have seen coming. One that the folks at DIF tried to flag at the last minute. They knew that proceedings for international adoptions must formally begin in the child's country of origin, following the framework of the Hague Convention on Protection and Co-operation in Respect of Intercountry Adoption. Indeed, that was the reason for Ms Gonzalez's last-minute urgent email, the one Larry failed to receive: Enrique Escorza of the Mexican embassy had written to Representative Granger that very morning to suggest placing Keyla with DIF until, "a Judge may authorize her leaving the country."

But the likely culprit at play that day was the William Wilberforce Trafficking Victims Protection Reauthorization Act, TVPRA. As Team Brownsville's Sergio Cordova told me my second day in Brownsville, in January 2020: though family separation was made policy under Trump & Co, it had been Border Protection practice long before that. The TVPRA is the reason why.

The 2008 TVPRA was hailed as a rare bipartisan achievement to counter the rise in sex trafficking of women and youth. But it held a sting in its tail for many adults and children seeking safety together. The law interprets "family" through the US-centric and outdated lens of biological mom, dad, and the kids. To avoid being separated from their younger companions at the US border, adults must prove biological parentage with a birth certificate authenticated by proof of name. In many cultures, however, especially those ripped apart by war and violence, the notion of "family" can extend beyond birth parent to include, for example, great-grandmother Antoñia or adoptive father Larry.

The TVPRA has led, therefore, to the separation of untold numbers of families in search of safety, especially if they'd had to flee without warning and the time to gather documents they might not know they'd need; or if, given the threatening realities of today's migratory trail, their vital papers have gone missing. They may not be criminals, felons, perverts, or invaders, but the law requires adults in search of a better life for their children, whether biological or otherwise, to prove that assumption wrong. On the other side, the TVPRA allows border officials to separate children from the adult in their company if a that person is perceived to be a threat.

llllllllllllllllllllllllllllllllllllllllllllllllll

No doubt eyebrows were raised the day Larry showed up on the Gateway International Bridge calling Keyla his daughter without documentation to back that up, just minutes after his spiteful sister-in-law leveled a defamatory accusation against him. And because Keyla, due to her disabilities, was unable to communicate to anyone that she felt safer with Larry than just about any other person in the world, US border officials took her away.

But then they lied to Larry, which they did not need to do.

They told him that Keyla was to be flown to Chicago the next day. She wasn't. She was taken, ironically, to a makeshift child detention facility in Los Fresnos, which was also her and Larry's final destination that awful day. She was held there for approximately one week.

What compelled them to lie rather than let the law and humanity do their job? The TVPRA also contains provisions that echo and even strengthen the legal agreements kicked off by Messrs Schey and Holguín on behalf of Jenny Flores twenty-five years before: In particular it calls for immediate family reunification. This provision should have brought Larry and Keyla together again within seventy-two hours.

But that did not happen.

llllllllllllllllllllllllllllllllllllllllllllllllll

Twelve-and-a-half years after Schey and Holguín first filed their class-action suit defending the rights of migrant children and youth, a deal was finally reached in *Flores v. Reno* on January 28, 1997. The resulting Flores Settlement Agreement required federal officials to meet minimum standards of "safe and sanitary" treatment of young people detained by US authorities. It mandated their "prompt" release from custody, later defined to be no more than three days in borderlands hieleras and no more than twenty days under the auspices of the Office of Refugee Resettlement.

The agreement further stated that children be held in the "least restrictive settings possible"—not "secured" facilities, such as Sam endured at the Nixon Center from 2006–2007; and not in prisons posing as hotels, like the Mardi Gras. The Flores Settlement required that both educational and recreational programs be delivered to youth in US immigration detention by trained and licensed providers. Finally, it broadened to whom minors can be released: if not to an available parent, which is the best-case scenario, then to another relative, including sibling, aunt, uncle, grandparent; an approved sponsor, which could be a family friend or legal guardian; or a provider licensed to care for the needs of children and youth   in that order.

The suit's key asks were for no detention, or as little as possible, as it was already understood that such loss of freedom causes potentially irreversible psychological harm to youth and children. The Settlement demanded the swiftest path to reunification with loved ones as possible.

When they propelled Keyla into the bureaucratic rabbit hole that is the Office of Refugee Resettlement, agents of Customs and Border Protection and the US Customs and Immigration Services denied Keyla her freedom and trapped her family in a Kafkaesque nightmare that persisted for seven long heartbreaking years.

The moment he told Keyla, "You are going on vacation; you are going to be fine," and pushed her away, thinking he could fix things the next day, haunts Larry to this day. Because it would be seven years before Larry and Nancy would embrace their Keylita again. Seven years of missed birthdays and unopened holiday presents. Seven years of hearing her cry out to them, night after sleepless night. Seven years of searching for her, wondering if she was being cared for with love approaching their own. Seven years of crushing guilt that Larry's final heartbreaking goodbye with the child he loved and had vowed to protect was a push and a lie. Seven years robbed of watching their daughter grow into adulthood, during which strong, beautiful, brilliant, dedicated Nancy would fall ill, then fall apart.

As the sun set on the day of June 7, 2011, Keyla Eulalia Ruiz Guajardo was seized by agents of the US federal government. The next day, she was "kidnapped"—her attorneys' term—by the US Office of Refugee Resettlement. Agents James de la Cruz and Maureen Dunn, the same individuals sued for denying Tía Jennifer's client Sam his right to freedom, thwarted Keyla's right to freedom as well. They, among others, refused without explanation to reunite her with her family again and again and again in multiple legal actions Larry took over the course of many years with the help of several lawyers to the tune of $200,000 in legal fees.

Because here's this story's shocking twist: Larry is a former corporate executive and self-made Christian white male. He's a Texan, to boot! If he's not safe from family separation, who is?

⸻

In September 2011, four months after Keyla had been forcibly separated from Larry and six-and-a-half years before she would be returned, the Resettlement Office tracked down her closest biological relative in the US—a grandfather named Sergio, who was living undocumented in North Carolina. The one and only phone call that Keyla had been granted in seven years was with this man, who did not know her and wanted nothing to do with her.

According to witnesses, Keyla told Sergio to "please call Casa Bugambilia and tell Larry and Nancy that I'm tired of vacation." She wanted to go home, she said.

She proceeded to repeat the only phone number she'd ever learned, over and over again: uno-once-quince-cincuenta-y-tres—111-1553.

Keyla spent the next seven years bouncing from Resettlement Office shelters and hospitals and foster homes in Illinois, Pennsylvania, and California, clutching a toy phone. She called Larry on it every day, says a staff social worker of her final provider: Crittenton Family Services. Every day, on every call, she begged a pretend Larry to come get her, that she was tired of vacation.

"[Refugee Resettlement] never allowed her a real call with us," Larry states. "Can it be that Keyla worked harder than anyone to get back?"

CHAPTER EIGHTEEN

Who Built the Cages?

In March 2015, Guerline Jozef received an unexpected call. There were Haitians at the San Ysidro, California border crossing, she learned. They didn't speak English and appeared to be in need of help. Could she come?

"I thought it was a joke. I'm like, 'What are you talking about? We Haitians, we go to Florida. We don't go to the US-Mexico border.'"

Guerline didn't respond, she told me as we meandered through leafy central London. She was on her way home to Orange County, California, from Geneva, Switzerland, where she had testified before the UN Committee on the Elimination of Racial Discrimination about the anti-Black racism embedded in the US Border Industrial Complex. She had a nine-hour layover at Heathrow, so she came into town, giving us the pleasure of a day together. It was August 2022.

Seven years earlier, when she received that fateful call, Guerline was a talk-radio host and program manager. She coordinated ten shows, including her own, and produced fashion exhibitions highlighting the talents of up-and-coming Haitian designers, all while mothering a young child. She was already a burgeoning public figure as a promoter of Haitian culture, art, fashion, and music, and a rare Black person in her politically conservative corner of the US: the same place from which Harold Ezell and John Tanton championed their anti-immigrant Proposition 187 in 1994.

The lack of diversity was sheer culture shock after growing up between Haiti and New York City. But even behind "the Orange

Curtain," Guerline developed a large and caring network of supporters and friends within her family's church, school, and professional communities.

Two weeks went by. The caller reached out again. More Haitians had gathered outside the McDonald's on the Camino de la Plaza at the shopping mall next to the San Ysidro port of entry. They had nothing. They needed, at the very least, the benefit of a speaker of Haitian Kreyol.

Guerline, who works "at the crucible of poverty, race, and immigration," in the words of Kerry Kennedy, president of Robert F. Kennedy Human Rights, decided to go. It was just a ninety-minute drive away, if there was no traffic. Of course, there's always traffic in Southern California. The trip took two hours each way. But the call was not a prank.

She found twelve Haitian men and women. They were hungry, exhausted, penniless, and stuck, desperate to call the friends and relatives in the US who'd been waiting to hear from them and were surely worried. ICE had dumped them at the McDonald's without returning their phones and other belongings. Now they had no way of securing the aid of those prepared to get them plane tickets to homes of welcome in Miami or New York. They weren't even given a voucher for a cup of coffee.

Guerline handed over her mobile. She watched it pass from person to person, while she ordered up Big Macs, Chicken McNuggets, Cokes, and fries. As they ate, she worked her way up to asking the questions burning at her brain: *What are you doing here? How did you get here?*

||||||||||||||||||||||||||||||||||||||||||||||||||||

Theirs was far from a straight shot to the US. These individuals had lived through the massive earthquake that struck Haiti in January 2010, and its tragic aftermath. The quake flattened the capital, Port-au-Prince, killing 220,000 people. Within weeks, the island nation experienced the worst cholera epidemic in recent history, taxing an already overburdened health system with 820,000 cases and resulting in nearly 10,000 more deaths.

"These were survivors of that terrible chain of disasters," Guerline recounted in our 2021 podcast interview for *From the Borderlands*. They had lost everything. Homes. Loved ones. There was nothing left for them but grief and heartache. "So they left."

Brazil was offering work and visas at the time. In anticipation of the 2014 FIFA World Cup and the 2016 Summer Olympics, the country needed laborers. Lots of them. All the Haitian refugees had to do was get there. The government would take care of the rest.

Of course, the reality was much different. The Haitian workers toiled in inhospitable conditions on these multimillion-dollar projects, earning a fraction of what they'd been promised by mercenary recruitment agencies. Once the stadiums were built and the games were over, Brazil went into political and economic meltdown. The first to feel the impacts were the guest workers. When right-wing former military officer, Jair Bolsonaro, stepped into the presidency, they were shown the door.

Some trickled to the US. But most continued on to nearby Chile, then one of the region's most robust economies. Plentiful work and a relaxed visa system drew them to jobs in restaurants and hotels, on construction sites and in mines, as factory and maintenance workers. In 2012, fewer than two thousand Haitians resided in Chile. By 2020, their presence had increased almost a hundredfold.

The sudden influx of so many Haitians, as well as Venezuelans also seeking employment, led to an anti-immigrant backlash that tightened visa rules, making it harder for Haitians to stay. The men and women Guerline met in March 2015 had abandoned their dead-end prospects in Chile, embarking on an extremely hazardous 14,000-mile journey by foot, bus, and boat, over the Andean mountains, through rivers as wide and as wild as the Amazon, and across Panama's perilous Darién Gap jungle. They traveled the same cruel route through Central America and Mexico that has claimed the lives of untold thousands. Now they were in the US—home to the world's largest Haitian diaspora—sitting with Guerline at a San Ysidro McDonald's, recounting bone-chilling tales of the latest leg in their five-year, multi-nation exodus.

"You walked here from Chile?" she asked them.

Yes.

"How long did it take you?"

Five months.

"How did you survive?"

Many didn't. They started in a much bigger group, burying their friends along the way. Of the remaining twelve, only two were women.

Guerline drove north that day perplexed, as I was upon first discovering the US "deterrence through cruelty" Border Industrial regime. "Even as a Haitian woman and a promoter of Haitian culture," she told me. "I didn't know about any of this."

<hr>

Guerline is no stranger to life in the diaspora. As a child, she and her parents were visiting relatives in the US when a military coup, predating the 2010 earthquake by nineteen years, prevented their return home. It was September 1991, and the country had been so hopeful. After more than two hundred years of plunder, following the 1791–1804 war of independence against France, the Haitian people had finally achieved democratic rule.

First came a century of paying crippling reverse reparations—winner to loser—to avoid another war. The historic aberration known as the "double debt" enslaved France's former slave colony once more, forcing the world's only independent Black nation to empty its treasury again and again and again for over one hundred years. The monies, equal to $560 million today, enriched French bankers and the descendants of former plantation owners at the sacrifice of Haiti's own economic and infrastructure development, leading to an estimated loss of $21 to $115 billion in untapped growth.

This suited successive US administrations just fine: they could not allow Black revolutionaries to prosper lest their own enslaved and oppressed peoples rise up and revolt by the Haitian example. When funds from coffee and sugar production fell short, however, Frank Stillman's National City Bank (Citibank) was happy to provide the Haitian leadership with hefty Wall Street loans for money that filled French pockets until 1947.

In 1914, US gunboats pulled into Port-au-Prince, disgorging Marines sent by President Woodrow Wilson, who'd been convinced by Stillman's bank that the US needed to take control of Haiti's political and financial interests. The succeeding nineteen-year US military occupation, carried out by Major General Smedley Darlington Butler, aka "Old Gimlet Eye," and "the boys" from 1915 to 1934, hamstrung Haiti's ability to develop once more.

While being fleeced by France and the US, Haiti was also tempest-tossed by devastating natural disasters. But each time, the country lacked the financing to rebuild. By 1947, when Haiti's "double debt" was finally paid off, many Haitians lived at starvation level. Only one in six children went to school. There were few roads; inadequate potable water sources; little electricity; and no sanitation. Hospitals were scarce. Medicines and health-care providers were scarcer still.

An elite class rose out of the once-rich, now-depleted earth, giving rise to the father-and-son Duvalier dictatorship. "Papa" and "Baby" Doc ruled with iron fists for thirty long years (1957–1986), plunging their countrymen and women further into poverty as they enriched themselves with the aid of their brutal paramilitary, the Tonton Macoute.

||||||||||||||||||||||||||||||||||||||||||||||||||||||||||

Finally, in 1990, democratic rule had come to Haiti. The Salesian priest and liberation theologian Jean-Bertrand Aristide won the general election with 67 percent of the vote. From the pulpit, he sounded a lot like Archbishop Oscar Romero, pledging to put food on the tables of Haiti's slum dwellers and rural poor, and to redistribute property concentrated in the hands of the few wealthy landowners. One of his first tasks, after being sworn into office on February 9, 1991, however, was to dismantle the military force that had, for decades, so terrorized the Haitian people. Naturally, the goons didn't think much of that plan, so they drove the former priest into exile just seven months after he took up residence in the presidential palace.

At that time, Guerline, her parents, and younger brother were on a family visit to New York. The military dictatorship's next targets were Aristide's known supporters, such as Guerline's Maman, a business entrepreneur, and her Papa, a community organizer turned mayor of Petion-ville. At least fifteen hundred, possibly as many as three thousand, Aristide supporters were tortured and killed. The Jozefs could not go back.

As violence engulfed the country in which Papa had had his own driver, he made ends meet driving a New York City taxi. Maman took care of other people's children, while fighting tooth and nail to be reunited with two of her own: they had not joined the trip to New York. Then, without warning, the family was torn asunder and forced to start over in a foreign land.

⠀

|||||||||||||||||||||||||||||||||||||||||||||||||||||||||||||

Through the winter of 1991–1992, nearly forty thousand Haitians took to the Caribbean Sea in dinghies and fishing boats, fleeing rape, repression, and extrajudicial massacres, forced disappearances, and the violent plundering of entire neighborhoods.. "You don't take your life into your own hands like that unless it's more dangerous to stay," Guerline is known to say. Many of her Haitian brothers and sisters perished, buried at the bottom of the ocean. That's when the Windward Passage, like the sandy Sonoran, became a migrant graveyard.

Like his presidential predecessor with regard to Central Americans, Bush 41, the elder, refused to acknowledge that Haitians were fleeing a "well-founded fear of persecution." He labeled them "boat people" rather than "refugees" and instructed the US Coast Guard to interdict them outside US territorial waters and "push" them to the US naval base at Cuba's Guantánamo Bay.

There, everyone—even children—were held in a vast cage encircled in chain link and barbed wire until their asylum claims could be processed by immigration judges brought to them. The Defense Department called the Guantánamo detention center a "humanitarian mission," but the refugees were subjected to deplorable conditions. They slept without privacy in rows of military-style canvas cots in barracks with a leaky tarpaulin roof and garbage bags taped over windows to stop the screaming ocean winds. They were given inedible, spoiled, often maggot-infested food. The medical care was, at best, ineffective and, at worst, abusive, with treatments sometimes denied, sometimes performed without informed consent.

The Bush 41 administration and Centers for Disease Control harnessed the "diseased migrant" myth, as in the El Paso of Carmelita

Torres's day, to claim that these "boat people" were all potential carriers of HIV-AIDS, dehumanizing them and whipping up a moral panic at the same time. The AIDS epidemic had been with us for a decade then; we knew it was passed through blood, saliva, and semen. It was ludicrous to claim that an entire nation group was a vector. And yet this group was tarred as among the 4-Hs—homosexuals, heroin users, hemophiliacs, and Haitians—and vilified, though fewer than three hundred of the twenty thousand Haitians then trapped in Guantánamo tested positive for HIV. And though these few were denied medical attention—because Congress had, in 1987, barred the entry onto US territory of any HIV-positive foreign person—AIDS never took over the camp.

The refugees were cycled through the asylum review process at rocket speed, without legal representation, and without the time or resources, like telephones and fax machines, to gather evidence to support their claims. Most were deemed to be coming to the US to work, even orphaned children, and dropped back into a country embroiled in a military and paramilitary reign of terror against civilians. When the Guantánamo facilities began to groan under the weight of the increasing refugee numbers, Bush 41 just ordered the US Coast Guard to push everyone back to Haiti, regardless of whether they had a credible fear of return or not.

The narrative justification for keeping Haitians in Cuba was to keep HIV-AIDS out of the US. But the effect was to keep Haitians in search of safety from stepping foot on US soil where they could request protection under the 1980 Refugee Act. By caging the refugees indefinitely at Guantánamo, then sending them back to harm, the US was "offshoring" the asylum process.

And it wasn't the first time.

"Offshoring" asylum started in 1980, the same year Dora Rodriguez nearly died crossing the desert, for Central Americans were not the only people on the run that year. That's also when we witnessed the largest mass migration from across the Caribbean. Approximately 125,000

Haitians and Afro-Cubans alighted in Florida between April and October that year. It was called the Mariel Boatlift.

Many Cubans were riding the wake of relatives who'd immigrated to the US two decades before, following the 1959 Revolution. The now established and politically powerful Cuban Americans met their boat-lifted brethren at the Miami docks. Some even sent boats to Mariel, Cuba to retrieve friends and family members. They were taken into homes and guided through the adjudication of their asylum claims while free to walk the streets of "Little Havana."

Those who did not benefit from welcoming family and friends were detained under the auspices of the Federal Emergency Management Agency in a decommissioned Cold War–era military defense base in Krome, Florida, on the edge of the sweltering Everglades. They slept under threadbare blankets in dilapidated army barracks infested with mosquitoes and snakes. They, too, were made to survive on barely edible food. As the "crisis" wound down and those individuals deemed "accept-able" had been released, the remaining refugees—all Black and mostly Haitian—were dispersed to newly conceived long-term lock ups in the Deep South.

The first US immigrant "detention center" popped up in Oakdale, Louisiana, an isolated rural region then suffering the highest unemploy-ment rate in the state. The three-hundred-acre facility, which cost $17.5 million to build, was able to accommodate "1,000 aliens who have no known criminal record." And because some within the Reagan admin-istration feared that it would "create an appearance of 'concentration camps' filled largely by [B]lacks," Reagan declared that henceforth *all* new arrivals, including those seeking asylum, would be jailed, instituting mandatory imprisonment as a staple of today's US immigration system even before the Clinton crime-trifecta.

The Oakdale prison augured the creation of the immigration detention industry. In 1983, the world's first private prison company—Nashville-based Corrections Corporation of America, today known as CoreCivic—was established to take advantage of a forecasted lucrative opportunity. The GEO Group, formerly the Wackenhut Corporation, followed, winning its first federal contract in 1987 for the Aurora Detention Facility in Colorado. The two companies remain the main immigration detention players in the world today, operating facilities that jail people not charged with a crime in the US, UK, South Africa, and Australia.

By the 2016 presidential election, CoreCivic and GEO Group were each bringing in annual revenues in excess of $2 billion, between them running more than 170 facilities in the US. With more than 200 prisons in operation in the US today, the for-profit immigration detention sector is consistently a "no-brainer" investment recommendation of bullish retiree-portfolio managers.

||||||||||||||||||||||||||||||||||||||||||||||||||||||||||||

Four years after the Boatlift, in 1984, most Afro-Cuban Marielitos had been granted permanent legal status, their homeland still being a Cold War foe of the US. The Haitian Marielitos, on the other hand, despite harrowing claims of persecution by the horrifically brutal Tonton Macoute, were labeled "economic migrants" and denied legal protection. Seven years later, in 1987, several hundred Haitian refugees were still locked up in US prisons. While a few Haitian Marielitos had managed to secure their release, most had been expelled by Reagan right back to the harms they fled.

The resistance to providing legal status to Haitians fleeing the Duvalier dictatorship brought the racialized nature of US asylum politics into focus, even at the tiller of the president most committed to human rights than at any other time in US history: Jimmy Carter. The Black-owned *Miami Times* newspaper stated in 1980 that "the treatment of Black refugees mirrored the treatment of native-born Blacks, as both were disproportionately subjected to incarceration." A federal class-action lawsuit brought on behalf of four thousand Haitians subsequently found that the INS had deliberately denied plaintiffs due process in its determination to expel them despite a "substantial danger" of being tortured or killed on return.

Ten years later, in 1991, Bush 41 baked further anti-Blackness into US immigration-detention when he offshored—or "externalized"—the asylum processes of Haitians by incarcerating safety seekers at Guantánamo Bay: the facility whose name would become synonymous with torture under the presidency of his son, Bush 43. It was an end-run around the 1951 Refugee Convention. And coming from the leader of the free world, it gave first Australia, then Europe, tacit permission to do the same.

In 2015, Guerline was about to discover firsthand an all-new, land-based version of "externalizing" asylum when the Obama-Biden administration began metering the Haitians then arriving in Tijuana after walking 14,000 miles from Chile.

||||||||||||||||||||||||||||||||||||||||||||||||||||||

Following those first twelve people she met in San Ysidro, Guerline told me, "we had forty. Two weeks later, it was two hundred. Then three hundred. And I'm like, "How many of you are there on this godforsaken journey?"

The answer: a lot. Guerline sprang into action. She states, "We cannot have people showing up out of desperation after that terrible journey and have no structure to receive them."

She co-founded the Haitian Bridge Alliance to advocate for fair and humane immigration policies and, with a particular focus on the Black community, to connect safety seekers with legal, humanitarian, and other social services. Harnessing the kindness of her community back in conservative Orange County, she set up a *Welcoming the Stranger* program. Neighbors of all colors, economic backgrounds, and creeds pitched in to support the needs of people seeking asylum at the border, Guerline recalls. "Church people, Republicans, it didn't matter—they provided money, encouragement, time, prayer. They brought folks into their homes. They offered kindness and really great support."

Arriving Haitians, like all asylum seekers prior to Trump & Co, were detained, but they were eventually released or "bonded out"—a system in which they put up money as a guarantee that they will show up in court. After the first middle-of-the-night phone call requesting help with bond money, Guerline set up the Black Immigrants Bail Fund with Dr Seydi Sarr, a Senegalese native and the Founder/Helmswomxn of the African Bureau for Immigration and Social Affairs in Detroit, Michigan. The Bail Fund had raised over $1.5 million at the time of Guerline and my 2022 London rendezvous. The previous year, in October 2021, Haitian Bridge Alliance launched the Cameroon Advocacy Network in collaboration with RFK Human Rights and other immigrant rights organizations. Today, Guerline and the members of her expanding community are saving lives everyday, acting as a bridge for seekers of asylum of all origins, ensuring they get safely out from under the knee of Customs and Border Protection or ICE and on to their networks of support.

||||||||||||||||||||||||||||||||||||||||||||||||||||||||||

But the sheer numbers of Haitian arrivals in 2015–16 apparently overwhelmed the San Ysidro port of entry—at least that was the narrative coming out of the Obama-Biden Department of Homeland Security. Customs and Border Protection agents claimed they were unable to manage all of their priority missions—national security, drug interdiction, facilitation of lawful travel and trade—with their attention turned to "processing" undocumented arrivals.

Note: the humanitarian needs of people seeking safety is not considered a priority of the so-called Border Protection regime.

Instead of surging more asylum officers to San Ysidro, Homeland Security instructed agents to impose daily limits on the number of people who could present themselves; and Mexico was suddenly seen to station guards on its side of the bridge to block safety seekers from crossing the line. This especially hindered Haitians for, as Guerline states, "we cannot hide in these Black bodies."

Border Protection officers instructed people determined to enter the US legally to add their names to a list, then they pushed both individuals and families, who'd managed to survive a five-month, 14,000-mile overland trek, back into the violence of northern Mexico to wait for their names to be called. Only when on US soil could they request protection.

The practice of metering rendered thousands of Haitians homeless in cartel-controlled Tijuana. Unable to work and with no home to go back to, men, women, and children, who posed no threat to US security, were put in a state of indefinite limbo. Waiting times stretched into weeks, then months, as Customs and Border Protection officials called only twenty to thirty names a day, while many more than that were added to the list.

Tent cities blossomed as shelters overflowed, drawing in transnational criminal organizations like moths to a flame. This resulted in a spike in folks attempting to cross the line *between* ports of entry—aka "illegally" or "without inspection"—which, in turn, led to an uptick in border-related injuries and deaths.

Recognizing that pushing asylum seeking refugees back into Mexico under metering had caused multiple humanitarian crises, the Obama-Biden White House ordered Border Protection officials to deal with the backlog, then abolish the practice.

But the precedent had been set.

Trump & Co would make metering (aka land "pushbacks") standard practice in early 2017, though without making any effort to resolve the backlog of humanity the policy created. The bottlenecks at the US-Mexico ports of entry did not just include Haitians. As Guerline would later say, "We went to the US-Mexico border for the Haitian community, but then we saw our African and Central American brothers and sisters. So we stayed for them all."

Unfortunately, metering and indefinite, mandatory detention for all safety seekers was not then the only evil precedent left for Trump & Co to exploit.

CHAPTER NINETEEN

Locking Up Family Values

Trump loved to say that Obama built the human cages of the US Border Industrial Complex. He was wrong, as we've seen. Carter started the practice; then Reagan turned cages into big business. Clinton continued the trend. But it was the younger Bush, 43, who introduced the idea of imprisoning whole families in what Georgetown University Professor Philip Schrag calls in his book of the same name, "Baby Jails."

In 2004, the number of non-Mexican southern border arrivals jumped to a record 65,911 from 28,769 in 2000. It doubled again a year later to 154,995, according to Border Patrol data. Primarily Central Americans, they included close to 20,000 children and youth presenting with adult family members, mainly mothers: a historic new phenomenon. They claimed a need for protection from the gangs the Clinton-era "crime-trifecta" deported to the region from LA.

Of these childhood arrivals, 7,767 were labeled "unaccompanied," document researchers Jacqueline Bhabha and Susan Schmidt. But we'll never know for sure if they really were traveling alone, for then-division director of the Resettlement Office's Unaccompanied Children's Services unit, Maureen Dunn, admitted that kids were initially separated from their parents *because the new border protection regime had no idea what to do with families.*

"Children apprehended by DHS even as young as nursing infants, are being separated from their parents and placed in shelters," concludes a 2005 report by the House Appropriations Committee. One year later, in *Seeking Asylum Alone: Unaccompanied and Separated Children and Refugee Protection in the US*, Bhabha and Schmidt sounded the alarm that the federal bureaucracies were not capturing custody data critical for intra-agency record-keeping and family reunification—the same issue Jodi Goodwin and her colleague Efrén Olivares, author of *My Boy Will Die of Sorrow* (2022), would encounter, still unresolved, twenty years later.

Having added antiterrorism to their anti-drug trafficking and anti-immigrant mandates, the new Homeland Security bureaucracies were instructed to consider everyone a suspect, and lock them up. They did not pivot this approach when new arrivals to the southern border included mothers with children and babies. Bush 43 had already declared war on the standing practice of allowing folks seeking asylum to walk free while their legal processes wound their slow way through the immigration court system. It was he who dubbed the practice "catch and release," beating Trump to that linguistic punch by two decades.

The second Bush administration reverted to the universal application of mandatory detention until the culmination of one's legal claim. But the only existing immigration lockups then were intended for adult men. So, as would happen twenty years later—but without the cameras—families were separated. Possibly forever.

Untold numbers of separated children were classified as "unaccompanied" and sucked into the Resettlement Office ecosystem before advocates from the Women's Refugee Commission, Lutheran Immigration and Refugee Service, and US Conference of Catholic Bishops got wind of it. These groups demanded that the federal government stop separating families, and release the kids, per the Flores Settlement Agreement, within twenty days.

But Flores, as originally written, did not stipulate what to do with *accompanied* children: those arriving with adults who could prove parentage.

A kinder, gentler administration would have released the women and children together, because the agreement prioritizes freeing a young person to the care of a parent. But Bush 43 chose, instead, to appropriate ninety million taxpayer dollars to jail families. They would remain locked up, indefinitely, by the "Family Values" president, to await the outcome of their asylum applications, together.

|||||||||||||||||||||||||||||||||||||||||||||||||||||||||||||

The first "Baby Jail" to open under Bush 43 was in a former nursing home in Pennsylvania, called Berks. But Berks only had room for forty families. So Congress contracted the Corrections Corporation of America, then the largest for-profit prison company in the country, to convert a medium-security penitentiary in rural Taylor, Texas. They named it after the company's founder: the T. Don Hutto "Family Residential Center." But that was just another euphemism. Hutto was a jail. A jail run by jailers.

A 2007 report by the Women's Refugee Commission and partners, entitled *Locking Up Family Values*, brought to light the truth of mass, aka "congregant," family internment. Children and youth living with high levels of trauma confined to cells for twelve hours in twenty-four, without books or drawing materials or toys, subjected to seven head counts a day, each lasting up to one hour, and given only fifteen minutes to eat food described as "watery and unappealing."

If they fell ill, as many did with persistent diarrhea, the only medical advice was to "drink more water." But the water was said to be undrinkable and the likely cause of gastrointestinal illnesses that, if left untreated, could take a dangerous turn.

Everyone was forced into prison garb; even newborns wore prison-issued onesies. And as laundry facilities could not keep up with the needs of menstruating women and children not yet potty trained, Hutto "inmates" had no other choice but to wear soiled clothing much of the time.

Lights were kept on all night, making sleep elusive, especially as prison guards made constant rounds, banging noisily on the bars of cell doors and shining lights into the eyes of incarcerated children, who were mostly under the age of twelve.

Privacy was impossible in cells shared by multiple families where toilets sat out in the open. Visits were rare, and when they happened, communication was by phone, with interlocutors separated by thick panes of bulletproof plexiglass.

Children were threatened with separation or time in "the hole," aka solitary confinement, if they misbehaved. But misbehavior was subjective, determined by guards who had no training in the care, developmental needs, or behavioral stages of children.

The American Civil Liberties Union filed suit against ICE in March 2007 on the grounds that conditions at Hutto violated not only the Flores Settlement Agreement but also the UN Convention on the Rights of the Child. The ACLU won the argument for improved conditions: The children were allowed more time outdoors; they were no longer made to wear prison uniforms; educational programming and an on-site pediatrician were brought in; the prison count system was eliminated and privacy curtains installed around toilets; field trip opportunities were promised as were toys and books; food was made more varied and nutritional.

But the suit did not achieve the release of families. The decision hinged on a single word, for the Flores Settlement Agreement, as then written, only applied to "unaccompanied" children.

Hutto was finally closed to families in August 2009 due to the gross human rights violations. But a military coup in Honduras that year presaged another shock to the system. Putting an abrupt end to the liberal reform agenda of President José Manuel Zelaya Rosales, the coup brought obscene levels of violence into the streets. The homicide rate in Honduras doubled to 90.4 per 100,000 people, earning it the distinction of "murder capital of the world." For perspective, the global average rate that year was 6.2 per 100,000.

The brutality sent hundreds of thousands of children northward in the early years of the 2010s just as Obama-Biden prepared to roll out the first immigration reform since Reagan's 1986 amnesty program. Their 2012 Deferred Action for Childhood Arrivals, or DACA, offered protection from deportation and work authorization to "talented, driven, and patriotic" US residents brought to the country as children and who knew no other home. With the stroke of a pen, Obama-Biden changed the lives of 800,000 young people, for the better.

Sadly they locked up thousands more. Then, they sent Department of Justice lawyers into the courts to chip away at the protections afforded to children by the Flores Settlement Agreement.

One year after the launch of DACA by executive order, children younger than ever before crossed the line—an unprecedented 68,541 in fiscal year 2014 alone. They came with the names and phone numbers of relatives sewn into their clothing or written on scraps of paper stuffed into their pockets or tied to their wrists. Parents, as Sam's mother had done and Dora's mother before her, were sending their kids to El Norte on their own to save them from the most violent countries on the planet.

Obama-Biden threw money at the Office of Refugee Resettlement to scale up its system as quickly as possible: $175 million, according to Jonathan Blitzer in his indispensable book *Everyone Who Is Gone Is Here* (2024). Contractors licensed to care for children twelve and under created "tender age shelters," reviving then-bankrupt Southwest Key. And borrowing from Carter's Mariel Boatlift model, an emergency tent city was erected to house teenagers—this time on the unused Homestead Air Reserve Base in Florida.

Nearly as many families crossed the line that year as well: 68,445, mostly women and children. No more willing than their predecessors to explore alternatives to family detention, Obama-Biden contracted for-profit prison companies Corrections Corporation of America and GEO Group to build three more large, congregant-style family prisons: in Artesia, New Mexico, and in Karnes and Dilley, Texas.

As at Hutto, children and adults imprisoned at Karnes, Artesia, and Dilley suffered an abusive loss of liberty and dignity. They were refused medical services and visitors. They grew lethargic and depressed. They lived in a constant state of fear and anxiety. They lost weight. They lost hair. Older children regressed to younger developmental states. Tantrums were frequent and bed-wetting ran rampant.

Dean of the School of Social Work at the University of Texas Luis Zayas declared after meeting with families at Karnes, "Untold harm is being inflicted on these children by the trauma of detention." He warned that the toxic effects of prolonged incarceration will leave long-lasting, likely permanent, scars on their mental, emotional, and physical well-being. But because the Flores Settlement Agreement stressed the prompt release of *unaccompanied* minors in the custody of the Office of Refugee Resettlement, all energies were focused on them.

Detention for *accompanied* children of roughly 3,600 families stretched on and on and on.

"The network of pro bono immigrant lawyers and legal clinics was amazing in providing resources at the family detention centers to counsel the detained families prior to their credible fear interviews, resulting in a very high rate of credible fear being found," Professor Schrag told me. This did lead to the eventual release of some on parole or bond. Still, many languished.

The American Civil Liberties Union brought suit again. The Obama-Biden administration was forced to justify the detention of immigrant families as a matter of national security. It could not. So, the government claimed the mothers were flight risks and jacked up their bond commitments to unaffordable levels.

The only weapon the ACLU had left to get these families released from jail was to facilitate the reinterpretation of the Flores Settlement Agreement to include *accompanied* children and their parents.

In 2015, Schey and Holguín were back in court, this time in front of Judge Dolly M. Gee in the Central District Court of California. They argued that in 1985 no one could have foreseen that children would be arriving "accompanied," but that the needs and rights of these kids were no different from those who were "unaccompanied." They stated that prisons cannot be licensed as child welfare facilities, even with nice names like "family residential centers." The Flores Settlement must be reviewed within this 21st-century context, they argued. The population under its jurisdiction should be understood to include not just *unaccompanied* but *accompanied* minors as well, *and* their adult companions.

The only solution "in the best interest of the child," the standard promulgated by the UN Refugee Agency, was to keep families together through parent-and-child mutual release.

Obama-Biden saw family release as tantamount to political suicide. They signaled their Department of Justice to go on the attack. And without giving you the blow-by-blow, the results were both welcomed and devastating.

On the upside, as Karnes and Dilley were not licensed by the state of Texas to care for kids, Judge Gee agreed they could no longer be used to house families. The remaining adults and children interned at these facilities were released within the twenty-day window governed by Flores.

On the downside, however, Judge Gee held that only the rights of children were recognized in the Flores Settlement—*accompanied* and *unaccompanied*—not the parents. That left families imprisoned at Berks, which held the requisite state license as it was also a home for orphaned, runaway, and wayward youth.

The fight to get families freed from Berks would continue. But mass family detention was no longer a legal option. If the government insisted on caging everyone, it would have to find a way to criminalize parents as a means to justify taking their children away.

As it turns out, that idea—first floated in 2014 by Thomas Homan, then-executive associate director of ICE Enforcement and Removal Operations—was being tested in El Paso even with Obama still sitting behind the Resolute Desk.

CHAPTER TWENTY

Barbarians at the Gate

"Toward the end of the Obama administration, we saw an increasingly harsh application of US immigration laws here in the El Paso borderlands, particularly by ICE, and particularly with respect to asylum seekers," recalls Dylan Corbett, founding executive director of the El Paso–based Hope Border Institute (HOPE). Working across borders of geography, ethnicity, and race in an area of roughly one million people spanning three Catholic dioceses and two countries, HOPE builds bridges of solidarity between communities of faith, social justice, and politics. HOPE does "good theology in a practical way," states Bishop Mark Seitz, leader of the US Conference of Catholic Bishops, head of the El Paso Catholic Diocese, and an outspoken voice for US immigration reform.

For Bishop Seitz, Dylan, and their allies, "practical" involved no small dose of "political" when a shift in ICE tactics rolled into town with a new agency boss in December 2015. His name was Corey Price. And as ICE field office director of the El Paso Sector, he brought with him a culture of legal and human rights abuses that spread like a cancer through ICE "detention centers" from West Texas through New Mexico—and one hundred miles northward.

It wasn't until late March 2016, however, when the El Paso community really felt the sting of change. That's when the National Border Patrol Council, the 18,000-member labor union representing agents and support staff of the US Border Patrol, endorsed a presidential candidate for the first time. That candidate was Donald Trump. And the symbiosis seemed to embolden not just the Border Patrol, but all law enforcement agencies associated with the Department of Homeland Security in the El Paso Sector, including ICE.

Historically, Dylan explained to me, ICE has had broad discretionary powers to keep families together. Customs and Border Protection, too. This is essential in borderlands everywhere, where extended families live, work, worship, marry, give birth, and bury loved ones in regions that extend across two sides of a mapped line. But as spring 2016 rolled into summer, Border Protection and ICE appeared to pivot away from case-by-case humanitarian determinations. Without warning, the decisions of immigration judges were ignored and asylum candidates were being unexpectedly deported directly from their scheduled, in-person ICE check-ins. Those who'd requested asylum and been detained, what's more, were bringing to their lawyers reports of troubling ICE behavior.

||||||||||||||||||||||||||||||||||||||||||||||||||||

Dylan was not alone in his alarm. Faith- and community-based organizations, advocates, and attorneys, even El Paso federal court judges, were witnessing an increase in due process violations; the arbitrary use of prolonged detention; and the near-blanket denial of humanitarian parole. But more sinister still, the Diocesan Migrant and Refugee Services came to suspect that kids sent into their care had been taken from their parents.

Under federal contract and muzzled by strict nondisclosure agreements, however, they *couldn't* talk about it.

Private, low-cost, and pro bono attorneys, particularly at Las Americas Immigrant Advocacy and Catholic Charities of Southern New Mexico, were picking up clues from their adult clients in ICE detention centers that their children had been taken from them. Shelter providers such as El Paso's Annunciation House were hearing similar stories.

But it was so unthinkable, they didn't know *how* to talk about it.

"It was like a strong undertow that took everyone by surprise," states Dylan.

They decided to set up a new research body to document the patterns and look for trends. They called their forum the Borderland

Immigration Council, and from September 2016 to January 2017, participating members conducted in-depth research on enforcement and detention policies and practices in the El Paso Sector. Attorneys recorded 120 interviews with clients detained under ICE. Researchers catalogued the emerging themes. It proved a critical and prescient move, for not only did it get area human and migrant rights stalwarts collaborating across traditional lines, states Dylan, "but that's also how family separation got on our radar."

The resulting study, *Discretion to Deny: Family Separation, Prolonged Detention, and Deterrence of Asylum Seekers at the Hands of Immigration Authorities Along the US-Mexico Border*, was issued in February 2017, concurrent with Trump's inauguration. It documented, among other things, that the separation of families by Customs and Border Protection and ICE was becoming disturbingly routine. And that the practice had detrimental impacts on legitimate asylum claims, as well as the mental and physical health of separated adults and children.

||||||||||||||||||||||||||||||||||||||||||||||||||||||||||

"So, everyone saw it, or thought they did," continues Dylan. "But there was no memo, no indication that families were being separated as a matter of policy."

Then, out of the blue, Dylan received an off-the-record phone call from a federal magistrate. "He told me that more and more parents were coming into his courtroom distraught, asking what happened to their kids." Because Border Patrol agents are always present in immigration court hearings, the judge would turn to them and ask. But he never got an answer. "The caller implored us to act."

Unable to get a meeting with local Homeland Security leadership, HOPE and the Borderland Council turned to Representative Beto O'Rourke, from their local Texas congressional district, for help. It took a while, but the Democrat's office eventually convened a community meeting with the alphabet soup of federal law enforcement agencies on October 24, 2017. They gathered in a ballroom at the El Paso Community Foundation. ICE, CBP, and the Homeland Security Investigations teams all sent their local top brass. They were joined by the general counsel of El Paso's immigration court, under the jurisdiction of the US Department of Justice.

As for the Border Patrol, it sent only a couple of line agents.

"Buried way down on the agenda was the issue of family separation. When I asked if it was happening," says Dylan, "the heads of all the agency leaders shook, *No*. But the Border Patrol agents volunteered that, *Yes*, they were separating families."

They quickly qualified their actions, Dylan told me. "They said, *but it's only policy in the El Paso Sector and only with fathers traveling with children over ten.*"[6]

So, it wasn't just a few agents gone rogue in the midst of a leadership change, which was their best-case scenario.

||||||||||||||||||||||||||||||||||||||||||||||||||||||||

"That moment, when family separation was acknowledged in public, the air got sucked out of the room," states Camilo Perez-Bustillo. Previously the director of the Border Human Rights Documentation Project at New Mexico State University, Camilo had joined HOPE as director of advocacy and research just that month. "We suddenly knew that what we most feared, what the federal magistrate blew the whistle on, was true."

The next day, the assistant chief counsel for Customs and Border Protection, Lisa R. Donaldson, sent an email to all Borderland Immigration Council members, trying to walk back the officers' statement. "But that looked to us like a semi-veiled confession, too," says Dylan.

The key part of the message read: "As a point of clarification: the Border Patrol *does not* have a blanket policy requiring the separation of family units. Any increase in separated family units is due primarily to the increase in prosecutions of immigration related crimes." (Emphasis in the original.)

Just as with the Mounted Guard in 1904; the Border Patrol's first headquarters in 1924; the border fumigation baths, 1914–1954; Operation

---

6. This was a feature of the pilot, not a bug, according to journalist Jonathan Blitzer. The "braintrust" behind Family Separation wished to ensure, at the very least, that the initial batch of children kidnapped by Uncle Sam would be able to identify themselves to authorities; state where they'd come from; and to whom they were meant to be going.

Blockade, aka Hold the Line, aka Operation Gatekeeper from 1993—El Paso was again the launchpad for border policy experimentation.

"Family separation was beta-tested here by local DHS leadership before being adopted in Washington as national policy," says Dylan.

The practice had begun while Obama-Biden were still in office, possibly without their awareness. By October 2017, however, it was happening with the full knowledge of and in coordination with the US Department of Justice. According to government reports and a Border Patrol whistleblower who worked on the project, Sessions was applying the arcane Emergency Quota Act of 1921 in the El Paso Sector to criminalize asylum-seeking parents traveling north with children. Yet, Trump's second Homeland Security secretary, Kirstjen Nielsen, was denying that family separation was policy—just as her predecessor, General John Kelly, had done even after telling Wolf Blitzer on CNN in March of that year that Trump & Co were considering taking children away as a means to deter migration.

Now the Borderland Council had confirmation that Trump & Co had lied.

|||||||||||||||||||||||||||||||||||||||||||||||||||||||||

Word flew from community to Congress with the speed of a text message. Representative O'Rourke's Washington office, however, brushed it off as a mistake, as something that could be fixed.

"But this was no mistake," states Dylan. "We had a double admission."

Local ICE stonewalled the Borderland Council. Even the agency's community engagement officer, a Protestant minister named Bryan Van Dyke, refused to engage. Dylan remembers feeling threatened when Van Dyke told him, *There's a new sheriff in town. You better watch yourself.*

The El Paso migrant rights community had solid data, a double confession, and alarming new suspicions that parents were being deported without their children, too. Kids, moreover, were being disappeared into the black hole of the Resettlement Office as its shelters began to swell. But even as these abuses accelerated under Trump, the borderlanders struggled to get anyone beyond Texas to care.

Writing for the *Houston Chronicle*, journalist Lomi Kreil first disclosed the Border Patrol agents' screw-up on November 25, 2017. She went on to uncover additional instances of family separation, including that of a Congolese mother and her seven-year-old daughter at the San Ysidro port of entry. The mother, Ms. L, was held in California, while her daughter was sent to Chicago. Border Protection agents claimed they had doubts about Ms. L's maternity, yet ICE waited a full four months to administer a DNA test.

Lomi's reporting sparked an American Civil Liberties Union class-action lawsuit: *Ms. L v. ICE*. Led by attorney Lee Gelernt, the suit would bring a legal end to family separation under District Court Judge Dana Sabraw the following June. But Lomi's scoop could have—*and should have*—put an immediate stop to the heinous practice.

"It's as bad as anything I've seen in thirty years of doing this work," Lee told me. "Little kids begging and screaming not to be taken from parents as they were being hauled off."

"Media outlets outside Texas simply weren't interested," says Dylan. Frustrated and incredulous, disappointed but undaunted, HOPE and the Borderland Council carried on documenting the horrors. Their next report, *Sealing the Border, The Criminalization of Asylum Seekers in the Trump Era*, presaged the official rollout of zero tolerance, which would become commonplace along the two-thousand-mile line in a matter of months. This time, their research revealed that 94 percent of asylum-seeking adults arriving in the El Paso Sector between July and November 2017 had been separated from their children. Yet, as of the January 2018 release of the Borderland Council's second study, Trump & Co were still claiming that family separation wasn't a thing.

Jonathan White, then–deputy director of the Refugee Resettlement Office's children's programs, had been left out of the policy loop. When supposedly "unaccompanied" infants and toddlers began to arrive in unprecedented numbers on his proverbial doorstep, he surmised what was going on. White warned his new boss, Trump-appointee Scott Lloyd, that the practice would cause lifelong trauma for everyone involved. Lloyd told White: "There was no policy that would result in the separation of children."

‖‖‖

Finally, Molly Hennessy-Fiske of the *Los Angeles Times* brought the story to national attention on February 3, 2018. Beating Jeff Sessions by six weeks, she warned us of what was soon to come: "According to public defenders and immigrant advocates, more and more immigrant families who come to the southern border seeking asylum are being charged in federal criminal courts from El Paso to Arizona. . . . Once a case becomes a criminal matter, parents and children are separated," she wrote.

The Tanton network's Center for Immigration Studies pushed out the counter-narrative that parents making the dangerous trek with children were no better than human traffickers. Criminal charges were, therefore, warranted, they argued.

In the El Paso Sector, the detention of people seeking asylum had become the rule, not the exception, despite objections from public defenders that prosecuting this population was not permitted under federal or international law. Parents were promised their children back if they renounced their asylum claims and "volunteered" for their own refoulement. This, too, was a lie, for as Trump's Homeland Security operatives failed to keep records, they couldn't reunite families even if they wanted to. Many asylum-seeking parents were returned to harm under false pretenses, without their kids.

Criminalizing asylum was now the latest chapter in the thirty-plus-year "prevention through deterrence" playbook. The new policy, which Sessions announced on April 6, 2018, declared zero tolerance for all who dared to cross the border between ports of entry, even those seeking asylum. However, the accompanying practice of metering effectively closed ports of entry to this population. Made to wait in Mexico, families were sitting ducks for organized crime syndicates, driving them to entrust their lives to traffickers ready to cross them over the line for ever-increasing sums of money.

It was the perfect government-sanctioned Catch-22, forcing folks wishing to immigrate "the right way" into the water, through the desert, or over the wall now as high as a three-story building in some places—a fall not easily survived.

|||||||||||||||||||||||||||||||||||||||||||||||||||

The world beyond El Paso was finally catching on that Trump & Co were ripping families apart. Scenes of barbarity made international headlines, shaking us to the core: A mother shackled by agents of the federal government for protesting when her suckling infant was pulled from her breast. A man dead from suicide on being denied information regarding the whereabouts of his wife and three-year-old son. A little girl in a red sweater, no taller than an officer's knee, appealing to her captor with tears welled up in her eyes and streaming down her face.

It was so hard to believe, let alone to feel. Then an insider—someone protesting their odious job—snatched an eight-minute recording from deep inside the Ursula hielera.

The largest Border Patrol station in the US, Ursula is a sprawling 77,000 square foot warehouse, retrofitted under the Obama-Biden administration to detain up to 1,500 people at a time. Outside, it looks like it could be part of the IDEA Los Encinos Secondary School complex on McAllen's Ware Road, right next door. Until you spot the US and Border Patrol flags waving above the screened, razor wire–topped fencing requisite of all Border Industrial Complex fortifications.

Inside, off-limits to all but guards and prisoners, are chain-link cages like those containing captive dogs at a pound. But in 2018, the cages contained kids.

In one, a little girl, Alison Jimena Valencia Madrid, is heard begging a Border Protection officer to call her auntie. She has memorized the phone number. She is reciting it, through sobs, over and over and over. She is six.

The recording, which at times sounds muffled, as if it was made from within the whistleblower's pocket, was passed to Tía Jennifer, who shared it with journalist Ginger Thompson, who shared it with the world via *ProPublica*.

|||||||||||||||||||||||||||||||||||||||||||||||||||

In early June 2018, the Department of Homeland Security disclosed that 1,995 minors had been separated from 1,940 adults from April through May 31. As of June 26, that number was revised to 2,047 kids. But when Trump & Co finally owned that they'd been experimenting with separations in El Paso from July 2017, affecting another 281 families, the official tally of children kidnapped by Uncle Sam jumped to nearly 4,000. Then, reports emerged that the Department of Health and Human Services, the Resettlement Office's parent agency, had previously lost track of another 1,475, which brought the number of children rendered "unaccompanied" by the family separation policy closer to 5,500.

Faith leaders decried the practice as "deeply immoral." Amnesty International said family separation was "tantamount to torture." The American Academy of Pediatrics warned it would trigger "toxic stress" in the young, disrupting and potentially arresting brain development. Physicians for Human Rights predicted—and has since proven—that the mental, emotional, and physical toll of both family separation, as well as prolonged detention away from loved ones, will hamstring its victims for a lifetime.

In protest, Texas State Judge Kathleen H. Olivares resolved to leave the bench for good and join the fast-growing campaign to end the monstrous practice.

CHAPTER TWENTY-ONE

#ElPasoStrong

It's the mark of a good judge—a fair judge—to remain dispassionate, beholden not to personal beliefs or politics, but to the US Constitution and the law. And for twenty years, Judge Kathleen Olivares lived this oath with pride. But when confronted with the sounds of children crying for their lost parents in federal "ice boxes" and scenes of them wrapped up in mylar "blankets" in crowded Border Patrol "dog pens," she told me, "I felt compelled and driven to assist."

She renounced her judgeship, harnessed a life's worth of El Paso connections, and transformed into a community organizer—a role she'd never played before—as #ElPasoStrong would be stretched again.[7] Just when they thought things couldn't get any worse, residents of a desert hamlet located forty miles southeast of El Paso on the US-Mexico border realized to their horror that a city of khaki canvas was going up in their actual backyard. Tornillo, Texas, population 1,568, where everyone attends the same public school and shops at Don Pancho Supermarket, was suddenly home to an internment camp. An internment camp for teens.

---

7. On August 3, 2019, Patrick Wood Crusius, a 21-year-old of German and Italian descent, drove approximately 650 miles (1,050 km) to the borderlands city of El Paso and opened fire on shoppers at the Cielo Vista Walmart in an act of domestic terrorism fueled by white-supremacist hate. We know this because shortly before the attack Crusius published a manifesto on the Neo-Nazi image-board 8chan. Sounding much like Trump & Co and its propaganda arm, Fox News, Crusius declared his crusade of stopping the "Hispanic invasion." He murdered twenty-three people and injured twenty-two others in the deadliest attack on the Latinx community in modern US history. The El Paso population rallied, uniting in solidarity as they expressed strength amid adversity. That's #ElPasoStrong: a tribute to diversity and inclusion as well as to the lives the world lost that dreadful day.

The desert prison opened on Father's Day, June 17, 2018, with one hundred "inmates"—none charged with a crime. It was just far enough away to be out of view. But El Pasoans mobilized. The sleepy borderlands backwater was thrust into national headlines.

More protesters than prisoners met at the barbed wire–laden fences and gates that separated them from the twenty massive soft-sided structures erected in a parched field within the Tornillo-Guadalupe port of entry. The tents provided space, protesters were told, for a reception center, medical clinic, cinema, and dormitories big enough to sleep twenty teenagers each in bunk beds. Demonstrators did not know if these claims were true, however, for no one but guards, detainees, and truck drivers making deliveries were allowed inside. Not even Beto O'Rourke.

Now running for Senate, O'Rourke finally spoke out. At the event that day, organized by his office, he declared that locking immigrant children up besmirched the name, values, and global reputation of the USA. As activists held up signs that said FIGHT IGNORANCE, NOT IMMIGRANTS and THIS IS HOW THE HOLOCAUST STARTED, he beseeched borderlands communities to shine a bright light on the need for immigration reform.

"It's no accident that this is in Tornillo," he said. "It's in a remote location on purpose so the American people don't know what's happening here."

⁂

Four days later, on June 21, mayors representing twenty cities and both major political parties held a press conference in 99°F (37°C) heat at the locked threshold of the desert prison. It was the day after Trump signed an executive order ending the policy his administration had maintained, for over a year, did not exist. Hosted by El Paso Mayor Dee Margo, that delegation, too, tried to get inside the tent city and was thwarted.

June 24 drew yet another crowd, including the activist Dolores Huerta, the director Rob Reiner, and the politician Julián Castro. Addressing the crowd, then-California Secretary of State Alex Padilla said, "Detaining children, taking little babies away from their mommies and daddies, is not who we are as Americans." But it was wishful thinking at best, an example of "American amnesia," writes Laura Briggs, author of *Taking Children: A History of American Terror*. "Child taking," as she calls it, is deeply woven within the US white supremacy story.

When Judge Kathleen laid eyes on the Tornillo encampment for the first time, she told me, "Seeing buses carrying kids enter the facility, I was filled with disbelief and rage. I was reminded of our government's shameful and inhumane internment of Japanese American citizens during WWII. It was a detention camp, for children."

She decided to be part of the solution.

She found immediate allyship with her close friend and community activist, Analisa Cordova Silverstein; as well as student volunteers from senior class of their high school alma mater, Loretto Academy, who joined the effort with their parents' blessing; and from Camilo at HOPE. They would soon be joined by El Paso newcomer Ashley Heidebrecht.

||||||||||||||||||||||||||||||||||||||||||||||||||||||||

Ashley landed in El Paso just as the internment camp arose from the desert floor. To complete her Masters in Social Work, she volunteered with Fernando Garcia, executive director of the Border Network for Human Rights, a seven thousand-member coalition that has been leading the charge for immigration reform in the US since 1998. Ashley pitched to Fernando the idea of organizing a series of rallies to keep the Tornillo protests going.

"There was a lot of buzz after Beto, the mayors, and activists went to Tornillo," she told me. "A foundation had been laid. Now it needed momentum."

The Border Network was heavily involved in campaigning to stop Trump's border wall with the second annual *Hugs Not Walls Community Action*. It provided a rare opportunity for family members separated by US immigration policies to hold each other. Fernando and his wife, Adriana Cadena, coordinator of Reform Immigration for Texas Alliance, described the event to me over lunch at El Paso's famous Rainbow Fountain: "Members of nearly four hundred families, who had not seen one another in years, waded into the water from the Juarez and El Paso sides of the Rio Grande." Loved ones stood on platforms raised over the water enfolded in each other's arms.

The Border Patrol gave them only three minutes to embrace.

It wasn't enough. Still, everyone wanted to hug again.

The second rollout of the event was coming up on September 22, 2018, and it needed Fernando and Adriana's full attention. If Ashley wanted to spearhead a series of Tornillo rallies, Fernando told her, she could count on the Border Network's communications team for support.

Simultaneously, HOPE was preparing a gathering of national faith leaders from communities across the denominations to hear for themselves the cries emanating from the border. "We just wanted folks to come," says Camilo. "We wanted them to understand that the borderlands are not dangerous and that people in search of life are not criminal invaders."

"We craved renewed moral clarity," states Dylan. "In a world where cruelty was swiftly becoming normalized, we feared our own faith might be slipping away."

They called their meeting *El Grito de la Frontera* (The Cry from the Border). This time, they put family separation at the top of the agenda. "People came from all parts of the country," says Dylan: "Catholics and Protestants, a number of academics, some angry grannies, Sanctuary International, and a Jewish component as well."

HOPE and the Border Network had both platform and audience. Ashley and Judge Kathleen had, between them, time, connections, and organizational acumen.

"All we had to do was get people to the Tornillo gates," says Ashley. "Because once you see, that changes everything."

That's when a retired software developer from Brooklyn pulled into town to bear witness, too.

|||||||||||||||||||||||||||||||||||||||||||||||||||||||||

Even before Alison Jimena's cries heard 'round the world moved us from outrage to action, Joshua Rubin and his wife, Melissa Bowen Rubin, had joined a neighborhood coalition in politically liberal Brownstone Brooklyn. Called *Don't Separate Families*, it was a small group with a big heart that assembled shortly after Jeff Sessions' April announcement of zero tolerance to organize lobbying efforts, circulate petitions, hold poster-making parties, and populate New York–area protests. They also set out to organize a delegation to go to the border.

Joshua blazed the trail. And he didn't waste time. By mid-June, he was standing on McAllen's Ware Road outside the Ursula hielera, a lone protester holding a poster that shouted FREE THEM to all who went in and came out. An artist, Melissa applied the two simple words in bold black letters to glossy white foam core.

"I just wanted to put myself in front of it," Joshua told me, "to see what, if anything, would come of it." Within a week, he was arrested for criminal trespass and locked up for a night in the county jail. His rental car was towed. "There was nowhere to sleep but the floor. The lights were never turned off. And it was shockingly cold," Joshua recalls. He couldn't catch a wink, which made him empathize with asylum seekers detained by ICE all the more.

By imprisoning him, if only for one night, US law enforcement had radicalized him.

On the opposite edge of Texas, when El Paso/Ciudad Juarez native and history professor Diana Martinez learned that a child prison had popped up "right in our own backyard," she created a private Facebook page: *S.O.S. For The Detained Children: What Are We Going To Do?*

Before one week was out, she had a thousand followers, first from El Paso, then more far-flung. It became a kind of clearinghouse for information about how to get involved: "We would post with ideas about shelters that needed donations; where to meet to help stuff bags with toiletries; who needed legal support; about all the protests that were going on around town."

||||||||||||||||||||||||||||||||||||||||||||||||||||||

Though a lone protester standing vigil outside Ursula, Joshua was rarely alone. McAllen locals organized by the Texas Civil Rights Project joined him, as did members of the Carrizo/Comecrudo Nation of Texas. A young Democratic politician from Maine, Zak Ringlestein, showed up with a pickup truck full of water and toys and bedding—gifts from his constituents he was not permitted to deliver. A documentary film crew from Springfield, Missouri, Carbon Trace Productions, arrived in late June to collect footage.

Joshua and the Carbon Trace crew traveled together to attend the June 28 *Families Belong Together* rally in Brownsville, forty-five minutes to the east. Then they immediately reversed course and hightailed it 1,000 miles west, to join the June 30 mobilization in El Paso, one of 750 in cities worldwide—600 in the US alone.

"It was the biggest El Paso protest I'd ever seen," recalls Diana.

Armed with clipboard and pens, having volunteered to register new voters at the rally, she approached two men: "One carried a sign that said FREE THEM; the other carried a professional video camera." On learning that they were registered to vote in New York and Missouri, respectively, Diana was blown away: "It really moved me that people from so far away cared about my city and what was going on here."

When Joshua told Diana that he was considering shifting his vigil from Ursula to Tornillo, she confided to me, "I was immediately worried. I had been there for Beto's Father's Day rally, and it's desolate."

She told Joshua: "I don't know how many people will see you or your sign." What she left unsaid was that growing up as a *fronteriza*, a borderlander of Mexican origins, surrounded by an increasingly aggressive law enforcement apparatus whose trigger-happy agents sometimes killed innocent people who posed no threat, at other times wrongfully detained and deported US citizens, she'd learned to be fearful and distrustful. Not of border crossers. But of both Border Patrol and Texas state authority.

"I stay away from the border wall," she told me, "unless I'm in a group."

<hr />

Tornillo was not unique. Jails for kids were then spreading like weeds: in empty office buildings, abandoned big-box stores, and old hotels. Many, like the old Mardi Gras, were clandestine. Trump's Resettlement Office wasn't forthcoming about the location of these shelters or who was running them. Not even attorneys, like Jodi Goodwin, were given access to that information.

ProPublica reported on June 27, 2018, that a network of approximately one hundred shelters and foster homes in fourteen states run by an assortment of nonprofits was then housing 8,886 children, all of whom had crossed the border before April. When the Department of Health and Human Services updated its numbers again, it was to admit it had 10,773 youth in custody and that shelters were at 95 percent capacity. That's when Trump & Co announced no-bid contracts to build more emergency shelters.

One million dollars a day, at least, went to San Antonio–based BCFS Health and Human Services between June and November to operate the Tornillo internment facility. Comprehensive Health Services, a subsidiary of Homeland Security contractor Caliburn International LLC, which had links to now White House Chief of Staff John Kelly, won $31 million in February 2018 to turn the underutilized former Air Reserve base at Homestead, Florida, into another 3,200-bed prison for immigrant kids. It obtained at least $222 million more to operate Homestead between July 7, 2018, and April 20, 2019.

Crucially, because the Tornillo and Homestead prison camps had been erected on federal lands, Trump & Co maintained—as Reagan and Bush 41 had at the Guantánamo detention camp decades before—that they were subject *neither* to state licensing requirements *nor* to federal agreements, like the Flores Settlement Agreement.

They also said the Tornillo encampment would be temporary, and that it would house no more than 360 children. But within one week of its opening, talk shifted to expanding the facility to ten times its original projected size.

"It's not the kind of place you just walk out of," Joshua told Diana. "And if no one sees it, who will know?"

In September, after a short stint back home in Brooklyn, Joshua returned to attend HOPE's Grito de la Frontera. By then, Amnesty International calculated that another 6,022 children, at least, had been snatched, suggesting that Trump & Co had gone right on taking kids even after the June 30 executive order ending family separation as policy. Caitlin Dickerson of the *New York Times* scooped the world that teenaged boys in detention facilities all over the US were being rounded up and sent to Tornillo, which had reached peak capacity of 3,800. But it wasn't until an El Pasoan attending El Grito made a piercing comment that Joshua's resolve to hold vigil at Tornillo became solidified: she said she was tired of people coming to the border for a few days and thinking they'd "done" something.

Three weeks later, Joshua phoned HOPE. "He told us of his intentions to hold a vigil at the gates of the Tornillo encampment," Camilo recalls. "He was already making calls to the county commission, looking to secure permission to park on county property so he couldn't be removed by the authorities. He wondered if HOPE could help push any buttons."

Camilo and Joshua devised a plan: Claiming to be part of the Carbon Trace documentary crew, Joshua obtained a commercial permit to park a camper van on the El Paso county line, just across from the ever-expanding tent city. He packed up his FREE THEM sign once more, as well as a new one. It read: WITNESS TORNILLO. He kissed Melissa goodbye as September turned into October and promised to be back in Brooklyn for New Year's Eve.

||||||||||||||||||||||||||||||||||||||||||||||||||||||||||

Arriving in El Paso for the third time that year, Joshua was whisked off to Loretto Academy by Camilo before he'd had a chance to pick up his camper. They were needed for a planning meeting with Ashley, Judge Kathleen, and representatives of the school's senior class. Their action, called *El Paso Cares—Liberty for All!* was set for October 27, three weeks into Joshua's vigil. It would begin with a morning protest in Tornillo, followed by an evening fundraiser at El Paso's historic downtown concert venue, Tricky Falls.

Before the big day, Judge Kathleen drove out to Tornillo to see Joshua and tour the site. When she asked him, *What do you need?* he channeled Diana's wise counsel: "Judge," he said, "we could use a Port-a-Potty."

So Judge Kathleen figured out how to obtain a small patch of land from the county onto which she had installed a portable toilet. "And that's how I became the Port-a-Potty judge!"

The potty remained with Josh throughout what Ashley would describe as his "occupation."

CHAPTER TWENTY-TWO

Ninety Days in the Desert

Wearing a wide-brimmed olive green Tilley camping hat and binoculars slung around his neck, Joshua was largely alone his first month and a half in Tornillo. "It was like my forty days in the desert," he states.

To help pass the time and coax up intelligence about the goings on inside the Tornillo teen prison, he'd chat up the delivery drivers and service contractors. The encampment's lifeline, they brought in generators, tents, beds, and Port-a-Potties, as ICE brought in busloads of boys and girls, ages twelve through seventeen.

"More kids went in than came out," Joshua witnessed.

They trucked in potable water, "at the rate of seventy thousand gallons a day," and hauled equal amounts of gray and black water out again. "I learned the most from the guys who moved water from the hydrants into the camp tanks."

He'd ask them: *Do you know what you're supporting?* If they didn't, he'd tell them: *It's a jail. A jail for kids.*

When he wasn't interrogating service and delivery men, he was walking the camp's perimeter, sometimes more than once each day. The youth were brought into the yard in formation, "marched, single file, like soldiers, like prisoners," continues Joshua. "Once there, they were allowed to be 'at ease.' But they remained under constant surveillance."

He tried to communicate with the teen "inmates" when they were outside—contact the guards roundly discouraged. One day he managed a short conversation.

"I found out that a Salvadoran boy had been inside for three months. Another boy shouted, *cuatro meses*, four months, and another said, *cinco*, holding up five fingers." That would put him on the inside since the opening of the camp—a clear violation of the Flores Settlement.

"That was the last time I had anything close to a conversation with the Tornillo teens," Joshua recalls. "A guard hurried over, and the boys shut down." The next time Joshua walked along the soccer fields, the fence had been screened to block his view.

Joshua joined Facebook, creating a page he called *Witness Tornillo*. There, he began to share his daily observations as the camp continued to expand. "If there were one thousand kids there when I arrived, there were at least three thousand in the end."

HOPE calculated that, all told, six thousand boys and girls passed through Tornillo's patrolled gateway from June–December 2018, rivaling in size the largest federal penitentiary.

The kids weren't just "inmates." Taking a page out of Harold Ezell's book, they were also being used as bait. Trump & Co obligated *all* members of a potential sponsor's household to be fingerprinted and undergo background checks—not just the sponsor him or herself per previous practice. Information would be provided to authorities to hunt down and deport undocumented relatives. When intelligence resulted in raids on private residences, at school bus stops, and in churches, etc., many households ceased to cooperate, like Jenny's mom had back in 1985. This trapped kids inside even longer, slowing the vetting process such that time served at Tornillo was stretching to a new average of ninety days in the desert.

By bearing witness, Joshua opened up space for others, near and far, to do the same. "In particular," says Ashley, "the Jewish community. I had no idea how engaged they were, but they would give our organizing efforts both capacity and national attention."

Congregation Hakafa in Glencoe, Illinois, for example, felt a kindred connection to the migrant children. For decades, Hakafa members, including Lee and Nancy Goodman, had been involved with immigrant justice issues. Since 2016, they had helped to resettle newcomers to the US. So, when the horrors of family separation became public knowledge, the Hakafa membership, led by Rabbi Bruce Elder, resolved to take action.

Though small, Ashley's rallies had attracted a bit of media attention, "which made our efforts more visible. So, in a quick Google search," she states, "Rabbi Bruce found me."

He sent Lee to El Paso as Hakafa's emissary to scope out opportunities for action. Ashley acted as Lee's ambassador. They visited the internment camp with Joshua.

Meanwhile, Rabbis Josh Whinston and Miriam Terlinchamp from Ann Arbor, Michigan, and Cincinnati, Ohio, respectively, were separately underway with plans for a nationwide caravan, destination: Tornillo. That summer, Rabbi Josh had met a mother whose three children had been taken from her at the border.

"Listening to her speak of such a harrowing experience sparked the beginning of my activism in this arena," states Rabbi Josh. "As someone who believes deeply in Judaism's justice texts, which espouse values that have been with us for thousands of years, whose passages I love to talk about and reflect on and quote, I had to ask myself: *Was I willing to step up and take action in accordance with those principles?*"

The answer was, *Yes.* By the time he and Rabbi Miriam joined forces with Rabbi Bruce, they had secured the participation of several congregations. "We knew we weren't going to be getting kids out. So we decided our trip was to be about coverage," states Rabbi Josh.

Faith In Action, a national network dedicated to dismantling systems of racial and hate-fueled injustice, agreed to set up rallies in the cities the caravan was to pass through—Indianapolis, St. Louis, Oklahoma City, and Dallas—en route to the Tornillo gates, where they planned an interfaith vigil for Thursday, November 15.

Then, on the day of Judge Kathleen's community protest and fundraiser, everyone's commitment was tested.

|||||||||||||||||||||||||||||||||||||||||||||||||||||||

An anti-Semitic attack at the Tree of Life Synagogue in Pittsburgh, Pennsylvania, violently cut eleven lives short on October 27, 2018. The connection the Jewish community felt to the migrant youth was never more stark. It paralleled the exodus of the Israelites from Egypt. It recalled the centuries-long diaspora history; forced to move from place to place; refused welcome when most in need, even the children. It brought to mind the concentration camps of the Holocaust, and the US's shameful turning away of roughly nine hundred Jews aboard the MS *St. Louis* in 1939. It summoned up the bone-chilling chants of *Jews will not replace us* by tiki-torch-bearing white supremacists in Charlottesville, Virginia, the summer before.

"Rather than let some guy with a gun stop us," Rabbi Josh told me, "in many ways, the hate crime energized us."

Which is not to say he wasn't scared. "I was nervous about attracting white supremacists, yes. They'd been given license by the Trump administration, and what we were about to do would be very public."

The caravaners were fine until they reached Texas. "Then, a Reform synagogue in El Paso began receiving threatening calls." But rather than back off, that congregation joined the pilgrimage to Tornillo, too, as did Christians and Muslims, who joined the caravan over the course of their four-day interstate drive.

An estimated two hundred people convened at the doorstep of the Tornillo internment camp on the morning of November 15 to send a message, states Rabbi Josh, that: "As one of the wealthiest countries in the world, it is our responsibility to welcome asylum seekers, rather than treating them as criminals."

"You can't imagine the scene," recalls Camilo. "Into this sea of yarmulkes and prayer shawls came the busloads of girls from Loretto Academy, all dressed in their red and gray school uniforms. They descended the buses like a flock of beautiful birds."

Also rolling into view during the rally were ICE buses—their blackened windows shut tight. "You couldn't see kids," Rabbi Josh remembers, "but you knew they were there."

When they disappeared behind the fortress of metal and barbed wire, states the Rabbi, "It shocked me just how easy it was to hide several thousand teenagers. You could be outside the gates and have no idea what was going on inside."

〰〰〰〰〰〰〰〰〰〰〰〰〰〰〰〰〰〰〰〰〰〰〰〰

Thanks to the mounting activism, Father Rafael Garcia, from South El Paso's Sacred Heart Parish, gained entrance to the tent city to celebrate Sunday Mass. He was followed inside by monitors for the Flores Settlement Agreement, including Stanford University child psychologist and trauma specialist Ryan Matlow, as well as Camilo. Their assessment was unequivocal: "The kids of Tornillo were by all indications suffering." They painted a picture of psychological distress due to the indefinite confinement. They noted little to no psychosocial support.

Meanwhile, Trump touted Tornillo as a model, with talk about creating another child prison inside El Paso-based Fort Bliss. Equal in size to the state of Delaware, the Army base's impenetrablility sparked additional public outrage.

Tornillo had become a national flashpoint. The *Washington Post* updated the number of children and teens then in the custody of the federal government to roughly 14,600. Not since the Japanese internment have so many young non-offenders been imprisoned. Yet, Congress allocated another $367.9 million in the last quarter of 2018 to keep Tornillo operational.

Then, CNN and the Associated Press disclosed that, among the more than 2,100 Tornillo employees, none had undergone rigorous FBI background checks. This was in violation of Health and Human Services' and the Resettlement Office's own guidelines.

Exhausted but undaunted, El Paso activists and their allies picked up their protest, heading into the holiday season with a plan. Ashley secured the participation of US Representative-Elect Valerie Escobar (D-TX) for a rally on December 15. Representative Judy Chu (D-CA) and Senator Jeff Merkley (D-OR) agreed to come, too. Three days later, they introduced their Shut Down Child Prison Camps Act.

Diana began to organize the first in a series of events that would come to be called Christmas at Tornillo. The Carbon Trace crew teased the outside world with images from their coming documentary, *Witness at Tornillo*, alongside invitations to attend.

As Joshua continued speaking through Facebook, his following grew and grew. Word began to spread.

Actress and activist Alyssa Milano came to interview Joshua outside the detention site. Their conversation reached tens of thousands over Twitter.

More people came, showing up from far and wide. They arrived in camper vans. They slept in cars. They pitched tents.

The caroling began on Sunday, December 23, and continued into January.

‖‖

Tom Cartwright, a retired financial executive, came with a massive professional sound system, which sent participant speeches and songs soaring right over the encampment walls. "When the kids were outside and waving to us, we knew they could hear our music and messages," recalls Tom.

Camilo remembers seeing soccer balls fly back over the fortification in response—"the perfect symbol of resistance." In "Ode to the Soccer Ball Sailing Over a Barbed Wire Fence," 2021 National Book Award winner for *Floaters*, Martín Espada, transformed the bid for freedom into poetry.

During Christmas at Tornillo, Beto O'Rourke, again at the gates, promised that the encampment would be shut down. Sure enough, the Tornillo teen prison operator, BCFS Health and Human Services—the second-highest grossing kid-jailer that year after Southwest Key—gave in to the mounting negative press attention. Its director, Kevin Dinnin, announced that the camp would be emptied and broken down by the end of January 2019.

This forced Trump & Co to rescind the background check requirement for all members of a sponsor's household. Suddenly, twenty-five hundred young people were released to loved ones, proving that the unnecessary and prolonged incarceration at Tornillo had always been at the discretion of the administration. It was cruelty for cruelty's sake. Another attempt to deter the inevitable, for human migration is a fact of life. Especially when forced to run for your life.

‖‖‖

"I feel so grateful and appreciative of anyone who did anything," states Ashley. "From every phone call made and dollar donated to every song sung and letter written, it's testament to what humankind *can* achieve when we work together for a common cause, regardless of belief systems or methodologies. If any one component had been missing," she believes, "it would not have been a success."

Joshua's vigil at Tornillo was over. He returned home to Melissa for New Year's Eve, as promised. A new pair of witnesses, now forever committed, took over to see the Tornillo internment camp all but erased.

"Once the last of the children were gone," remembers Karla Barber, "our role was to watch and document the dismantling of the place to verify that is was taken down."

"All fencing, tents, toilets, generators, mobile kitchen, soccer goals, everything, were packed up and carted away," says Julie Swift. "They literally scraped the ground clean. Like there were never children there. They even swept the sand to remove any traces that the camp ever existed."

PART IV:
DESCENT

CHAPTER TWENTY-THREE

~~Six Seven~~ Eight Degrees of Family Separation

Tía Lizee's warmth and exuberance are matched only by her infectious ear-to-ear smile. But the day we met, in early 2020, she was downcast, broken-hearted. One of the hundreds of families in the Matamoros refugee encampment had shrunk in size from three to one the day before.

Sixteen-year-old "Pedro" couldn't take it anymore. He, his mother, and sister, along with 2,500–3,000 other safety seekers, had been living in tents meant for weekend camping for months.

They were not protected from the weather. When the rains came, their tent leaked and the walkways turned to mud. When the winds kicked up, they huddled together, shivering. When the sun bore down, they sweltered atop the grassless floodplain of the temporary "home" that was feeling all too permanent.

They were not protected from violence. In Matamoros, they experienced the same ongoing threats that forced them to flee Honduras. Returning home, where they faced routine abuse from an angry, broken husband and father was out of the question.

Three of the seventy thousand people forced into the Remain in Mexico program, they would have had no protection at all were it not for the humanitarian leaders, like Lizee, of the Dignity Village Collaborative. They would have had no tent or mat to sleep on. No access to potable water. No basic health care. No legal support.

No self-supporting community. No teachers to aid their continued learning. No books to help them pass the time. No way to charge their cell phones.

And they would have no guarantee of at least one daily meal.

Despite the tireless efforts of Team Brownsville and its vast volunteer network, which had been providing breakfast and dinner for the stranded refugees since early 2018, there was never enough for a growing boy to eat. Notwithstanding the help of the Angry Tías and Abuelas to keep the camp's four "free stores," las tiendas, stocked with cooking oil, rice, and beans for the shared cocinas, Pedro lived in constant, gnawing pain. The hunger left him cranky and listless and prone to colds and other ailments. His mother, "Marta," could do nothing to help her son, and it was tearing her apart.

She was determined to bring her children to safety, to provide for and protect them, to give them a future. Yet under MPP, she could do none of these things.

Lizee admitted to me she saw it coming. "He kept asking me for new shoes." He'd laugh, "like he was making a joke," she said. "He'd say that with new shoes he could swim the Rio Grande more swiftly and move more quickly once inside the US to avoid the Border Patrol."

Lizee sensed a seriousness beneath Pedro's coy smile. "I had shoes to give him. But something held me back. Perhaps I knew that if I did, he'd be gone. And if he drowned in the river, that would be on me."

She had taken a rare day away from the camp to prepare a coordination plan for the Dignity Village Collaborative when it all went down. Tracking who was doing what and where the gaps were was one of Lizee's many contributions to the intergroup structure that consolidated when MPP descended on Brownsville in July 2019. From individuals to ragtag groups to a grassroots network of now-formal organizations, each took on a specialized role, from providing food and shelter to serving medical needs to developing the camp's infrastructure. By December 2019, their collaboration had a name and a mission as well as a designated cohort—including the Angry Tías' inseparable dynamic duo of Lizee and Susan Law—who met weekly with Mexico's National Migration Institute. This binational coordination betrayed the unspoken reality: that as much as everyone knew MPP was illegal and would be made to end, eventually, it wasn't going away as long as Trump & Co remained in the White House. And neither was the Matamoros tent encampment.

||||||||||||||||||||||||||||||||||||||||||||||||||

On the evening of the day Lizee decided to work from home, Pedro was waiting with his family in the Team Brownsville dinner line when someone accused him of going for seconds before others had been served their first. He tried to defend himself, for it was patently untrue. But he was ordered to step to the back of the line.

Pedro turned to his mother, the look on his face beseeching her to do something, anything. He was starving. He *had* to eat.

"Go," said Marta.

Did she say this without thinking? Or had she been considering this for some time? Lizee didn't know. Before becoming an Angry Tía, Lizee was a mental health professional. "If I heard too many of their stories, I wouldn't be able to function," she told me. She received whatever they were willing to share. But she never asked and she did not probe.

"Better they save sharing their experiences of terror and heart-wrenching brutality for their credible fear interviews," she said, "so they aren't further re-traumatized."

Truth is, Lizee didn't need to hear what drove the refugees to make the perilous journey to the US. She could see it in their eyes and in their body language. She was also a daily witness to the toll that living under MPP took on each and every person caught in its web, no matter their age. MPP was a steady, dehumanizing grind, an endless purgatory that chipped away at the spirit and soul. Behind each asylum seeker was a story of persecution, violence, or poverty so crushing there was only escape. Ahead of them, the Promised Land. Or so they thought.

Lizee and I struggled to understand how politicians and policy-makers would knowingly drive families into such appalling circumstances, and force upon parents the most atrocious worries and abhorrent choices. States Lizee: "I don't believe an inhumane idea like MPP would have ever made it onto paper if anyone had looked into Pedro's or Marta's eyes."

We imagined Marta, stony-faced, gesturing with a tiny turn of the head northward toward the Gateway International Bridge. We imagined Pedro shocked, not expecting this reaction from his mother. But neither of us imagined that it would be Pedro's nine-year-old sister, "Esmeralda," who would break the ice. According to Lizee, she shocked everyone when she blurted out: "Can I go, too?"

Marta's look of astonishment must have matched Pedro's then. If Esmeralda had been as miserable as Pedro, she hadn't let on, at least not to Lizee.

Lizee and I imagined a tearful goodbye—the three holding each other, unnoticed by the community of tent city residents and Team Brownsville volunteers that buzzed around them. We don't know if the kids ate first, then left; or if they left right away, still hungry. But at some point that evening, Pedro and Esmeralda clasped hands and set off together in the direction of perceived safety in El Norte, raggedy shoes and all.

There, they turned themselves in to US Customs and Border Protection.

This is Family Separation 6.0, by my count. It isn't the first example of family separation I've described so far. We've seen five degrees of family separation already. And in talking to separated families for this book, I found two more.

That's eight degrees of family separation created by US immigration policies.

||||||||||||||||||||||||||||||||||||||||||||||||||||||||

It starts with migration stories as old as recorded time. A parent or parents take off first to blaze the trail to safety, in search of opportunity and a better life. Once settled, they send for those they left behind, as illustrated by the story of Jenny Flores and her mother. Like the story of Karla Cornejo Villavicencio, author of *The Undocumented Americans*, who felt she could only come out of the shadows and write her truth as a childhood arrival once protected by DACA. Or like poet Javier Zamora, who recounts in *Solito: A Memoir* the experience of crossing the Sonoran desert as a nine-year-old. He is alive today thanks to the kindness of strangers. We'll call this Family Separation 3.0.

With Family Separation 2.0, we see mothers, like Sam's and Dora's, forced to kick their young out of the nest prematurely in order to save them from dangers they cannot control: forced military or gang conscription; death squads, bombardment, and village massacres; abusive fathers, starvation, climate-related devastation; corrupt authorities, displacement by transnational extractive industries, land depletion, and more.

Family Separation 3.0 takes place when adoptive fathers, like Larry, or other non-parental relatives, including the grandparents, older siblings, aunts, uncles, and guardians, who show up at the southern border every day, only to have their beloved charges taken from them because of culturally biased rules written into laws, however well-meaning, like the Trafficking Victims Protection Reauthorization Act.

Family Separation 4.0 occurs when flawed policies enacted by folks too far removed to experience the human fallout pull families apart, even if it means falsely labeling children as "unaccompanied" and sending them into a bureaucratic purgatory; even if it means parents and children might never see each other again.

Family Separation 5.0 ups the ante by putting human trauma and pain on public display as Trump & Co did in 2018 when they ordered border agents to separate families for the cameras—and they did. It was the ultimate expression of "prevention through deterrence"; a marketing message: *Do Not Come. Do Not Come.* It was cruelty for cruelty's sake.

Parents like Marta are too often forced to weigh only heartbreaking choices: *Do I keep my kids with me despite the hunger, despite the daily threats of rape or kidnapping, where I am helpless to protect them? Or do I send them across a bridge on their own to a future I cannot see?*

Under MPP, *families* were forced to remain in mob-controlled Mexican border towns. But *unaccompanied children* were not. They could cross the line. So, Marta made a Sophie's Choice.

Marta was not the only parent I encountered in January 2020 who made the dreadful, desperate decision to send their kids northward without them. Another couple refused to come out of their tent the whole time I was working in the Matamoros encampment. They blasted music from a battery-operated boombox set just outside their zipped-up "door," located beside Team Brownsville's food service line, to drown out the sound of their remorseful, uncontrollable sobs. The volume made it hard to eat, hard to chat, hard to think. But no one dared ask them to turn the music down.

MPP was a lie, a mirage. That was part of the program's cruelty. By design, it gave folks in need of protection false hope. They were made to believe that if they just waited in Mexico long enough, the gates to the US would eventually open to them. But even with the aid of the Dignity Village Collaborative, there was no childhood, no sense of control. The future stretched infinitely into the horizon, indefinitely on hold. Being exposed to danger every minute of every day transformed past traumas into toxic stress. And there was the constant, gnawing hunger, not just for food, but for freedom.

"I wanted to scream and shake her and yell, *Why did you let them go?*" Lizee told me on learning that Marta had let Pedro and Esmeralda cross the line alone. But how could Lizee reprimand a grieving mother? How could she tell her that in "the Promised Land" Pedro and Esmeralda would be separated by virtue of their age and gender and sent in different directions? How could she break the news to a heartbroken Marta that her children would likely lose contact with each other until they made it to their sponsor, if they ever did? How could she even breathe the words that one or both children might be sent back to Honduras without her?

Lizee certainly could not let slip that Trump & Co had been holding kids in concentration camps, like Tornillo and Homestead; or that they were using young people as bait to hunt down and expel their loved ones in the US. For there is another face of family separation that the US public tends to overlook: when families are ripped apart as a consequence of ICE raids, as happened with Robert Vivar's second deportation.

After living in the shadows for a decade, Robert stood up for his daughter and two granddaughters and against an abusive son-in-law when the man then under a restraining order showed up at the family's door. In the act of protecting his loved ones, he did not consider that the angry younger man would turn on him and turn him in. But soon after, Robert was cornered at his workplace in a sting operation, involving four ICE officers dressed up as Los Angeles police accompanied by a local TV talking head and cameraman.

This is Family Separation 7.0, a tragedy from which even US citizens and Trump voters are not immune. It took place under Obama-Biden, evidenced by Robert's second eviction from the only home he'd ever known. But Trump & Co turbocharged the practice. Ten thousand additional ICE officers were hired in the initial months of their one-term administration. As illustrated in the Netflix documentary *Immigration Nation*, they grabbed fathers at church and cuffed mothers waiting for the school bus with their kids. They raided homes, without warrants. They picked locks and knocked down doors. They sowed terror in immigrant communities on behalf of the US federal government.

Local police departments were deputized under a revived, and reviled, Section 287(g) of IRA-IRA, which allows ICE to sic local police—after a mere four weeks of ICE training—on undocumented residents living and working in the US during "the course of daily duties." The job depends on racial profiling, which ICE and ICE wannabes did with impunity and without accountability during the Trump years.

Profiling coupled with unnecessarily harsh imprisonment prevailed in the 142 state and local municipalities deputized under the program by Trump & Co's ICE. This perversion of police power led to uncountable civil rights violations, the subject of an ACLU report entitled, *License to Abuse: How ICE's 287(g) Program Empowers Racist Sheriffs and Civil Rights Violations.*

The surge in ICE arrests rendered thousands of US-born children orphans overnight, inflicting lifelong psychological harm, and propelling remaining family members into destitution. Broken families were suddenly plunged into housing and food insecurity; even the youngest expressed depression and suicidal ideation. Mothers and children fell into a decimated and underfunded welfare system, chipped away at since Gingrich's 1994 "contract *on* America." Many were forced to move from friends and communities of caring, all because of a loved one's incarceration and deportation.

It may not have happened at the border, but it was family separation.

||||||||||||||||||||||||||||||||||||||||||||||||||||||||

The unjust impact 287(g) had on communities goes a long way to explaining why we saw a revival of the Sanctuary Movement in the Trump years. This time, however, it wasn't just places of worship that were pushing back against the intersection of racist laws and unjust governance. This time, whole cities and states got involved in acts of civil disobedience.

Some adopted policies prohibiting local authorities from questioning individuals about their immigration status. Others simply refused to honor ICE's requests to hold unauthorized immigrants in custody. Police chiefs rightly worried about the strain hunting law-abiding community members would put on local resources, keeping them from doing their real job of targeting bad actors. Police officers felt that if the community saw them as an arm of federal immigration enforcement, undocumented residents would be less likely to come forward as victims of or witnesses to crimes. Local legislators took issue with the potential legal liabilities of doing ICE's job.

By 2018, 564 states and municipalities had taken up the mantle modeled by John Fife and Jim Corbett, adopting sanctuary policies. ICE raids without warrants were unlawful, they declared. They would play no part in enforcing 287(g).

Trump & Co declared war on these "uncooperative jurisdictions." Armed with subpoenas, lawsuits, and the Border Protection SWAT team, BORTAC, they sought to strong-arm sanctuaries into compliance. They called for cutting off access to federal monies by executive order. These efforts were largely frozen by the courts. But that didn't stop ICE and local police in jurisdictions where 287(g) was enforced from shackling mothers and fathers in front of their terrified kids and sending them into exile.

One mother, Cecilia Rochester grew so anxious her hair fell out in thick clumps. She stopped driving altogether and became fearful of taking her son, Ashton, to school in the affluent Atlanta suburb where she lived and owned a home with her Georgia-born husband, Jason.

‖‖‖

Jason met Cecilia while on the job, delivering packages for UPS, in 2004. It was love at first sight. "She was so pretty and funny. She had such a beautiful smile."

He wooed her for nearly two years. Though he felt she reciprocated his love, she refused his advances. It turned out, she was afraid to tell him that she was among the eleven million US residents without status. A co-worker finally spilled the beans: "She's undocumented," he said.

An easygoing guy and evangelical Christian, Jason didn't care. In his eyes, she was neither "illegal" nor an "alien." She was the woman of his dreams. They were meant for each other.

Under Obama-Biden, ICE granted one-year, renewable work permits to many law-abiding immigrants who had been in the country for at least five years. Cecilia had one, making it possible for her to earn a living. But it also put her on ICE's radar. And though Jason voted for Obama in 2008, hoping he would fix the immigration system and make it easier for Cecilia to pursue citizenship, by 2016 immigration was not his main concern. Overturning *Roe v. Wade* was.[8] So he swung conservative. He voted for Trump.

Even when the candidate's campaign rhetoric caused Cecilia great worry—she felt personally attacked when Trump painted all Mexicans as rapists and criminals—Jason had faith that he didn't mean her. He believed that the candidate, as president, would not target "good" immigrants.

"Cecilia had never even gotten a traffic ticket. I never imagined she would be considered a 'bad hombre.'"

Jason assured her that the US government wasn't interested in them. But early in 2017, it was clear he was mistaken: "Cecilia had been lumped into the same category of felon as a drug dealer or known member of MS-13."

---

8. *Roe v. Wade* was the landmark 1973 decision of the US Supreme Court that upheld a woman's legal right to seek and obtain an abortion. Conservatives have been trying to overturn the protection ever since. They finally succeeded on June 24, 2022.

With her next ICE appointment and work permit renewal coming up in November, Jason and Cecilia faced a no-win situation: "If she went, she risked being arrested and deported on the spot. If she didn't, we all risked the possibility of ICE agents knocking down our door," recalls Jason.

Ashton was only four years old. Cecilia would do anything to shield him from the trauma of seeing his mother being shackled and hauled away. She and Jason sought legal counsel. They were advised that if Cecilia agreed to "voluntary departure," she could avoid a deportation order, and re-start the process of becoming a legal citizen from Mexico, and immigrate "the right way" under the long-standing scheme that privileges family reunification.

But Trump & Co even took "the right way" away. Leaning on the 1952 Immigration and Nationality Act, they penalized not one's unlawful acts, but one's "unlawful presence" in the US. After Cecilia told Ashton, "Mommy will be back soon," and returned to Mexico, her attorney shared the bad news that she was barred from coming back to her son, in perpetuity.

Once again, uninformed lawyering bumped into racialized legislation.

Jason, Cecilia, and Ashton's story is hardly uncommon. More than one in ten individuals living in the US without legal status is married to a US citizen, according to the Migration Policy Institute. Nearly a third of these are parenting US-citizen children under the age of eighteen.

Since January 2018, however, Cecilia has been mothering Ashton via FaceTime. Even when, a year later, five-year-old Ashton was diagnosed with kidney cancer and had to undergo surgery, chemo, and radiation therapy, the Trump administration refused Cecilia the possibility of returning under humanitarian parole.

She wasn't even allowed to enter the US temporarily to nurse her gravely ill child.

||||||||||||||||||||||||||||||||||||||||||||||||||||||

As Jodi Goodwin said, "A body politic that will separate families will stop at nothing." Even immigrants who come to the US "the right way" wait in a long, invisible line to adjust their status, during which time they are denied the freedom to visit the families they left behind. As a result, their children will never know their extended relations. They are the link broken: Family Separation 8.0.

But Lizee couldn't tell Marta any of this. Recognizing the devastation and regret on her face, hearing in Marta's words her desire to believe she'd done the right thing, all Lizee could do was console the bereaved mother. So, she powered up her lovely, calming, awe-inspiring smile and she did what anyone with a heart would do: she gave the mother hope.

With me, however, Lizee could crack. "If I hadn't taken a day at home, I could have stopped them," she said, forcing back tears.

Lizee wasn't always an activist. But when she heard the infamous recording of Trump & Co's tiniest victims, crying out for their missing parents, reciting an auntie's phone number while detained in her hometown of McAllen, it woke her up.

"I realized then, if I don't act to stop these crimes against humanity, I'm complicit."

CHAPTER TWENTY-FOUR

The Gulag

Summoning my father's perennial advice, delivered from a place of white male privilege, to "just act like you own the place," I turned right off Brownsville's Ruben M. Torres Boulevard to try to get a look inside the infamous Walmart turned child-detention center. It had become a national flashpoint in 2018, when Trump & Co promised Southwest Key another $458 million to scale up. Despite the hundreds of violations attributed to Southwest Key's twenty-six facilities nationwide, under fire for lax hiring and vetting procedures that led to sexual and other abusive misconduct, more bed space was needed to accommodate the children torn from their loved ones under zero tolerance.

In 2020, this boys-only kids' jail may well have been where Pedro was taken after turning himself over to Customs and Border Protection. I wanted to see it for myself.

A yellow and brown sentry hut and speed bump made it impossible to blow right past the security detail. As I slowed, a woman about my height and shaped like a square in her high-visibility vest stepped right out in front of my rented Kia Sorento, signaling me with her hand to "Halt." I stomped on the brakes. Expressionless, she gestured for me to roll down the window.

This time calling forth my father's mastery of sweet-talking bullshit, I flashed the sunniest of smiles as I sent the window glass gliding into the doorframe.

"Can I help you?" she asked with a scowl, seeing right through my faux-friendly posture.

"I'm just here to do some shopping," I said, switching from owning the place to playing dumb blonde.

"There is nothing to buy here, ma'am."

"This isn't Walmart?"

"No, ma'am, it is not. Put your car in reverse and kindly back out." She cocked an arm at the elbow and began thrusting it forward and back, forward and back, like a traffic cop, her index and middle fingers pointing toward the four-lane commercial highway.

"Back into oncoming traffic? That looks dangerous," I responded. "Surely you don't want me to get into an accident. I'll just pull up ahead and make a U-turn."

I punched the accelerator before she could say "No." But I didn't immediately turn. I headed deep into the crowded parking lot, because I knew I could. I snapped photos of the facility with my iPhone as I rolled, and I didn't care if anyone saw me do so.

The building resembled the ubiquitous big-box store in shape only. The characteristic blue highlighted by a yellow starburst had been replaced with the same yellow/brown palette of my greeter's hut. The name SOUTHWEST KEY PROGRAMS CASA PADRE replaced the Walmart logo, topped with the bright orange half-sun branding of the highest-earning "tender age" shelter operator, whose CEO Juan Sanchez was pocketing $1.5 million a year.

Before banking left to carve a slow, wide arc back to the sentry, I glanced in my rearview mirror. I saw two security guards come bursting through the facility's front doors as I steered the Kia toward the exit. Of course I knew that no one except employees with ironclad non-disclosure agreements and detained individuals ever got inside. Not even members of Congress. Senator Merkley had been turned away when he tried to visit in June 2018. He was able to force the company's hand, however, leading to a few strictly monitored tours for a limited number of congressional delegates, child health advocates, and media representatives. The pictures that turn up in a Google Image search of Casa Padre today are few—all taken then, at the climax of Trump & Co's family separation debacle. They show that at the entrance, under a black-and-white stencil of Trump, was this quote: "Sometimes by losing a battle you find a new way to win the war."

I wish I were making that up.

As I rolled back to the hut and the exit beyond, the square sentry blocked my path again and the two burly uniformed guards approached my car on each side from behind, like cops expecting a threat.

"Good morning," said the one to my left. "Please be advised that this lot is for authorized personnel only."

"Yes. I get it now," I said, meeting his eye. "This is that kids jail, isn't it?"

Silence.

"How do you feel about working for a company that incarcerates children?" I asked. I really wanted to know.

He stepped behind the car, jotting down the Kia's license plate number as I continued toward Ruben M. Torres Boulevard. As soon as I hit my first red light, I texted Tía Cindy: "Can you get me into a detention center?"

She responded within seconds: "I can't," she wrote. "But Tía Madeleine can."

Tía Madeleine calls herself "an accidental activist." Yet, she has been at the forefront of many social justice causes since her arrival in South Texas in 1969. She's a voting rights advocate, an environmentalist and birding enthusiast, and a fundraiser for Alzheimer's research. She helped to organize Brownsville's January 2017 Women's March. She and Tía Joyce mounted the June 14, 2018, rally against family separation that resulted in her becoming the fifth Angry Tía. Because she lives just miles away from the Port Isabel Detention Center, where Border Protection officials were then sending the parents of seized children, that became Tía Madeleine's "beat."

Her role back then was to provide hope to the anguished mothers and to connect them with lawyers, like Jodi Goodwin and ProBAR's Kimi Jackson, who were tirelessly—and without pay—trying to track down the kids that had been kidnapped by Uncle Sam. To do that, Madeleine had to school up quickly on Trump & Co's shape-shifting anti-immigrant agenda, making her the Tías' expert in all matters related to detention.

By the time I arrived in the Rio Grande Valley in 2020, the Port Isabel jail contained only men—fifteen hundred of them. They slept seventy to a dorm in bunk beds spaced three feet apart. There were only four toilets per dorm, though at least one was always a clogged, stinking eyesore. The toilets had no privacy doors.

Tía Madeleine focused her energy on the safety seekers among the incarcerated, distinguishable from those imprisoned on criminal charges only by their blue prison-issued jumpsuits. All others wore red or orange. The "inmates" were made to buy their own soap, at inflated commissary prices. They were fed often spoiled, always nutrition-deficient food, "just enough calories to keep them alive," says Madeleine, who then as now adds money to their commissary accounts monthly for ramen and other processed foodstuff.

Madeleine comforts the men by phone or text when their anxieties spike or when they lose hope. She secures legal counsel for the unrepresented, raises bond money, and is always available to ferry those released from jail to the first bus or plane that will get them out of Texas. She refers to them as "my boys." They all call her "mama," "mummy," and "maman."

Madeleine presents a surprising package. Her petite, soft-spoken stature masks a fierce dedication to justice. A naturalized immigrant herself, she's now standing up to the very system that once showed her welcome.

"What moved you to take on such a Sisyphean challenge?" I asked her.

"Because what's happening in this country today is not what I signed onto when I became a US citizen."

The rule for non-lawyers in January 2020 was one inmate per visit. But on learning that I speak French—a rare find in the Rio Grande Valley—Tía Madeleine passed me the A#s of three safety seekers from former French-colonized West Africa, "Just in case the guards are feeling generous." They were all in dire need of human contact, she said; even if such contact, she warned, would be through a thick plexiglass barrier and over a 20th-century-style corded telephone with a crackling receiver speaker.

Having already been denied entry to Casa Padre, I checked my expectations as I wound my way up the long, landscaped drive of the national wildlife refuge in which Port Isabel Detention Center hides—a collection of low-slung brick structures circumscribed by razor wire–topped chain-link fencing rising out of the Port Isabel wetlands. The silver barbs glistened in the sunlight—out of place under this flight path for myriad bird species.

I parked the Kia, locking my iPhone, notebook, and mechanical pencil into the glove compartment, per Madeleine's instructions. I stopped to read the plaque affixed to a stone monument placed where the lot met the entry walkway. It dedicated the site to the victims of 9/11.

I spat out a sarcastic laugh. My friend Dave Fontana sprang instantly to mind. He died that day, alongside eleven other members of New York Fire Department Squad Company 1, as I watched the North Tower implode and collapse in a cloud of dust from my Brooklyn rooftop. Dave would not have appreciated having a place that robbed peaceful people of their freedom dedicated to his memory. He would not have wanted to be associated with the corruption and human rights abuses documented in former Port Isabel prison guard Tony Hefner's 2011 memoir, *Between the Fences*. He would not have liked learning that a 2015 report by the US Commission on Civil Rights found that in its quest for ever higher profits, the prison operator, Ahtna Support and Training Services, regularly put at risk the health, safety, and Fifth Amendment rights of immigrants caught in its grasp.

I emptied my pockets of coins and car keys and passed through metal detectors. I spread-eagled my legs and arms for the obligatory wanded pat-down. I received nothing but polite interaction from my khaki-clad minders, who handed over my change, but placed my keys in a metal locker and slammed it shut. I would get them back on departure.

I approached a clerk's security window and pushed three forms through the gap between glass and narrow laminate counter, each one filled out with the A#s of the men I'd come to see. Again pressing my privilege, I asked the guard behind the bulletproof plexiglass to kindly grant me an exception to the one-inmate rule: I was just passing through, I told him, all the way from London, I added. This would be my only chance to visit.

He made no promises, inviting me to take a seat in the antiseptic waiting room where rows of hard-backed, scoop-seated metal chairs stood bolted into a cold, gray cement floor. A reverse ATM machine—allowing visitors to deposit money *into* detainee accounts for overpriced commissary purchases, like the soap the prison refused to provide—nestled up against a vending machine offering bottled water, sodas, candy, and junk food. Above them, a single soundless television monitor projected *The Hunger Games*—a coincidence, surely, but also a way too obvious metaphor for the bizarre world I'd entered.

Stripped of phone, paper, and pencil, I had nothing to do to pass the time but stare at the muted transmission of the Mockingjay's struggle against The Capitol. My mind scrolled back through all the dystopian films of my youth, landing on those set in or around 2020: The year after "the future" envisioned in *Blade Runner*, *Akira*, and *Running Man*; a few decades past the world of *Escape from New York*; still two years away from "It's people! It's people!" *Soylent Green*, starring five-term president of the National Rifle Association Charleton Heston paired with the outspoken critic of fascism and Nazism, Edward G. Robinson. But none of these films portrayed a darkness as banal as what I encountered at Port Isabel Detention Center, where freedom-seeking refugees were locked up, no matter who sat behind the Resolute Desk, no matter which party controlled Congress. Orwell's *1984* struck me as more apropos; or Terry Gillian's *Brazil*.

Located just a few flaps of a migratory bird's wings away from the tourist beaches of South Padre Island and roughly thirty miles north of the two-thousand-mile humanitarian crisis that stretched from Matamoros to Tijuana, the Port Isabel Detention Center provided the key to my expanding witness. I understood instantly that Trump & Co's manufactured border crisis was not limited to the south side of the line, out of sight and out of mind for most of us to the north. Indeed, the crisis was out of sight and out of mind on our side, too, in this cancer of human captivity, where people innocent of any crime are locked up and tucked away from prying eyes, sometimes for years.

Looking back toward the security gauntlet I'd just been made to pass through, I suddenly realized that no one person resembled the

"Good Ol' Boy" jailer of my imagination. The prison guards looked much like the imprisoned.

"In the poorest counties in the United States, the best-paying jobs are with ICE, the Border Patrol, or some other iteration of law enforcement," Michael Seifert told me when I brought my surprise to him. Michael served the residents of borderlands colonias for twenty-three years as a Roman Catholic priest. He personally knows dozens of US-citizen children of undocumented residents who grew up in miserable poverty only to become Border Patrol agents. It's common, he says, to find Border Patrol and military recruiters behind desks in high schools throughout the border region.

"The money, the job security, the social status of wearing a uniform and carrying a weapon—it all goes a long, sad way to erasing all of the other deficits of being a child of a Mexican immigrant," he says.

At Port Isabel, the phenomenon is not limited to the regional population: the prison is part of a portfolio of businesses run by an Alaska-native shareholder-owned corporation.

I may have been watching *The Hunger Games*, but I was in *The Matrix*—another member of the cast, or "caste" as Isabel Wilkerson would spell it, in a world where abnormal is made normal; where injustice is made to look just. And where a machinery "whose purpose is maintaining the primacy of those hoarding and holding tight to power" commits atrocities that are brushed off as collateral damage, as unavoidable.

‖‖‖

I waited an hour. Finally, a heavy bolt turned, a metal fire door opened, and a youthful Latinx guard beckoned me inside. He ushered me down a long, cheerless hallway of two-toned gray-on-gray walls, then through another imposing door leading into a large, windowless room painted yet a darker shade of gray and carved up by mirror-image cubicles. Within each open-backed cubicle, white facing tables, three feet wide by two feet deep, were split in two by transparent plexiglass barriers that rose to the ceiling. I felt as though I had stepped inside a fun-fair maze of repeating mirrors. The fluorescent lighting buzzed in my ears like angry bees. And just as pictured in every prison movie you've ever seen, the headset of a gray phone sat perched in a cradle bolted onto the perpendicular partition wall to the right, also painted gray.

There, in this room of white-accented gray and no natural light, I met "Manny" and "Keith" from Guinea, as well as "Valery." Though hailing from majority French-speaking Cameroon, Valery was an English speaker—part of the minority Anglophone population targeted for persecution in a country, then as now, gripped by intractable civil strife. He was new to Port Isabel. He'd been there for only three months. But he was lonely, according to Madeleine, and bursting to tell his story.

None of the three men could safely go home again. Yet, in Trump's USA, they were not viewed as humans, but detritus from "shit hole countries." They were well and truly stuck.

Manny became a marked man when the opposition candidate he'd worked to bring to power in 2015—the second democratic presidential election since Guinea gained independence from France in 1958—lost to the incumbent strongman amid claims of fraud and election mismanagement. Following the contested electoral outcome, Guinea experienced a dramatic spike in violence. High-profile opposition leaders were targeted for persecution. Manny was secreted out of the country, where he commenced the long journey to find safe haven.

When I met him, his imprisonment in the US was approaching three years. Port Isabel Detention Center was the seventh ICE prison to detain him, and one of the worst by his account. If returned to Guinea, he told me, slack shouldered, he'd be taken from the airport on arrival and executed. Denied books to read and paper to write on, he passed the long days making wallets out of trash. He gifted one to me.

Keith was born into a country that considers any expression of LGBTQIA+ identity both a punishable sin and a crime. When the man he loved was found out, community members dragged him through the streets and stoned him to death. Keith ran, certain his neighbors were coming for him next. He got away, living in the shadows for months before finally setting off in search of safety.

Keith had been inside Port Isabel for nearly two years and he was distraught. The appeal of his rejected asylum claim had been denied the previous day for lack of hard evidence. Keith's pro bono lawyer felt his case was worth appealing again, which meant imprisonment in the US for many more months to come. Meanwhile, ICE was hounding him to sign his own deportation papers.

His choices were to remain locked up under ICE, indefinitely, or return to probable death. Keith spent the entirety of our interview shrieking, "Aidez-moi! Aidez-moi!"—*Help me! Help me!*—into the crackling phone. I've never felt more impotent in all my life.

Valery hailed from bilingual, bicultural Cameroon, whose constitutional promise of equality for its French- and English-speaking peoples had been betrayed immediately upon independence in 1961. The fall of 2016 saw Anglophone lawyers and teachers take to the streets to protest nearly sixty years of marginalization and the extraction of their country's resources for the sole benefit of the Francophone population, while they went without adequate hospitals, schools, and roads. Though the demonstrations were peaceful, joined first by students then whole families, Cameroon President Paul Biya—in office since 1982—responded with force. Tanks rolled into Anglophone towns. The elite troops and paramilitary forces trained by French, Israeli, and US advisors, patrolled the streets. Military checkpoints went up. All English speakers were considered guilty until proven innocent, especially young men.

Sitting proud and tall, Valery explained to me the part he played in the Cameroonian equivalent of the US Civil Rights Movement. For this, he was targeted for persecution. He was arrested, detained, and tortured. Once released, Valery became the target of the Amba Boys: those Anglophones who'd eschewed nonviolent struggle. Assuming he'd won his freedom from Biya's goons by naming names, they went after Valery, too. If returned to Cameroon before the resolution of the conflict, he doubted he would make it out of the airport alive: "There's no telling which side will tear me apart first."

* * *

One by one, I learned their stories, both harrowing and heroic, of fleeing certain death back home and enduring a monthslong marathon pursuit of freedom, during which their lives were further threatened and their wallets exploited at every turn. Though one and all entered legally, requesting freedom from persecution at a recognized port of entry, they were shocked to be shackled in five-point restraints and transported, enchained, to jail, locked up under punishing conditions in the "Land of the Free" after surviving not just the trek through Mexico, but a sixty-mile bottleneck through hell on earth, too.

It is now that I admit that I only learned of the dreaded and perilous Darién Gap trail on that January day in 2020. I have since heard countless accounts, and have recorded many—mostly of people now in hiding back in their homelands after being refouled by agents acting on behalf of the US federal government.

"HOWARD": *My family decided that, for my safety, I should leave Cameroon. I would fly to Ecuador, because it was then a visa free country. I left Douala and traveled by land to Benin, then to Nigeria. From there I flew through Dubai, Argentina, Peru, finally landing in Quito, [Ecuador]. I stayed at Big Mama House Hotel. A lady at the hotel advised me how to get to the US. She made all the arrangements. She assured me it would be easy. It was not easy.*

"GODSWILL": *From Quito I crossed Ecuador, over land into Colombia. From there, I traveled by boat into Panama, where I entered the Darién jungle.*

"OSCAR": *We each paid Colombian traffickers $250 to take us by boat across a bay that is part of the Caribbean Sea. The journey we were told would take five to six hours. It took three days. A storm capsized the boat, and we had to hang on for our lives until the driver could get it under control. Three adults and one child died.*

GODSWILL: *Believe me, no one travels that route if they don't have to. The trail is littered with the dead—men, women, and children. The traffickers take your money and lie about how much food and water you should bring. Sometimes they just leave you in there. It's very easy to get turned around in the jungle. When the rains come, the river rises quickly with a force able to carry you away.*

OSCAR: *The jungle is so dense with trees that it's impossible to see more than fifteen meters ahead. It's easy for the slow ones to get lost. And they do. It is a world where dead people talk.*

I traveled with Indians, Nepalese, Ghanaians, Nigerians, Cubans, and Cameroonians. Climbing and descending hills and valleys, my legs grew weak, I had muscle cramps, and blisters. The soil was so slippery, I fell several times. My clothes grew heavy with filth, my skin became covered in bites from mosquitoes, ants, centipedes. The group just before us was attacked by bandits who stripped them of their money and phones. They raped the women.

One day in the Darién, I was out of water and so anxious to quench my thirst, I knelt in the mud to drink from a river. Oh my God, lying just about ten feet from me was the corpse of a Black man already half-decayed.

"JOEL": *I saw many people die in the jungle: by hunger, lack of medicine, mosquitoes, drinking bad water, drowning. I will never forget it as long as I live. We spent close to $200 each to be guided through, stepping over the dead. But we were the lucky ones. We made it.*

We finally arrived in Matamoros on March 1, 2019. I asked for asylum, but I was turned away. I was given a number and made to wait, forced to sleep on the street for one month and ten days in this very dangerous border town. I would have died of cold and hunger if it were not for Team Brownsville, who fed me and gave me a tent.

I finally was allowed to enter the United States on April 9, 2019. I was so tired and so happy. My mum and older sister were waiting for me in Little Elm, Texas. But I was detained: thrown first into a "cold house," then taken to a prison camp near Brownsville, called PIDC.

They chained us! I never knew about that. I said, "I'm not a criminal." I started crying, really shedding tears. I had no idea why. No idea what was happening.

GODSWILL: *At the time, I thought crossing the Darién was the hardest thing I would ever have to do in my life. But that was before I met US ICE.*

"RAY": *I was brought up to believe that the United States was a land of laws where human rights were valued and respected and where I could request asylum from the persecution I had suffered back home. It was a lie. They imprisoned me for nearly three years. And then they sent me back. In chains. To die.*

That day, Tía Madeleine provided me a peek inside the US immigrant-detention gulag: the largest for-profit prison system for non-criminals in the world. What began in 1980 as an Emergency Influx Shelter in a decommissioned missile defense site in Krome, Florida, managed by the Federal Emergency Management Agency, has metastasized into a living, breathing many-headed Hydra that needs constant nourishment.

Its fodder, as in *Soylent Green*, is people.

Its fertilizer, as in *The Hunger Games*, is dehumanization.

Its method of survival is manufacturing fear and loathing of a convenient "folk devil." In this case, the so-called "alien invaders coming for your wives and daughters and jobs," who include doctors, lawyers, translators and teachers, former government officials who exposed corruption, and tiny babies.

Its mouthpiece is the Tanton network propaganda machine, with its disinformation "think tanks" and institutions, like FAIR, the Center for Immigration Studies, and the cult of Fox News and Breitbart, which highlight and regurgitate *ad infinitum* the lies of Tanton network disciples, who now include governors, members of Congress, attorneys general, and others inside the US judiciary, not to mention the 45th US president.

These folks love to squawk about how migrants are a strain on local economies. But the business of jailing migrating children and adults is a booming business, particularly in Greg Abbott's Texas, Ron DeSantis's Florida, Arizona, California, and throughout the Deep South. From the Reagan era, Corrections Corporation of America (CoreCivic) and the GEO Group knew a cash cow when they saw one, and they are loathe to let it go. According to the Sentencing Project, an advocate for "decarceration," aka the end of prisons in the US, 4,841 immigrants were detained by the US government in 2000. By 2016, that number had soared to 26,249—more than a fivefold increase.

In the early years of the Trump administration, that number doubled again. Keith, Manny, and Valery were among more than 52,000 new arrivals detained in two-hundred-plus prison camps all over the US. Seventy percent of these were operated by profiteers, including GEO Group, CoreCivic, LaSalle Corrections, and Ahtna.

With a worldwide footprint, the GEO Group oversaw approximately 85,000 prison beds in the US in 2020—one out of five, or

19.4 percent, for ICE. The richest prison operator in the world, GEO gained 22 percent of its total revenue that year from ICE contracts. But in 2016, GEO and its closest rival, CoreCivic, faced an existential threat when Congress under Obama–Biden green-lighted the end of privately run detention centers. A scathing Department of Justice review cited shocking conditions: abuses and assaults were rife, including at Port Isabel.

GEO's stock price dropped 6 percent. CoreCivic's fell 9.4 percent. But shareholders were responding not to the human rights abuses. They knew that federal contracts were integral to both companies' revenue model and profitability.

So, their lobbyists got to work, though they didn't have to work too hard. Following a combined contribution of a mere $500,000 to the Trump campaign, the then-candidate began weaving the need for more private prisons into his already polished anti-immigrant rhetoric. The morning after the 2016 election, GEO Group and CoreCivic stock rose 18 percent and 34 percent, respectively.

Once named attorney general, Sessions revoked the Obama administration's prison-reform initiative and began requesting bids from profiteers again. Within a month, GEO Group won a $110 million contract to build the first ICE detention center under the new administration, and moved its annual conference to the Trump-owned Doral resort in Boca Raton, Florida.

Keeping Black and Brown freedom-seekers locked up is considered such big business, one investment analyst recommended putting "GEO Group's 16% yield in solitary confinement deep in your portfolio." Take a look at yours. GEO Group and CoreCivic's biggest shareholders— Vanguard Group, BlackRock, and Fidelity Investments—may well be managing your money.

While ICE doled out $807 million in fiscal year 2018, Trump & Co exploited every gap in congressional legislation that fails to limit detention duration. By 2019, the average stay in a for-profit prison was 87 days, as against the 33.3-day average for immigrants held in publicly run facilities. But Black people seeking asylum, like Manny, Keith, Valery, and myriad others I would speak to through the extortionist GEO Group–controlled phone-calling app, Getting Out, would remain locked up for years. One Nigerian-born man I know was imprisoned by ICE—separated from his wife and kids—for nine years, despite having no criminal record and having established a credible need for protection from persecution.

"This is governmental kidnapping," he told me. "We were kidnapped by ICE and denied our freedom, guarded," in his words, "by sadists. And the Blacker you are, the harder you have it."

Rather than reaching the Beacon of Hope, asylum seekers to the US are trapped in *The Matrix*.

||||||||||||||||||||||||||||||||||||||||||||||||||||||

It had been a long, hard day. But *I* was able to leave.

I pulled into the Texas Roadhouse on I-83E, Frontage Road, for a meal and a beer before returning to my hotel. There, I made the acquaintance of twenty-two-year-old Maria. She was my server and she was captivating. Beautiful and confident, sporting a long, single black braid that dripped down her back, she spoke with me in English, then pivoted on her heels to speak Spanish with the party just adjacent. It was a large, multigenerational group and they appeared to be celebrating. It turns out, they were celebrating her. She had just finished an undergraduate program and this would be her last night waiting tables.

"What did you study?" I asked.

"Criminal justice," she answered. This put her on track to pursue a career as a police, corrections, or ICE deportation officer; a prison warden or coroner; or perhaps she intended to start as a paralegal, if she wasn't directly en route to law school.

So I asked her, "What will you do next?"

"I just signed a contract with Southwest Key." Indeed, that day while at the Port Isabel prison, I had seen an advertisement for a Southwest Key job fair in neighboring Raymondville, Texas. The company was opening yet another jail for kids in yet another emptied former Walmart.

Even in January 2020, the child incarceration industry was still expanding. The year before, the US detained more children away from their parents than in any other country: 69,550. That's enough infants, toddlers, 'tweens, and teens to fill the Dallas Cowboys' home field.

"Why did you choose criminal justice?" I asked her.

"I didn't, really. I was tracked into it as a high school student."

CHAPTER TWENTY-FIVE

Under the Big Top

I now know what a "kangaroo court" is, for I've been to one. Surrounded by a razor wire–topped chain-link fence, intimidating police dogs, armed guards, and surveillance drones, this one sat under a series of circus-style canvas tents that covered a warren of rooms assembled Lego-like from converted shipping containers. A constant thrumming of portable air conditioners pumped frigid gusts into makeshift inter-view and court rooms, as well as waiting areas replete with backless metal benches that were ice-cold to the touch. These were separated, in contrast, by sweaty, airless corridors where asylum seekers and attorneys alike lined up on a rug of faux grass, advancing only when directed by a member of the internal security detail.

Those who'd previously entered the bowels of this cursory nod to jurisprudence wore or carried jackets. Unfortunately, I was dressed for the balmy Texas temperature outside, so my time in each enclosure was spent shivering and blowing warm air into my cold, cupped hands.

This was the second border-hugging immigration tent court to open for business, following the first in Laredo, Texas. The cost to the US taxpayer to raise and operate the two facilities was roughly $155 mil-lion in 2019, monies that were shifted from the Federal Emergency Management Agency and went largely to a private contractor called Deployed Resources, according to *Forbes*. Known for providing tempo-rary solutions in emergency settings as well as for supporting popular music festivals such as Bonnaroo, Lollapalooza, and Firefly, the company that was paid to "establish and operate temporary Migrant Protection

Protocol (MPP) Immigration Hearing Facilities along the Southwest border" also built the child internment camp in Tornillo.

The court I penetrated in Brownsville was built into the Customs and Border Protection parking lot on the US side of the Gateway International Bridge. The canvas structure, shrouded in technology and metallic barriers, shared a driveway with the manicured campus of Texas Southmost College where Team Brownsville's Melba Salazar-Lucio worked as a professor of English. When MPP's bureaucratic wall went up there, the roughly one hundred people seeking asylum but halted in Matamoros by metering were switched automatically into the new program, though they did not know it.

It was a heartbreaking awakening when, on the day their numbers finally came up, Doctor Dairon Rojas and Professor Ray Rodriguez went to the bridge to request asylum. Dairon had been sheltering with his wife in a church, supporting their needs from his meager sweatshop earnings. Ray had been surviving in a tent with his friend and travel companion, Tito. Only then, on the day they expected to lawfully enter the US, did they learn that they would be remaining in Mexico—and for who knew how long.

"I fell to the ground and cried like a baby," recalls Ray.

Asylum applications of southern border arrivals had experienced a nearly fivefold increase between 2014 (31,517) and 2019 (154,368), according to the National Immigration Forum. Staffing at the federal agencies in charge of screening and hearing asylum claims, however, had not kept pace. Depending on the jurisdiction, immigration courts were already backed up by four to six years when MPP began. It was now here, under the Big Top, that their asylum cases would be adjudicated, for having trapped Ray and Dairon south of the line, Trump & Co brought the US immigration courts to them.

They hailed the program—this one the brainchild of Homeland Security Secretary Kirstjen Neilsen—as progressive and innovative. They referred to Mexico as a "non-detained setting," suggesting that living in tents and shelters in some of the most fearsome places on Earth was a positive step up from indefinite detention north of the line. Their tent court complexes, however, were said to be "detained" settings, requiring airport levels of security. As such, press and public were largely barred from the covert goings-on, shielding the border regime and its agency actors, yet again, from scrutiny.

||||||||||||||||||||||||||||||||||||||||||||||||||||||

On my first attempt to get inside, an officer barred my path. Hearings were not open to the public, he stated. But I was welcome to request permission from "headquarters."

"Where is that? And who should I contact?" I asked. He refused to say.

I was not the only person for whom this opacity raised alarms. The American Civil Liberties Union of Texas was well ahead of me, holding court-watch trainings facilitated by now-border advocacy strategist Michael Seifert. He encouraged us to embed with attorneys or members of the press, who'd obtained pre-clearance. So, I approached an immigration lawyer who'd flown in from Washington to meet her new client, "Marisol," on the occasion of her first tent court hearing. An Iranian-born political refugee, the attorney agreed to present me as her translator, though we both knew her Spanish was equal to mine.

By the time we'd passed through metal detectors; waited for a portly guard to approve us for admission; surrendered our passports; and been "invited" to leave our smartphones, cameras, notebooks, pens, and pencils in a lock-box; we had less than thirty minutes to consult with Marisol. That was only enough time for her to express, through anxious tears, the threats she and her baby sons faced every day in Matamoros, where they'd been encamped for nearly two months. The situation in Matamoros was no less dangerous than what they'd fled back home in Honduras, she said. In fact, it was worse: without her husband, she and the kids were especially vulnerable.

Every day my children and I are threatened with kidnapping, she told us. *They say they will take my boys and I will be forced to work in a brothel to get them back.*

Marisol's husband had blazed the trail upon the assassination of his brother by Honduran security forces, which coincided with the birth of the couple's second son. The cops were coming for him next, they said. So he fled, crossing the line at a southern port of entry and requesting asylum before zero tolerance reared its ugly head. Once he was safe and settled in the home of a relative in Maryland, he hired the lawyer to handle the family's asylum case and signaled to Marisol that it was time for her and the boys to follow. But their plan was foiled by Trump's election and his administration's attack on an already beleaguered asylum system, which should have worked like this . . .

||||||||||||||||||||||||||||||||||||||||||||||||||||||||

The first ring in the US asylum protection circus is proving to the government that it shouldn't expel you as quickly as possible. Every safety seeker to the southern border, upon requesting asylum, is supposed to be put directly into "expedited removal" proceedings. To advance to the second circus ring, you must express to an *immigration officer* that you fear persecution if removed or returned—what's known as the "shout test"—and hope the official follows procedure (which they don't always do) by referring you for the required screening: the "credible fear interview." Once inside the second ring, the onus is on you to prove to an *asylum officer* that you will likely suffer harm, even death, if refouled—a challenge further complicated by a perennial staff shortage. Yet, that test must be passed to move to the still stressful but slower-paced third ring, called "removal proceedings." Only in this third circus ring do you get access to the immigration court system; only here are you permitted to file an asylum application; only here can you hope to eventually present your request for protection before an *immigration judge.*

Until a judge hears and decides on the merits of your case, you are protected from expulsion—as long as you don't fall on the wrong side of the law, which is easy to do in a world where misdemeanors can rise to the level of felonies just like that. Only upon the successful conclusion of your asylum claim does your status lift from asylum seeker to the official designation of protected refugee, opening up a pathway to apply for US citizenship, all of which can take years. And where you must wait for the opportunity to plead your case while in the US asylum circus is highly unpredictable, made more so by Trump & Co.

You could be released to join your husband in Maryland, for

example, with a "Notice to Appear" in the nearest immigration court and your leg weighed down by a stigmatizing GPS-enabled ankle bracelet. Another revenue stream for GEO Group, these monitoring devices are notorious for burning the skin, causing swelling, and creating wounds that cannot be easily cleaned. Their heft makes sleeping difficult and has left many a wearer with a lifelong limp. They lose charge quickly, which sets them off beeping, making for always embarrassing situations if they start screaming in public. And though being phased out by less-physically damaging smartphone device tracking, living under full-time surveillance has been likened by many to a "virtual prison" as you can be located, snatched, and detained by ICE at any time. It exacts a mental and emotional toll.

Still, it's better than the alternative: being shackled, handed over to ICE, and made to wait your turn to plead your case to a judge in chains and a prison jumpsuit.

If enrolled in MPP, as Marisol was in November 2019, you would be made to wait in northern Mexico, even though the data then showed that asylum-seeking families with access to legal representation complied with immigration court obligations 98 percent of the time. Trump & Co said without evidence, or using spurious statistics prepared by Tanton network–linked organizations, that they didn't. So, they created MPP and commenced their takedown of asylum by one thousand cuts, while tapping the age-old eugenicist tropes—of "surges" and "tsunamis" of "invading criminal hordes," "flooding" the border to whip up fears of such "folk devils" as Professor Ray, Dr. Dairon, Marisol, and her tiny sons.

⁓⁓⁓

When Marisol arrived at the US border, she followed internationally recognized procedures for requesting refuge in El Norte: She presented herself to Customs and Border Protection officials at the Gateway International Bridge. She asked for protection from harm, citing a credible fear of return to her homeland with evidence tucked into a folder stashed in the handbag hooked under an arm. She provided her husband's and attorney's names as well as the address of her intended destination.

She and her boys should have been paroled into the US right there and then, placed in "expedited removal" proceedings, given a Notice to Appear with the address of the ICE office and nearest federal court in her Maryland jurisdiction, and sent on their way. But in Trump's USA, the ability to immigrate had become a crapshoot, a lottery without a ticket.

Marisol was ordered to remain in Mexico and sent back to Matamoros with her babies and a court date. Since then, she'd been stuck in a place closer to hell than purgatory where Human Rights First would document nearly ten thousand instances of kidnapping, rape, and other assaults against safety seekers stranded in Mexico by mid-2022. That's one in seven people seeking asylum, and wishing to immigrate the "right" way, subjected to violent harm as a result of MPP. And given folks' fear of speaking up in places where "the cartel has ears" and the murdered cannot talk, the researchers, themselves, maintain that ten thousand was a vast undercount.

<hr />

Finally, the day of Marisol's first hearing had come. As it was scheduled for 8:30 a.m., Border Protection officials instructed her to join the queue on the Mexican side before dawn. This required her to navigate the streets of Matamoros in the pitch dark with two little boys, for there was no one in Mexico to whom she could entrust their care.

Holding babies and toddlers, propping up the less-abled and elderly, the people on the tent court docket that morning stood in orderly single file well before the sun peeked over the Texas horizon. They were tired but hopeful, believing their turn for justice had come. As 8:30 a.m. approached, federal officers ushered them through the border checkpoint on the Brownsville side of the bridge and into the Customs and Border Protection offices. From there, they entered the Big Top via a back door, all the while under armed guard.

Marisol's lawyer and I entered through the front. By the time we met mother and sons, they had been on their feet for hours. Marisol's one-year-old was draped heavily over her left shoulder, fast asleep. She gripped her three-year-old's hand tightly in hers. His complaints of hunger and exhaustion threatened to hijack the already-truncated initial meeting.

The only "food" among us was a Milky Way bar the lawyer found buried at the bottom of her purse. It calmed the little boy for a time. But the sugar rush eventually whipped him up again before a displeased judge.

Despite the fact that Marisol and her sons had been living for two months in a tent and prepared for court in the middle of the night, the boys were smartly dressed in clean and pressed white button-down shirts, blue slacks, and mini man-like loafers. Marisol was freshly coiffed and remarkably well pulled together in a fitted beige skirt secured with a leather belt into which she'd tucked a long-sleeved floral blouse. We complimented her outfit. She said she'd splurged on it out of respect for the process.

〃〃〃〃〃〃〃〃〃〃〃〃〃〃〃〃〃〃〃〃〃〃〃〃〃〃〃〃〃〃〃

Though only Marisol's *master-calendar hearing*—the start of the asylum screening process and when the *merits hearing* can be scheduled—she and her lawyer were hopeful that mother and sons would be paroled this day into the US. Marisol's case was a slam dunk, her lawyer told me without going into confidential details. In addition to legal representation, she had support in place and a home to go to as well as hard evidence to back up the family's persecution claim. She was separated from her husband with two small kids, and US legal precedent dating back decades should have privileged family unification. In a "normal" world all these factors would have provided the keys to unlock the multi-bolted door and send them on their way.

But things didn't go as planned.

For starters, US immigration judges are not Senate vetted and confirmed specialists in this area of the law. They are Department of Justice employees—many political appointees, including former ICE attorneys trained to argue for denial and removal. What's more, MPP court judges weren't even there. They were beamed into the shipping container courtrooms from far-flung places via teleconferencing, and by design: for seeing asylum applicants on-screen, rather than in person, further reduces their humanity. Over TV, there can be no eye contact that might stir empathy; there is little hope that the tear dripping down a traumatized cheek will be seen. And the stories that bodies communicate are much harder to perceive in 2-D.

In addition, the judges were swamped, processing forty to fifty asylum claims per session, or "docket," and handling two dockets per day. This was two to three times the number of cases they would otherwise be assigned, the president of the National Association of Immigration Judges, Ashley Tabaddor, told the *Texas Observer* in 2019.

"The sheer volume of cases that judges are being assigned," she stated was "[an] unsustainable demand." One judge famously described the job as akin to "holding death penalty cases in a traffic court setting."

The odds were certainly not in Marisol's favor. The number of positive asylum rulings under MPP amounted to 1.1 percent—732 individuals out of 67,694 cases—or 1 in every 100 requests. And even these so-called winners had to suffer through an average of five tent-court hearings spaced out over the course of eight months.

|||||||||||||||||||||||||||||||||||||||||||||||||||||||||

On the day I went to tent court, Judge Barbara Cigarroa loomed over our frigid shipping-container courtroom via a large-screen TV from an immigration court building in Port Isabel. A lawyer representing the US government was also present, but in voice only. Neither her face nor that of the court-appointed Spanish–English interpreter could be seen. Their speech was barely audible on our side of what was looking more and more like a reality TV show in which no interpreter role had been cast for the speakers of Guatemala's indigenous languages.

By the time of my visit in January 2020, 5,596 cases had been reviewed and concluded under the MPP Big Top. Just 81 of these had been supported by a lawyer, according to tracking by Syracuse University. Less than 2 percent of those seeking asylum who'd been forced to remain in Mexico had legal representation—a statistic that was alive and well in Courtroom C that day where only two individuals before Judge Cigarroa had a lawyer present: Marisol and Professor Ray. Everyone else was left to navigate on their own the highly complex US asylum process, in an inhospitable environment, through a tongue they did not understand, over TV.

By concentrating cases that would otherwise have been spread across the country into border-based tent courts, Trump & Co knew they were unfairly stacking the odds against people. Everyone knew. Border cities claim relatively few immigration attorneys, and many of them were reluctant to play party to what was an obvious affront to due process. Indeed, the potential for error was staggering. The crowded temporary courtroom complex was not conducive to recounting personal stories of persecution, abuse, or desperate escape. Even those who'd been placed into MPP who did have attorneys struggled to keep calls privileged back in Mexico, if they could make contact at all. Preparing, exchanging, and signing documents would have been impossible in Matamoros were it not for the law office Charlene D'Cruz established.

ıllllllllllllllllllllllllllllllllllllllllllllllllllllllllllllll

It was a sham; it was theater, posing as jurisprudence; a dystopian, Kafkaesque travesty of justice that hopped—like a kangaroo—right over legal due process; another arrow in the quiver of "prevention through deterrence." In the words of Trump's third and now-merely "acting" Homeland Security secretary, Kevin McAleenan,[9] "This will deter people who don't have valid asylum claims and allow us to get to those who do have valid claims more quickly."

In going for "a more expeditious process," McAleenan & Co disadvantaged non-English speakers without access to counsel, forcing them to face off with government attorneys they couldn't even see, who were trained to argue for their removal. Expediency exacerbated, rather than minimized, the chances that vulnerable people were returned to places where they'd suffered persecution. And it wasn't all that different for those trapped in the US immigration gulag, according to Texas A&M University Law Professor Fatma E. Marouf.

"It used to be that all those requesting asylum at a port of entry were paroled out," she states, "but under Trump more than 90 percent were detained."

---

9. Trump eventually sidestepped the Senate-based process of vetting and confirming Cabinet-level secretaries. He leaned on existing legal authority that allows appointees to assume their roles as "acting" officials until their congressional confirmation is realized. But he made this temporary status effectively permanent, awarding himself the "flexibility" to send packing anyone who displeased him. McAleenan was the fourth of five homeland security secretaries to serve during Trump's four years; the second of three to hold the role in this unvetted, unconfirmed, "acting" capacity.

Following the rollout of zero tolerance, asylum hearings were similarly conducted en masse by judges beamed in or brought into immigration prisons. In some situations, detainees were bused to federal courtrooms to make their bid for protection dressed in prison jumpsuits and bound in five-point restraints. And whereas in criminal court, guards almost always un-cuff petitioners' hands when in front of the judge, "they don't remove the shackles in immigration court," says Fatma.

"As an attorney, I can ask that my client's hands, at least, be unshackled. But it is up to the judges' discretion, and they often say no. So, asylum seekers can't take notes on their case or anything."

Virtually no one seeking asylum without representation fares well under these conditions. "And keep in mind," Fatma stresses, "being present in the US without authorization is not a crime."

‖‖‖

When our turn finally came, Marisol's lawyer requested that her client be given a non-refoulement interview. Only a positive non-refoulement interview with an asylum officer would keep mother and sons out of Mexico and allow them to pursue their claim with her husband in their Maryland jurisdiction, as was standard practice pre-Trump. It was the last ticket remaining to both attorney and client, and it was golden: for under the Big Top only about 5 percent of non-refoulement interviews were then being approved. The lawyer needed to convince Judge Cigarroa of both the danger of sending Marisol back to Matamoros as well as the logic of reuniting her separated family.

The judge granted the non-refoulement interview request. But she also had Marisol's lawyer and me promptly removed to await its conclusion on the other side of the razor-wire fortified fence. Marisol was not allowed to prepare for the critical procedure to come. There was not even an attempt at transparency. Secrecy was at the heart of all things.

The next thing we knew, Marisol and the boys were back in Mexico, unable to explain what happened. Depressed and despondent, her mind began spinning worst-case scenarios: *If I am to be sent back to Honduras, I prefer that my children go to the US. Even if they kill me, I don't care. As long as my boys are OK.*

She'd arrived at having to consider the now common Sophie's Choice.

At least six other women seeking asylum in court that day articulated fears of returning to Mexico—two others cited kidnapping or forced prostitution threats, like Marisol. But all were sent back to the encampment before Team Brownsville showed up with dinner.

|||||||||||||||||||||||||||||||||||||||||||||||||||||||

As I drove back to my hotel that evening, a report came in over the local radio station that unleashed sobs buried deep within my core: thirty-something-year-old Jesús García Serna had requested asylum at the Customs and Border Protection office on the Reynosa-Pharr bridge in Texas. He insisted that his life was at stake, that he was hunted by criminal gangs. He pleaded that if made to remain in Mexico, he would be tortured and killed.

At about 5:00 p.m. that day, his insistence that he be allowed to pursue asylum in the US flatly denied, Jesús began to make his way back across the bridge. Just a few feet past the international boundary into Mexico, he stopped. He drew a knife from a pocket, reached up to his neck, and slit his own throat. By the time US federal agents reached him, Jesús was dead, lying in a pool of his own blood.

I pulled into the hotel parking lot feeling drained, feeble, impotent. Tears streamed down my face, which I was too tired to wipe away. My phone pinged. It was Tía Cindy.

"Pass it on," read the brief message she forwarded via WhatsApp. A link to a PDF popped onto the screen. With a tap, it opened to a press release, announcing a vigil to be held in Xeriscape Park, just across from Trump & Co's Kangaroo Court, until MPP was terminated and the right to asylum restored in the US. The vigil was to launch that weekend on January 12, 2020. I messaged Cindy right back. "C U there."

Scrolling through my newsfeed before drifting off to sleep that night, I noticed a World Health Organization announcement that a mysterious and highly contagious pneumonia-like virus was wreaking havoc on the population of Wuhan, China. Several of my Nanjing University students were from Wuhan. I fell asleep thinking about them, hoping they weren't among the fifty-nine people hospitalized at that time.

CHAPTER TWENTY-SIX

No Place for Kids

The crowd was already buzzing by the time I arrived at Xeriscape Park on the morning of January 12. Located across the street from the Kangaroo Court and just steps from the Border Protection offices on the north side of the Gateway International Bridge, it was the perfect spot from which to mount a visible, long-term vigil. A municipal signpost at the park's entrance, welcoming arrivals from Mexico, set a caring, inclusive vibe. The park's palm trees and scattered concrete benches offered a pleasant place to find respite from the Texas sun. And with the Brownsville bus station just across International Boulevard, there was no need to rent potties.

Amongst the now familiar faces of RGV humanitarians—Team Brownsville's Andrea Rudnik and Sergio Cordova; Tías Lizee, Susan, Cindy, and Joyce—were many people I had yet to meet. They'd come to bear witness from as near as Austin and as far as Anchorage. The League of United Latin American Citizens, LULAC, arrived en masse from neighboring San Benito. The Carbon Trace crew returned from Missouri. And members of such organizations as Reunite Migrant Families and Grannies Respond/*Abuelas Responden* had flown in from various points north. I thought I might win the prize for farthest flung, but that accolade went to a woman from Italy.

Most came bearing protest posters, their corners flapping in the cool breeze of this cloudless day. They held messages that really hit home: PEOPLE ARE NOT ILLEGAL one read; another stated SECRET COURTS ≠ DUE PROCESS. A double-sided sign of a pair of eyes stapled around a long pole stood head and shoulders above the gathering assembly, reminding us that WE ARE WITNESSES TO AMERICA'S SHAMEFUL PRESENT. A witness from Seattle wore an olive-green jacket with a message hand-painted in white on the back in a nod to Melania Trump: WE CARE Y DON'T U?

I recognized Joshua Rubin instantly, even from a distance. His signature sign, this time cut from red letters vibrating on a purple foam-core background, shouted FREE THEM to all who cared to listen.

From a makeshift outdoor office set up in front of a religious-themed sculpture gifted to the city of Brownsville in 1959, the leadership team that emerged from the grassroots movement to end child detention had broadened its scope by January 2020. "We turned our attention to bringing down MPP, because of the cruel impact the policy was having on families," states witness Julie Swift. She, Karla Barber, and Margaret Seiler directed me to a stockpile of posters with prewritten slogans. Some were scrawled in thick black marker, others rendered with calligraphic flair—like the one intended for Melania's husband, or perhaps his sidekick, Stephen Miller. Recalling reports of actual conditions inside the same Customs and Border Protection "dog pens" that had taken the lives of at least seven children,[10] through negligence and a lack of human decency, it read: I DON'T WANT HIM IN PRISON. I WANT HIM IN A CAGE WITHOUT TOOTHBRUSH OR SOAP, SLEEPING ON THE FLOOR AND DRINKING FROM THE TOILET.

Another, painted in red-lettered cursive on a sky-blue background, asked: WHAT IF IT WAS YOUR FAMILY?

||||||||||||||||||||||||||||||||||||||||||||||||||||||||||||

The largest banner of all was made of fabric and intricately sewn. Unfurled, it stood almost as tall as me, at 5'2", and stretched many more feet as wide. It had to be handled by several people at once. Created by Miami-based artist Alessandra Mondolfi, the banner superimposed a map of Mexico over the Stars and Stripes, producing a tattered flag effect. Within the ripped stripes was a list of MPP's greatest hits:

---

10. No child had perished in US Border Protection custody in the previous ten years, reports Jacob Soboroff in his sobering first-hand witness to the Family Separation crisis, *Separated: Inside an American Tragedy* (2020). In Jacob's words, zero tolerance was "the most spectacular policy fail" of the US government and the greatest human rights crime of a lifetime.

EXTORTION, HUNGER, RAPE, HUMAN TRAFFICKING, FAMILY SEPARATION, KIDNAPPING, SICKNESS AND DEATH.

Another textile banner sewn by Alessandra positioned a "moral gauge" over an upside-down image of the US flag. The gauge was, naturally, set to zero.

Alessandra had been one witness among many who had gathered at the child internment camp a year earlier in Homestead, Florida. In fact, no sooner had Joshua aired out his Tilley hat after spending ninety days in Tornillo than he was back on the front lines again. This time, however, his vigil was not lone: He joined advocates from the American Friends Service Committee-Miami and the Florida Immigrant Coalition, who organized protests and petition campaigns, as well as local stalwarts, who'd been showing up everyday since February 2019. They waved huge, homemade red hearts at the kids to let them know they had not been forgotten. They targeted the camp staff and management with placards that read FREE THE CHILDREN and HOMES INSTEAD.

In a simultaneous action that set its sights on members of Congress—all 535 of them—Rabbi Bruce Elder, Lee and Nancy Goodman, and other members of Chicago's Hakafa congregation turned their outrage over child imprisonment into political action. They circulated both local and *Move On* petitions, garnering more than 65,000 signatures, while raising awareness of the for-profit imprisonment of children.

The expanding movement to bear witness to the US government's un-American activities would eventually draw to the Homestead gates folks from all fifty states. As Alessandra joined those on the ground in February 2019, Rabbi Bruce, Nancy, Lee, and others descended on Capitol Hill. They informed legislators of the harm done to children by detaining them. They reminded lawmakers of the constitutional obligations and international treaties they were complicit in breaking. They stood with Senator Merkley and Representative Chu in announcing the Shut Down Child Prison Camps Act. They urged members of Congress to support the Family, not Facilities Act, brought by then-Senator Kamala Harris (D-CA) and Senator Ron Wyden (D-OR).

"Our message was simple: close the child prisons and stop separating families," says Nancy.

Rabbi Josh Whinston was among the very few to be offered a glimpse inside Homestead. "Staffers at the Department of Health and Human Services invited me to DC for a full day meeting with political appointees. I thought it was to do with our advocacy *against* child detention, because of our caravan and rally at Tornillo. But it turned out they were looking to the faith community to run overflow shelters. They were looking for *more* space to house kids, not less."

Health and Human Services flew him, along with a retired Unitarian minister and representatives of Evangelical and Catholic social-services programs, to Homestead for a tour. Despite the prison operator being aware they were coming and ready to put on what they deemed an impressive show, Rabbi Josh was shocked by what he saw.

"It was crowded. The kids were made to march in single file. The educational offerings were not up to any standards. There were kids that had been there for more than three months. That was not right. It was upsetting being in there."

Towering chain-link fences concealed the Dickensian daily reality that began at 6:00 a.m. in the hot and barren environment for legions of children who knew neither where they were nor how long they would be made to stay there: Massive white tents and former barracks that contained rows of bunk beds no more than a shoulder-width apart; hour-long lines for the privilege of a ten-minute shower; counselor-accompanied bathroom breaks; rumors of sexual misconduct alongside testimonies of shouted insults and obscenities, "the worst and ugliest words imaginable"; LGBTQIA+ kids being kept "safe" in solitary confinement; children crying everyday, unable to sleep, having lost all desire to eat or to play, told to remain quiet and threatened with deportation if they misbehaved; a ban on physical contact of any kind with each other; and two short phone calls a week with parents who implored them to *be patient and don't cause trouble*. Some said youths too angry, confused, or depressed to comply with orders were controlled with psychotropic drugs.

These were just some of the descriptions that trickled out of Homestead in reporters' notebooks and from snatched conversations with attorneys and witnesses, like Rabbi Josh, who managed to get inside.

From its opening in March 2018 until June 2019, when Democratic presidential hopefuls came to take a look, over 13,053 kids were cycled through the facility equipped to detain up to 3,200 at a time. By the time activists showed up to bear witness, the grounds were monitored by private security contractors.

||||||||||||||||||||||||||||||||||||||||||||||||||||||||||

It was from Alessandra that I first learned who ran the camp; and how much they were estimated to have been paid: $775 per inmate, per day, as against ICE's average allocation of $133.99 a day to detain an adult in 2018. At that cost, you might expect luxury digs. But Homestead is a truly inhospitable place.

Hot year-round except when pummeled by tropical winds and rain, the Florida Air Reserve Base buildings—said to be crawling in mold—sit atop soil and groundwater enriched with hazardous contaminants, such as heavy metals, pesticides, waste oils and gasoline, hydraulic fluids, paints and paint thinners, as well as solvents relating to military and industrial processes. All are known to be cancer-causing. They can lead to kidney failure, blood disorders, and developmental damage in the young. A US Environmental Protection Agency Superfund site since August 30, 1990, Homestead—like Tornillo, like Ursula—was no place for kids.

Yet, in April 2019, Comprehensive Health Services, a subsidiary of Caliburn International LLC, won its third no-bid contract to manage the facility. The first, awarded in February 2018 to get it ready, was worth $31 million. The second, to operate the internment camp between July 2018 and April 2019, totaled $222 million. This third one put another $341 million in the company's coffers and was meant to cover costs to run the place for another year, into 2020.

Joshua Rubin was on-site when the news of the $341 million contract broke. He happened to be talking with a reporter and camera crew from the *Miami Herald* when a golf cart shot passed with a familiar figure sitting at the back.

"That's John Kelly!" Joshua exclaimed.

Heads and cameras turned, catching the Homeland Security secretary turned Trump chief of staff on tape touring the grounds. This forced Caliburn to confirm that upon leaving the White House at the end of 2018, the retired Marine General had joined its board of directors. Kelly knew Homestead well, having led the US Southern Command from there from 2012 to 2016. During that time, according to the Washington Office on Latin America, SouthCom funneled $13.4 million to Guatemala to train its border patrol force: the Chorti.

Caliburn was then making so much money off detained kids that it was considering going public with a $100 million initial stock offering.[11] While Kelly was still a member of Trump & Co, the average length of stay for an unaccompanied non-citizen child in US custody skyrocketed. By 2019, Comprehensive Health Services had become one of the dominant players in the child-prison industry, holding one out of every four kids in the entire system, depending on the day. It acceded neither to routine inspections by state child welfare experts nor to employee background checks under the Statewide Automated Child Welfare Information System.

⁂

Outside the prison gates, witnesses suffered through constant skirmishes. They would pitch tents to ward off the Florida sun in unclaimed, open areas. Prison management would insist they were occupying a staff parking lot and shoo them off; send drivers out to repark trucks and vans to block witnesses' views; and force them to park as far from the detention center as possible. Even the Miami-Dade superintendent of schools was rebuffed when he, a local teacher, and some students attempted to deliver more than 2,500 letters addressed to the detained youth from their New York and Florida age-mates.

Fortunately, the movement that drew a through line from Tornillo to Homestead did find a few sympathetic ears in Congress, in addition to Merkely and Chu. South Florida Representative Debbie Mucarsel-Powell had gone to the mat with the federal government, the Office of Refugee Resettlement, and Comprehensive Health Services early on, insisting they provide local legislators with a hurricane evacuation plan.

---

11. The IPO never came to pass.

How would a prison camp located in Florida's second most vulnerable area for hurricanes and made of tents easily blown away in the wind keep its "inmates" safe during a storm? she wanted to know.

By June, Mucarsel-Powell still had no answers. And after nearly five months sweltering on protest lines, witnesses had yet to spark national outrage about the long-term internment of kids at the Homestead Air Reserve Base.

Ali Wicks-Lim and her children, eight-year-old Summit and fourteen-year-old Mason, were about to change that.

||||||||||||||||||||||||||||||||||||||||||||||||||||||

Hailing from western Massachusetts, the three had been bird-dogging their senator and preferred presidential candidate, Elizabeth Warren, for months, which is to say they had been strategizing with activists nationwide to steer both Democratic platform and candidate talking points toward the issues most important to voters. Ali and her kids had waited in numerous interminable handshake lines for a selfie and a pinky swear that Warren would make the twin injustices of family separation and child detention central to her candidacy. But frustration grew from New Hampshire to Iowa to South Carolina when bird-doggers, like the Wicks-Lims, couldn't get anyone in the crowded Democratic primary field to commit to speaking out against Homestead.

The national media didn't seem to care, either. Only the local Miami press corps deigned to come out.

Then, the Democratic National Committee announced that its candidates would debate in Miami on June 26 and 27, providing the advocates a tactical opening. Instead of merely asking their candidates to comment, they would implore them to go bear witness to the youth prison when in the Magic City.

Because where the candidates go, so goes the press.

Ali's colleague in political activism Tina Marie Davidson pulled up stakes and went to Florida. She joined witnesses, both constant and intermittent, for the long haul. She provided daily observations of the internment camp to bird-doggers nationwide: Children's medical and other documents were being trashed; a portable ultrasound machine seen shuttling between girls' dormitories suggested pregnancies or the tracking of menstrual cycles; the arrival of an ambulance and team of Emergency Medical Technicians wearing masks raised alarms of illness inside the camp; the number of armed ICE and Border Protection personnel was growing along with the intensity of their bullying of witnesses.

Pressure built with the onset of the summer heat as Mucarsel-Powell and other legislators made attempts to tour the facility only to be turned away, repeatedly. Following the witnesses' lead, the congress-woman, too, shifted her focus to gaining the attention of Democratic presidential candidates. But even as they bore down on Miami, only US Representative Eric Swalwell (D-CA) had committed to visiting Homestead. Some had already said, "No."

Tina Marie texted Ali: *We need you here. Bring the kids.*

⁕⁕⁕⁕⁕⁕⁕⁕⁕⁕⁕⁕⁕⁕⁕⁕⁕⁕⁕⁕⁕⁕⁕⁕⁕⁕⁕⁕

"It was not my plan to go. But I piled two kids and a tent into the car and we went." Ali, Mason, and Summit arrived, sweaty and exhausted, the day of Elizabeth Warren's pre-debate Town Hall. "We went straight to Homestead."

Summit climbed the ladders set up by Karla in March when man-agement, perhaps taking cues from Tornillo's operators, screened the facility's perimeter fencing. Mason, an aspiring photographer and videographer, documented Summit as she stood vigil on the top step, taking it all silently in.

"Kids were waving to us and making heart signs," remembers Ali. "I kept thinking, my kids get to go home; these kids don't. It was really overwhelming."

At the height of the midday heat, Ali took a break. As she tried to catch her breath for a moment under the shade of a tent, her phone pinged. It was a Warren staffer. "I'm sorry, the senator can't make it," the text read.

"Everyone's hearts fell," remembers Ali. Their months of passionate, unrelenting work to get the candidates to focus on Homestead could be coming to nothing, and "according to Tina Marie," who was already at the Miami athletic facility that was doubling as Senator Warren's Town Hall venue, "EW was our best hope."

||||||||||||||||||||||||||||||||||||||||||||||||||||

At that point, adrenaline took over. Ali made the snap decision to drive straight to Miami and try to engage Senator Warren directly. There was no time to waste. The Town Hall would be starting soon. She would have to bring the kids. She texted Tina Marie to tell her they were on their way.

"We were hot and sweaty and needing to pee. We gassed up, grabbed some hummus and chips at a mini-mart, and ate dinner in the car en route. I got lost, broke any number of traffic laws, losing my mind that we would arrive too late."

They got there just minutes before the event began, covered in hummus and crumbs. But there was no time to freshen up, for as Ali, Mason, and Summit made their circuitous way toward the athletic center, Tina Marie made certain the senator knew that a family of constituents had driven all the way from Massachusetts and wanted to speak with her.

"We were ushered directly into a squash court, where we came face-to-face with Elizabeth Warren. She was with several staffers, Tina Marie, and a group of other witnesses."

Summit didn't skip a beat. "She looked right at the politician and said, 'We've just come from Homestead. And those children need you. I think you should go.'"

"We'll do what we can," was all Senator Warren would commit to. Three minutes later, she was onstage before an adoring audience. The Town Hall had begun.

||||||||||||||||||||||||||||||||||||||||||||||||||||

Tina Maria had one trick left.

Warren's campaign events featured a limited Q&A session by lottery. If you wanted to address the candidate, you requested a ticket.

Tina Marie suggested pooling all witnesses' tickets to increase their chances of getting ahold of the mic.

Then it was up to Lady Luck. And boy did she deliver.

One of three winning numbers was, indeed, among their own. Tina Marie handed the golden ticket directly to Nannette Bartels, a grandmother and former inclusion specialist with Miami-Dade County Child Development Services. And in an eloquent speech she had not known until minutes before that she would be asked to make, Nannette informed candidate Warren that "just twenty-some-odd miles from here, there is a children's prison." She refused to use the government-preferred moniker of "temporary influx shelter," because she knew better.

"Witnesses have been there every day for 135 days," she stated, forcing back overwhelming emotions, for she was one of them.

"We are there, standing vigil to shine a light so this country will see what is happening in our name. We need you there," Nannette concluded to a standing ovation.

"So," Warren began, glancing at the floor when the mic passed back to her. "I'm going to Homestead tomorrow," she stated as she looked up and out over the spellbound crowd. "Come with me."

||||||||||||||||||||||||||||||||||||||||||||||||||||||

Warren had been to McAllen the year before, she said. She'd seen the kids in cages, and spoken to frightened mothers, on the run from violence and hunger.

She instructed her staff to rent several buses and the next morning an entourage escorted her to the walled-off eyesore "twenty-some-odd miles away." Naturally, the press and other candidates followed.

"From maybe eight witnesses the day before," states Ali, "to press tents, talking heads, candidates—hundreds of people—the next, it went from calm to chaos."

When Warren's bus arrived, Summit stepped out of the crowd. The candidate held out her hand to the eight-year-old as Mason and the press corps rolled tape.

"I'll show you how to witness," Summit offered. And the two climbed the ladders together. Summit pointed out everything she'd absorbed the day before: *That is the yard where kids go out to play but only once a day, for an hour.*

Warren nodded.

See their hats? The kids didn't have that until the witnesses fought the prison administration to provide them sun protection.

The hats were prison-issue orange.

Don't be upset if you wave and they don't wave back, Summit warned. *Sometimes they get punished and sent inside, losing their recreation time. Sometimes they get threatened with more time in prison.*

The candidate bit her lip.

‖‖‖

Representative Swalwell beat Senator Warren to Homestead, posting on Monday, June 24, "These children need homes, NOT a privatized prison."

Then-Senator Harris was among the many candidates to follow in Warren's footsteps on June 26. After an impromptu press conference, she climbed right back into her car. Joshua ran up to the driver's side as she tried to pull away. He knocked on the closed window. As the glass descended, he stuck his head inside the air-conditioned cool: "Don't you want to see the kids?"

The future US vice president stammered that she assumed they were out of view.

"Come with me," Joshua said. He led her to the nearest ladder to peer into grounds made off-limits by a company that, in Warren's words, "has built its profits from running a facility to lock up children." He handed over his binoculars so Harris could better see what nearly $600 million in congressional appropriations can buy.

"She had tears in her eyes on her way back down," recalls Joshua.

That day, Elizabeth Warren made a statement shared by many: "An immigration system that can't tell the difference between a terrorist, a criminal, and a little girl is not an immigration system that is keeping us safe. . . . It certainly doesn't reflect our values."

She later tweeted: *There's no place in this country for operating private prisons that profit off of cruelty. At $775/day, there is no incentive to return* *kids to families. The system is working great for the rich and powerful. For the investors in private prisons. But it is not working great for American citizens. Locking people up for money is not what the US should be doing.*

॥॥॥॥॥॥॥॥॥॥॥॥॥॥॥॥॥॥॥॥॥॥॥॥॥॥॥॥॥

Three days after that, back home in Massachusetts, Ali was called to speak at a national day of action to abolish ICE involvement at her county jail. She spoke on the importance of *just showing up*, whether that means confronting your political representatives, protesting on-site, making calls and writing letters from your kitchen table, or educating others in your proverbial backyard.

"The people profiting off what is happening to these children would like it to happen in secrecy," she said. "Bearing witness interrupts that. Witnesses hold up a mirror for all of us. So that we have to look closely at what we will and will not allow." Ali told the crowd, "Ultimately we want Homestead and every place like it shut down."

Ali was keen to acknowledge everyone who contributed, whether seen or not: "That moment with Summit on the ladder with Elizabeth Warren was a big moment, and one we'll personally never forget. But it was made up of countless smaller moments, involving people who may never be known or recognized or named. It's easy to look past the million, smaller moments but that's where the magic happens, because that's where true change is made."

A month later, Homestead was shut down. No one knows what happened to the kids.

CHAPTER TWENTY-SEVEN

Death by a Thousand Cuts

As sunrise accompanies sunset and low tide accompanies high, the dark side of offering asylum is denying refuge through expulsion. It has been part of humankind's good/evil struggle forever, even before there were nation-states with borders to patrol. Communities have long harnessed fearmongering to justify banishing or barring entry to one folk devil or another: Foreigners, criminals, and the poor; indigenous people, religious groups not like one's own, and those thought—or said—to be carriers of communicable diseases.

In this, the US is no exception and Trump & Co were no originals. The US practice of legislating expulsion began in 1882 with the Chinese Exclusion Act; continued through the 20th century, targeting Mexican migrant workers most notably during the reprehensively named "Operation Wetback"; and hit a peak under Obama-Biden, who removed some three million people in eight years. These campaigns have accompanied periods of nativism and xenophobia. In the US that has led to the demonization of Asians, Central Americans, Haitians, Arab Muslims, Africans, among others. At the time of Adam Goodman's 2020 publication of *The Deportation Machine: America's Long History of Expelling Immigrants*, the Land of the Free had deported 57 million people—more than any other country in the world.

Texas-based journalist and writer Debbie Nathan was working to unmask the deportation machinery in El Paso when the Witness #EndMPP vigil began. It was a challenge, however, to track ICE operations at the city's sprawling airport, with its many impenetrable nooks and crannies. She reached out to the leadership team of what would eventually take the name Witness at the Border with a request: might they steal some time to see if deportation flights were easier to track from the smaller Brownsville-South Padre Island International Airport?

Then-Executive Director of the American Civil Liberties Union of Texas Terri Burke was in Brownsville when Debbie's email landed—and good thing, too. The day Terri left the vigil to return home, she called Karla from the airport. *I see a deportation flight on the tarmac right now*, she reported.

"We jumped in the car and drove the fifteen minutes to the airport," states Karla. En route, she downloaded a free flight-tracking app, called FlightAware, at Debbie's suggestion. Sure enough, when they arrived they saw men, women, and teens shackled in five-point restraints, as if they were hardened criminals. They were being being loaded onto a Boeing 737, along with younger children and toddlers.

Goodman shows us that from its beginnings the US "deportation machine" was cruel and dehumanizing by design: built from a make-it-hurt-so-badly-they-never-come-back mentality. And that is just what Karla and the other witnesses found.

Linked like a Jim Crow chain gang, the shackled people stood in a demoralized line. All that remained of their belongings lay strewn on the tarmac, stuffed into white plastic bags. One by one, ICE agents wearing high-visibility vests and bearing stun guns subjected each individual to a pat-down. They barked "open" and peered into the mouths of the enchained. They checked the necks of all the women sporting long hair. They searched in vain for contraband that would have been impossible for anyone to transfer from an hielera or ICE prison to a removal transport while bound in wrist cuffs and leg irons attached to waist chains.

From that day, Witness at the Border folded deportation flight tracking into their group mission. States Karla: "We started checking FlightAware frequently, often in the middle of the night, to monitor when planes were going out. If we saw a flight, we would get the word out and meet at the airport. We were often there before sunrise because the flights were usually scheduled very early in the morning."

In an essay for the *Brooklyn Rail* entitled, "Diary from a Genocide in the Making," Margaret Seiler recounts dragging herself out of bed on February 14. It was still dark when roughly thirty witnesses gathered. There was a chill in the air. The silhouettes of palm trees stood out against a sky growing rosy with the rising sun. They walked to the lot. There, four buses sat. "They were full of human cargo," recalls Margaret.

Behind the buses' tinted windows, they could make out the forms of the people inside. They held up their cuffed hands, displaying their shackles, as the witnesses held up the red cardboard hearts they'd made for Valentine's Day. They sang out, "¡No están solos! (*You are not alone!*) and ¡Te queremos! (*We love you!*)."

"What was most disturbing was the banality of it all," says Margaret. "This was just another morning at the border: our government deporting the unwanted and ignored back to danger."

Unbeknownst to the group then, the routine had been going on for decades.

‖‖‖

The modern deportation machine began as a government-run operation managed by the US Marshals Service on government-owned planes. It ran out of five airport hubs: Mesa, Arizona; Miami, Florida; and Alexandria, Louisiana; as well as San Antonio and Brownsville, Texas. That changed from 2011, documents Goodman, with the hardening of ICE interior enforcement. Deputizing local police under 287(g) agreements sparked the development of the private-public transport infrastructure of buses, airports, and planes that, under Trump, merged with the immigrant detention industry, becoming a multi-billion dollar business.

Today, that detention-to-deportation pipeline has ballooned into a sprawling, semi-secret network, within more or less thirty-five airports. The machinery benefits "fixed base operations" at these hubs—services such as fueling, hangaring, tying down, and parking—as well as privately owned charter airlines used by ICE, collectively referred to as "ICE Air." In addition to the three dozen domestic ports, ICE Air's international infrastructure extends to 134 airfields in 119 countries worldwide, having doubled in size in the second decade of the 21st century.

Prior to February 2018, ICE contracted with CIS Aviation to operate ICE Air flights. Since then, the contract has been under a new broker, Classic Air Charter of Huntington, New York, which subcontracts the bulk of the ICE Air deportation machine to private aviation companies. The two most frequently used subcontractors are Swift Air, owned by iAero Group, and World Atlantic Airlines, also flying under the name Caribbean Sun. Other airlines include GlobalX as well as Gryphon Air and Eastern, which fly less frequently, clocking in a few flights per month. Omni Air International, a US Department of Defense troop mover, also moonlights as ICE Air's mass deportation flyer to far-flung places, like Africa and Southeast Asia. It handles what ICE refers to as "High Risk Special Charters."

This shadowy industry transfers safety seekers from borderlands hieleras, to the two-hundred-plus ICE detention facilities, to their expulsion across borders in daily departures, always in chains, on privately hired Boeing 737s, McDonnell Douglas M-80s, and General Dynamics Gulfstream jets that can transport a dozen passengers and remain in flight for as many hours. Like the detention economy, ICE Air is making a lot of people rich, including folks who have no idea what's fueling the mutual funds in their investment portfolios.

"Although ICE's current contract with [Classic Air Charter] has not been made public," states the April 2019 report by University of Washington human rights researchers, *Hidden in Plain Sight: ICE Air and the Machinery of Mass Deportation*, "the Government Accountability Office's resolution of a February 2018 protest filed by a competitor company described its value at $646 million."

This is, of course, courtesy of the US taxpayer. More than that, the US deportation machine makes accomplices of every industry it touches—airports, cabin and flights crews, security and medical teams, food service providers and cleaning staff, control tower logisticians, hangar space and fuel operators, all their labor unions, and, of course, the aircraft companies themselves.

At the old-school Brownsville–South Padre Island International Airport, witnesses enjoyed great sight lines. They captured videos and pictures—for a few days. They could anticipate the ICE bus routes and plant their cars in the way to gum up the flight schedules—at least at first. But it didn't take long before airport personnel began to block their views with fuel trucks and mobile hydraulic stairs. They turned the deportation planes around to board their human cargo from the far side, where witnesses could only see the enchained from the knees down.

The Matrix is a complex mechanism containing many cogs that are endlessly churning. It only takes one break to stop the gears turning and force a reset. Likewise, it only takes one evil engineer, tinkering at the back end, to crank the cruelty to the next level.

The evil engineer of this story is Stephen Miller.

IIIIIIIIIIIIIIIIIIIIIIIIIIIIIIIIIIIIIIIIIIIIIIIIIIIIIIIIIII

Born in 1985, the grandson of Ashkenazi Jews who fled early-20th-century Russian pogroms, Miller was still a high school student when he became a committed acolyte of Wayne LaPierre, CEO of the National Rifle Association, as well as of the rabidly racist, homophobic, and misogynistic climate-change denier Rush Limbaugh. Already a fixture of conservative talk radio-host Larry Elder's show and a practiced provocateur at the age of sixteen, Miller would go on to become Trump's speechwriter and right-hand man, responsible for the hyperbolic vitriol about people on the move.

Miller engineered the Tanton network-inspired project to end asylum in the US, bringing about more than four hundred changes to immigration-based rules and regulations in less than three years. With the patience and long-term vision of John Tanton himself, Miller began to plan his attack on asylum when, as a staffer for then-Alabama Senator Jefferson Beauregard Sessions III, he pored through the entire federal code to look for provisions and legal loopholes that might be exploited to halt immigration to the United States.

Once unleashed as Trump's immigration czar, his mission began. It was a bloodletting by a thousand cuts, aided more quietly by another Tanton-network adherrent, Gene Hamilton. Alongside the Muslim ban, stepped-up ICE raids, family separation, and MPP, they slashed the refugee cap, threatened DACA and TPS, and put into place myriad less visible actions. Many required negotiating Asylum Cooperation Agreements with third countries vulnerable to being strong-armed.

||||||||||||||||||||||||||||||||||||||||||||||||||||

For context: the 1980 Refugee Act established that anyone physically present in the US or its territorial holdings may apply for asylum, no matter how they arrived or what countries they passed through on the way. The legislation permits the attorney general to designate, through bi- or multi-national agreement, "safe third countries" where folks unable to reach the US may remain under protection until refugee status is conferred. These "safe third countries," by definition, must boast a robust and accessible—aka "full and fair"—asylum system and, following the 1951 Refugee Convention and 1967 Protocol, be places where people will enjoy freedom from persecution.

When I worked for the Hebrew Immigrant Aid Society in the 1980s, for example, the former Soviet Jewish refugees we welcomed had all been offered safe haven in Italy before transiting to New York. This is an example of the original spirit of the safe third country provision: to encourage nation-state responsibility sharing. Miller twisted the safe third country ideal into a weapon, making it part of an arsenal of policies intended to *prevent* folks seeking safety from stepping foot onto US soil where national and international obligations toward them would kick automatically into gear.

As with the high seas interdiction of Haitians and their forced displacement at Guantánamo Bay under Reagan and Bush 41, Miller's goal was to move, or "externalize," the asylum process—to push it away from US territory—far from the courts and public view.

MPP was such a program. It required the agreement of the Mexican government. But Mexico was too close. Tent encampments hugging the US border drew witnesses. And as Jill Biden recognized on her December 2019 visit to Matamoros, the existence of refugee camps at its very doorstep was not a good look for the leader of the free world.

Also, as we've seen, Mexico is not safe for stateless and poor people on the move. And while it does have a refugee agency tasked with processing asylum applications, its Comisión Mexicana de Ayuda a Refugiados is under-resourced and inaccessible. It is not "full and fair."

||||||||||||||||||||||||||||||||||||||||||||||||||||||||||

Mexico only acquiesced to a "safe" third country deal when Trump & Co threatened crippling tariffs. With that, the floodgates opened. The Orwellian-named Humanitarian Asylum Review Process (HARP) followed. Also piloted in El Paso, HARP sped up the processing of credible fear screenings of Mexican asylum seekers to ten days. It removed the mandate that officers ask new arrivals if they feared being returned to Mexico. Thus, unless an asylum candidate stated such a fear without prompting, passing the "shout test," their so-called "humanitarian" review resulted in rejection and prompt ejection. Once denied refuge, Mexican asylum seekers subjected to this fast-tracked credible fear process could appeal the decision to an immigration judge, but over the phone, while still in frigid holding pens, deprived of a nourishing meal, and still in filthy traveling clothes. If denied again—which is most often the case without the benefit of legal due process—they were expelled right back to the places they fled.

Trump & Co next forced a similar deal on Guatemala, despite the US embassy assessment there that it was "among the most dangerous countries in the world," where violence against women goes unpunished. Guatemala is also notoriously poor, compelling thousands of its own citizens to emigrate each year. It has a rudimentary asylum system, at best. There are few shelters there dedicated to aiding people on the move, and Miller's plan did not provide funding for such care.

For all these reasons, the Asylum Cooperation Agreement with Guatemala got hung up in the US courts. So, Miller turned his attention to the next biggest brick in the big "beautiful" bureaucratic wall: a unilateral policy that barred everyone, no matter their country of origin, from seeking asylum at the US border if they hadn't first applied for, and been denied, asylum in a country through which they transited.

Variously called the "entry ban" or "transit ban," it was really an asylum ban—the most far-reaching of Miller's surgical stabs. Simultaneously, negotiations for a "safe" third country agreement with Honduras—the homicide capital of the world—lacked only the signatures when, in November, then–Attorney General William Barr certified Guatemala as a "safe" third country over continued strong opposition from the US Department of State and UN Refugee Agency.

Miller was armed and ready, as well, with a policy meant to bypass further MPP enrollment of Salvadorans and Hondurans and expel them directly to Guatemala, instead. Called the Prompt Asylum Claim Review (PACR) and fashioned after HARP, PACR led to the refoulement of nearly one thousand people, mostly women and children, before Miller was handed the best possible answer to his asylum death wish: the coronavirus pandemic.

Miller's toolkit included an obscure public health order known as Title 42, which he pushed regularly as a legal silver bullet. Title 42 of the 1944 Public Health Service Act conferred authority on federal officials to screen and detain people at US borders in order to mitigate the spread of infectious disease. Title 42 enabled the US surgeon general, the nation's top doctor, to prohibit the introduction of people into the country thought to pose a danger to public health. It was originally created in response to post–World War II concerns about the spread of malaria and tuberculosis by soldiers returning home from far-reaching corners of the world. But barring entry to one's own was felt to be too unfair. So, Title 42 was buried and forgotten.

Until it was unearthed by Miller.

He first attempted to harness Title 42 against members of the fall 2018 migrant caravan, determined to find evidence that they carried communicable illnesses. He tried to invoke Title 42 two more times in 2019: when an outbreak of mumps spread through immigration detention facilities in six states; then again when Border Patrol stations were hit with the flu. He was known to ask often for updates on communities receiving newcomers, hoping to find the spread of new diseases there.

COVID-19 handed him the perfect pretext to enact the border blockade of his dreams. And in an election year, too.

On January 21, 2020, the US Centers for Disease Control confirmed the first coronavirus case in the US: a Washington State resident who'd returned from Wuhan, China, six days before. The city's known cases having climbed to three hundred from fifty-nine not two weeks before, Wuhan made the unprecedented move of quarantining its entire population of eleven million on January 23.

That's when Miller's campaign to shut US land borders to all "nonessential" travel began.

Trade would not be affected—trucks and trains packed with consumer goods could cross the line as before. Kids attending school on the other side of the line and professionals crossing for work could carry on doing so. Of the tens of thousands of pedestrians and passengers, including nearly 35,000 truck drivers who traverse the busiest border in the world every day, none would be subjected to testing against, or even questioning about, their potential contact with the virus.

But folks in need of refuge? They would not be allowed to cross. Even though the coronavirus was already present in the US and spreading fast.

||||||||||||||||||||||||||||||||||||||||||||||||||||||

We saw disaster coming like a slow-motion train wreck. "We were still making jokes about the coronavirus in late February," says Sam Bishop of GRM, the Dignity Village Collaborative healthcare provider. But when Milan, Italy, went into lockdown on March 9, and people began to show up at hospitals all over the US with a constellation of symptoms medical providers didn't really understand or know how to treat, the collaborative realized the perfect storm they and the camp residents faced: it was no longer just the threat of cartel and gang violence that lurked outside their zippered doors as they waited for their turn in Kangaroo Court.

"One case of COVID and the whole camp could be wiped out," says Sam. Yet, an informed global response was as scarce as the personal protective equipment essential workers needed to stay alive. So the Dignity Village Collaborative took matters into their own hands.

Going into overdrive, Team Brownsville purchased old shipping containers, which they hauled to the encampment and, repurposing them as storage units, stuffed to the ceilings with rice, beans, cooking oil, and other nonperishable food items. The Tías located and delivered used sewing machines and bolts of fabric, passing them to Gladys

Aguilar as well as to Gaby at the Resource Center, who set up a cottage industry of mask makers. Charlene amped up her efforts to get the most vulnerable of the vulnerable paroled into the US while there was still time. Tucker and another cadre of camp residents commenced building 88 four-sink water, sanitation, and hygiene—or WASH—stations for installation throughout the tent city. His simple, affordable design become a template for refugee encampments worldwide.

It was all part of a COVID-19 prevention program developed by the GRM leadership. Helen and Blake cast their gaze back in time, studying responses to past epidemics—Ebola, the Swine Flu, even the Spanish flu of 1918–1919—to inform a rapid behavior and culture change within the camp. And with the help of the nation-group leaders, the collaborative launched a community campaign to educate everyone as to the importance of regular hand-washing, mask-wearing, and social-distancing. Drawing from protocols Helen found in early-20th-century army manuals, they rearranged camp beds, with tent-sharers sleeping head to toe; they requested the Resource Center sanitation team to disinfect the Port-a-Potties after each use; they passed out zinc tablets and vitamin C, then thought to mitigate COVID's ability to attack the human organism; and they required that, henceforth, floor coverings be mopped rather than swept.

<hr />

North of the line, witnesses carried on their predawn trips to observe ICE Air operations at the Brownsville airport. Karla, a technologist by profession, began to capture information about carriers as well as flight times, domestic paths, and international destinations. Tom Cartwright organized Karla's data into spreadsheets and charts to see what patterns might emerge.

But the Ides of March brought bad news: Joshua announced that the #EndMPP vigil would be shuttered on its now-sixty-fourth day. Four days earlier, on March 11, the World Health Organization declared COVID-19 a pandemic. On March 13, while calling it a "hoax that would be over by summertime" out of one side of his mouth, Trump declared a national emergency out of the other.

Also that day, Andrea Rudnik informed Team Brownsville's nation-wide community of volunteers that they were passing their refugee food service to Chef José Andres and his World Central Kitchen: "This will be the first week in over a year that I'm not making a bridge calendar," she wrote. "[W]e've been told not to take extra people unless necessary for [asylum seekers'] protection as well as ours. We are continuing to supply food, medicine, clothing, hygiene supplies through our tiendas, so don't worry. People will be taken care of."

Though the kitchen handover had been in the offing for weeks, it, too, would soon get scuppered.

As of midnight, March 18, the US Department of Justice suspended the nation's immigration courts. This brought an abrupt halt to all asylum adjudication processes indefinitely, including in Trump & Co's border-hugging Kangaroo Courts.

Then came Miller's final parry: The Centers for Disease Control announced on April Fool's Day that it was invoking Title 42. Goods, money, commerce—and the coronavirus— were still free to cross the line. But Customs and Border Protection agents would, henceforth, no longer be processing southern border arrivals. All newcomers would be transferred immediately to ICE Enforcement Removals Operations, boarded onto ICE Air planes, and flown back where they came from.

Mexico would accept no one from third countries.

There would be no judicial review of this procedure.

The US southern border was "closed."

PART V:
RETURN

CHAPTER TWENTY-EIGHT

Locked Down

No one slept well in the summer of 2020.

"We felt so defeated," says GRM's pharmacist, Perla, about her family's asylum proceedings being put on hold. "We couldn't go back to Nicaragua." Not only were their lives in danger if they returned, but air and land transportation systems were, little by little, shutting down worldwide. One of the few camp residents working with a lawyer, Perla had been assured the family had a winnable asylum case. "We had come through so much and had waited so long already. We knew if we wanted to enter the US legally, we would have to stay put."

They were not alone. Though most far-flung witnesses, like me, scattered before commercial airlines were grounded, the camp population did not significantly shrink at that time.

To mitigate potential exposure to the virus, the Dignity Village Collaborative cleaved itself in two. The Resource Center and GRM teams stayed in Matamoros. Team Brownsville and the Angry Tías, having laid in ample food stores, identified proxies among the leaders of the camp's nation groups. They set up remote communication systems via WhatsApp and Zoom. Then they proceeded to lock themselves down in homes from Port Isabel through Brownsville and Harlingen to McAllen.

The void they left was slowly, inevitably filled by both Mexico's National Migration Institute and the Gulf Cartel. It's hard to say which stepped into the gap first, for, as we've seen, after prevailing over Los Zetas in 2011, the cartel and Tamaulipas State authorities were effectively one and the same. In 2020, that dynamic had little changed.

No sooner had Trump closed the border to people seeking asylum than Migration Institute officials were agitating to move the tent city off the Civic Plaza. Neither Matamoros residents nor town leaders relished the encampment in their midst—a daily reminder that they lived at the mercy of their bullying northern neighbor. Promising newer, sturdier tents big enough to stand up in, officials swept the plaza clean of refugees, relocating everyone to the other side of the levee.

Now thousands of people, including children and the elderly, were rendered invisible by not one, but two national governments. And if being forced to live in a tent during a deadly global pandemic weren't bad enough, they were perched atop a sloping floodplain—and hurricane season was right around the corner.

Fortunately, GRM leadership had been thinking ahead. Long before Helen, Sam, and Blake threw themselves into designing, sourcing, and building a COVID field hospital to serve the refugee encampment, they had been searching for experts in stormwater management. Three young female engineers, Erin Hughes, Christa Cook, and Chloe Rastatter, all separately answered the call.

Coincidentally, they had each learned of the Matamoros refugee camp thanks to a November 2019 four-part podcast series by *This American Life*. When each woman heard Helen, interviewed for Episode One: "The Out Crowd," talk about the camp residents' limited access to clean water and sanitation, she thought, "I can help with that." One by one, all three reached out. One by one, they were welcomed to come down. By the time they arrived, the need for their expertise had greatly expanded.

Erin, a licensed professional engineer with a Masters in environmental engineering from Drexel University, landed just days before Trump & Co closed the border to people in need, and mere weeks before Mother Nature gave everyone a taste of what was to come. Spring showers pummeled the refugees, turning their Rio Bravo floodplain home into a mud slick. The deluge leveled tents and took down tarps. Belongings were ruined by waters that coursed through the encampment like rivers. Folks went from sweltering in triple-digit heat to being drenched to the skin.

Many turned up at GRM's Mobile Medical Unit with broken bones and twisted ankles from falls attributable to the slippery footing.

Having survived tragedies most of us will never imagine, they now faced new hardships in addition to mud, like ravenous mosquitoes, mold, mildew, and more rain.

|||||||||||||||||||||||||||||||||||||||||||||||||||||||||||||||||

Shifting into high gear as the camp's principal engineer, Erin got right to work. She mapped the topography of the floodplain using data compiled by the United States Geological Survey and studied the archives of the National Oceanic and Atmospheric Administration to develop a plan for securing the topsoil from future inundations. All meteorological predictors pointed to a very active hurricane season in the summer of 2020—about 140 percent above average. She would need to dig thousands of feet of half-foot-deep dykes and drainage channels to direct stormwater around tents and living areas to the river. She would need to source, purchase, and have delivered hundreds of tons of gravel to reinforce the walkways and utility roads. She would have to fill tens of thousands of sandbags to stack at the camp's lowest elevation points to create a berm to stave off water in the event the river breached its banks. She would need shovels and wheelbarrows and sturdy gloves; as well as water pumps to whisk away puddles and bogs where bloodthirsty mosquitoes might lay their eggs. And the six hundred tents absolutely had to be lifted off the ground to keep them watertight in a storm.

Erin, it should be said, carries her smarts in a slight, delicate frame. And by April, when she tied back her brunette bob-cut hair and donned her work cap to begin slicing and shifting sod, temperatures were steadily climbing into the sultry hundreds.

Fortunately, she would soon have plenty of help. Chloe, then in her final year as an undergraduate student of engineering at the University of Colorado Boulder, came down during her spring break and stayed, electing to finish her degree remotely. Christa followed in June, freshly graduated with a Masters in sustainable engineering from Villanova University. The three formed an unstoppable team alongside Tucker, with whom they additionally constructed showers, engineered clean water access and solar power for GRM's field hospital, and added to Blake's existing water filtration efforts. Most importantly a crew emerged from the camp community itself, led by Honduran preacher Dison Valladares, who became instrumental, Erin recalls, in guiding both project prioritization as well as implementation. He was, in short, the team's right-hand man.

Meanwhile, Helen raised $250,000 to build a COVID field hospital and isolation area, following a treatment plan devised by the GRM medics: If someone presented with mild symptoms, they would be sent to the "cool zone" for isolation and observation. If symptoms progressed to full-blown COVID, they would be transferred to the "hot zone," equipped with beds and oxygen to support twenty people. If intubation was required, the patient would be transferred to the nearest available hospital. And if the hospitals refused treatment— which they did when Matamoros, like nearby Cameron County, Texas, hit widespread community transmission—the team would be ready with palliative care to keep the dying comfortable.

With only eight ventilators to support a population of five hundred thousand, "Matamoros hospitals literally locked their gates. Mexican citizens were seeking health care in the US because their own hospitals were doing nothing," says Helen. "We even trained Pastor Abraham on how to use personal protective equipment so he could come into the hot zone safely to give last rites."

GRM's field hospital opened on May 2. "Of all the things we did in Matamoros, our COVID prevention response and field hospital are what I'm most proud of," says Helen. It was indeed a sight to behold: state-of-the-art medical technology, incorporating lots of ingenious, cost-saving hacks, under a tent completely powered by solar energy.

\|\|\|\|\|\|\|\|\|\|\|\|\|\|\|\|\|\|\|\|\|\|\|\|\|\|\|\|\|\|\|\|\|\|\|\|\|\|\|\|\|\|\|\|\|\|\|\|\|\|\|\|\|\|

In a video introducing the field hospital, Tucker states: "We built the hospital a few hundred meters away from the entrance to the residential area." The key word in that sentence being "entrance," because prior to the hospital becoming operational, workers sent by the Mexico's Migration Institute showed up with enough fencing to enclose the encampment in a twelve-foot chain-link barrier.

They did it, they said, to keep residents "safe." And at first, some of the Dignity Village Collaborative leaders were okay with the idea. But when workers returned with spools of concertina wire, weaving the barbs into the top of the wall tilting inward, not out, everyone understood that Mexico's real intention was to lock the refugees down, indefinitely. Suspicions were confirmed when, once residents were fenced in, the government dispatched guards to patrol the entrance gates built into the fortification at its southern end.

The camp now resembled an outdoor prison. And as with all prisons, the guards brought new rules.

No newcomers would be allowed. If a current resident left the area for any reason—to bid goodbye to a dying loved one back home, for instance, or to ride out the pandemic under safer conditions—they would not be permitted back in. Camp residents had to be back inside before curfew or risk being left out on the streets for the night. Reentry was subject to temperature checks and symptom controls by authorities positioned at the prison gates. If found to be symptomatic, camp residents would be referred to GRM and isolated until they tested negative for the coronavirus. Though GRM would be in charge of their care, all positive tests had to be reported to the Mexican government.

The Migration Institute "offered," with attitudes bordering on insistent, one-way chartered bus trips to Tapachula, on Mexico's border with Guatemala, "for a limited time." Buses showed up once or twice to transport anyone interested in going to a new shelter that purportedly had running water and private rooms. But when takers ended up in Tapachula, "bus arrivals took on a very negative, threatening connotation," says Helen.

Because of the concentration camp–like optics, media outlets were also barred from entering. Migration Institute officials argued that it was a COVID risk. Residents felt it was meant to render them further invisible.

"International rules say that we have to attend to them," Matamoros City Hall spokesman Miguel Garay told an Al Jazeera reporter in February. "We can't kick them out by force." But following the example of their northern counterparts, they could sure make the refugees feel as menaced and uncomfortable as possible. And that is just what they did.

Through the spring and into summer, as the GRM and Resource Center staff and crews sweated and labored, the progressive takeover of government/cartel control showed itself in numerous ways: ransacking tents and burning them; threatening to take kids and turn them over to Mexico's child protective services, DIF; random teens watching over GRM's operations by day; strangers approaching and confronting the staff at all hours.

"Our presence kept the worst of the harassment in check," Helen believes. "Human rights abuses are much easier to get away with when they go unseen. Being in the camp, we could keep an eye on things."

In the same Al Jazeera interview, Garay stated that the Mexican government had covered most costs for camp infrastructure. This simply was not true. The only costs the Mexican government shouldered were to erect the domes to cover tents—"which collapsed!" recalls Helen—and to encircle the camp in razor wire and send in their own security detail to police the gates. Everything of humanitarian value, anything that brought the refugees even a modicum of dignity—food, shelters, medical care; drinking water, solar power, and Port-a-Potties; the forty-four outdoor showers and laundry facilities; cooking stoves and the contents of the free stores—was financed and provided by Team Brownsville, the Angry Tías, the Resource Center, and GRM—all members of the Dignity Village Collaborative. GRM's Matamoros budget for 2020 alone was in the neighborhood of $1.2 million.

⁕

The stormwater management and implementation plan wasn't the only crushing responsibility Erin Hughes took on that summer. The refugees trapped on the Matamoros floodplain were still not out of danger in the event of a hurricane. Intense rainfall upriver feeds myriad tributaries, creeks, and streams, all of which lead to one place: the Rio Bravo. This can cause the river to rise dramatically from its usual nine feet, the width of a two-lane byway, to a thirty-foot high-speed torrent, as wide as a six-lane highway.

"Such an overflow," Erin informed me, "would flood the entire encampment," whose lowest point stood at twenty-three feet. What's more, the river is always the highest and fastest as it sluices past Matamoros before washing into the Gulf of Mexico. So Erin took on developing a flood watch and evacuation plan as well.

When she submitted her draft proposal to both the Migration Institute and her Dignity Village collaborators on June 23, the GRM field hospital had still not seen any action. Refugees they suspected might be coming down with the virus had been sent into isolation. But so far, though COVID raged all around them, not a single case had breached the camp gates, exploding Trump's second big lie: that people seeking safety were all vectors for disease.

GRM's prevention protocols were working. Residents were taking them seriously, following all precautions.

A month later, on Friday, July 24, when a tropical storm formed in the Gulf at the mouth of the Mississippi River, save for three mild cases, there was still no sign of coronavirus in the camp.

||||||||||||||||||||||||||||||||||||||||||||||||||||||||

At 11:00 a.m. Central Time on July 25, the storm had picked up speed. Clocking in at eighty knots, close to one hundred miles per hour, it was now officially a hurricane. And it was heading straight for Matamoros.

When Hurricane Hanna made landfall, reaching Texas's South Padre Island at 5:00 p.m., the refugees were already zipped up tight inside their tents. But the driving rains and gale-force winds were punishing for those who had nothing but canvas and nylon to shield them from the elements. At 6:15 p.m., Hanna sat right on top of them. She raged on throughout the sleepless night, bringing down trees and hurling debris as she dumped eighteen inches of rain in a matter of hours amidst children's screams and the prayers of Pastor Abraham. He stayed with the camp residents, leading a community prayer vigil throughout the night in the former World Central Kitchen mess tent. When Sunday, July 26, dawned, the winds calmed and the clouds parted, somewhat. The refugees stepped out of their rudimentary shelters to find that both camp and residents survived the inundation.

Erin's storm plan had worked. The on-site interventions of culverts and berms protected living areas as intended. Except for puddles and pools that had to be pumped out to mitigate bug infestations, the water found its way around people and tents and into the river. In fact, the encampment had fared better than in the spring when a normal downpour left whole areas underwater.

"God protected us," states Pastor Abraham. Now it was time to clean up and kick Erin's flood risk assessment and evacuation plan into gear, which she based on the following elevation markers:

- 19 ft = Warning. Begin to pack. Clear the hospital of all equipment.
- 21 ft = Too close for comfort. Move the lowest dwellings to higher ground.
- 23 ft = Flooding begins at the lowest elevation. Evacuate to the Plaza.
- 30 ft = Total inundation will reach the top of the levee.

However, a fifth and final step in Erin's plan had yet to be resolved: where to take the refugees in the event of an evacuation.

"Asylum seekers would be sitting ducks for contracting the deadly disease in the city shelters," states Erin. With Matamoros then registering COVID death tolls equal to neighboring Cameron County, that was a risk no one wished to take. Erin's flood models predicted that the water would reach twenty-three feet, overflowing the banks but not for a few days. "There was plenty of time to relocate individuals and families whose tents were pitched in the risk zone," she felt.

Sam agreed. "It was my role to validate Erin's data and predictions," he told me. He called the International Boundaries and Water Commission and they, too, confirmed that the river, while on the rise, would not reach its highest level until Wednesday or Thursday. It would likely surpass twenty-three feet, compromising GRM's field hospital and flooding about half the encampment. But the highest points of the floodplain would be safe. So all hands were on deck to break down and move "anything of value not nailed down." Shelters went closer to the berm. The hospital's component parts went into the Resource Center building.

Then, on Monday, July 27, came a force potentially more devastating than anything the camp residents and humanitarians had encountered thus far.

Migration Institute officers barged into the encampment at approximately 11:00 a.m., shouting for everyone to clear out, immediately. They had received a call—no one could say from whom. Floodgates upriver had been opened or a dam had crumbled—they weren't sure which. Details aside, it was time to go. *Now!* The camp would be underwater by nightfall. *Go!*

The refugees, many of them people of the land, looked at the river. It was moving no more quickly than an hour, or even a day, before. They looked at the officials who had been trying to get rid of them for more than a year and they had no doubts: they were being lied to.

Without data and charts, they sided with *Las Ingenieras* (the lady engineers). They refused to budge.

The officers retreated. They called Sister Norma, who called Gaby. Preferring to err on the side of caution, Norma sent Gaby into the encampment to try again. She arrived at 3:30 p.m., this time bearing an updated message: *The floodplain would be underwater by midnight.*

"We were put under tremendous pressure," states Sam. "Lives were at stake. They were in our hands. With Norma contributing to the fears being kicked up by INM, we humanitarians were ready to move. But not the camp residents."

Even threats and language like *this is not up for discussion* didn't work. The camp residents simply did not trust what they were being told.

Sam phoned all the experts again, including the Brownsville Fire Department and the Cameron County Council. Everyone told him the same thing: *If floodgates had been opened or a dam had been breached, Reynosa would be underwater by now.*

"This is when we realized the refugees would resist being further displaced to the death," recalls Sam.

"If, and when, they saw the water coming they would adjust but they would not take the word of people who'd repeatedly tried to force them back home. For many, that *would* be death," adds Helen.

In the Migration Institute officials, they saw only duplicity—a manufactured crisis. They threw in their lot with the river. It turned out to be a good decision. No dam broke. No floodgates were opened. The river rose, slowly and steadily, just as Erin predicted, hitting its peak on Thursday.

"We were blown away by the bravery of these people to live through all that," says Erin, meaning the hurricane, rising waters, and the authorities' attempts to sow distrust and create division. In subsequent days, the team followed the asylum seekers' lead. Resident safety became their sole preoccupation.

But the aftermath was costly.

〰〰〰〰〰〰〰〰〰〰〰〰〰〰〰〰〰

The encampment was a mess following Hurricane Hanna. The rising river brought polluted water, rats, and venomous snakes. Mosquitoes proliferated in the post-storm humidity, feeding without mercy on human flesh. Suspicions grew among residents and humanitarians alike that their newest neighbors were not limited to critters.

Had the camp been infiltrated by the cartel as well? Was this INM's retaliation for their not moving?

Morale fell to an all-time low as those with still-pending asylum claims saw the end of the pandemic, and the resumption of their legal processes, stretch ever farther into the horizon. The Dignity Village collaborators sensed it, too.

"In spring we felt invincible, driven by adrenaline and a creative energy born of the tremendous responsibility to keep people safe and alive," remembers GRM's Andrea Leiner. "After the hurricane, we felt a collective sadness. We feared we'd lost control."

Three weeks after the hurricane, their suspicions were confirmed when the Guatemalan nation-group leader, Rodrigo, was found floating face down in the river. Official reports were that he drowned trying to save some pregnant women who were attempting to cross, though he didn't know how to swim. But everyone knew that was a fiction to rival the post-hurricane opening of the floodgates upriver.

Desperate, Rodrigo had tried to get his wife, two daughters, grandmother, and sister to safety on the other side of the line. But with the drug trade hammered by COVID lockdowns, kidnapping, extortion, and the trafficking of folks trapped by Title 42 were on the rise as the cartels' most lucrative revenue stream. They could not let Rodrigo get away with taking his family across without payment.

More crucially, they had to send a message to everyone else considering a DIY approach to crossing the line.

So, yes, media reports were not entirely wrong. Rodrigo did drown in the river. He couldn't "swim" because staying afloat is impossible when you've been beaten unconscious or forced to wear cement shoes.

So, no. No one slept well in the summer of 2020.

CHAPTER TWENTY-NINE

Locked Up

When COVID also caused ICE to suspend advocate and family visitations to its immigration gulag nationwide, on March 13, 2020, Pastor Steven Tendo's immune system was already shot. A lifelong diabetic, he had been able to control his condition, while he walked free. But since December 2018, when he presented himself at the Gateway International Bridge and requested asylum in the US, he'd been locked up inside the Port Isabel Detention Center. There, he'd been given the same moldy-bologna-on-frozen-white-bread sandwich—with chips or a cookie on the side—as everyone else. Not a diabetic's diet. His blood sugar levels were checked only every three months and his medications had been altered to half his necessary daily dosage, according to court filings signed by his three-attorney appeals team, which included Tía Jennifer.

His glucose readings had reached such dangerous levels by the spring of 2020, he was going blind—though that may also have been due to developing cataracts, diagnosed when Pastor Steven began to experience headaches behind his right eye. He was plagued by an itchy rash and painful, recurring boils. His toes were green with fungus and his feet emitted an embarrassing odor that would not be washed away. He suffered from constant exhaustion. He was thirty pounds underweight. He reported numbness and tingling sensations he'd never felt before. He grew so worried about dying of COVID that his blood pressure went through the roof—another health condition his minders ignored.

It was with such negligence toward the imprisoned in mind that Al Otro Lado, a binational immigrant advocacy and legal aid organization, joined forces with a coalition of more than thirty-five human rights groups and private attorneys to file a nationwide class-action lawsuit on August 19, 2019. *Fraihat v. ICE* charged the federal agency and its parent, the US Department of Homeland Security, as well as all the profiteers acting under their auspices, with failure to provide a class of 55,000 people, incarcerated without charge on any given day, adequate and appropriate medical and mental health care.

The suit charged ICE, furthermore, with making no provisions for the special needs of immigrants living with disabilities, and for routinely punishing those who dared to protest their lack of care with time in "el pozo"—aka "the hole," aka solitary confinement—what ICE refers to by the understated label of Special Housing Unit, or "the SHU." Forced isolation in tiny, windowless cells where the lights never turn off, the temperature is set to bitter cold, and mattresses and blankets are seldom provided only exacerbated frail health.

It's also the very definition of torture as codified by the UN.

Seven months later, in the midst of a global pandemic, counsel for the plaintiffs in *Fraihat v. ICE* sought an emergency order in the still-untried suit. They demanded an immediate process that would allow those with special risk factors, like Pastor Steven, to be released to shelter safely with sponsors or families.

⠀⠀⠀⠀⠀⠀||||||||||||||||||||||||||||||||||||||||||||||||||||||||||||||||

Pastor Steven had already survived arbitrary torture at the hands of a cruel government. His "crime"? Registering new voters and educating people about their human rights.

By the time he fled his native Uganda in September 2018, he had been arrested without charge and held against his will at least twelve times. The abuses he suffered included the severing of two of his fingers; burning his flesh with molten, dripping plastic; beating him with methods that left no physical scars, referred to euphemistically as "VIP treatment"; leaving him to hang from rafters for hours with a brick tied to his genitals; and making him share a pit with an angry, frightened python that whipped the pastor mercilessly with its powerful, stinging tail.

His wasn't a special case. When Yoweri Museveni grabbed his country's top job for a fifth time in 2016, he declared that it would be "the term of no games." Amnesty International confirmed in 2017 that rights to freedom of expression, association, and assembly were being increasingly severely restricted in Uganda. The US State Department concurred, writing in time for Pastor Steven's asylum hearing that the Ugandan government was "reluctant to investigate, prosecute, or punish officials who committed human rights abuses, whether in the security services or elsewhere in government, and impunity was a problem."

Pastor Steven was clearly persecuted for his political views: he supported the opposition candidate, who almost forced Museveni into retirement, Bobi Wine. Museveni's goon squad, the Black Mamba, had already assassinated Steven's uncle, a police officer thought to be protecting his nephew, when Steven's brother was also killed on August 13, 2018. He was Bobi Wine's personal driver.

"I knew that I was the next target," Pastor Steven told Immigration Judge Frank T. Pimentel in May 2019. "I ran out of my country to save my life."

Pastor Steven's credible fear of persecution if returned to Uganda was topped off with a signed medical examination, stating that his head, chest, back, legs, buttocks, genitals, and hands all showed signs of torture. Still, Judge Pimentel denied Steven's request for political asylum that June.

Appointed to the immigration bench by Attorney General Sessions in 2017, Judge Pimentel had no background in immigration law. And he didn't really seem to care, according to attorneys and advocates. Pimentel denied asylum cases nearly 90 percent of the time.

"Judge Pimentel sentenced me to death that day," says Pastor Steven.

।।

When the coronavirus was declared a pandemic nearly a year later, Pastor Steven was still locked up under ICE. Prisons across the globe were letting their occupants out, lest COVID turn them into death traps. UN High Commissioner for Human Rights Michelle Bachelet called on governments worldwide to release "every person detained without sufficient legal basis." She meant political prisoners denied freedom without charge for expressing critical views. Folks seeking asylum fall into that bucket, too.

Even Iran set 80,000 prisoners free, cutting its prison population in half. But not ICE. It still held over 38,000 adults in its custody when much of the world locked down. Former acting head of ICE John Sandweg reminded the agency that, "Unlike the Federal Bureau of Prisons, ICE has complete control"—that's 100 percent discretion—"over the release of individuals."

Inside ICE prisons, it was fear and chaos, and quite a lot of loathing, too.

On March 23, sixty immigrant detainees at GEO Group's South Texas Immigrant Detention Center in Pearsall, Texas, rioted after learning about the pandemic on TV. Their demand for immediate freedom was greeted with a "use of force" protocol: guards doused them with pepper spray. Though considered a poison by the US Centers for Disease Control and said to be able "to stop a grizzly bear in its tracks," pepper spray is allowed throughout the US prison-industrial complex, even against people seeking protection.

On March 24, at GEO Group's Pine Prairie Detention Center in Louisiana, eight guards and an assistant warden dressed in riot gear overpowered seven panicked individuals incarcerated without charge, pepper spraying them from less than two feet away. Then they threw these non-criminals into solitary confinement. The dousing they suffered was so severe, according to victims' statements, that it was too painful to wear clothes even the following day.

Also on March 24, seven women imprisoned at GEO Group's LaSalle Detention Center in Jena, Louisiana, protested the lax social distancing measures and lack of hand sanitizer, disinfectants, and personal hygiene products. They, too, were showered in asphyxiating levels of pepper spray.

On March 31, at the Port Isabel Detention Center, where Pastor Steven languished, a staff member was confirmed to have contracted the virus. Yet life went on as before: Guards and staff continued to pass in and out of the facility with no precautions. They prepared and served inmates' meals without wearing masks or gloves. They supplied neither criminal nor immigrant detainees with soap or hand sanitizer—only those with commissary funds could purchase such lifesaving items, and at inflated prices. Social distancing remained impossible where 1,500 men slept seventy to a dorm in bunk beds set a mere three feet apart. And where four toilets for seventy men stood out in the open, clogging often, bacteria was allowed to spread freely as management denied detainees disinfectant and masks.

Scared that they would never see their loved ones again, an estimated ninety individuals at Port Isabel initiated a hunger strike on March 31. Hunger strikes were already underway at three ICE facilities in New Jersey—all protesting the lack of COVID precautions. The Port Isabel strike was quashed immediately with guards sending its leaders straight into "the SHU."

llllllllllllllllllllllllllllllllllllllllllllllllllllllll

On April 3, attorneys for plaintiffs in *Fraihat v. ICE* argued that an ICE facility outbreak not only put the lives of detainees at risk, but would menace the non-detained population as well, further straining local hospitals. On April 20, US Judge Jesus Bernal of the Central District of California decided in the plaintiffs' favor, finding ICE's response to the pandemic to be "systemically deficient, deliberately indifferent, and in violation of the US Constitution and federal disability laws."

Bernal ordered ICE to conduct release redeterminations for every person under its custody at heightened risk of contracting the coronavirus and let them out. He also ordered ICE to create a free, confidential hotline to ensure that incarcerated asylum seekers could reach *Fraihat* class counsel. A tsunami of calls from people in crisis followed, exposing the panic that gripped ICE prison populations at the time.

In May, ICE had released some 900 individuals, but it continued to hold over 30,000 asylum seekers, many of them African nationals. Anecdotal evidence from inmates, advocates, and attorneys alike confirms that while Latinx asylum seekers without criminal records were let go, ICE kept its Black population locked up tight. Given that, as we've seen, the agency's roots can be traced to the Slave Patrols, this probably shouldn't surprise us. Even the UN Committee on the Elimination of

Racial Discrimination says it's time for the US government to take seriously and dismantle its racially discriminatory immigration practices. Backing up a multitude of statements that "the Blacker the skin, the worse you have it under ICE," is a mountain of reporting from human rights watchdog groups. Despite impeccable records and clear paths to sponsorship, single African men suffer, on average, longer terms in ICE detention, increased punishments, worse job assignments, higher bond fees, and withholding of prison privileges, if they get privileges at all.

"There is the verbal abuse," says Pastor Steven, "calling you monkey, boy, and other racial slurs, telling you 'go back to the jungle.' There is the emotional abuse from constant threats of deportation or time in the SHU. There is the physical abuse of denying medical care and feeding us only enough calories to keep us alive but not to thrive."

Even in the wake of the *Fraihat* ruling, a Texas district court judge denied Pastor Steven's request for immediate release, twice.

⁜⁜⁜⁜⁜⁜⁜⁜⁜⁜⁜⁜⁜⁜⁜⁜⁜⁜⁜⁜⁜⁜⁜⁜⁜⁜⁜⁜⁜⁜⁜⁜⁜⁜⁜

COVID, of course, didn't respect court orders. On June 12, Port Isabel management acknowledged twenty-six confirmed cases and another twenty-three "under observation." Steven counted "more like fifty-eight or sixty people down with virus" at that time. "They were taken to isolation. Some we never saw again. It's hard to say if they died—ICE never said. People were leaving, and not coming back."

On June 26, a Port Isabel security officer died. Cause of death: coronavirus.

Yet, "they kept bringing in new people," states Pastor Steven, "literally spreading the virus around, transporting the virus between jails."

In early July, a second hunger strike erupted at the lockup in Port Isabel. This time, 120 non-criminal immigrant inmates protested their detention in the midst of the pandemic. "I consoled myself with the Bible," states Pastor Steven. "I convinced myself I was brave enough to fight through it."

Pastor Steven's prayers caught on. Inmates flocked to him for comfort. "They drew strength from his sermons," says Tía Madeleine. A ministry grew, with up to eighty people at a time attending his services.

On July 4, Steven circulated a letter to the media written by his dorm mate and friend Carl, a Cameroonian who had then been separated from his wife and daughter for nine months. *Dear US Taxpayers*, the letter began. *Did you know? Your hard-earned dollars are being used to fund the torture of asylum seekers. I know, because I am one of them.*

When I asked if this would put him in danger of retaliation, Pastor Steven replied, "I'm either going to die in ICE prison or in Uganda." He resolved to speak with anyone willing to listen, which is to say, with anyone willing to pour money into his Getting Out phone account. Inside ICE, you must pay to play. And though it killed me to give my hard-earned shekels to GEO Group, which milked me of a small fortune that summer, I became one of many lifelines for Pastor Steven and other ICE inmates at that time.

With the in-person visitation programs shut down, these fifteen-minute, monitored phone calls became their only contact with the outside world—the only non-detained human contact some would have for two years. Attorneys and advocates for the incarcerated began to coalesce, first in a shared email listserv, then in a WhatsApp chat group. Among them was Witness at the Border's Tom Cartwright, who, unable to sleep while locked down at home in Columbus, Ohio, continued to bear witness to the unfriendly skies of ICE Air. Ironically, with global commercial flight movements virtually grounded, Tom found it easier to track ICE Air's chartered operations: "By midsummer, they are just about the only planes in the air," he recalls.

|||||||||||||||||||||||||||||||||||||||||||||||||||||||||||

In July, Pastor Steven lost his appetite and sense of smell. He found it difficult to breathe, "like my diaphragm was unable to work properly." He described the pain as "like a fire in my chest, like I'm exploding from within." He experienced discomfort in all his joints. He began to sneeze and cough, uncontrollably. But he declined to disclose these symptoms to his minders.

"I didn't want to go to isolation. Being locked up all alone is worse than anything."

Week two was really hard. He spent his days curled up in prayer on the bottom bed of the bunk that had been his home now for nineteen months. "By day fourteen you know if you are going to recover or die." Sometime in the third week, he felt his energy return. By week four, he not only felt better, he'd lost his fear: of both the virus and ICE retaliation.

In August, the frequency, urgency, and reach of his calls increased. "The world must know what is going on inside ICE prisons," he stated. In a letter to the press, he wrote, "A dead body cannot be detained."

That's when ICE moved to stamp out Pastor Steven's growing influence and public profile.

On August 30, an ICE deportation officer told him: *Pack your things. We are transferring you tomorrow.*

Steven tried to refuse. He had waited five months for cataract surgery, which was scheduled for September 3. He was no longer able to see out of his right eye, and his left eye was going. He had lost his sense of balance, so was no longer exercising.

He called Tía Madeleine and each of his three lawyers in turn, Tía Jennifer, Lisa Brodyaga, and Cathy Potter. They all said the same thing: *You have the right to resist.*

When the officers came to his dorm the next morning, he stood his ground. With Carl bearing witness, he told them, "I'm not going anywhere. Not until I have my surgery."

"They tell me, *we don't care. You're leaving come rain or come shine.*"

Suddenly, "maybe eight, maybe ten guards surrounded me." Carl says it was more like fifteen. "I can only describe it as a SWAT team," says Steven. Carl referred to it as "the ICE military."

ICE calls it the Special Response Team, or SRT. A branch of the Department of Homeland Security, they are trained "to deal with extreme/dangerous situations," according to the American Special Ops website. There are twenty-two deployable ICE SRT teams, each consisting of sixteen to eighteen agents—so Carl's guess was closer. They are trained at the former Fort Benning, now Fort Moore, US Army post in Georgia.

"They swarmed the dorm," says Steven. "They jumped onto beds. They were everywhere."

Through shock and fear, Carl described to me how the ICE SRT "wrestled Steven to the ground, flipped him face down, and put a knee on his neck, like George Floyd." They restrained Pastor Steven—and not just in five-point shackles. "They rolled him up in a kind of thin black mattress, like a tortilla. They treated it like sport."

Pastor Steven describes it differently: "I was bagged and tied," he told me. And when I asked for details, he said, "I was stuffed into a sack. They bound my legs together. They cuffed my hands so tight they damaged the nerves in my thumbs. You cannot resist them, Sarah. They are an overwhelming force. They will tase you, render you numb, powerless. They lifted me up on their shoulders and carried me out of the dorm like pallbearers carrying a coffin."

That's when advocates, attorneys, and friends alike lost sight of Pastor Steven.

⁣⁣⁣

"First, they put me in a cold room. They came to tell me they were trans-ferring me for medical reasons. But they handed me over to ICE ERO."

That's ICE Enforcement and Removals Operations, the sub-agency that manages the ICE Air deportation machine.

"These guys are terrifying. Unapproachable. They are trained soldiers. Maybe ex-Marines. They are tough guys. Very rough. You find only brutality in their hands."

They conveyed Pastor Steven to a white van, still "bagged and tied." Though like a jail cell on wheels—a fortified armored vehicle that locked from the outside—they kept him bound for the entire trip to the Laredo International Airport, three-and-a-half hours away. Loosening only the center of the three yellow straps that constrained his legs in black mesh, they bent his knees as they placed him on the seat and belted him in. His arms remained immobilized and cuffed behind his back, forcing his body to pitch painfully forward.

"Hands tied behind you is the worst because the body is not used to being in a position like that for very long."

It's defined as a "stress position" by the UN Convention Against Torture, making it illegal under international law. Steven had to work physically very hard not to topple over to the left or right each time the van turned a corner or followed a bend in the road.

Terrorized, Pastor Steven soiled himself. But rather than releasing the bonds and letting him get cleaned up on arrival at the Laredo airport, his ICE handlers "cinched the black and yellow 'tortilla' that made me look like a bumble bee," back up and carried him onto a plane. It held two other passengers already. Both Ugandans. Both similarly enchained and restrained.

En route to GEO Group's Alexandria Airport and ICE Staging Facility in Louisiana, Pastor Steven had to sit in his own excrement. Only there was he escorted into a shower and told to strip off his garments.

It took him three years to tell me this part of his tale. "They exhume pain and shame. They were so inhumane. I never wanted to talk about that."

Alexandria, by all accounts, is a strange facility: a panopticon,[12] a prison in which inmates are made to believe they are under surveillance at all times. The interior walls are all transparent so that immigrant inmates can be observed at all times. It has dorms big enough for 70 men, which face the airport runway. There is a large central room, where people are bound and shackled before being boarded onto flights. It also has two-person cells, reserved for those ICE deems to be "high security," I'm told by Sarah Decker, attorney with RFK Human Rights. "Though it's rarely clear why people are given that classification," says Sarah, "it often seems to be applied without justification, and sometimes in retaliation."

While at Alexandria, Pastor Steven witnessed six other men, three at a time—all African nationals—get tackled to the ground and "bagged and tied" before being removed from the facility. He saw it all through the see-through walls. Two days later, they bound him in the full-body black-and-yellow human restraint again. He was carried onto another plane, with another forty or so people.

He had been lied to. He was being deported. There was little he could do. "Once you are in their hands, you have to go."

"At each stop," he says, "ICE was picking up new people." From Louisiana, they were flown to CoreCivic's Florence Detention Center

---

12. French philosopher Michel Foucault was an outspoken critic of the panopticon. He considered it, though ingenious, to be the cruelest, most inhumane, and degrading of human cages. Making them believe they are being watched even when they aren't, panopticon policing induces prisoners into a perpetual state of heightened anxiety and paranoia.

in Arizona via "somewhere in Texas," where ICE loaded on more Black people in chains. "The plane was full, approximately 150 people." Everyone was manacled in leg irons and wrist cuffs attached to chains draped around waists. Movements were commanded, not requested. Orders were shouted. No one was kind.

"Under ICE, we are treated like criminals. Under ICE ERO, we were treated like terrorists," says Steven.

"The cuffs around my wrists were so tight, I started to bleed. When I asked that they be loosened, they cinched them up tighter," he continues.

"What would we do in an accident? We couldn't get to our oxygen masks!"

Pastor Steven tried not to think about being enchained like this all the way to Uganda, "a trip that can last more than twenty-four hours. We were bound and enchained from Louisiana to Arizona—for seven hours. There is no humanity on an ICE Air flight. When I asked to pee, they said, *NO!*"

He told his handlers, "There are laws against treating even terrorists this way!"

They told him, "We're just doing our job."

||||||||||||||||||||||||||||||||||||||||||||||||||||||||||

Pastor Steven would have been deported on September 3, the same day of his intended cataract surgery, had Tías Madeleine and Jennifer, attorneys Lisa and Cathy, and an army of other advocates—I was one of them—not waged an all-out campaign on Capitol Hill. In a letter to then-Acting Secretary of the Department of Homeland Security, Chad Wolf, forty-four members of Congress demanded that the agency release him on medical grounds, while the motion to reopen his case was still pending with the US Fifth Circuit of Appeals. Amnesty International and other human rights organizations mobilized to save Pastor Steven as well.

At around midnight on September 7, while still imprisoned in Florence, Arizona, Pastor Steven learned that he would not be deported after all. At least not yet. He stayed awake and prayed with at least ten other Ugandans, many of whom had also been victims of torture. Then he watched as they were bound and moved toward the small Gulfstream aircraft that awaited to refoul them. One man, Cebufu, tried to shrug off the ICE ERO agents who came for him. He, too, was knocked to the ground, flipped face down, and stuffed into the black and yellow sack, then carried onto the plane, "bagged and tied."

"I will never forget that day," Pastor Steven told me. "I was in so much fear." He was actually relieved to be returned to his captors at Port Isabel. "I would rather be in ICE detention than under the knee of ICE ERO on an ICE Air deportation flight."

When I shared news of Steven's odyssey with Tom Cartwright, he wondered out loud, "Is ICE rounding up Africans, now?"

As for me, I couldn't stop imagining how a grown man gets stuffed into a sack.

CHAPTER THIRTY

Locked Out

Through the spring and summer of 2020, complaints against ICE piled up. They landed in the inboxes of Department of Homeland Security Inspector General Joseph Cuffari and Officer for Civil Rights and Civil Liberties Cameron Quinn. Buried unseen within the bowels of the US government, like the innermost figurine of a Russian nesting doll, the Office for Civil Rights and Civil Liberties was established to ensure that the multilayered post-9/11 law enforcement bureaucracies didn't lose sight of the rights guaranteed by the US Constitution—even to noncitizens—as they steered us toward a security-first paradigm.

A forum for internal oversight and policymaking, the civil rights office has the power to investigate grievances, write reports, and recommend fixes. But it cannot enforce its prescriptions. Its advocacy, moreover, is not for public view—only the investigations of the Homeland Security inspector general are posted. And although staffed by experienced attorneys in the area of civil liberties and human rights, the office is not empowered to give legal advice.

That is why Scott Shuchart quit his job as senior advisor to the chief of the office, known to insiders as CRCL, when Trump's Tanton network cabal dreamed up zero tolerance and started tearing families apart without checking with experts, like him, first. "I thought that was illegal (contrary to treaties and to the substantive due process prong of the Fifth Amendment), un-American, and seriously wrong," he told the nonpartisan Project On Government Oversight in December 2018.

Shuchart left his post, publicly, after eight years. Writing for the Center for American Progress, he states that Trump & Co "exposed long-standing limits on CRCL's ability to meaningfully fulfill its mission in the face of political leaders who continuously aim to violate the US Constitution."

Which comes down to this: if you combine a Homeland Security secretary who, as Shuchart states of John Kelly, "did not have the minimum level of basic education on the subjects DHS manages to lead the organization," with a bad watchdog, ICE and Customs and Border Protection impunity can go unchecked. And it did in the Trump years, because Inspector General Cuffari and Officer Quinn were very bad watchdogs, indeed. As I write these words, Cuffari still is.[13]

While those who've been imprisoned in Ohio's Morrow County or Colorado's Aurora lockup might dispute the claim, many say that the barbarity inside ICE's New Orleans Field Office knows no equal. Invisibilized in the Deep South states of Alabama, Arkansas, Louisiana, Mississippi, and my home state of Tennessee, incarcerated African nationals seeking asylum were neither getting out nor getting relief during the Trump years.

This was in large part due to immigration judges like Scott Laragy. Appointed by Sessions in 2018, Laragy had denied asylum to Cameroonians 100 percent of the time when "Tikem," a shop owner from the northwestern, Anglophone-speaking region of the bilingual nation, stood before him. By then, thousands of Anglophone Cameroonians had lost their lives in Francophone President Paul Biya's "Unseen War," called that due to the negligence of the international community to check the dictator's war crimes and other abuses. Millions of Anglophone Cameroonians had already been forcibly displaced; millions more still in country were in need of urgent humanitarian assistance.

---

13. Despite a blistering letter delivered to Joe Biden by Cuffari's own staff, begging the new president to remove their boss due to his lack of integrity and impartial, independent thought, and similar criticisms from congressional committee chairs, Cuffari was still the bad watchdog of the world's largest, and most troubled, law enforcement apparatus as this book went to press. This is because, while on the campaign trail in 2020, Biden promised that he would not repeat Trump's serial removal of inspectors general who did not hew to his version of reality and the law.

Cameroonians seeking asylum in the US should have been a shoo-in under the 1951 Refugee Convention, by virtue of their social group. This was especially true if, like Tikem, a credible fear of harm if returned had been established and past persecution could be proved. But those trapped in the New Orleans Field Office of ICE were twice as likely to be denied asylum than similarly situated applicants from non-African countries—which was new.

At the end of the Obama-Biden administration, the same ICE Field Office granted parole for individuals seeking asylum three-quarters of the time. By 2018, however, that rate had dropped to 1.5 percent. Under Trump & Co, immigration detention grew by over 50 percent, according to the American Civil Liberties Union, with contracts for forty new detention facilities that overwhelmingly benefitted private prison companies.

Money flew, in particular, to the Deep South. ICE beds skyrocketed from 1,000 to about 13,000 in Louisiana alone.

⸻

"Even before we had a chance to present our cases," says Tikem, "Judge Laragy would tell us, *Better just sign your deportation papers, even if you appeal I will stop you*. He told us that we were wasting our time because we were going back no matter what."

In protest, Tikem donned his Black Lives Matter T-shirt—bought at inflated prices from the GEO Group–controlled commissary of the ICE prison in Pine Prairie, Louisiana—and joined forty-two other men, mostly Africans. The men wanted a fair shake, at least; at most, they wanted to be heard. So, they initiated a hunger strike on March 3, 2020, to denounce their prolonged incarceration and the biased court judgments of Laragy.

Tikem and an Oxford-educated Nigerian lawyer named "Bernard" ingested no food or water for nearly two weeks. Even when guards tried to break them with time in isolation—it's called Echo at Pine Prairie—the two persevered.

"We kept it peaceful," Tikem told me. "We gave them no cause to abuse us."

Finally, when their physical condition tipped toward critical, ICE sent an officer—Officer Don—to talk with the men. Every person locked up under ICE is supposed to be assigned a deportation officer, or DO. But the dozens of men and women I have spoken to who had the misfortune of being locked up in the New Orleans Field Office jurisdiction had DOs in name only. Each asylum-seeking inmate's name was paired with a DO written on a document attached to a facility wall. Next to each phantom officer's name was a phone number. Calls were never answered. And the assigned DOs changed every few months. Basically, there was no one inside ICE that asylum-seeking individuals could talk to.

Officer Don was nice, according to Tikem. He and Bernard agreed to end their strike if Officer Don promised to go to the Oakdale Court to investigate their claims. "He did. He confirmed that Laragy's ruling was wrong, that our documents were fit for parole. He told us we were right, that Laragy was giving no one from Cameroon protection."

A lawyer representing five other Cameroonians also incarcerated at Pine Prairie reported the same: Laragy was letting no one out. "With those two things aligned," says Tikem, "we understood ourselves to be victims of routine bias."

When COVID struck, Tikem was stuck.

"I was brought up to believe that the US was a land of laws, a beacon of hope for the oppressed, a champion of liberty and human rights. But the US enslaved us. As long as we were locked up under ICE, people were making money off us." About $7 million a day calculates writer John Washington in his inspired 2024 book, *The Case for Open Borders*.

‖‖‖

The prisoners of Pine Prairie went on hunger strike twice more in the summer of 2020, the second and third times to protest being imprisoned during the pandemic. On Monday, August 10, a group of roughly forty-five Black, majority Cameroonian asylum-seeking inmates entered the mess hall. They picked up their unappetizing servings of rice and beans and expired, spoiled chicken. They walked across the cafeteria to the dishwashing station and slid their untouched meals through the window to be discarded. Then they went into the hallway and sat on the floor. They put their hands in the air, signaling their peaceful intentions.

A fifteen-member SWAT team descended upon the men dressed, recalls Tikem, "like they were going to war." They were armed with tear gas and pepper spray, handcuffs and batons. They climbed on top of three of the peaceful protesters, locking them into painful choke holds. Panic took over the group as the three men struggled to breathe. But they refused to fight back.

Tikem pleaded with the officers, his hands still in the air. He said, "We are peaceful. We have committed no crime. We just want to talk. Someone needs to listen to us!"

Miraculously, the SWAT unit backed off. The facility guards promised to bring someone to speak with the hunger strikers. But after four days had elapsed, no one came.

So the men renewed their hunger strike. This time, they each prepared a bag first, expecting to be thrown into Echo. And they were, two to a cell. Amid the yelling and screaming and rough-handling of guards, some of the cells had to be emptied of quarantined COVID patients first. The cells were not disinfected. The men were given no water. They were forced to drink from the toilet.

||||||||||||||||||||||||||||||||||||||||||||||||||||||||||||||||

The incident resulted in another legal complaint against ICE. Brought by the Cameroon American Council, Freedom for Immigrants, New Orleans-based Immigration Services and Legal Advocacy, and the Southern Poverty Law Center on August 26, it beseeched Cuffari and Quinn, "in the name of integrity and accountability," to investigate and remedy the racist violence leveled against detained peaceful hunger strikers at Pine Prairie.

But Cuffari and Quinn did not act. Instead, ICE split the men up and sent them in different directions.

When Tikem and Bernard arrived at ICE's oddly named Allen Parish Public Safety Complex in Oberlin, Louisiana, the assistant warden, a man everyone called King Chavez, met them with a gun. "He put us into isolation to quarantine. He told us we were sent there because he heard we were 'troublemakers.' He told us, *There are no troublemakers here. I have a gun. And I will shoot you.* He said it while laughing, but we never took it lightly."

"In the whole of my career," says Luz Virginia Lopez, senior supervising attorney at the Southern Poverty Law Center and co-signer to the August 26 complaint, "I've never seen anything like the lawlessness and corruption, the brutality and complete disregard for human life, the xenophobia and anti-Blackness." Luz calls ICE's New Orleans Field Office "a microcosm of the worst of the Trump administration's immigration agenda."

And then there's the ICE Atlanta Field Office, which includes Georgia, North, and South Carolina, where the next complaint would originate thanks to ICE whistleblower Dawn Wooten.

|||||||||||||||||||||||||||||||||||||||||||||||||||||||||||

When I try to calculate the number of people on the inside of the many-headed Hydra that is the US immigration-industrial complex, I wonder why there aren't more voices like Dawn's. There is a mechanism: the Government Accountability Project. It has worked for more than forty years—since Daniel Ellsberg blew the whistle on government lying about the Vietnam War—to support and protect whistleblowers when their own ethical compass compels them to speak up for the truth.

Given the vast number of people contributing to the dehumanizing deterrence to detention to deportation system that robs one and all of due process under the law, it would only take a few Davids to take this Goliath down for good. With the help of Project South, Georgia Detention Watch, Georgia Latino Alliance for Human Rights, and South Georgia Immigrant Support Network, Dawn Wooten tried.

The September 14 complaint documented not just the same flagrant flouting of COVID safety protocols that we've seen at Port Isabel and Pine Prairie. Dawn also blew the whistle on the rogue medical treatment of women at Irwin County Detention Center in Ocilla, Georgia.

Irwin is run by a relative latecomer to the for-profit immigrant enslavement business, LaSalle Corrections, the family-owned and

-operated ICE contractor that allegedly sent female "inmates," including those seeking asylum, to the same gynecologist over the course of several years even when Dawn and her colleagues remarked to management that he might be performing nonconsensual medical procedures. If he was, then Dr. Mahendra Amin was making money off women jailed under ICE, billing the government for operations they did not need.

Even before Dawn came forward, a Cameroonian mother and teacher we'll call "Faith" told me, "All the women suspected something was happening." When she arrived at Irwin in the fall of 2018, Faith says, "The women told me they were killing our organs." The rumor going around at the time was that it might be something in the water.

Dawn and the other nurses found that the women in their charge would go outside the prison for gynecological checkups and return having undergone surgical procedures. The women didn't always understand what happened or why. They certainly had not given their informed consent.

One such person was Pauline Binam.

Pauline was told she needed surgery to remove one or more ovarian cysts. Upon waking at the Irwin County Hospital post-procedure, however, she learned that part of one of her fallopian tubes had been excised.

"I was shocked and appalled, hearing Nurse [Dawn] Wooten confirming what Pauline had been telling me all through 2019," says her attorney at the time, Vân Huynh. "She was adamant that she did not give consent."

||||||||||||||||||||||||||||||||||||||||||||||||||||||||||||

Pauline came to the US, like Robert Vivar, as a child. She was then just two years old. Born in Cameroon, she grew up in the US. It was the only home she'd ever known. Also like Robert, Pauline pled guilty to a shoplifting charge. It happened on her eighteenth birthday. She had no legal counsel. It marked her, following the dictates of IRA-IRA and other 1990s anti-immigrant legislation, as a "deportable alien."

At the time of Dawn's whistleblower disclosure, Pauline was thirty years old and had been locked up under ICE for almost three years, separated from her US-citizen daughter. She agreed to be publicly identified as a victim of and witness to medical abuse, and Vân Huynh sought an emergency pause on her removal orders. But two days after Dawn's complaint was filed, ICE tried to get rid of Pauline.

"[J]ust as we were learning about all these things that were coming out from Nurse Wooten—they wanted to put [Pauline] on a flight and try to deport her as soon as possible," Vân Huynh then stated.

There was no way Pauline was going back to a war zone, and a place where she knew no one, without a fight. Fortunately, she had a witness. With her at O'Hare airport, awaiting a one-way flight out of the US, was "Confident," a Cameroonian beautician and salon owner. Through the window of her shop back home, Confident saw members of the Francophone military murder two civilians, then frame them as separatist fighters in an attempt to justify the assassinations. When she, like Dawn, spoke out about what she knew, Confident became a target for persecution. She was arrested, detained, raped, and brutally beaten. As soon as she found freedom again, she ran. And like so many other Anglophone Cameroonians at that time, she opted to seek safety in the US, rather than follow the previously more typical route for Africans to that point: northward and across the Mediterranean to Europe.

In late 2016, when the lawyer- and teacher-led peaceful protests in Anglophone Cameroon were first violently repressed, Europe was closing up. Greece and Italy, with the blessing of the European Union, were paying Libya and Turkey to stop people in motion, prohibit pro-immigrant groups from rescuing those in distress, and drive folks back to Northern Africa and away from European borders. Tunisia and Libya are now paid handsomely to incarcerate people fleeing harm. Libya is a death trap, implicated in selling safety seekers into slavery or simply executing them.

After former German Chancellor Angela Merkel opened her borders to one million Syrian refugees in 2015, the EU and the UK were taken over by nationalism fueled by a xenophobic fervor to rival Trump's. The twenty-seven-member European Union began walling itself off then, earning it the moniker "Fortress Europe." It has since turned the Mediterranean Sea—like its Caribbean counterpart—into a migrant graveyard. That is why, despite the dangers of Panama's sixty-mile Darién Gap jungle and the multi-nation migratory trail, African refugees now opt to take the longer, land-based route from South America to the United States.

In 2017, Cameroonians began to arrive at the US-Mexico border for the first time. They were among the top ten nationalities seeking asylum in the US that year. It was bad timing and worse luck that they arrived in Trump's USA. When Trump & Co instituted their "travel ban"—aka asylum ban—in July 2019, anyone who didn't apply for protection, and get denied, in a pass-through country could be ruled ineligible for asylum.

In addition, many, like Confident, were forced to represent themselves *pro se*—on their own. Confident, who speaks a dialect of English called Pidgin, was not offered a translator and became quickly lost in the rapid-fire questions hurled at her by Immigration Judge Randall Duncan. The result was, of course, the denial of protection. Duncan moved her immediately back into expedited removal proceedings.

"When ICE tried to deport us through Chicago," she told me, "Pauline's lawyer advised her to make sure we were allowed to see our travel documents and to make sure they were signed by the ambassador." They weren't. They had been issued by ICE and signed by a Methodist minister in Houston named Charles R. Greene, who claimed at that time to be a "pending Honorary Consul of Cameroon."

"So, we sat down at the airport and raised our voices to create a scene. We shouted, 'This is fake!' We told our ICE escorts, 'What you're doing isn't right.'"

The women asked a passerby if they could borrow a phone. They called Vân Huynh and their families, who in turn called members of Congress. Representative Pramila Jayapal (D-WA), then-vice chair of the House Immigration Subcommittee, and Representative Sheila Jackson Lee (D-TX) came to the ladies' rescue. They led seventy-two other congressional representatives in demanding Cuffari to open an investigation into Dawn's allegations. He did, eventually. But not until late 2021. And only after intense advocacy.

Dr. Amin has denied any wrongdoing.

CHAPTER THIRTY-ONE

Locked On

ICE tried to whisk Pauline away but, like Steven, she had helpers in high places. The two were among the very, very lucky few. Confident was transferred in shackles right back to an ICE lockup for women in Conroe, Texas: the Montgomery Processing Center. This confirmed anecdotes by Tikem and Steven that ICE continued moving people around the country, even during the pandemic.

By that point, Tom Cartwright had amassed enough data to prove, beyond any reasonable doubt, that the agency wasn't just spreading the virus around its prison population. It was transporting COVID throughout the world, too, sending it to countries far less equipped to deal with it than even the US.

In Brownsville the previous January, while out at the airport each crack of dawn with Karla and the other witnesses, Tom became overwhelmed, imagining the magnitude of the ICE Air operation. "There were then over fifty thousand people imprisoned in over two hundred ICE facilities across the nation," he remembers.

And they were looking at just one airport.

"When we were forced into our homes by the pandemic, we realized we had already developed the methodologies and obtained the right tools to go on witnessing the ICE Air machine virtually," says Tom, whose goal was "to bring some transparency to this issue."

He began with a single research question: *Would the ICE Air operation change, either in deportation or domestic transfers, because of COVID?*

To answer that, he needed data from before the pandemic to compare with flight patterns after it was declared. He sought out other researchers working to unmask ICE Air's machinery. He found two: Professor Angelina Snodgrass-Godoy, director of the Center for Human Rights at the University of Washington, and Jake Johnston, senior research associate at the Center for Economic and Policy Research. They were happy to help.

"Basically nothing changed," says Tom. "We were seeing people being ferried between detention centers just as before, spreading the disease throughout the detention population."

After three months, his methods in place and the world still in lockdown, Tom decided to carry on. "The major contractors for ICE Air, Swift and World Atlantic, were not flying for casinos or music groups or professional and collegiate athletic teams and so forth. Those all came to a halt. So it was easier then to establish ICE Air's flight patterns and hub locations, to learn more about the types of planes being flown and under what circumstances."

By September 2020, Tom already had a monthly report with data and analysis going out to the press and members of Congress. He had graduated from using the free FlightAware app he and Karla began with in Brownsville to a paid version that allowed him to track each of the ICE Air contractors' combined fleets of one hundred planes. Triangulating airlines, aircraft tail numbers, and airports, he was able to isolate ICE Air's daily missions.

He has since built a system that distinguishes between ICE Air's domestic and international routes: "Shuffle flights" move people from prison to prison, while "removal flights" ferry people out of the country. Shuffles include two subcategories: "connecting flights," a shuffle that delivers to a removal flight; and "lateral flights," which move safety seekers from one southern port of entry to another to ease congestion in Border Protection hieleras. Finally, there are "return flights," the planes coming back empty after delivering their human cargo to worldwide locations.

Each hop, point-to-point, Tom calls a "leg." Of the one hundred planes he tracks, ten to fourteen planes regularly fly thirty-five to forty legs a day. While "laterals" hug the border, bouncing from Brownsville to San Diego and all points in between, a single plane might "shuffle" from Washington State to one of several places in Texas, picking up people along the way; then finish the day's mission in Louisiana, where it "connects" with a "removal" to Guatemala City, which then "returns" to Miami.

|||||||||||||||||||||||||||||||||||||||||||||||||||||||

By late Summer 2020, Tom had found a logic and predictable timing to the machinery, at least as far as the Western Hemisphere was concerned. The mysteries still yet to crack were the removal patterns to farther-flung places, like Africa and Asia. From April, Jake had tracked Omni Air International flights to Guinea and Liberia; India, Bangladesh, and Pakistan; Vietnam and South Korea; as well as to a handful of international locations more associated with US military bases than with forcibly displaced persons. But neither Jake nor Tom could say for certain who or what was on those planes: people deemed "deportable" or US troops and materiel.

On September 30, they were handed a massive clue when Omni Air International, tail number N207AX, took off from a private airport in Fort Worth, Texas, called Alliance Field. A hub for FedEx and Amazon, Alliance Field mainly serves cargo operations and defense contractors. The Omni Air International flight made multiple stops in Africa: Senegal, Liberia, and the Côte d'Ivoire, returning to Senegal before touching down in Ghana. The pattern gave credence to our hunch, following Pastor Steven's enforced odyssey from Texas to Louisiana to Arizona, that ICE was indeed rounding up African-origin individuals seeking asylum and removing them.

If you've been wondering how such a massive operation as the US Deportation Machine can grow so big and remain so hidden for so long, this is how: It exists between the cracks, churning away at odd hours and in out-of-the-way places where even a Boeing 767 wide-body can lift off without notice. Unless you know what you're looking for.

By late September, Tom and Jake knew what they were looking for.

Three days later, activist-scholar Anne-Marie Debanné, a French speaker who grew up in Canada, provided the key to solving the puzzle as to why ICE wasn't letting Black immigrants out of jail.

|||||||||||||||||||||||||||||||||||||||||||||||||||||||

Anne-Marie entered the world of immigrant rights advocacy in 2017 as a volunteer French translator for the San Diego–based Casa Cornelia Law Center, a public interest firm that provides pro bono legal services to victims of human and civil rights violations. She was then a professor of geography at San Diego State University. In early 2018, she and her colleagues and students began a letter-writing campaign to boost the spirits of immigrant inmates at the nearby Otay Mesa Detention Center, run by CoreCivic under contract for ICE. She was paired, as I had been at Port Isabel Detention Center, with French speakers.

One day the campaign coordinator gave her the name of a young political activist from Cameroon named Achiri. She wrote to him, in French. Achiri wrote right back, saying, "Yes I'm Cameroonian, but I'm actually an English speaker." The two began to correspond regularly, growing from pen pals to close friends.

On the day of Achiri's bond hearing, a Ukrainian refugee, who had entered the US with a phony passport, received a bond price of $1,500 to earn his provisional release. Moments later, the same judge set Achiri's bond at $50,000.

Anne-Marie was outraged. This was clearly discriminatory. She determined to help Achiri raise such an unjust and inappropriate amount in order to see him released. Until then, he was locked out of liberty and locked up under ICE for more than 900 days—180 of which he could not see the sky or sun.

"Achiri was the catalyst for everything," says Anne-Marie, for as she proceeded to organize his bond money, she became a dedicated immigrant rights activist and developed an expansive network of advocate and attorney contacts. She connected with Freedom for Immigrants, volunteering with the organization's call center and emergency hotline. She met and began working with Guerline Jozef and her growing team at Haitian Bridge Alliance and the Black Immigrant Bail Fund.

Perhaps most profoundly, Anne-Marie was moved to take up the cause for prison abolition. Not prison reform: the attempt to improve conditions of imprisonment from the inside. But the dismantling of our carceral systems that, as we've seen, are the modern legacy of the historic enslavement of some for others' economic gain.

When Anne-Marie visited Achiri at Otay Mesa for the first time, the scales fell from her eyes. "This wasn't *detention*. This was imprisonment. This was confinement. This was the systemic criminalization of safety-seeking people."

"We shouldn't be treating *anyone* this way," states Anne-Marie.

Indeed, there's no way to roll back the morally bankrupt practice of indefinite mandatory detention—what many call the "crimmigration" gulag—that daily drags into its cruel, dehumanizing grasp permanent residents, like Robert, as well as individuals seeking asylum, like Achiri. The only logical response is to tear it apart.

It's certainly not the right place to house an asylum adjudication system. We need practices of welcome and support, not an operation built to make money off misery wherein human rights violations are normalized as "just doing our job."

||||||||||||||||||||||||||||||||||||||||||||||||||||||||||

One morning in December 2018 at 5:00 a.m., Anne-Marie's phone rang, waking her up. It was Achiri. "He thought he was being deported. He was so scared."

She and Achiri's lawyer, Nanya Thompson, traced him to a GEO Group jail in Jena, Louisiana, population 3,398, where jobs are few and the average hourly starting wage as a prison guard is only slightly higher than at Walmart. But Achiri was destined for the Etowah County Jail in Gadsden, Alabama. Run by the county sheriff, Etowah is a 950-bed facility that was then paid to hold 90 beds in reserve for ICE. At Etowah, incarcerated seekers of asylum were treated with cruel neglect; the sick had to "literally beg" for medical care.

Searching Google, Anne-Marie learned in article after article that "Etowah was said to be the worst place ever." Nanya confirmed her worries: "Etowah is where ICE sends asylum seekers to convince them to give up on their cases."

Due to a plethora of advocate complaints backed up by gruesome evidence, ICE stopped using Etowah. But not before Achiri was forced to spend six months there under a jacked-up bond levy of $75,000. Meantime, thousands of miles away and no longer able to visit him, Anne-Marie's network grew from California to Florida; and from the Texas legislature to the Canadian Parliament. It included other incarcerated Cameroonians seeking asylum and their detention visitors, too.

On October 3, 2020, she would put her contact list to good use.

|||||||||||||||||||||||||||||||||||||||||||||||||||||||

In two identical messages to roughly thirty-five recipients, Anne-Marie sounded the alarm that Cameroonians were possibly being targeted for deportation. "Maxwell," imprisoned at LaSalle Corrections' Richwood, Louisiana facility, reported that his property had been tagged by an officer who said they are getting ready to deport him. "Denis" at Pine Prairie said his bag had been tagged and his commissary account frozen; he was told he would be leaving the following Monday. "Lenny," recently transferred from Pine Prairie to Jena, said that he wasn't alone: a number of Cameroonians had arrived from Etowah, as well. Among them was "Ernest," a Nigerian-Cameroonian dual-national, whose lawyer had heard he, too, could be facing deportation.

"Castillo," a professional electrician, told Anne-Marie that ICE seemed to be "rounding up all the Cameroonians and corralling us at Jena for a mass deportation prior to a possible change in presidential administration." It was the same phenomenon Pastor Steven witnessed in early September, while at GEO Group's Alexandria Staging Facility.

The first person to respond to Anne-Marie's group message was a volunteer advocate we'll call "Hannah." She seemed to have observed the start of what culminated in the late-September Omni Air International hop around Western Africa: "It also happened to folks from Ghana last month," Hannah wrote. She had disturbing news from Natchez, Mississippi, as well.

"Thomas" told her that "Cameroonians at [the Adams County Correctional Center] were sprayed with something, one man was beaten, eight are in isolation, two on suicide watch, one was hospitalized." Attorneys with Southern Poverty Law Center were taking sworn statements as quickly as possible in preparation for yet another complaint against ICE because "they'd heard that Cameroonians at

Adams would be gone in two weeks. If we don't get sworn statements, we'll never be able to hold ICE accountable for these horrors."

It appeared to Tom and me that our worst fears were confirmed: Trump & Co were gathering Africans seeking asylum in the US, some of whom still had cases open and pending, many of whom had been locked up under ICE for more than two years. It was to be a mass refoulement, likely on Omni Air International N207AX, probably out of Alliance Field.

||||||||||||||||||||||||||||||||||||||||||||||||||||||

"And so it began," Anne-Marie says, referring to a spontaneous grassroots eruption, akin to the explosion of the *Families Belong Together* movement, though not as big or as visible. It involved myriad individuals, community- and faith-based organizations, legal nonprofit entities, and national advocacy groups whose selfless simultaneous actions included, in no particular order:

Lawyers demanding emergency stays of removal for their clients. Castillo's attorney even got him an asylum interview in Canada.

Representatives from Cameroon American Council, Haitian Bridge Alliance, Ohio Immigrant Alliance, Human Rights Watch, and Amnesty International arranging emergency meetings with members of the Congressional Black Caucus and Homeland Security Oversight Committee to express their outrage and grave concern.

Family members, pen pals, detention watchers, and hotline volunteers fielding calls with panicked ICE inmates, urging them to keep up the fighting spirit, giving them reason to hope, and taking notes to feed back to the growing group all that they learned; then beseeching family and friends to contact their members of Congress and implore them to "Stop the Plane!"

Press releases were written. Everyone with any links of any kind to media outlets worldwide reached out to interested journalists.

Tom suggested finding someone on the ground in the Dallas/Fort Worth area to scope out the Alliance Field airport for viewing spots. He wanted witnesses.

Anne-Marie agreed, advocating for direct action alongside the lawyering. The folks at Refugee and Immigration Center for Education and Legal Services (RAICES) delivered. Enter: the North Texas Dream Team, who put protesters at the ready to hold a rally at the ICE staging facility nearest Alliance Field, Prairieland Detention Center, and to form a human chain to block ICE buses from getting to the airport forty-four miles north.

Family, sympathetic diplomats, human rights defenders, and media on the ground in Cameroon were alerted. If a flight were to land there, witnesses would be needed to document the fate of refugees being refouled by the US federal government aboard ICE Air's Omni Air International N207AX, which by now we'd dubbed "The Death Plane."

When the email traffic became too much, Tom created a WhatsApp group. Notifications sounded 24/7.

〈||||||||||||||||||||||||||||||||||||||||||||||||||||||||||〉

On October 7, 2020, another complaint landed in Homeland Security watchdog inboxes, this time directed to Cuffari and a new head of the Office for Civil Rights and Civil Liberties: Patricia Nation. Complainants were eight Cameroonians, all asylum seekers, imprisoned at Adams. Submitted by an equal number of advocacy organizations, the complaint detailed egregious human rights violations, including "coercion and unwarranted use of physical force tantamount to torture," by ICE officers in league with guards in the employ of CoreCivic.

The assaults, which took place over two days, September 27 and 28, revealed a singular motive: to force compliance with a long-standing deportation machine "option" unironically called "voluntary departure."

The complaint proves it is seldom what its name implies.

The eight men would like you to see them as representative of what happens to so many under ICE: they did not drop their asylum claims and agree to sign their own deportation orders, as the agency would have us believe. Indeed, ICE habitually provides patently false statements to the media, such as, "ICE is firmly committed to the safety and welfare of all those in its custody," which ICE spokesman Bryan Cox claimed at the time. Cox, who was captured in a lie on the Netflix series *Immigration Nation*, also stated that, "ICE provides safe, humane, and appropriate conditions of confinement for individuals detained in its custody," which we know, now as then, to be untrue.

An ICE Special Response Team and their CoreCivic counterparts overwhelmed the men, restrained them, and dragged them to facility locations out of range of security cameras. Through various acts of physical and psychological violence, including beatings and the breaking of fingers; the deployment of pepper spray directly into eyes; the stripping off of clothes and the shaming of naked bodies by female officers; as well as the abusive use of solitary confinement, where basics such as mattresses and blankets and food and water were withheld, the guards took complainants' fingerprints.

ICE had been shuffling Ray around, always in chains, for two years and ten months, even in the middle of the pandemic. "No precautions were ever taken to preserve my health," he told me. Though Ray, a teacher of physics, wears the evidence of his torture in Cameroon on the soles of his feet—they were whipped with a machete blade until sliced to ribbons—he was denied protection by another immigration judge with a disproportionately high denial record of 94.7 percent: Rex Ford.

"For a full year, he had not granted a single positive asylum case—so many people denied. He failed to really consider my situation. He found the smallest things to deny me."

Adams was Ray's last stop. "Things were very bad there," he recounts. He told me he experienced such a high level of stress at Adams that he almost committed suicide.

That September, he says, "They took me into the game room where there was no camera. There, a large group overpowered me. They held me down. One took my hand by force—it felt as if it was about to break—and stole my fingerprint."

When the cadre came for "Cornelius," they took him to Zulu, "the place where they punish people." First, they put paper and pen in front of him and insisted that he sign. "It was a deportation order document with my picture." He declined.

"They said, *Do you want to fight?*" And when they rushed him with handcuffs, ankle irons, and chains, he gave in "to avoid physical coercion."

An hour or so later, while still locked up in Zulu, Cornelius witnessed ICE officers "bringing other Cameroonians to Zulu forcefully with cuffs on their hands and legs. They were crying and screaming. They had been pepper sprayed in their eyes. Some were being dragged, others carried."

One of them was "Julio Franc." He'd previously been part of a hunger strike at Adams, he told me, to protest "the lack of social distancing in this large dorm where we were 120 people with beds squeezed tightly together." The strike didn't last long. On day two, he recounts, a large group of prison guards dressed in black uniforms and wearing helmets advanced on the imprisoned individuals.

This description mirrors the Special Operations Response Team—SORT for short—deployed by CoreCivic when journalist Shane Bauer went undercover in 2014 to expose another Louisiana-based contributor to the ICE crimmigration gulag: Winn Correctional Center. The men in black carried tear gas, says Julio Franc. They walked into a crowded, windowless dorm and shot two loud blasts—*Boom-Boom*—into the air.

Julio Franc and the others ducked for cover. Then, "We all started having tearing and pain in our eyes. We couldn't see . . . we were suffocating." On that day, he states, "I saw the same thing that happens in my country happens in the United States, too. I understood that I was no safer in the US than I was back in Cameroon."

From that point forward, Julio Franc believes he became a target for officer abuse. He was in and out of solitary confinement. On the day of the assault and battery at Adams, documented in the October 7 complaint, he was returning to his dorm from the mess hall when two ICE officers and two CoreCivic guards blocked his path. One said, *We told you that we were going to deport you and we will torture you until you sign your deportation order.*

They eventually got what they came for under conditions so grizzly Cornelius and other witnesses assumed Julio Franc had been hospitalized. The last anyone saw of him, he was being rushed out of the facility strapped to a wheelchair.

Though wounded and in pain, Julio Franc was not taken to the hospital. He was stripped naked and thrown into solitary. He was given neither blanket nor mattress, though the temperature in his cell was bitterly cold. He was hardly fed. And there he remained until he was transferred, first to GEO Group's Alexandria Staging Facility, then to Prairieland prison, before being deported out of Alliance Field with eighty to ninety Cameroonians, Kenyans, and Congolese aboard The Death Plane, Omni Air International N207AX, on October 13.

Despite the most valiant of efforts on the part of the coalition that formed thanks to Anne-Marie's October 3 email, the ICE Air machinery would not be stopped.

||||||||||||||||||||||||||||||||||||||||||||||||||||||

"I felt betrayed," states Hannah, a retired US civil servant. "As a career government employee, I took an oath and I took it seriously. I believe in the government and I believe civil servants are good people. I try very hard to see both sides. But ICE is an aberrant entity."

As Tom tracked the safety seekers by satellite from Alliance Field to Douala, Cameroon, with a stop in Dakar, Senegal, he believes for refueling, we struggled to sleep, awaiting news from our friends. But there was no time to rest because history was already repeating itself: reports of excessive use of force to falsify deportation orders were coming out of Louisiana's Jackson Parish Correctional Center as well, resulting in the fourth multi-person civil rights and civil liberties complaint on behalf of Cameroonians seeking asylum to hit Cuffari's desk in three months. This one, dated November 5, 2020, also implicated ICE officers and private prison guards in the New Orleans Field Office jurisdiction with deliberate acts of assault and battery to forcibly steal fingerprints.

It happened to Godswill on October 8 or 9, he states. A deportation officer by the name of Contreras came with deportation documents for Godswill to sign. "I said that I would not because I have a pending motion to reopen my case," which his lawyer confirmed. "I said I could not because it would be like signing my own death warrant."

Seven other male officers were standing around ready, Godswill continues. On Contreras's signal, they pounced. They snapped handcuffs over Godswill's left wrist. Then ICE Officer Contreras and a facility guard held down his right arm and the two teams, as Godswill describes it, pulled in opposite directions, "like they were going to rip me apart."

"I was crying and saying they were taking me to my death. They never explained themselves." They eventually succeeded in forcing Godwill's fingerprint onto the document. Then, they laughed and told him not to worry; it was "just a formality."

It wasn't. Godswill saw that the document pertained to Section 243(h) of the Immigration and Nationality Act. Dating to 1952, the law protects from removal anyone seeking asylum that the US government has agreed will face persecution if returned. Godswill's fingerprint on this document effectively voided his right to protection from deportation.

He and roughly twenty-four other Cameroonians seeking asylum were sent back across the Middle Passage in chains on ICE Air's Omni Air International N207AX, The Death Plane, on November 11, 2020, just as fifty-seven Cameroonians had been refouled the month before. Both flights took place on US national holidays, making it harder for lawyers to obtain emergency stays of removal. Some lawyers did succeed. Even at the last minute, men and women in chains were pulled off the planes. Still other lawyers were betrayed by the judicial system they were brought up and trained to believe in.

Tikem was jostled awake in the middle of the night while still at Allen Parish, in Louisiana. He was told to pack. He was not told why. He was not told where he was going. He was returned to the lion's den from which he ran, "in violation of a Court-ordered stay of removal based on his pending Petition for Review before the [5th Circuit Court of Appeals]," according to his legal representative. A "Stay of Removal" is a legally binding pact between attorney and the US courts. But ICE removed Tikem in what he and his lawyer believe was an act of retaliation for the role he played in the Pine Prairie hunger strikes.

CHAPTER THIRTY-TWO

Locked In

I had hoped our friends would tell this part of the tale themselves, but it was too re-traumatizing. They invited me to do it. They implored me to do it, as Godswill states, "So that nothing like this ever happens to another person again."

Be advised: The rest of this narrative could be triggering.

The Death Flights sparked a spontaneous collaboration among me, Anne-Marie, Hannah, and Lauren Seibert, researcher in the Refugee and Migrant Rights Division of Human Rights Watch. We tracked down and interviewed more than five dozen people on those two journeys back to harm. We spoke largely to Cameroonians, though I made contact with several Congolese and Angolans, too. Lauren's research focused on what transpired upon their refoulement; mine was to document the conditions of their deportation. Except for Rebecca Sharpless's book, *Shackled* (2024), about a thwarted 48-hour ICE Air removal mission to Somalia in December 2017, what follows is perhaps the only public account of what happens on over one hundred ICE Air flights every month; impacting an estimated average of 11,500 individuals, according to Tom.

As I am not one of the directly impacted persons whose horrors I've been permitted to share here, I can only imagine the terror and humiliation they felt based on the experiences they shared with me. I, therefore, must ask you to imagine, too…

|||||||||||||||||||||||||||||||||||||||||||||||||||||||||||||||

If you've ever been on a long-distance, economy-class flight, you will know that the body fatigues from sitting in the same position for too long. Though seat backs recline, it's challenging for many to rest with knees bent and legs dangling. The joints swell, both from inaction as well as from the cabin's lower than normal humidity, which sucks moisture from the tissues and cells, causing dehydration. Shoes become uncomfortably tight; hands lose their grip. Even a six-hour journey across the continental US can be taxing to the lower back, hips, knees.

Now imagine being forced to fly across half the US as well as the Atlantic Ocean with your ankles in manacles, your hands bound in cuffs, and tied tightly to a waist chain. Imagine the links of the waist chain planting themselves into your spine and back muscles. Imagine not being able to shift or adjust them because you are bound—for sixteen, twenty, twenty-four, thirty-six, even forty-eight hours in the case of the botched Omni Air International flight to Somalia documented in *Shackled*.

Imagine sitting for sixteen hours to Douala, Cameroon, your ankles and hands swelling, causing the metal hardware to pierce your skin and eat into your nerves. You are unable to kick off your shoes and shake off the wrist guards. You are unable to reach the button to push your seat back to relieve the pressure on your hip joints. Imagine your panic at a moment of turbulence when you realize that in the event of an emergency you will not be able to place over your nose and mouth the oxygen mask that drops from above; you will not be able to open the hatch if the aircraft lands on water; you will not be able to grab a life buoy or to tread water in the event you must deplane in a hurry. You will not be able to hurry. You will be helpless.

Imagine being fed nothing but stale white bread and potato chips. Imagine having to bend over, like a dog, to eat the tasteless, salty fare because your chains are so tight, you cannot bring your hands to your mouth to feed yourself. Imagine not wishing to eat like a dog and going without, for sixteen hours, maybe more.

Imagine your mouth and nose so parched, the natural, human act of breathing causes you pain. Imagine hours passing before anyone offers you water. Now imagine being physically unable to raise the plastic bottle up to your bone dry lips and throat.

"To get a drink," recounts Oscar, "you had to squeeze both your hands around the container to push the water out the top and try to catch a little on your tongue."

Imagine not being allowed to go to the bathroom without the escort of an armed guard. Imagine having to shuffle your way down the aircraft aisle in manacles and chains with a bladder full to bursting only to find, when you reach the cabin restroom, that the guard refuses to close the door. It is impossible, of course, to lower zipper and trousers with your hands enchained. Imagine missing and soiling yourself. Imagine your escort erupting in laughter, shaming you. Imagine returning to your seat, made to sit in your own urine and feces.

Imagine being a menstruating woman denied a fresh pad; or given one but unable to apply it to soiled panties with bound hands. Imagine even wanting to try with the toilet door left open, and a male guard peering in. Laughing. Imagine.

Imagine that for sixteen hours, or more, no one has cleaned the toilets. The November Death Plane did not touch down in Luanda, Angola, for thirty-four hours and forty minutes after takeoff from Alliance Field, according to Tom's data. Imagine being enchained for that long in a cabin overpowered by the stench of human excrement. Imagine trying desperately to hold it, but finally giving into the call of nature and the stench being so bad your body takes over. You pee in your pants as you retch, adding to the unholy mess.

I'm told it wasn't just the raw essence of human waste, moreover, that infused Omni Air International N207AX. There was the constant sobbing of passengers; the ceaseless yelling of guards dressed for war and toting guns; and the odor of nervous, panicked sweat. Again quoting Oscar: "It was torture. You could smell the trauma."

Oscar wasn't the only one to say so. The four-dozen-plus testimonies I collected from those forced into this ICE Air torture chamber collectively describe a flying Abu Ghraib.

The stench of trauma began long before the sixteen-hour flight in chains, however. It takes a long time to shackle eighty to ninety people, I'm told. Even with a sixteen-man ICE ERO Special Response Team, it takes hours. They bind each person one at a time, while still locked up, while still at the nearest pre-deportation "staging facility."

That prison, in the case of these two flights, was Prairieland Detention Center in Alvarado, Texas, where our friends, clients, brothers, sisters, sons, daughters, aunts, and uncles had been corralled. It took ICE days—and a lot of taxpayer dollars—to orchestrate the transfer of this many people. They arrived on ICE buses or on ICE Air shuffle flights from Louisiana, Texas, Minnesota, and Ohio.

Though some figured out what was coming while en route, others only understood once at Prairieland that this was the last stop in the Land of the Free. Most, like Tikem, had been lied to, if they were told anything at all. ICE and ICE ERO agents said only, *You're being transferred.* They didn't say, *You're being expelled.*

Therefore, few among our friends had destroyed the documents they once assumed would save them: the asylum case files, containing descriptions of the tortures they'd endured in their homelands; reports by Human Rights Watch and Amnesty International, documenting unsafe country conditions; witness statements signed by loved ones; and other sensitive—and confidential—affidavits that would signal to the persecutors they'd fled that they had sought asylum in the US.

In Cameroon, this is considered treason.

In Cameroon, treason is a death-penalty offense.

Some of our friends, moreover, had defected from Paul Biya's army—an act that would put them in a hood before a firing squad.

That is why, once at Prairieland, our friends' panic pivoted from the threat of expulsion to the likelihood of execution. Their goal became focused and singular: they had to destroy their case files.

It was a matter of life and death.

They pleaded for days—as many as five—before both the October and November flights. When the jailers answered, it was to say, *Only ICE can authorize that.* Yet no one from ICE ever came.

Fright turned to terror. Some of our friends went quiet. Others fell to pieces, curling up on their cots, begging the guards to *just take out your gun and kill me now.* Still others escalated to communicating their human rights with their fists. They pounded on the one-way mirror in each of their twenty-five-person cells, hoping that someone on the other side might still hold enough compassion in their heart to comprehend our friends' cries.

When that didn't work, "Renny" reached a breaking point. He picked up a mop and used the handle to try to smash the window. When that didn't work, he went for the TV.

That worked, sort of. A guard came immediately. He shackled Renny; he threw Renny into solitary. Then he returned to allow the others, for a few rushed minutes, to claw through their belongings, stored in a cramped hallway closet, in search of all contents that held the power to condemn them.

It wasn't enough time, though. And not everyone was given the opportunity. Those who were couldn't finish, much less think, with the guard urging them to *Hurry! Hurry! Faster! Faster! Let's go!*

When ICE Air Omni Air International N207AX landed in Douala, Cameroon, on October 14 and November 12, 2020, respectively, the cabin doors opened and the tropical heat rushed in, mingling with the stench of terror, vomit, and shit. "Kyle" states that agents of ICE ERO's Special Response Team stopped Cameroonian officials from getting onto the plane.

"They didn't want us to be seen in chains. They unshackled us one by one while still on the plane." The women were last.

In the theater of "voluntary deportation," representatives of the US government created a stage that made it look as if our friends were returning home at will. But the farce was immediately betrayed.

"Meeting us at the Douala airport were the military, gendarmes, the local police," recalls Kyle. He and the others were filed into a large room by fifty or so men bearing arms. They were interrogated, their bags gone through. Anyone still in possession of incriminating evidence was taken away.

"ICE gave all our documents to the Cameroonian military," states Kyle, who was imprisoned for five months on return. "Several of us were taken to prison straight away, some ex-military men that had defected from Biya's army because of what they were being forced to do their Anglophone brothers and sisters. They were likely killed."

Indeed, several men were never heard from again.

Imagine, once again, being a woman—Faith or Confident—now considered a traitor to her nation thrown into a medieval prison, packed into crowded cells with dirt floors and no windows, no toilets, made to sleep on the ground. The only food or water you get is whatever your loved ones manage to have smuggled in—if they even know you're there. Imagine the advantages taken during the daily tortures, if you're a woman.

Imagine.

Others were taken to "quarantine" in a place called Yasa. But it was really an excuse to extort their families. Everyone was made to pay to win their release.

One of our allies in Douala snapped a picture of the flight manifest—an item the Center for Constitutional Rights (CCR) requested from Homeland Security under the Freedom of Information Act and have yet to receive, as I bring this book to a close. States a February 6, 2023, CCR brief: "To date, it remains unclear whether [ICE, Homeland Security, and the Department of State] even have policies regarding" decisions to remove non-citizens to areas of conflict where they may experience life-threatening consequences. "Instead, the documents we have received over the past several months show federal agencies defying federal court orders despite recognition of unfair treatment of Black migrants."

The manifest smuggled back to us was in the possession of someone from the Biya regime. It had the names of all our friends on it, even those pulled off the planes at the last minute. This suggested only one thing: state-to-state complicity. The US deliberately refouled our asylum-seeking friends and clients. Their former persecutors knew who was coming. And they were waiting.

||||||||||||||||||||||||||||||||||||||||||||||||||||||||

Then came the coup de grace—as if the above terrors were not terrors enough: officers of the US government handed over to the Biya regime all passports and national identification documents. Without a national ID, you cannot move freely in Cameroon. Even if not behind bars, therefore, our friends had been robbed of dignity, shut out of justice, and were now locked out of their human right to liberty and freedom of movement—all things guaranteed in the Universal Declaration of Human Rights—by the leader of the free world.

Now considered criminals by their nation, those of our friends that managed to survive their refoulement are still on the run or living in hiding—three years later.

The human rights violations were so egregious, the tortures so numerous, the international crimes committed so myriad, the WhatsApp chat of the group Anne-Marie now called the Alliance in Defense of Black Immigrants threatened to explode my phone. As I scrolled through the stories trickling back from The Death Plane passengers, I recognized some familiar language.

One advocate reported that her client was "bagged and tied."

Another one said hers was "stuffed into a sack."

Still another used this language: she said her client had been "tortillu'd."

The US-citizen sister of "Robert," a nurse and resident of Delaware, told me her brother had been "entombed." She feared his mind had snapped: "It was too much."

CHAPTER THIRTY-THREE

Like Boxcars in the Sky

I t's called The WRAP. The brainchild of former cops, it's 100 percent Made in the USA.

Manufactured by California-based Safe Restraints, Ltd., The WRAP is marketed as a "humane restraint": intended for use in law enforcement contexts when individuals are perceived to be a danger to themselves and in need of urgent medical care; permitted for use when individuals thought to be resisting arrest, or help, have become "combative," *when handcuffs just aren't enough.*

When I spoke with President & CEO Charles Hammond in December 2020, he touted The WRAP as a "lifesaving device." I asked him how restraining a person can ever be humane. He said The WRAP is meant to be used "only as a last resort."

There are now more than ten thousand WRAPs in use across the US and Canada. ICE is Safe Restraints' biggest customer. Investigative journalist Angelika Albaladejo reported in February 2022, that since the agency's initial purchase in 2016, "ICE has spent about $235,000 on WRAP restraints for its detention centers and private jets transporting immigrants among those facilities and for deportations abroad." (That's about the cost of GRM's Matamoros field hospital.)

The WRAP is registered with the US Food and Drug Administration as a medical device, sharing the same designation as a wheelchair. Though unlike its rolling cousin, it is far from benign.

In contrast to the straitjacket, which binds the torso, The WRAP immobilizes the legs, viewed by law enforcement as weapons when they kick or cycle. Application of The WRAP, therefore, begins with a yellow ankle strap, which "goes on easy and firm and fast."

Then comes the leg harness. Made of robust black mesh fabric, it spreads flat along the ground, like a tortilla. A team of two to eight officers—the more, the better—can easily roll a human face down onto the tortilla, with a "1-2-3," then wrap the tortilla "nice and tight" around the legs, securing it with a *snap-snap-snap* of three bright yellow straps that each bind calves, knees, and thighs, respectively.

The third piece, the chest harness, is then laid onto the back of the prone body, which officers then flip over and push into a seated position while bringing the harness over the head and securing it with a seat belt–like buckle below the rib cage. Another seat belt–like strap, extending from the chest harness, is clipped to a buckle at the ankle end of the leg harness, and cinched up "to remove any slack."

Binding the legs, rather than the torso, states Hammond, allows "WRAPped" persons to remain upright, at a 90° angle to their lower extremities, so they can breathe. It's the mirror image of the hog-tie or hobbling practices, which leave victims lying face down, on their bellies, kissing the ground, causing too many accidental deaths by "positional asphyxiation." That is why the hobble, hog-tie, and fetal-tie methods are prohibited by agencies of the US Department of Homeland Security—although they did play a part in the inter-agency killing of Anastasio Hernández Rojas in 2010.

Per Safe Restraints' training manual and guidelines, no one should be left alone and unmonitored while WRAPped; they should only remain WRAPped for as long as it takes to achieve calm; and their hands must never be cuffed at the front. There, they can push into the belly, forcing the gut and diaphragm into the lungs, and cutting off respiratory passageways.

That would defeat The WRAP's purpose, says Hammond. "When used correctly," he claims, "The WRAP's design ensures that breathing is never compromised."

But ICE, ICE ERO, and the ICE "military," aka Special Response Team, do not use The WRAP correctly.

As Pastor Steven observed during his swing through multiple ICE facilities in September 2020, WRAPpings appear to come in threes. The first among the Cameroonians to be WRAPped was Ray. It happened at the Alexandria Staging Facility prior to the Swift Air shuffle flight that transferred many of our friends, clients, and family members to Prairieland Detention Center in October.

RAY: *At around 6:00 a.m., ICE agents came and cuffed my hands and my feet and attached them to a chain around my waist. We remained shackled like that for hours in our little cells. I grew more and more anxious. When they came back at about 9:00 a.m., I told them I did not want to go. I told them, "You are sending me back to my death."*

I was in the first cell, so the first to be called out. I refused. So four big officers dragged me out of the cell. They carried me out of the facility and threw me to the ground. They rolled me on my belly. A fifth man put a knee on my neck. I could not breathe. Then they tied me up in something made of stiff black fabric and secured with straps. When I protested, they told me, "We are just doing our job."

The cuffs around my ankles were so tight, and the pain in my feet so acute, I started to cry. Then they attached a cord from a buckle at my chest to a buckle at my feet and they pulled my body together so tight my lips were touching my knees. I could not breathe well. I was completely immobilized.

Ray's cellmate, Maxwell, bore witness.

MAXWELL: *There were four of them. They showed no emotion. They tackled [Ray] to the ground, onto his front, and dragged him out of the cell. I watched them pick him up and carry him out of the facility. The next time I saw him, he was tied up in a black bag with yellow straps, his knees pulled up to his nose. His body was locked in that position. He was screaming in pain. He couldn't move.*

RAY: *They left me like that for at least an hour—on display so the others would think twice about protesting their deportations as I did. They left me on the ground, crying in pain, until they loaded everyone onto a plane.*

Oscar told me that he had planned to protest his removal, too. But when he saw what had happened to Ray, he decided to comply.

OSCAR: *Outside the detention center, there were these mats laid out on the ground in front of the building. This one guy, even shackled by his hands and legs and no longer able to fight, had been wrapped up in that mat. They tied his face to his knees. He was crying, sweating. They left him there, on the ground screaming in pain, as a warning to the rest of us. We had to pass right by him as we were pressed toward the plane. He was the last to get boarded.*

In December 2020, ICE spokesperson Mary G. Houtmann told me that "ICE only uses The WRAP if a deportee becomes 'noncompliant' and a threat to crew and other passengers, *while onboard the plane*" (emphasis mine). Ray's testimony proves Houtmann's statement untrue. He even heard the name of it invoked by ICE officers while bound and writhing in pain on the ground at the Alexandria Staging Center.

RAY: *Once everyone had boarded, two guys from the ICE military came. They told me, "We want to remove The WRAP, but you must remain calm. If you continue to fight, we will leave it on." They removed it. I was so sad, so tired, so depressed. It was so hard to walk, they had to help get me to the plane. On the way to the plane, I noticed several WRAPs laid out on the ground. They were there to warn the others not to protest or risk being treated as I was.*

Rather than using an additional restraint on top of five-point shackles to "save lives," ICE has transformed The WRAP into an instrument of coercion through the example of torture—a means to deter protest by instilling deliberate fear—all to keep the planes flying on time. Even when wrist and ankle cuffs *are enough.*

Robert refuses to speak of it. Eyewitnesses say he was "entombed" for the entire sixteen-hour October flight. Unable to see, to breathe, to eat, or take water, he suffered numerous panic attacks. Unable to get up, he could not get to the restroom and was thus forced to go on himself. He suffers from post-traumatic stress disorder as a result of these tortures under ICE.

Ernest was also WRAPped. Twice. He was hooded while WRAPped. Twice. Both times his torso and legs were cinched together at an acute angle, nose to knees. Both times his hands were cuffed in front, compromising his breathing. Both times he was already constrained in five-point restraints and a threat to no one.

Ernest was boarded onto—and pulled off of—both the October and November flights. He protested his removal, both times, because he was leaving a wife and two children behind in the US; because their asylum cases were still open; because he feared he'd never see them again. Both times he struggled to be understood. Both times, if anyone spoke to him, it was to say, *We are just doing our job.*

Ernest has a history of heart disease. He lives with an arterial stent. ICE knew this.

Ernest's attorney intervened. He was able to get Ernest successfully removed from the October flight at the eleventh hour. One month later, however, ICE loaded Ernest onto Omni Air International to Cameroon again. This time, while WRAPped and hooded, Ernest suffered a cardiac episode. He may have lost consciousness.

JOEL: *They wrapped him in that black mattress with yellow straps. They folded him up and pulled his chest to his legs and locked his body at 30°. You could hear him screaming, "I'm dying. I'm dying. Just kill me now."*

HOWARD: *They put a cap over his head. It was more like a mask. It covered his whole face. The kind of thing kidnappers use to cover your face so you can't see where you are or where you're going. They had to remove him from the plane because of a chest issue.*

We will never know, however, if Ernest had a heart attack that day, because once revived by emergency technicians called to Alliance Field, ICE sent him right back to prison at Prairieland.

||||||||||||||||||||||||||||||||||||||||||||||||||||||||

Ernest wasn't the only person to be pulled from the October flight and returned to Prairieland. Castillo, too, was spared that day; saved by his lawyer's last-minute intervention. Because Castillo had a real shot at finding freedom, though in Canada.

His asylum interview was scheduled for October 30—*just two weeks away*—at the Buffalo, New York, port of entry. Though his advocate had arranged transportation for both him and a security escort, ICE tried to remove Castillo before his Canadian asylum hearing. Then, ICE hid him: they kept him in solitary confinement at Prairieland for the next two weeks.

CASTILLO: *Even though they wanted me out of the US, they would not permit me to have a chance of a future in Canada.*

When they finally let me out of isolation, they put me in a cell with a glass door, so I was under constant watch. For two more weeks, I watched more and more Africans arrive: Cameroonians, Congolese, and Angolans. We were sixty to seventy detainees. One evening, I noticed my commissary account was blocked. The next morning at 5:00 a.m., two officers woke us up and told us to pack.

I told them, "No. My case is still pending. I won't go without a conversation with an ICE officer." They left.

They came back, saying, "You're right, you're not going to be deported. You are a special case. Come with us."

So I did. But they lied. They took me to isolation again. The two guards were replaced by a team of eight or ten men dressed like military officers in khaki and green uniforms with badges on their arms that read something like, "ICE Special Forces."

They shot me four times with rubber bullets: two on my left thigh, two on my right shin. It was a shock to my muscles. I was powerless. I fell to the ground and they fell on me and dragged me out of the cell. They pushed my face to the ground, like they did to George Floyd. One pressed on my back, two held my hands, two held my feet, someone said, "Get The WRAP."

It was like being rolled into a bag. They tied my feet together, then they tightened the bag around my legs with three straps. They put something over my neck and around my torso and arms. They cuffed my hands in front of me and attached them to a chain around my waist.

They snapped a rope or strap or cord from my neck to my feet. They leaned on my back and pushed my face toward my knees, and pulled the strap tight.

My body was at about a 40° angle. I was left completely immobile. Zero movement.

I was forced into The WRAP while we were still at Prairieland Detention Center. I was left in The WRAP from 10:30 a.m. Texas time on November 11, 2020, until halfway across the Atlantic at about 7:30 p.m. that night. They carried me all the way—four to six guys—from the detention center onto the bus. Then they carried me off the bus and onto the plane. The position was very stressful for my body; my muscles were shot with pain the entire bus ride and flight back to Cameroon. I tried not to cry.

They eventually took The WRAP off, but I remained shackled all the way to Douala—sixteen hours. I couldn't talk. I couldn't eat. I went two days without eating. All I remember is the pain, and the yelling of the officers.

Castillo lives with chronic back pain still today. He cannot sit up for any length of time. He cannot work. He was re-incarcerated on arrival back in Cameroon. The conditions were medieval.

⸻⸻⸻⸻⸻⸻⸻

Godswill was the third man ICE WRAPped on November 11, 2020. He was the first of the estimated eighty-three Cameroonians to be refouled by the US government that I spoke to after the two Death Plane flights touched down in Doula. I located him through his brother, who lives in Maryland. When Godswill and I first made contact, on December 5, 2020, he was in hiding, unable to speak to his loved ones without falling apart. He was so traumatized and broken after sixteen months imprisoned under ICE, then being WRAPped and "treated like luggage," that he worried about traumatizing *them*. He was also, like Castillo, in terrible pain but unable to see a doctor for fear of being seen, arrested, jailed, and tortured, again.

Sometimes it's easier to unburden yourself to a total stranger. And thanks to Godswill, the poetry of his speech and his detailed descriptions, I was able to identify the human restraint device that ICE uses daily, as many as three times per flight, to keep the gears of the ICE Air machinery turning.

On November 11, 2020, Godswill was not combative. He was already lashed in five-point restraints, *which should have been enough.* He was not out of control, not a danger to others, nor to himself. In fact, though afraid, he was not protesting. He merely missed his step as he tried to mount the air-stairs leading to Omni Air's Boeing 767 wide-body, disrupting the rhythm of the chain-gang.

GODSWILL: *Then, I was forced to live through treatment that was so bad, I understood that, to the US, I am not regarded as a human being . . .*

They came for us very early in the morning. They came in a battalion of facility officers and ICE military. We pleaded, we cried. We tried to resist, but they said: "We're taking you to the airport whether you like it or not, whether we have to tie you down or not."

They put cuffs on our ankles and wrists, they shackled our cuffed ankles and wrists to chains. They filed us onto a bus and drove us to an airport. They forced us off the bus and onto the tarmac just in front of a large airplane.

I was so depressed. I felt so broken. I hadn't eaten and I was weak. When I arrived at the steps taking us to the plane, I tripped and fell. The officers didn't ask me what was wrong. They didn't ask if I was okay. They dragged me across the tarmac, they climbed on me, and they stuffed me into a kind of bag. I later learned it is called The WRAP.

They pulled the straps so tight, I couldn't move. They pushed my upper body down and pressed on my back to the point where my head was almost touching my knees. The whole time they were yelling at me. Then, they attached a strap from my chest to my feet, and folded me up.

There was so much pain, in my waist and in my back. My lungs were compressed, I couldn't breathe. I couldn't sit up. I was immobilized. My body was in so much stress. I truly felt I was meeting my death in that moment.

Six officers, three on each side, picked Godswill up and carried him onto the plane.

GODSWILL: *They plopped me down, like luggage, like a load of wood, across a center row of seats. They left me like that for several hours—more than three, maybe four. The WRAP pressed into the shackles which dug into my body, my skin. My back was killing me. I couldn't breathe.*

Godswill, it should be noted, is asthmatic. ICE knew this. Yet, they WRAPped him. They cinched his body into a "stress position," with his hands cuffed in front and pressing into his lungs. They put him at deliberate risk of "positional asphyxiation."

"Benedict" was next to be boarded onto The Death Plane. He was made to sit just across the aisle from Godswill, who he had befriended while imprisoned under ICE. The two had passed the endless hours studying the Bible together.

BENEDICT: *When I saw what they had done to [Godswill], I started shaking and crying as I looked at him struggling to breathe and being tied as if he was not a human being. With tears running down from my eyes, I had to shout: He is asthmatic! This is triggering his medical pre-conditions!*

No one paid attention to his cries. An officer finally came. Godswill begged for his inhaler. The officer walked away!

I had to ask: How can a human being treat another in that barbaric way?

GODSWILL: *Finally, a doctor came to check on me. I begged him to take me out of The WRAP but he only reached into my pocket to get my inhaler. He put it to my mouth. He allowed me only one pull. Then he tossed it onto the seat and he walked away.*

BENEDICT: *A doctor left my friend trapped in the same painful position. When Godswill begged another officer to please loosen the The WRAP, he only fastened it tighter!*

‖‖‖

It took months and hundreds of hours to track down the passengers from those two planes. I found as many people as I could. So did Lauren. We searched until we hit dead ends. When I shared my findings with Luz Lopez of the Southern Poverty Law Center, she arranged for us to meet with Fatma Marouf. We all agreed: The WRAP is a highly problematic device being wielded by ICE—a problematic agency with historic ties to yesteryear's Slave Patrols—in a manner consistent with torture or cruel, inhumane, *and* degrading treatment in violation of the UN Convention Against Torture; US civil rights laws, as well as state criminal and tort laws; ICE's so-called detention standards and use-of-force policies; and Safe Restraints' guidelines.

At least, that is the contention of the fifth complaint against ICE brought on behalf of Cameroonians seeking asylum in the US during the Trump years, filed on the anniversary of the first Death Plane, October 13, 2021, by Fatma's law clinic, with the backing of six other human and immigrant rights' defenders: African Communities Together, Black Alliance for Just Immigration, Cameroon Advocacy Network, Haitian Bridge Alliance, UndocuBlack Network, and Witness at the Border. The WRAP complaint, like its four predecessors, urged Inspector General Cuffari to "promptly investigate ICE's use of The WRAP and to grant humanitarian parole to the complainants so that they might fully participate in an investigation."

Cuffari passed.

However, all five complaints had been taken under investigation by the Homeland Security Office for Civil Rights and Civil Liberties as the mercury rose to record levels in mid-2022, owing to ongoing efforts of a coalition of groups and individuals that refused to look away: Guerline's Haitian Bridge Alliance, Anne-Marie's Alliance in Defense of Black Immigrants, Fatma's Immigrant Rights Clinic; Human Rights Watch, RFK Human Rights, and the Center for Constitutional Rights, represented by Lauren Seibert, Sarah Decker, and Samah Sisay, respectively; and independent researchers, like Hannah and me. We became the Humanitarian Parole Working Group of the Cameroon Advocacy Network, led by Daniel Tse.

Further fueled by the horrors laid bare in Lauren's February 2022 report, published by Human Rights Watch and entitled, *"How Can You Throw Us Back?": Asylum Seekers Abused in the US and Deported to Harm in Cameroon*, as well as the first-hand testimonies shared with investigators via Zoom that summer, we succeeded in securing a meeting with ICE counsel. Our goals were to convince them that due to grave agency malfeasance, ICE should bring back to the US everyone it so viciously refouled aboard the October and November, 2020, Death Planes; and to allow them to restart their asylum cases without threat of further detention. The man representing ICE was former senior advisor to the head of CRCL, Scott Shuchart, now a Biden political appointee.

‖‖

Two years after the five complaints hit Cuffari's inbox, CRCL investigators confirmed their concerns, disclosed to me during our summer 2022 Zoom meetings, that ICE had never reviewed The WRAP to establish policy protections limiting officers from transforming it into an instrument of coercion. A letter to Fatma, dated September 29, 2023, cites a "lack of policy, oversight, documentation, justification," and recording as well as agency training in the use of The WRAP by ICE and ICE ERO "at detention facilities and during transport." The probe had been concluded, it stated, with all findings sent to agency top brass "in the form of a recommendation memorandum *for their consideration.*"

The emphasis is mine, because that may be all we ever know. For as I stated above, the human rights watchdogs inside the largest law enforcement agency in the land can only suggest remedies to check illegal practices. It cannot mandate them or police their implementation—a weakness Shuchart, himself, flagged in 2018 when he quit his eight-year run at CRCL over Trump & Co's family separation debacle.

CRCL's recommendations, what's more, may never be made public. That's up to ICE. It could be years before we see the report Fatma sought under the Freedom of Information Act. Even then, it's likely to come back too redacted to read.

Meanwhile, hundreds of thousands of mothers, fathers, sisters, brothers, uncles, aunts, and just plain folks are daily, monthly, annually removed from the US on ICE Air flights under conditions so egregious they rival those committed at the torture chambers of Guantánamo Bay and Abu Ghraib.

‖‖

On May 13, 1939, a passenger ship called the MS *St. Louis* set sail from Hamburg, Germany, with more than nine hundred Jews aboard. Hitler's rise to power had emboldened followers of Nazi ideology. They were confiscating Jewish homes and burning down synagogues and Jewish businesses. In the face of such unabashed, unacknowledged, unpunished hate-based crimes, the nine hundred Jews took flight. Now refugees, they were determined to seek safe haven in the United States of America.

They were prescient. The development of the Nazi gulag was already well underway.

The Jewish exodus faced an unforeseen hurdle, however, for such concepts as "crimes against humanity" and "genocide" had not yet been defined, much less codified. There was no Universal Declaration of Human Rights to provide a framework upon which to build a global refugee protection regime. There was no Refugee Convention to value the right to asylum and ensure that no human being ever face refoulement ever again.

The US had long been a Beacon of Hope for European Jews, and many of the refugees had family there. So the ship captain steered the *St. Louis* toward the so-called Land of the Free. But Cuba, then the gateway to the US, would not let the refugees dock. They met the same chilly response in sunny Florida.

After three weeks sitting with the Land of Immigrants in sight, the refugees were running out of food and water. The *St. Louis* was forced to reverse course and return its passengers to potential harm. It landed in Antwerp, Belgium, on June 17, 1939, minus a few individuals, who'd hurled themselves into the sea in fear of what was to come. Another 254 would number among the six million Jews rounded up, corralled, and deported in boxcars on one-way journeys to Nazi death camps, like Auschwitz.

Tracking Omni Air International N207AX as it flew its reverse course back over the Middle Passage was for me like witnessing boxcars in the sky.

CONCLUSION

Buried Dreams

It starts with a dot. A red dot. Which becomes a GPS coordinate.

"Ready?" asks Alvaro Enciso to no one in particular but to everyone present. Throwing me a friendly wink under bushy salt-and-pepper eyebrows, he rests a hand atop the open hatch door of the 4Runner. Piled into the back cargo area of the filthy, scrub-scuffed, gray SUV are two milk crates packed with 99-cent plastic gallon jugs of water, a construction bucket, a bag each of gravel and fast-setting concrete, several pairs of man-sized, heavy-duty work gloves, a shovel, and a pickaxe. Topping the utilitarian stack—and looking quite out of place— are five or six crosses made of 2x3-inch pine strips painted green, yellow, pink, and blue. Each is secured with a red metal dot constructed from a used bottle top nailed to the central meeting point. Some boast additional adornments of recycled metal trash, all simple.

"Yup," says David, heading to the passenger's seat.

"*Vámonos*," states Peter, buckling in behind the steering wheel.

Three doors slam, almost in unison. The final one, landed by Alvaro, brings into sudden reveal a red sticker, centered just above the ubiquitous Toyota logo of the vehicle's rear window. It shouts, SAMARITANS.

Peter steers the SUV out of the parking lot and onto Tucson's S. Sixth Ave. We're en route to Highway I-19, heading toward Mexico, as this three-man team has done each Tuesday for years. David powers up the GPS-tracking device in his hand and shows me a cacophony of red dots splashed across the map of the vast Sonoran—one of the most blistering deserts on Earth.

Many red dots mark locations far off the beaten path, often landing within the 2,900,000-acre Tohono O'odham Nation Reservation. We can't reach those without advance permission from tribal leaders and a guide, neither of which we have today. So David directs us to the east of the Buenos Aires National Wildlife Refuge in the foothills of the thirty-mile-long, north–south-running Baboquivari mountain range, the boundary of Tohono O'odham territory.

The range's granite peak, which towers over the vista like a monumental thumb at a dramatic 7,730 feet, makes the perfect landmark for travelers. Though Baboquivari Peak is the most sacred place of the Tohono O'odham people—the home of I'itoi, the Creator and Elder Brother of the Tohono O'odham homeland—it has stood just outside the Nation's current territorial boundary since 1853, when the Treaty of Guadalupe Hidalgo transferred over half of Mexico to the US and divided the Tohono O'odham lands. Mountain access privileged white colonial settlers. Since 1998, the Tohono O'odham Nation has fought to have the sacred peak returned to its custody. For now, it is the playground of hikers, climbers, and mountain bikers.

Our first stop this day will be a spot southeast of the Baboquivari Peak and just north of the US-Mexico border at the "blink-and-you'll-miss-it" Nogales exurb of Rio Rico. We pull into the weather-beaten asphalt-and-gravel roadside lot of Ruby Corners Inc. Motorway Services and park discreetly in a far-flung corner, well away from the semi-trailers lined up for repair. Using the bed of the 4Runner as a workbench, Peter pours a mixture of quick-dry concrete and gravel into the bucket, a recipe memorized from repetition. The rest of us grab water, tools, gloves, and a cross and follow David, now zeroing in on the sought-after coordinates, down a noisy, lonely length of highway.

"We try always to get as close as we can with the SUV," Alvaro explains. "Then we hike the rest of the way."

This hike will not take us far, for the red dot we seek marks the spot where Sergio Antonio Santiago, aged twenty-four, having successfully made it across the harsh Sonoran Desert and into the United States, collapsed by the side of I-19. Unlike most of those in search of life, he was found "fully fleshed," meaning his corpse was less than a day old when examined by the Southern Arizona Pima County Coroner's

Office. (More typically, the desert critters and climate in this area eat up a body, along with the origin tales it conceals, fast). Still, while we knew his name, thanks to identification found amongst his few things, Santiago's dream remains unknown. Whatever it was, it was denied him and his loved ones when he fell fifty-five miles from Tucson. Probable cause of death: hyperthermia, aka environmental exposure.

〜〜〜〜〜〜〜〜〜〜〜〜〜〜

Despite sizzling daytime temperatures that can climb as high as 120°F (49°C), shivering is likely the first symptom Santiago experienced—that and slurred speech or mumbling. Then his metabolism and heart rate surely slowed as his organs began, one at a time, to shut down. His breath grew shallow and his pulse weak, depriving him of life-giving oxygen, as his cells set off chemical toxins. When these hit his brain, the irreversible damage began. He felt drowsy, clumsy, confused. He lost his memory, along with his coordination, and probably started to hallucinate, forgetting to keep focused on Baboquivari Peak, before losing consciousness altogether.

Symptoms of exposure manifest so gradually, you might not even be aware of your condition until it's too late. It's always too late once exposure hits in the Sonoran Desert.

Now, it's up to local humanitarian volunteers to locate Santiago's family and reunite them with their lost loved one—that is, if they know about Humane Borders' efforts to map all desert deaths with a red dot or Colibri's Missing Migrant Project, and if they know to register him as "disappeared." Until then, his backstory will remain a mystery.

Until then, Alvaro, Peter, and David will follow red dots to remember the dead. Four, five, six at a time. Every Tuesday.

〜〜〜〜〜〜〜〜〜〜〜〜〜〜

It starts with a hole, determined by a red dot on a map, marking where Santiago went from standing to fallen. A hole, not too deep, cut into the earth by David with a pickaxe and shovel, then filled by Peter with moistened gravel and quick-dry cement as Alvaro plants into the mixture a simple cross made of rough 2x3-inch pine strips painted green. It's a solemn act, performed in silence, save the howling of traffic.

I eyeball the positioning of the cross, indicating to Alvaro with a slight wave to the left, then to the right, the adjustments necessary to settle it, straight and tidy, before the cement dries. David piles rocks, collected from the roadside and tossed into the now-empty bucket, at the base of the cross. They make it look pretty. They provide additional support. Peter draws a rosary from one pocket and drapes it over the cross. From another pocket, he pulls a vial of holy water. He sprinkles a bit on the fresh memorial, makes the sign of the cross, and whispers a brief prayer.

"The majority of the fallen are Christian, so we don't want to forget that part," Alvaro tells me, breaking the silence. "But it's ironic that an infidel is doing this for them." He laughs. He's referring to himself.

For Alvaro, the cross represents more than just a Christian symbol. "You're also looking at a geometrical figure," he explains. "The vertical line represents the living person with a future dream, still walking. The horizontal line is when that dream died with the human who, unable to remain upright any longer, collapsed. The red dot in the middle, where the criss and cross meet— that is the moment of death, the moment when, in this case, Santiago took his last breath."

Alvaro reminds me, too, of a pre-Christian legacy of the cross: "The Roman Empire used it to kill—to hang false prophets, enemies of the people, common criminals, and leave them out in the sun for days at a time, without any water, to die. That's exactly what's happening here. People dying from being exposed to the sun, without any water—and on purpose, because the US government has walled off the easiest points of entry, sending humans through the harshest, hottest, most difficult parts of the desert where they are bound to die."

Alvaro is talking, of course, about Operation Gatekeeper, launched on October 1, 1994, by the Clinton administration, which then caved to the same nativist, anti-immigrant fervor that squeezes the life from the soul of the US nation today. Operation Gatekeeper erected walls and fences in easy-to-cross border areas with the express purpose of funneling human beings into dangerous and inhospitable terrain, where they would either perish or be more easily spotted. Walls and fences went up alongside a dramatic rise in Border Patrol agent hires, as well as surveillance technology purchases. Ports of entry were added to the walls, as were interior checkpoints as far as one hundred miles from the border. Guns were surged to the gates and checkpoints, as prison beds were allocated for those "apprehended" before they could die.

As Operation Gatekeeper made its way east, from Imperial Beach, California, to Brownsville, Texas, it divided thriving bicultural communities, devastated natural ecosystems, and transformed the southern borderlands of the US into a militarized zone where law enforcement took on the job that would have been, then as now, better suited to humanitarians, like John Fife and the Tucson Samaritans; like the Dignity Village Collaborative in the Rio Grande Vally; like the Friends of Friendship Park, whose beautiful binational garden, once a place of calm and welcome, was reduced to rubble by the president who promised, "There will not be another foot of wall constructed on my administration," then waived twenty-three environmental and cultural protections to extend Trump's monstrosity across Starr County, Texas.

Operation Gatekeeper kicked off the now nearly three-decade militarization of the US-Mexico border, turbocharged after 9/11. It has led to the ruin of an uncountable number of lives. In 1994, fewer than thirty people were known to have died crossing the border. By 1998, the number had quintupled to 147. Deaths more than doubled to 387 in 2000. And the trend continues apace.

Conservative estimates suggest at least one person has fallen each day in the vast Sonoran since Operation Gatekeeper began. That's more than 11,000 dead, to date, in one discrete section of the border. Meanwhile, a high of 29.8 billion US taxpayer dollars were allocated for spending in fiscal year 2024 on the morally questionable belief that the human right to seek a better life can be deterred through cruelty.

As I bring this book to a close, Sally Hayden, author of *My Fourth Time, We Drowned* (2022), guesstimates that more than 27,800 people have died or disappeared in the Mediterranean Sea. That's since 2014, when the normalization of mass death began in Europe. *But who is really counting?*

Since Operation Gatekeeper—enacted eight years after the *last-ever* Congressional effort to legislate immigration reform, in 1986—it's been one policy of "prevention through deterrence" after another. Each one ratchets up the cruelty even more. Though the deterrence policies have caused the death, disappearance, and despair of hundreds of thousands, the strategy is and always has been a miserable failure, for folks just keep coming.

"The US government never understood," explains Alvaro, "that when you're poor and this is your only option, you do it. When facing the Sonoran Desert is a better path than a lifetime hiding from the gangs or watching your children starve to death, you do it. These people aren't looking for the tired 'American Dream.' They're just looking for better, so they do it."

Substitute Sonoran Desert with Caribbean Sea, Darién Gap, Mediterranean Sea, Mexico, Libya, the English Channel, and Guerline's statement—that no one puts themselves in such danger if it is safer to stay—rings ever louder. Somali British writer Waran Shire expresses the same truism in her poem "Home": "no one leaves home, unless home is the mouth of a shark."

⁂

We mark four more red dots this sacred Tuesday, one located within a ranch we enter on foot and without permission. When the owner speeds toward us, his dual-cab pickup kicking up a cloud of red desert dust, Alvaro throws up his hands and plants himself in the truck's path. My heart races, wondering if this will be the day that Alvaro becomes a red dot on a desert map. But on learning our purpose, the rancher humbly allows us to proceed. We leave a bright red cross in the memory of one who is welcomed in death, though in life he was not.

What started as a dream—"to reveal to the world the US government's responsibility for turning the Sonoran Desert into a graveyard"—has resulted in Alvaro transforming the desert into a cemetery, an art installation, and a memorial to the needless suffering of the great unknown. He has planted more than 1,600 crosses in vibrant colors, adorned with bits of metal trash found on the desert floor alongside the dead. More than 1,600 crosses—and counting.

"Alvaro will never finish in his lifetime," Todd Miller subsequently confided in me. "He can't keep pace with the number of fallen."

Was Santiago running from cartel or gang members, trying to force him to join their culture of brutality? Did his mother, like Sam's, wake him in the middle of the night, press her life savings of $30 into his hand, and whisper forcefully in his ear, "Run!"? Was he coming, like Jenny Flores, to meet an absent mother he never knew, the central figure of the family's only framed photograph, one of eleven million undocumented—yet essential—laborers that toil quietly, anonymously, to pick produce and slaughter livestock so we can eat, while their children back home cry from hunger? Or was he, like Godswill, fleeing a dictator's wrath with dreams of contributing his skills as a nurse, singer, and choir director to benefit US society?

Whatever the answer, a dream deferred—dried up like a raisin in the sun—is indeed justice denied. And the cruelty that drove it, was not, as Tía Madeleine says, what any of us signed up for.

AUTHOR'S NOTE

March 28, 2024

Dear Reader,

I'm overwhelmed with gratitude that you elected to take this journey of discovery with me. I am filled with appreciation that you've traveled with me this far. As I type these final words, my publisher is days away from sending Crossing the Line *to press. Yet, I continue to struggle with how to bring to a close what, it turns out, is a tale with no end.*

There was so much more I intended to share with you. About the failed promise of the Central American peace process. About how the now impossible DREAM went from bipartisan action in 2001, to DACA by executive order in 2012, to "unlawfully injurious" to Texas in 2023. About Lone Star State duplicity, in general—a topic that reads like dystopian fiction and features governors, attorneys general, high-court judges, and Border Patrol chiefs, squandering billions to stop an "invasion."

Except there is no invasion. There is no war. There are just people doing what people have done since time immemorial: move away from danger and toward opportunity.

Except at this historical moment, they crash into a reality so alternate, a mentality so destructive it finds justification in the unjustifiable: victimizing the victims, criminalizing the caregivers, and celebrating the true barbarians—elected officials and their gatekeepers—as the "good guys" keeping us "secure."

In this book, I refer to this twisted, upside down place as The Matrix, a metaphor I borrowed from Guerline. In his recently launched eponymously titled book, scholar-activist Kehinde Andrews speaks of it as an affliction. He calls it the "psychosis of Whiteness."

I was in Del Rio, Texas in September 2021, when an estimated fifteen hundred men, women, and children seeking safety appeared under the International Bridge. I bore witness through a sleepless night as Governor Greg Abbott militarized the borderlands against these individuals, most of them from Haiti, all unarmed and in need of food, shelter, water, life.

Dignity and respect should have been theirs by right. But when the sun rose over the Rio Grande, nearly one thousand federal and state vehicles stood side-by-side at the water's edge—a "wall" of weaponized metal reminiscent of Silvestre Reyes' 1993 Operation Blockade, aka Hold the Line. They were positioned to stop folks who'd traversed tens of thousands of miles, carrying children in their arms and all they owned on their backs, from entering the promised land.

It was a made-for-Fox-and-Breitbart spectacle; they were the only media outlets allowed on the ground. It was a set-piece enactment, recalling scenes from the Tanton network bible, The Camp of the Saints, *written by a celebrated Frenchman, who posits that racism and ostracism are necessary for white survival.*

"Paranoia is the recurrent symptom of Whiteness," writes Andrews, "there is a fear of the threat of immigrants, a fear of losing their traditions and a fear of Black people in general."

Most recently, in a charade worthy of cartoon villains, Abbott's lawmakers, who purport to be Christians, have targeted the leadership and volunteers of El Paso's Annunciation House, which has provided for tens of thousands of newcomers since Director Ruben Garcia opened its doors in 1973. Now, these Good Samaritans are threatened with ten to fifteen years in prison if they feed the hungry, clothe the naked, give the thirsty to drink, or ferry non-citizens in medical distress to the hospital.

There was lots more I wanted to illuminate, like all the ways in which the Border Industrial Complex inflicts lifelong trauma. But if you think this book is thick now, you should have seen it before we cut out 50,000 words!

There were deeper dives into the drug trade; how US policies created the cartels; where the US border can be mapped around the globe. But as others have written whole books on these subjects, I decided to refer you to them instead.

You'll find extensive End Notes *regarding their contributions in the* Resources *list my publisher and I decided, atypically, to move online, lest the book explode another third of its current size again. You'll find a QR code to take you there at the book's end.*

And with that decision came the realization—and relief—that while this book must come to a close, the narrative need not. I invite you, therefore, to join me on Substack @ Tales of Humanity *and wherever you listen to podcasts @* From the Borderlands. *There, I'll be publishing stories I once thought lost to the cutting room floor, as well as news, interviews, and more because some topics are just too big and too urgent to ever look away from again.*

They demand no less than a movement.

I hope in these pages you have found a manual for participation.

I hope that at least one person or group made your heart beat and provided you a personal pathway to action.

We need to grow a very large chorus, now, to sing in glorious harmony: Basta! Cruelty is not okay! This is not who we want to be!

You'll find more ideas in the Call to Action *below. But first, let's tie up some still loose ends, starting with the Biden–Harris record on immigration...*

EPILOGUE

Candidate Biden convinced us, in 2020, that the soul of the US nation *could* be restored, in part through compassionate, human-centered immigration reform. In some respects that has happened. But our global system is defined by borders. And borders are violent. They are tools of in-group/out-group exclusion. They exist to divide. So while Biden has succeeded in repairing some of the damage inflicted by the former guy, "prevention through deterrence" remains the basis of White House policymaking; and cruelty for cruelty's sake remains the strategy at its core.

Starting with the positive, legal immigration has reverted substantially to where it was before Trump & Co—another system they worked hard to destroy—with the US set to resettle more refugees in any year since 1995. Work-based H1A and H1B visas are back on track with solid bipartisan support for welcoming skilled workers. Another bright light is Biden's Humanitarian Parole Program for Cubans, Haitians, Nicaraguans, and Venezuelans (CHNV), which creates a legal resettlement pipeline for another 360,000 people a year.

The program is working. It is humane. It has saved many lives, enabling folks from these four countries to circumvent both human traffickers and the perilous Darién Gap. But only those who can pay. The CHNV program privileges people with access to visas, passports, and airline tickets, who have someone in the US willing to shoulder the responsibility of sponsorship. It exists on shaky ground, too, with the Tanton-network MAGA-party faithful trying to pull the plug on it by taking away presidential authority to offer relief on humanitarian grounds.

The ineligible poor, meanwhile, are still forced to run for their lives over land, through the dangerous Central American and Mexican gauntlet.

While newcomers under the CHNV program are provided work visas, which is good, families such as Jason, Ashton, and Cecilia Rochester, whom you'll recall was penalized not for her *unlawful acts* but for her *unlawful presence*, remain separated. Similarly impacted US-citizen spouses have been working tirelessly, and creatively, under the aegis of American Families United, to reunite the now hundreds of thousands of parents and children who have been unjustly pulled apart.

Likewise, the National Immigration Justice Center (NIJC) launched its Chance to Come Home campaign in early 2021, in response to the growing number of US organizations—the Ohio Immigrant Alliance, Unified US Deported Veterans, the Cameroon Advocacy Network—that are calling for the US government to develop processes for returning people it has so wrongly, and egregiously, expelled since the so-called immigration reform acts of the Reagan and Clinton eras.

Thus far, the Chance to Come Home campaign has reunified six families. Six. Out of tens of thousands.

"And nobody really talks about the civil and human rights being violated by depriving US citizen children the chance to grow up with their parents," Robert Vivar points out.

Robert understands this personally. After his second deportation in March 2013, the bank foreclosed on his family home. His wife left him. His son stopped talking to him. His daughter fell into destitution and onto the streets, propelling his granddaughters into foster care. All because Robert was not there to care for them.

I'm thrilled to tell you that Robert finally made it home on Veterans' Day, November 11, 2021, and not without first paving the way for others to return to their families, too. He was a major force behind a partnership between the Departments of Homeland Security, Veterans Affairs, and Defense called ImmVets, a resource portal for former military members to request assistance in being reunited with their loved ones. As I write, ImmVets has realized the repatriation of 105 deported US veterans.

Also while in exile, Robert became a lay minister with the bilingual-bicultural Border Church, which famously held outdoor services at the site of the binational Friendship Park and Garden. That is until Biden's border wall contractors bulldozed the oasis in late 2023.

Which brings us back to the border, where Biden's record has been less than stellar.

||||||||||||||||||||||||||||||||||||||||||||||||||||||||

Metering continues, though gussied up, now in the guise of a smartphone app called CBP One. The app is glitchy and as racist as the border regime's legacy itself, notoriously incapable of capturing the pictures of dark-skinned faces, thus slowing their access to the asylum circus. It's also only available in English, Spanish, and Haitian Kreyol, disadvantaging those who do not speak or read in these languages.

It's a newfangled quota system, to be sure. But CBP One right now allows 1,450 people to cross the line, legally and in an orderly manner, every day at eight different ports of entry. It has reduced the so-called "chaos" at the border, no matter what Fox News and Newsmax want us to believe.

On the other side of the border, however, things are still harrowing for CBP One applicants waiting their turn in cartel-controlled Northern Mexico. The Border Protection website claims it takes two weeks to get an appointment. A CBP One spokesperson recently disclosed that wait times are averaging ten weeks. But word-of-mouth testimony suggests four and five months is more the norm.

Any wait time leaves folks wishing to immigrate the "right" way vulnerable to rape, torture, extortion, enslavement, and even death. Many lose patience, hope, or choice. When it becomes more dangerous to stay, they react as people have for millennia, as my ancestors did and likely yours, too: they move.

||||||||||||||||||||||||||||||||||||||||||||||||||||||||

As yesterday's metering is to today's CBP One, so Stephen Miller's "travel ban" is to Biden's Circumvention of Legal Pathways rule. Both presume safety seekers ineligible for protection if they didn't apply for asylum and get rejected in a third, pass-through country first.

Miller's Prompt Asylum Claim Review (PACR) and Humanitarian Asylum Review Process (HARP) became Biden's Enhanced Expedited Removal (EER) program, which does exactly as advertised: conduct fast-tracked credible fear screenings within appalling Border Protection hieleras, without meaningful access to legal counsel. There, folks still captive, hungry, dirty, and exhausted are forced to disclose their worst nightmares and greatest fears to strangers in uniform. Never mind the potential language barriers, gaps in technological literacy, and difficulties comprehending the crazy complicated US asylum system.

When deployed by Miller, critics decried the practice as a travesty of justice that pushed many legitimate asylum claimants right back into harm's way. Not only is the Biden-Harris program modeled on Miller's twin abominations, their incarnation raises the fear standard as well, making the threat of future persecution even harder to prove.

||||||||||||||||||||||||||||||||||||||||||||||||||||||

Biden walked away from remunerative reparations for families torn apart by Trump & Co, too. Though he ultimately refrained from locking families up again—it was discussed—his administration has made virtual imprisonment the norm. The Family Expedited Removal Management, or FERM, and Alternatives to Detention, or ATD, programs now mean people seeking safety are constantly surveilled, sometimes with GEO Group's stigmatizing GPS ankle monitors; more often, these days, with another smartphone app, called SmartLINK. All families and single individuals currently enrolled in ATD—184,038 as of March 9, 2024—are on ICE's radar at all times. They must adhere to strict curfews or run the risk of immediate expulsion.

Biden's "safe" third-country agreements, furthermore, first negotiated with Northern Triangle countries in 2021 then with Colombia and Panama in 2023, put more boots and guns on the ground, resulting in the US border drifting ever-further south as more violent nets are cast for safety seekers to get caught in.

But the greatest mistake of the Biden-Harris administration, according to a Homeland Security insider who agreed to speak with me on condition of anonymity, was in not lifting Trump & Co's abuse of Title 42 of the US Public Health Code on inauguration day 2021, as promised. In this way, they let the most damaging legacy of the Trump administration live on: giving Border Patrol cowboys and Border Protection cops permission to kick everybody out as quickly as possible, with impunity and without legal due process.

"Both Title 42 and MPP moved the Overton Window as to what could be possible at the border," my source states.

As I hope to have illustrated in this book, the window of acceptability has been shifting relentlessly rightward for more than forty years. We are now so far to the right on immigration matters that many Biden-Harris policies resemble Trump & Co's in all but name.

||||||||||||||||||||||||||||||||||||||||||||||||||||||||

Meanwhile, the Dignity Village encampment is gone, destroyed following a rare week of joy in early March 2021, during which the Brownsville bus station parking lot became a place of celebration. There was music and laughter; there were tears of happiness; there were selfies and group shots and loads of hugs, COVID be damned, as Dignity Village residents finally, after as many as twenty months living in tents, set foot on US soil.

All Dignity Village humanitarians turned out to welcome their friends as they took their first long-awaited steps in the so-called land of the free. Sadly, the high times north of the line pulled focus. With the eyes of the leadership off the encampment, Mexico's Migration Institute pressed its advantage, sending in a wrecking crew to cut electricity lines, remove potties, and demolish WASH stations and other infrastructure even with sixty residents still living there.

The residents held firm, refusing to leave unless they could do so together and with a guaranteed roof over their heads.

Pastor Abraham Barberi opened his Matamoros Bible school to them, turning classrooms into dormitories, a communal mess hall, and kitchen. The *Dulce Refugio* (Sweet Refuge) remained in operation for the next two years, throughout the reign of Title 42, funded by Team Brownsville until the group exhausted its funds. Because another cruel result of the Democratic Party's return to the White House was that outrage-fueled donations to the borderlands humanitarians stopped flowing.

When the Texas courts rolled back Biden's MPP rollback, the president's Department of Justice didn't put up a fight. Rather, in late 2021, Biden brought back the newly minted Remain in Mexico program (RMX) and extended it to include arrivals not just from Central America but from the entire Western Hemisphere.

It wasn't the first campaign promise betrayed. There was also the 100-day moratorium on ICE Air deportations, also stopped by Texas and within five days of Biden taking his place behind the Resolute Desk.

By the Ides of March 2021, the immigration reform package Biden-Harris introduced on inauguration day was tossed to *el dompe* of history, never to be heard from again; ICE Air was back in business, with Biden en route to dropping more Haitians back into a house on fire than his three presidential predecessors combined; and the Dignity Village encampment was erased. Only the razor-wire-topped cyclone fence remains, even as refugees keep on coming.

Today, tents are once again being pitched on the floodplain atop the Rio Bravo levee park. Far from living with a modicum of dignity, however, folks are back to bathing in the fetid waters and defecating on the embankment under the Gateway International Bridge.

||||||||||||||||||||||||||||||||||||||||||||||||||||

The third week of March 2024 brought news both good and bad. On the upside, we at the Cameroon Advocacy Network received news from Scott Shuchart that at least some of the Death Plane passengers we've been advocating for since 2021 may be allowed to re-enter the US to start their asylum processes anew. On the downside, Congress boosted Homeland Security funding above its record-breaking haul of $29.8 billion for fiscal year 2024.

Despite reams of documentation proving the agency's propensity for committing human rights violations, ICE is now at liberty to incarcerate 41,500 non-criminal offenders on any given day—up from 34,000. This is a genie not easily rebottled, a win for only two groups: the demagogues and profiteers benefiting from the mass incarceration and deportation of people yearning to live free, in dignity and in peace.

In the words of my Homeland Security source: "The system is incredibly poorly designed. It's built around ensuring that the private prison companies make a profit, not around getting good detainee care."

Customs and Border Protection funding was also increased. An additional 19 percent will allow it to add 2,000 more cops to the largest, most-troubled, least transparent law-enforcement agency in the land: the 80,000-strong force that can be, and has been, turned against us at any time.

Meanwhile, federal contributions to nongovernmental organizations providing services for new arrivals—like Annunciation House and Sister Norma's Humanitarian Respite Center—have been slashed by 20 percent.

Democratic legislators didn't push back. There was no humanitarian quid to balance the law and order quo of right-wing lawmakers who refuse to believe that people are *pushed* to El Norte, fleeing endemic social dysfunction caused by US foreign and economic policies. Rather, they argue that heroes such as Dora Rodriguez—left for dead in the Sonoran desert in 1980, now giving aid to others suffering from exposure as she once did—*pull* people to the border through such simple, human acts as handing out water.

CALL TO ACTION

The late, great Toni Morrison stated in 1995, "Let us be reminded that before there is a final solution, there must be a first solution, a second one, even a third. The move toward a final solution is not a jump. It takes one step, then another, then another."

In today's global response to forced displacement and migration, we are careening down a similar course—one that history will not soon forgive, or forget—if we are not there already.

With one in every one hundred people on the planet right now displaced and seeking their human right to a safe and dignified life, we must do better.

We can do better.

Our perennial philosophies teach us that we have a responsibility toward one another. That cruelty for cruelty's sake is not okay.

Recorded history shows us, too, that people are always in search of something better—whether that means food on their tables or opportunities for their children—and that new arrivals make for healthier, more resilient, more diverse societies.

My story collaborators—and many others, besides— show us, every day, there is a better way. They compel us to ask:

Are we really okay with looking away as human rights are violated in our name? Is this who we really wish to be?

I don't think so.

It's time for a paradigm shift. And all hands are required on deck. Because we can no longer trust our elected officials to do it—if we ever could.

It's going to require a groundswell. And it must come from all quarters. It must start with bearing witness, *for who can stop the atrocities from happening if no one is there to lay eyes on and document them?*

The answer is: we can. Because the myriad ways in which the US government crosses the line, through its Department of Homeland Security agencies and actors, are paid for by us—and at a jaw-dropping expense, too.

Example: ICE Air's broker, Classic Air Charter, invoiced ICE $983,801.25 for a rescheduled flight to Somalia that never took off, following the botched deportation attempt documented by Rebecca Sharpless in *Shackled*, which we also paid for.

Is this how we want our taxes to be spent?

||||||||||||||||||||||||||||||||||||||||||||||||||||||||||||

We may not be able to change Congressional minds. But we can appeal to the corporate purse:

We can dump the GEO Group and CoreCivic stock from our mutual fund and retirement portfolios.

We can protest at local jails run by them, LaSalle Corrections, and Ahtna, Inc.

We can demand that fixed base operations and industry unions at our local airports cease to enable the ICE Air engine.

We can boycott the charter airlines that fly for ICE Air by refusing to attend the games and gigs of our favorite sports teams and rock bands they also ferry. We can inform both athletes and celebrities of how they are aiding the Deportation Machine. We can harness their solidarity, requesting that, like Colin Kaepernick, they take a knee on the tarmac of their next Swift or World Atlantic chartered flight.

We can try to avoid using the ubiquitous service that WRAPs people, then wraps packages, and delivers them to our doorsteps: Amazon.com. The company known by one and all—the fourth-most valuable corporation in the world, with a stock market value of $1.9 trillion as of March 2024, and tentacles reaching into all our homes—is also the largest shareholder, at close to 20 percent, of Omni Air International's parent company: Air Transport Services Group (ATSG).

The only ICE Air contractor willing to fly long-haul missions, Omni and Amazon-backed ATSG hold a monopoly over that aspect of the expulsion market. Also a Department of Defense contractor, Omni is double-dipping into the government purse.

We can let Amazon shareholders and leadership know that the company that WRAPs people isn't just violating its own stated Environment, Social, and Governance commitments, it has made us all accessories to crimes against humanity, such as torture and refoulement.

And that we don't like it.

<hr>

We can recognize that in our highly globalized and interconnected world, borders are no longer relevant. We can demand that they be opened to *people*, as well as to goods and money.

We can mobilize to tear down the walls of immigrant prisons. Then, we can tear down the walls of nations as well.

We can demand that our tax dollars be spent on healthcare and education, not on human misery and pain.

We can tell our leaders: *Cruelty Is Not Okay.*

We can demand that they stop asking: *How do we deter people in motion?*

And that they start asking: *Why are so many on the run?*

We can insist, as German-Jewish philosopher Hannah Arendt tried to do back in 1951, that we should all "have the right to have rights," just for being people. That the universality of human rights should be tied to our personhood, not to our nationhood; to the reality of our existence, not the location of our birth.

<hr>

The world's current extreme disorder has brought us civilian mass murder as a by-product of modern warfare. It has pushed our shared planet to a breaking point. It has produced increased human displacement and worldwide northward migration, year on year.

We are trapped in a cycle of violence that requires a collective global response, which is beyond our current nation-state system's ability to solve. But before we take on the world, we can start at the grassroots by agitating for better.

The once Nazi-sympathizer, Pastor Martin Niemöller, expresses in his famous poem, *First They Came*, how he lived to regret not speaking up for his neighbors when the "psychosis of Whiteness" allowed the worst human impulses to prevail.

I urge you to speak up on behalf of newcomers to your colleagues and neighbors, your family and friends. Recall your own immigration legacy, and ask them to do so as well.

Are your stories really so different to today's migration stories?

Remind everyone that we are all human beings; that no one chooses to pull up stakes and run unless they have no other choice; that we all deserve to live with dignity and in safety.

Point out that no one benefits from walls and divisions; from cruelty and fear. That fear is a trap, depriving us of empathy and human connection.

Volunteer at a welcome or "detention" center at the border or in your local area. Start your own *Welcome the Stranger* program. Bring friends and family along. Meet the young mother, the hardworking father, the teenager in need of a new pair of shoes.

Are they so scary?

Invite one and all to join our growing chorus.

It's time to turn back the tide of hate.

ACKNOWLEDGMENTS

This book was a vast collaboration, written not by me but through me, an undertaking chosen for me by the muse that stands on the strong shoulders of many. You've met my story collaborators in these pages. You've been introduced to the scholars whose research I've leaned on and whose points of view aided my subversive act of seeing. You've heard from individuals and families most impacted.

The depths of my gratitude to one and all knows no bounds. I remain in awe of their individual and collective resilience and generosity. But there are many people besides, at the back end of this endeavor, who you haven't met but without whom I would never have gotten *Crossing the Line* across the line. I'd like to shout to the rafters my love and appreciation for them here.

First and foremost: Thank you, James and Liliana Hertling, my better two-thirds, for your critical reading skills and keen editorial prowess; your tireless willingness to brainstorm with me and hold my hand through the murkiest, most difficult passages; for keeping me fed and caffeinated; for providing warm arms and a soft landing every time the darkness of the topic threatened to pull me under; and so much more. I would not have made it to the finish line without your emotional and editorial support, your love and belief in me, your shopping expeditions and myriad healthy meals.

Hats off, too, to Bob Marino, copy-editor extraordinaire, and to our now-decade-long partnership. I enjoy working with you, mate, and I look forward to our both making peace with the Chicago Manual of Style one day.

Thanks to Anne-Marie Debbané for pointing out where my language failed to be human-centered. Ditto to Lynn Tramonte of the Ohio Immigrant Alliance and Anacaona, LLC, for setting me straight with a dedicated sensitivity read. These were not always easy conversations to have. But I appreciate you sitting in the heat with me and telling me what I needed to hear. This is a better book for it.

To my colleagues at Witness at the Border and the Cameroon Advocacy Network, as well as to the entire Asylum Working Group and to all representatives, past and present, of the Welcome with Dignity campaign: Thank you for folding me into your communities, for trusting me to handle confidential information and conversations, and for introducing me to many of the teachers, mentors, and guides included in this book. I hope you feel I treated their stories the empathy and care they deserve.

To the ever-expanding community of witnesses, whose paths I crossed at the #EndMPP Vigil, during our pandemic webinars, on the Journey for Justice, at the Workshop for Justice, and on your own home turf. You are too many to name individually. Apologies. But please know that your support of my earliest story drafts, your enthusiastic response to my storytelling and concept, was wind in my sails every step of the way. At times, it was all I needed to keep going.

Special shouts of appreciation go out to Livia Brock and Margaret Seiler, my partners at *Witness Radio* (soon to be relaunched as *From the Borderlands*), who supported my foray into audio. Thank you.

I remain indebted, forever, to all my first readers: not just the one-hundred-plus kindred souls whose names and stories appear herein, the vast majority of whom fact-checked and verified their own passages, sections, and chapters. My profound thanks extend, as well, to every person who read part or all of the manuscript, *sometimes more than once!* And who provided straight-shooting, critical feedback whenever I needed it most: Tom Cartwright, Laura Dzurec (aka, the-lady-on-the-train), Joyce Hamilton, Merry Hancock, Luz Lopez, Fatma Marouf, Susan Morgan, Anne Marie Murphy, Aaron Reichlin-Melnick, Suzanne Pace, Camilo Perez-Bustillo, Madeleine Sandefur, Michael Seifert, Carey Shea, and of course Susan Law, RIP.

To all my blurbers: OMG! what a boost of confidence you provided me as I entered the final sprint of this marathon. Words cannot express the depths of my gratitude for making me feel seen after so many months spent alone, chipping away at the stone.

Shout-outs of thanks, too, to all the people who put me up (even during the pandemic) and fed me as I crossed lines: Susan Eaddy and David Ribar, Dora Rodriguez, Jack and Elizabeth White, Leslie Mullin and Terry Forman, Anne Reifenberg, Jay and Barbie Alman, Danton Miller and Karen Barcellona, Betty Anderson, Larry Rennick, Susan and Bob Greig, Peter Hamblin and Sandra Damm. Big waves, as well, to Kevin Brown, who connected me with Ken Burns—go *Hampshire!* To my fellow authors, Candy Gourlay and Patti Horvath, for your ongoing writerly advice. And to everyone who suffered through early readings and still loves me.

Big thanks to the folks who got me out of the house, even when I didn't want to go, and/or took care of Gryffindog when I needed to stay put and keep the pace: Anne Bagamery, Emma Noble and Luke Bowman, Rachel Skingsley, Nancy Janin, Tony Palazzo and Lonnee Hamilton. To Clare Shine for offering me a place at the Salzburg Global Seminar. And to everyone who kept me singing through it all: Marie-Claude Gervais, Sherman Carroll, Cindy Walters, Ronald Corps, and the entire family at the Highgate Choral Society. Thanks!

As for tending to my physical and mental wellbeing, all credit goes to Laura Brera, Lizzie Eshref, and Lisa Kaley-Isley, as well as to Gryffindog, who forces me into the park every day so he may attend to his job of chasing birds and hunting squirrels.

To Lily's friends, my personal fan club and posse: Thank you for keeping me young even as this topic and this effort aged me, and for making up the bulk of *Crossing the Line* pre-orders!

To my sisters, Cindi, Kati, and Marion, with whom I shared the crushing loss of both our parents in the years between my starting and finishing *Crossing the Line.* I cherish the kinship we rekindled in our grief. And to Marion, I send a special, additional shout of thanks for being my stateside offset printer, photocopier, and book fulfillment manager.

To all the Good Samaritans, keeping hope alive for the invisibilized masses trapped south of the line—Pastor Hector Silva, Lourdes "Lulu" Gonzalez, Gladys Cañas Aguilar, Felicia Rangel-Samponaro, Victor

Cavazos, Esther Garza, Jeef Nelson, to name but a few—I send kudos of recognition and strength to you. May you find blessings in abundance.

Thanks to all the folks who joined me in researching and exposing ICE's egregious and illegal use of The WRAP. In addition to those who already loom large in the book, hat tip to journalists Nadja Drost, McKenzie Funk, and Sam Biddle, as well as Dov Baum of the American Friends Service Committee for holding the torch with me. I'd also like to extend my gratitude to Pat Leach and Vicki Rosenthal, who provided the initial contacts I needed to get the boulder rolling uphill. And to Ruha Temlock for standing alongside me and aiding my research as a trustworthy translator.

Respect to Asong Divine for connecting me with Anye Alfred and Asongenyi Venart, all Cameroonians in exile, who helped me and Godswill set up the Ghana Sanctuary. More special thanks to Madeleine for joining me in the sanctuary endeavor. To all the friends and family who donated to our collective cause. And to Florence Selman for taking over funding the project when Madeleine and my money ran out.

Great wells of gratitude also flow to Anat Shenker-Osorio, communications guru, whose gift for formulating Values-Villains-Vision narratives changed my messaging strategy and talking points, forever—and for the better. And to Kimberly Glyder for the amazing cover art, Tabitha Lahr for the incredible interior design, and Madison Stevens for becoming my personal branding consultant.

Finally, my deepest gratitude to Brooke Warner, publisher of She Writes Press, for taking a chance on me and for seeing the potential in this book; to my perpetually gentle, yet always firm, production manager, Lauren Wise, who has been the perfect shepherd; and to Marissa DeCuir and Angelle Barbazon of Books Forward—thank you for believing and for always being there!

With so many people involved in a project of such magnitude, I have no doubt missed a name or two. Apologies in advance to anyone I've neglected to acknowledge here. Please reach out so that I may thank you directly.

In solidarity and in justice,
Sarah

ENDNOTES & RESOURCES

To access chapter-based endnotes, a bibliography, and a dynamic list of borderlands and immigrant rights organizations ever in need of volunteers and donations:

- Open the camera app on your phone
- Hold your phone camera up to the QR code below
- Tap the URL when it flashes over the image

You should leap seamlessly to Sarah's online home: www.sarahtowle.com.

Alternatively, just type the URL into your browser search bar and navigate to the ENDNOTES & RESOURCES page. We'll see you there!

ABOUT THE AUTHOR

Sarah Towle is an educator, researcher, and writer; a human rights defender, nature lover, and vocalist. She resides in an ephemeral borderlands, buffeted and buoyed by a diversity of languages, cultures, landscapes, and creeds. She has taught English language literacy, cross-cultural communication and conflict resolution skills, and the writing craft for three decades across four continents in myriad classroom contexts, including under the trees in refugee settings. An award-winning storyteller, Sarah has earned accolades for her interactive tales for educational tourism. *Crossing the Line: Finding America in the Borderlands* is her debut book.

Sarah is the proud mother of a powerful, confident adult woman. She is grateful to have found her soulmate, who triples as her editor and personal chef. She and her family currently share a home in London with their rescue hound, Gryffindog, who keeps everyone laughing and gets Sarah away from her desk and into the park every day (when she's not off crossing borders).

Subscribe to Sarah's Substack newsletter, *Tales of Humanity*. Find her audio-tales, *From the Borderlands*, wherever you listen to podcasts. Follow her on Instagram @sarahtowle_author. And visit her online home: sarahtowle.com.

Looking for your next great read?

We can help!

Visit www.shewritespress.com/next-read
or scan the QR code below for a list
of our recommended titles.

She Writes Press is an award-winning
independent publishing company founded to
serve women writers everywhere.